Discharge of Contractual Obligations

JORDAN ENGLISH

Associate Professor of Law, University of Oxford and Tutor and Fellow in Law, Magdalen College, Oxford

OXFORD
UNIVERSITY PRESS

OXFORD
UNIVERSITY PRESS

Great Clarendon Street, Oxford, OX2 6DP,
United Kingdom

Oxford University Press is a department of the University of Oxford.
It furthers the University's objective of excellence in research, scholarship,
and education by publishing worldwide. Oxford is a registered trade mark of
Oxford University Press in the UK and in certain other countries

Published in the United States of America by Oxford University Press
198 Madison Avenue, New York, NY 10016, United States of America

British Library Cataloguing in Publication Data
Data available

Library of Congress Control Number: 2024949634

ISBN 9780198906674

DOI: 10.1093/9780198906704.001.0001

Printed and bound by
CPI Group (UK) Ltd., Croydon, CR0 4YY

MIX
Paper | Supporting
responsible forestry
FSC® C013604

The manufacturer's authorised representative in the EU for product safety is
Oxford University Press España S.A. of El Parque Empresarial San Fernando de Henares, Avenida de Castilla, 2 – 28830 Madrid (www.oup.es/en or
product.safety@oup.com). OUP España S.A. also acts as importer into Spain
of products made by the manufacturer.

For Maddisyn

Foreword

This book provides a valuable account of a central part of contract law, specifically, the discharge of contractual obligations. It gets back to basic concepts and underlying principles. At the heart of it is an emphasis on certain ideas inherent in the reciprocity model of contract developed over centuries in English law, the implications of which have been explored in intricate detail over that time in a huge volume of case law.

Professor English quotes the legal scholar, Professor Francis Dawson, who said in relation to the contract of sale:

> It was one of the achievements of the early common lawyers that they recognised that in a bilateral contract parties enter into contracts in order to secure the performance of the return promise rather than bargain for a lawsuit and they were therefore prepared to find that in contracts of sale, the parties' promises of payment and delivery were implicitly conditioned on the concurrent tender of performance by the counterparty.[1]

This reciprocity model extends across the greater part of contract law. Professor English shows how the conditionality of performance obligations lies at the centre of it. This is particularly the case with mutual promises, where one party's promise of performance is given in return for a promise by the other party of performance on their side, often in the form of payment of the price at completion. As Lord Mansfield observed in the seminal case of *Boone v Eyre*,[2] mutual promises may constitute 'mutual conditions, the one precedent to the other'.

Lord Mansfield's remark is based on a conceptual picture, namely the idea of a condition qualifying an obligation to perform under a contract and governing whether it has yet fallen due. It explains how that picture falls to be applied in the case of mutual promises. The key difference is between independent promises and interdependent promises. This was explained in a set of notes written by Serjeant Williams to explain another seminal case, *Pordage v Cole*.[3]

[1] Quoted at para 1.59, infra.
[2] (1777) 1 H BL 273n, 126 ER 160n; see para 1.30 infra.
[3] (1669) 1 Wms Saund 319, 320; 85 ER 449, 451.

As so often, one finds Lord Mansfield standing at the start of the common law's journey from legal practice based on the forms of action towards coherence at the level of substantive rationality in the law, pointing out the way. And, as that substantive rationality is expounded in this book, one finds him patiently waiting for us at the end of the journey, perhaps pondering on why we have taken so long to arrive and wondering about some of the detours and confusions along the way.

The treatment of discharge of contractual obligations in this volume is profound. Professor English provides a rigorous and persuasive account of how the idea of a condition qualifying the existence of an obligation to perform under a contract underpins the reciprocity model of contract in the common law. The notion of legal obligations being subject to conditions is fundamental across many areas of law, and Professor English explains how an understanding of this conceptual tool provides a penetrating explanation for a range of features of contract law.

The book gives a careful and thorough account of how the idea of a condition applies in contract. The account uses the idea of a condition, and the meticulous examination of its application and implications, like a sort of acid to burn away conceptual confusions which have entered into legal doctrine, in an effort to take us back to a more principled and purer understanding of contract law.

Professor English's method is in the Hohfeldian tradition, involving examination of the nature of the core legal concepts in operation in the field. Chapter 1 sets out the key ideas and the intellectual map he lays out, to be developed in detail in what follows. It ought to be required reading for all students of contract law. Practising lawyers and judges will benefit from reading it as well, as an important aid to thinking more clearly about contract law and, indeed, about law more generally.

Bringing the idea of the conditional nature of contractual obligations fully into focus in such a lucid manner has the effect that differences between ideas can become obvious and relevant similarities can, equally, be identified.

The book explains clearly the conceptual difference between a promise and a condition which qualifies an obligation to perform under a contract. The language of 'promissory conditions' elides the two in a way which is liable to create confusion. As Professor Samuel Williston commented, 'The difference between conditions and promises is so radical in its consequence that there is no excuse for a nomenclature which fails to recognize the distinction'.[4] Yet the development of the law shows how inexact use of language in precedents, which later becomes the focus for legal debate between judges and lawyers, can generate incoherence. Inexact legal language obscures the intellectual picture and distracts lawyers and the judges to whom they present their arguments. This is always a risk, because lawyers and judges have to look up the law and understand it within very compressed timeframes and cannot always explore the full implications of a particular way of putting a point before repeating and reinforcing supposed doctrine with the same inexactitude. This book provides an antidote to this tendency. It draws a clear distinction between the non-occurrence of a condition (which may simply mean that the time for performance of a reciprocal obligation has not yet arrived) and discharge for the failure of condition, and it explains the relationship between the two.

On the other hand, the book explains clearly the underlying conceptual unity between conditions precedent and concurrent conditions, and between them and conditions subsequent. Developing the basic ideas thus set out, it also shows the affinity between discharge of obligations following breach of 'promissory conditions' and 'innominate terms', and for failure of conditions precedent in the cases of frustration and common mistake. It also offers a coherent and persuasive account of the doctrine of anticipatory breach. Professor English develops a sustained attack on the alternative theory of the discharge of contractual obligations based around discharge depending on the exercise of a power of termination, which seems prevalent at the moment. Even if the powerful analysis he offers is not accepted, opponents of it will have to face up to his arguments.

The scholarship displayed in this volume covers an impressive range, from legal history and the history of ideas within the common law through to contemporary legal theory. Many of the ideas in the book have been explained by other writers. It is noticeable how Professor English draws upon the great American contract scholars, Professors Samuel Williston and Arthur Corbin, and how he returns to early accounts, such as that by Sir William Anson, and cases from the period when contract law was emerging as a distinct legal category in the common law. In an important sense, the project in the book is one of recovery of an intellectual picture, not its invention.

[4] Quoted at para 1.40, infra.

The book provides detailed accounts of leading cases. In doing so it dissolves many legal puzzles which have grown up periodically in the common law, as ever more refined forms of contract doctrine have grown out of and become encrusted over the underlying principles. The analysis offered involves a perspicuous return to those principles. It is refreshing to read such a lucid account. In the final chapter, the book also provides an important account of how the idea of the conditional nature of contractual performance obligations interacts with the law of unjust enrichment, thereby providing a principled explanation for the interface between these two bodies of law.

Professor English seeks to offer important insights into contract law at the theoretical, analytical, and practical levels. He delivers on all three.

Philip Sales
Justice of the Supreme Court of the United Kingdom

Preface

This book is an updated and expanded version of my DPhil thesis, submitted to the University of Oxford Faculty of Law in 2022. Although the core claims developed in that thesis remain, the book has undergone substantial revision and expansion since then, including by the addition of chapters on anticipatory breach and restitution for failure of condition.

As originally envisaged, the doctorate was to explore the justification for the power to terminate in English contract law and to compare that to the justifications for the doctrines of frustration and common mistake. In seeking to answer that question, I spent many months in the first year of my doctorate trying to identify when English law definitively decided to shift from analysing the discharge of contractual obligations in terms of independent (unconditional) and dependent (conditional) promises, which it traditionally had done, to focusing instead on whether one party had exercised a power to terminate.

It was in those early days—working through the first thirty-three editions of *Chitty on Contracts* in the basement of the Bodleian Law Library in Oxford—that I discovered what I still believe to be a fundamental truth about English contract law, namely, that it did not consciously arrive at this position. Rather, as I explain in Chapter 2 of this book, English contract law arrived at the modern position, that discharge depends on the exercise of a power to terminate, through a series of missteps and loose language.

From there, the thesis as it now stands developed. Instead of asking what the justification for the power to terminate was, the project began to explore whether the concept of a power to terminate was necessary in the first place. And so was born the claim that discharge following breach, frustration, and common mistake traditionally have been, still can be, and certainly should be, explained as instances of the discharge of contractual obligations for failure of condition. The reason one or both parties are discharged from their obligations in such cases is that their obligations were expressly or implicitly conditional on the existence of facts that do not exist or the occurrence of events that have not occurred.

A book like this does not come into existence without the support of many people. First, I would like to thank my DPhil supervisor, Professor Birke Häcker. Birke was the best supervisor I could have asked for. She supported me in exploring what, at times, appeared to be heretical ideas, and challenged me when my work needed to be developed further. Birke entertained countless hours of conversations both in her office and online about how different pieces of the puzzle might fit together, all while juggling her own busy workload. At least equally as importantly, Birke took an interest in me as a person, not just as a DPhil student, and has been a mentor, source of support, and, now, friend.

Secondly, I would like to thank those who were involved in the examination of the thesis at various stages and the review of the book, including Professors Edwin Peel, Robert Stevens, Ewan McKendrick, and Paul S Davies. Ed examined the thesis at all stages. His careful comments and questions—often emphasising the need to set out why some proposition mattered in practice—have greatly improved the book. Rob, who I subsequently have had the great fortune of teaching with, encouraged me during my Qualifying Test to look at waiver of conditions, which has become a substantial part of the book. He was also a great supporter of my ideas generally, giving me motivation when my own self-doubt set in. Paul's questions in the viva voce examination also led me to consider how some of the arguments made here might work for employment contracts, which has since become a significant part of my research agenda.

I must make special mention of Ewan, who acted both as an examiner at the Confirmation of Status stage of the DPhil and as a reviewer of the book for Oxford University Press. Ewan has been exceedingly generous with his time, reading and providing feedback on every chapter in the book. His comments, in particular, helped me see where I was overstating the strength of my own arguments and understating the strength of others. His commitment to the book is a debt that I am unlikely to be able to repay to him personally, but it is one which I hope to pay forward in the future.

Thirdly, there are a number of people in my life that I have discussed ideas with (read: pestered with ideas) that ultimately found their way into the book. Aside from the above, these include Jonas Atmaz Al-Sibaie, Francis Dawson, James Edelman, Alexander Georgiou, Mohammud Jaamae Hafeez-Baig, Matthew Hoyle, Paul MacMahon, Catherine MacMillan, Ben McFarlane, Charles Mitchell, Robert Mullins, Timothy Pilkington, Magda Raczynska, Samuel Walpole, Simon Whittaker, Frederick Wilmot-Smith, Viktoria Winzer, and Reinhard Zimmerman. A special thank you is due to Jonas, Alex, and

Jaamae, who bore the brunt of said discussions. I would also like to thank Anna Kretowicz and Harrison Simons, who both provided excellent research assistance in proofing and editing the final chapters. All errors of course remain my own.

Fourthly, I would like to thank Lord Philip Sales who generously agreed to write the foreword to the book despite a demanding work schedule. As a fellow enthusiast about conditions (one of his first publications was an excellent article about the conditions of a contract of employment), I can think of no one better suited to the task.

With one important exception, these are the people who have helped bring this book to fruition. But of course, I have also benefited from a lot of institutional support. I am thankful to the Rhodes Trust for funding my DPhil and to the Sir John Monash Foundation and the Aurora Education Foundation for funding my BCL degree, which was a stepping stone to the DPhil. I am grateful to Magdalen College, Oxford, which took me on as a student for the BCL and DPhil, and to which I returned in 2024 as a Tutor and Fellow in Law. I am also indebted to St John's College, Oxford, where I was a Supernumerary Teaching Fellow in Law from 2021 to 2024. Much of the final work on the thesis and the book was done while I was a fellow at St John's and with the support of my colleagues there. I am forever grateful.

Last, but certainly not least, I owe this book—and so much more—to my wife, Maddisyn, who agreed to move to the other side of the world to support my studies and who has been a constant source of strength and support. That is why I have dedicated the book to her. Maddi also gave me the greatest gift in the world: our son, Arthur, who arrived the day after I completed the first full draft of the thesis. Naturally, he had very little to do with the thesis but I thank him for delaying his birth until I had finished and for filling my life with purpose and meaning in the two years since. As I hope this book shows, the study of contract law is endlessly rewarding and fulfilling—but being a husband and father is the true prize.

Oxford, 21 October 2024

Contents

Table of Cases

UNITED KINGDOM

INTERNATIONAL

Australia

New Zealand

United States

Table of Legislation

1
Introduction

Introduction

This book examines situations in which parties are discharged from their contractual obligations for reasons other than performance of those obligations. It explores cases involving breach, cases of frustration, and cases of common mistake and asks why parties are discharged from their obligations to perform. The core claim is that each of these seemingly disparate forms of discharge is in fact explicable as an instance of failure of condition. The reason one or both parties are discharged from their obligations to perform in such cases is that their obligations were expressly or implicitly conditional upon the existence of particular facts or the occurrence of particular events, which do not exist or have not occurred. To say that an obligation to perform is conditional means either that it will not fall due unless a particular fact exists or a particular event occurs (conditions precedent or concurrent conditions) or, if an immediate duty of performance has arisen, that duty will be extinguished if a particular fact exists or a particular event occurs (conditions subsequent). **1.1**

For many, this claim will not be new. Various arguments have been made in the past that discharge following breach,[1] **1.2**

[1] Most importantly, AM Shea, 'Discharge from Performance of Contracts by Failure of Condition' (1979) 42 Modern Law Review 623; AM Shea, *Analytical Problems of Discharge of Contracts on Breach* (DPhil thesis, University of Oxford 1977). See also Charles Bruce Morison, *Rescission of Contracts: A Treatise on the Principles Governing the Rescission, Discharge, Avoidance and Dissolution of Contracts* (Stevens & Haynes 1916) 5, 18–22; FMB Reynolds, 'Warranty, Condition and Fundamental Term' (1963) 79 Law Quarterly Review 534; Francis Dawson, 'Metaphors and Anticipatory Breach of Contract' (1981) 40 Cambridge Law Journal 83, 87–90; FMB Reynolds, 'Discharge of Contract by

Discharge of Contractual Obligations. Jordan English, Oxford University Press. © Jordan English 2025.
DOI: 10.1093/9780198906704.003.0001

frustration,[2] and common mistake[3] can be explained as instances of failure of condition. This is the way in which these instances of discharge were understood for hundreds of years. But few people subscribe to this view today. Instead, the modern view is that English law has a doctrine of termination for breach,[4] a doctrine of frustration, and a doctrine of common mistake, none of which depends on the conditional nature of obligations to perform. These doctrines are often seen as independent of one another, and where links based on their historical roots have been drawn between them, modern scholars have sometimes said that such links are 'misleading'.[5] The result is that we have three seemingly disparate doctrines all in want of a justification and each giving rise to its own difficult doctrinal problems.

1.3 This book takes aim at this modern orthodoxy. To repeat, the claim is not that these are three separate and unrelated instances of discharge, but rather that the reason for discharge in each case is a failure of the conditions that qualify the parties' respective obligations to perform. Insofar as the doctrine of termination for breach is concerned, it will have to be conceded that the 'power to terminate' model now coexists alongside the 'failure of condition' model. But, as we will see, the power to terminate model has created a number of problems in practice that do not arise on the failure of condition model. It also means that English law has lost sight of the relationship between these different instances of discharge and the important distinction between promises and conditions.

Breach' (1981) 97 Law Quarterly Review 541; Robert Bradgate, 'Termination for Breach' in John Birds, Robert Bradgate and Charlotte Villiers (eds), *Termination of Contracts* (Wiley Chancery 1995) 17.

[2] JC Smith, 'Contracts—Mistake, Frustration and Implied Terms' (1994) 110 Law Quarterly Review 400, 402–03; Stephen A Smith, *Contract Theory* (OUP 2004) 374; Jonathan Morgan, 'Common Mistake in Contract: Rare Success and Common Misapprehensions' (2018) 77 Cambridge Law Journal 559, 568; Paul S Davies, *JC Smith's Law of Contract* (3rd edn, OUP 2021) 353–54.

[3] S Martin Leake, *A Digest of Principles of the Law of Contracts* (3rd edn, Stevens and Sons Ltd 1892) 282–90; CJ Slade, 'The Myth of Mistake in the English Law of Contract' (1954) 70 Law Quarterly Review 385, 396–403; KO Shatwell, 'The Supposed Doctrine of Mistake in Contract: A Comedy of Errors' (1955) 33 Canadian Bar Review 164, 178–82; Arthur L Goodhart, 'Mistake and Frustration in English Contract Law' in *Aequitas und Bona Fides—Festgabe zum 70 Geburtstag von August Simonius* (Helbing & Lichtenhahn 1955) 99; Smith, 'Contracts—Mistake, Frustration and Implied Terms' (n 2); Smith, *Contract Theory* (n 2) 297–304; Morgan (n 2). For the similar, if not identical, view that it is a matter of the construction of the agreement see: PS Atiyah, '*Couturier v Hastie* and the Sale of Non-existent Goods' (1957) 73 Law Quarterly Review 340; PS Atiyah and FAR Bennion, 'Mistake in the Construction of Contracts' (1961) 24 Modern Law Review 421; Robert Stevens, 'Objectivity, Mistake and the Parol Evidence Rule' in Andrew Burrows and Edwin Peel (eds), *Contract Terms* (OUP 2007) 101, 105–06; Robert Stevens, 'The Meaning of Words and the Intentions of Persons' in Simone Degeling, James Edelman, and James Goudkamp (eds), *Contract in Commercial Law* (Lawbook Co 2016) 167, 178–79.

[4] Or 'after' breach: Frederick Wilmot-Smith, 'Termination after Breach' (2018) 134 Law Quarterly Review 307.

[5] See, eg, Andrew Burrows, *A Casebook on Contract* (7th edn, Hart Publishing 2020) 361.

As for frustration and common mistake, this book contends that the failure of condition model remains the best explanation of these doctrines. The reasons given for rejecting the implied condition view of frustration and common mistake—ie that both of these doctrines can be explained as instances in which the parties' obligations, as a matter of construction, were implicitly conditional—are 'superficial'[6] and the arguments made have tended to attack a straw man. **1.4**

Ultimately, this book sets out to prove that failure of condition is a basis for the discharge of contractual obligations in cases involving breach and the basis for discharge in cases of frustration and common mistake. And if this view were given more emphasis in the modern law, many of the problems faced today in the discharge of contractual obligations would fall away. **1.5**

Outline

Professor Peter Birks used to say that legal writing should not be like a 'mystery novel'; '[t]he reader should not have to wait until the end when, with a miraculous twist, the answer is produced'.[7] In that spirit, this first chapter aims to provide an overview of the claims made in this book, explain the key concepts, and persuade the reader why the argument matters. **1.6**

Discharge following breach

Chapters 2 and 3 are devoted to the claim that the best explanation of discharge following breach is that the innocent party is discharged because their obligation to perform was conditional, and the condition has failed. Chapter 2 (Promissory Conditions) focuses on cases where one party is said to have 'breached a condition'.[8] This chapter explains how it is that the modern law came to distinguish between a promissory condition in the sense of a duty the performance of which is a condition precedent or concurrent condition, and a promissory condition in the sense of an essential term breach of which gives rise to a power to terminate. The chapter shows how, historically, there **1.7**

[6] Morgan (n 2) 561.

[7] Stevens, 'The Meaning of Words and the Intentions of Persons' (n 3) 167. See also James Penner, 'Resulting Trusts and Enrichment: Three Controversies' in Charles Mitchell (ed), *Constructive and Resulting Trusts* (Hart Publishing 2010) 237, 238.

[8] On this loose and inaccurate phrase, see [2.38].

was no difference between a promissory condition and a promissory condition precedent (or concurrent condition). Rather, as traditionally understood, the phrase 'promissory condition' referred simultaneously to a promise to ensure that some event occurred (or that some fact existed) and to a condition that made the other party's immediate duty to perform depend on that promise being performed. Where one party failed to perform such a promise, the non-occurrence of the condition prevented the performance of the other party's obligation falling due and, where the condition could no longer occur, the condition 'failed'. The result of this was that, unless the condition was waived, the performance of the obligation could never become due and in this sense the party was 'discharged'[9] from their obligation to perform on account of the failure of the condition.

1.8 While accepting that the positive law, through a series of missteps and loose language, has come to recognise a power to terminate for breach of a condition, and that it may now be too late to turn back, this chapter highlights the problems that have arisen from this way of thinking, identifies the questions that are not being asked as a result, and provides a way forward that can provide just resolutions to contractual disputes.

1.9 Chapter 3 (The Substantial-Benefit Condition) addresses cases involving discharge following breach of so-called 'innominate' or 'intermediate' terms—the form of discharge commonly associated with *Hongkong Fir Shipping Co Ltd v Kawasaki Kisen Kaisha Ltd*.[10] It argues that this is also explicable as an instance of failure of condition, and that the best explanation of this form of discharge is the failure of what is termed the 'substantial-benefit condition': the condition that renders one party's obligation to perform conditional on that party receiving 'substantially the whole benefit which it was the intention of the parties as expressed in the contract that [they] should obtain as the consideration for performing those undertakings'.[11] This condition is sometimes referred to as the principle of 'failure of consideration'. As this chapter explains, the substantial-benefit condition has also been deployed in a great number of other cases, including those involving breach and not involving breach, in the context of instalment contracts, and also in the context of the so-called doctrine of substantial performance.

[9] See [1.50]–[1.55].
[10] [1962] 2 QB 26.
[11] ibid 66.

Waiver of conditions

A core claim in this book is that failure of a condition operates to discharge a party from their obligation to perform unless they waive (or have waived) the condition. Chapters 4 and 5 therefore consider what is meant by waiver and the circumstances in which conditions can (and cannot) be waived. Given that many doubt the existence of a separate body of law concerned with waiver, Chapter 4 (Waiver of Conditions I—Election and Estoppel) makes the argument that there is a distinct area of law concerned with waiver of conditions that is broader than 'waiver by election' and 'waiver by estoppel'. The chapter also argues that there has been a modern tendency to subsume cases of waiver of conditions into the doctrine of promissory estoppel, but the integration has not been altogether satisfactory. Chapter 5 (Waiver of Conditions II—Prevention and Repudiation) considers the waiver of conditions by prevention and on a repudiation. It argues that there is a distinction between the principle of waiver of conditions, which English law does recognise, and the 'fictional fulfilment' of conditions, which English law does not (or at least should not) recognise. Moreover, it argues that not all conditions can be waived, at least not for all purposes. In particular, a condition cannot be waived for the purpose of an action for the price if the performance of the condition is the consideration for the promise it qualifies. **1.10**

Frustration

Chapter 6 (Frustration) defends the view that the so-called doctrine of frustration is also an instance of discharge for failure of condition and can be explained on the basis of implied conditions. It considers the development of the various conditions in play in cases of frustration and explains that although both parties are discharged, it is often the case that each party is discharged for failure of a different condition. This chapter also criticises the development of a unified doctrine of frustration. Most importantly, Chapter 6 responds to common objections to the implied condition view and argues that the implied condition view has often been misunderstood. **1.11**

Common mistake

Chapter 7 (Common Mistake) argues that the doctrine of common mistake is also an instance of discharge for failure of condition and explicable in terms of **1.12** implied conditions. More precisely, this chapter argues that there is no doctrine of common mistake concerned with the parties' subjective states of mind that is capable of rendering a contract 'void'. Rather, where the obligations of each party are conditional on the existence of particular facts or the occurrence of particular events, and those facts do not exist or the events cannot occur at the time the agreement is made, the parties are discharged from their obligations *ab initio* or, to put it another way, their obligations are 'inoperative'.[12] It will be seen that the notion that there is a subjective doctrine of mistake (which is what the word 'mistake' most naturally connotes) is inconsistent with English law's objective approach to contract law formation and interpretation.

Anticipatory breach

1.13 Chapter 8 (Anticipatory Breach) explores the development of and justifications for the doctrine of anticipatory breach. According to that doctrine, where one party, in advance of the time for performance, renounces their obligations under the contract or disables themselves from performing—both commonly referred to as a 'repudiation'[13]—the other party can, on 'acceptance', treat the repudiation as an event discharging the parties from their contractual obligations to perform and immediately bring an action for damages for breach of contract. The doctrine is an eminently sensible one to have but it has proven difficult, on the orthodox account, to justify it as a matter of theory. The chapter therefore considers whether a failure of condition model—and the important distinction between promises and conditions—might provide a better explanation.

1.14 Anticipatory breach is also addressed elsewhere in this book. In Chapter 2, for example, we will see how the decision in *Heyman v Darwins Ltd*[14]—a decision about anticipatory breach—has contributed to the modern orthodoxy that following 'breach of a condition' the innocent party is given a 'power to terminate'.[15] And in Chapter 5, we will see how 'long before the doctrine of anticipatory breach of contract was developed',[16] a renunciation or disablement by a promisor operated as a waiver of the conditions to that party's obligation.[17]

[12] PS Atiyah and FAR Bennion (n 3) 427.
[13] See [2.47].
[14] [1942] AC 356.
[15] See [2.46]–[2.52].
[16] *Peter Turnbull & Co Pty Ltd v Mundus Trading Co (Australasia) Pty Ltd* (1954) 90 CLR 235, 246.
[17] See [5.37]–[5.97].

Restitution for failure of condition

Finally, Chapter 9 (Restitution for Failure of Condition) considers the implications of the arguments made in this book for the doctrine of failure of consideration in the law of restitution or, as it is sometimes referred to today, restitution for 'failure of condition'.[18] In particular, this chapter considers what exactly is 'conditional' in failure of condition claims and how this affects the justification for the claim. **1.15**

Key Concepts

Much of the difficulty faced in this area has arisen due to the use of loose language and the fact that in English we often use the same word to describe several different things. It is therefore essential at the outset to explain what is meant when certain concepts are deployed in this book. The key concepts that are commonly deployed throughout are 'condition', 'discharge', and 'failure of condition'. The hope in defining these concepts is that the reader will always be aware of the sense in which these words are being used and that any confusion about the arguments being made in this book will be avoided. A broader hope would be to encourage lawyers, academics, and judges to be precise about the same concepts. But to borrow a statement made by Professor Arthur Corbin with a healthy dose of realism before defining 'condition' in his own contract treatise: 'however, beautiful and exact may be the usage and terminology of this book, comparatively few people will read it; and it is impossible to compel millions of contractors to conform to it'.[19] **1.16**

Condition: a chameleon-hued word

The word 'condition' can be used in a variety of senses depending on the context.[20] To give just four possible meanings, 'condition' can be used to refer to: **1.17**

[18] Frederick Wilmot-Smith, 'Reconsidering "Total" Failure' (2013) 72 Cambridge Law Journal 414, 416.

[19] Arthur Corbin, *Corbin on Contracts: A Comprehensive Treatise on the Rules of Contract Law* (West Publishing Co 1960) vol 3A, 13 §627.

[20] Samuel Stoljar once identified no less than twelve, though query how many of these overlapped: Samuel J Stoljar, 'The Contractual Concept of Condition' (1953) 69 Law Quarterly Review 485, 486–88.

1. the terms of the deal (ie the 'conditions' of the contract);[21]
2. the state or quality of goods (ie the goods are in excellent 'condition');[22]
3. an essential term breach of which gives rise to a 'power to terminate';[23] and
4. an uncertain fact or event that qualifies an obligation (or multiple obligations) under a contract.[24]

As this short list shows, 'condition' is a 'chameleon-hued word', and 'in any closely reasoned problem, whether legal or non-legal, chameleon-hued words are a peril both to clear thought and to lucid expression'.[25]

A working definition

1.18 In order to avoid these dangers, unless otherwise stated, the word condition will be used in the fourth sense identified above to refer to an uncertain fact or event upon which the existence of an immediate duty of performance depends.[26] This is a working definition, but four points of clarification must be made.

1.19 First, '[i]t is a source of confusion of thought that the word condition is frequently used without exact recognition of what the supposed condition qualifies'.[27] Accordingly, to be clear, the conditions with which we are concerned qualify obligations of performance under a contract: either an obligation to perform will not fall due (condition precedent or concurrent condition)[28] or, if an obligation to perform has fallen due, the immediate duty of performance it creates will be extinguished (condition subsequent) if the condition is not fulfilled.[29]

[21] *L Schuler AG v Wickman Machine Tools Sales Ltd* [1974] AC 235. See also Corbin (n 19) 11 §627.

[22] Sale of Goods Act 1979, s 14.

[23] See Edwin Peel, *The Law of Contract* (15th edn, Sweet & Maxwell 2020) 981 [18-043]; Ewan McKendrick, *Contract Law: Text, Cases, and Materials* (9th edn, OUP 2020) 742; Andrew Burrows, *A Restatement of the English Law of Contract* (2nd edn, OUP 2020) 118.

[24] See American Law Institute, *Restatement of the Law Second: Contracts 2d* (American Law Institute Publishers 1981) 160 §224, comment (a).

[25] Wesley Newcomb Hohfeld, 'Some Fundamental Legal Conceptions as Applied in Judicial Reasoning' (1913) 23 Yale Law Journal 16, 29.

[26] See also to a similar, although not identical, effect: American Law Institute (n 24) 160 §224 ('[a] condition is an event, not certain to occur, which must occur, unless it non-occurrence is excused, before performance under a contract becomes due'); Corbin (n 19) 11 §627 ('an operative fact [or event], one on which the existence of some particular legal relation depends').

[27] Samuel Williston, *The Law of Contracts* (Baker, Voorhis & Co 1921) vol 2, 1283 §666.

[28] See American Law Institute (n 24) 165 §225.

[29] See [1.25]–[1.30] below. Technically, it can be said that in cases of conditions subsequent the party is discharged for the fulfilment of the condition rather than its failure. But this is just a matter of how the condition is phrased.

Secondly, the language of an 'immediate duty'[30] is a deliberate attempt to distinguish between an obligation that has fallen due, and therefore calls for immediate performance, and an obligation that requires performance only at some future date. The risk of confusion is that it is common to speak of a party having a 'duty' or 'obligation' to perform even though the duty to perform will not fall due until some future date. As Corbin has observed, '[i]t is our custom, both juristic and popular, to say that a contract creates rights and duties, even though the performance is not yet due and even though some event must still occur before it becomes due.'[31] Thus, a contract entered into on 1 January to deliver a book on 10 January is said to create an obligation to deliver the book. But that obligation is one which only calls for performance on 10 January. The seller is under no immediate duty to deliver the book until 10 January. **1.20**

The difference between the two is only in the level of abstraction at which the obligation is described. The risk of confusion will be avoided by distinguishing clearly between when an obligation—used in a more general sense—arises and when the duty to perform falls due. The language of an 'immediate duty' is simply a shorthand for this latter concept. Moreover, as the definition above makes clear, it is the existence of the immediate duty of performance that depends upon the fulfilment or occurrence of the condition, not the existence of the general obligation itself. Further, when referring to the 'existence' of an immediate duty of performance, what is meant is the creation of that duty or its continued existence. The former reflects the fact that often, a failure of condition will prevent an obligation from falling due in the first place. **1.21**

The third clarification is that '[n]ot infrequently a promise is subject to more than one condition.'[32] Thus in the context of a sale of goods by sample, the condition of the buyer's obligation to accept and pay for the goods may be both delivery of the goods and that the goods correspond with the sample. This proposition—that obligations in a contract may be subject to multiple conditions—is perhaps trite, but it appears, until recently, to have been forgotten in some contexts.[33] **1.22**

Fourth and finally, as the definition makes clear, when using the word 'condition' we are concerned with uncertain facts or events and not facts that are **1.23**

[30] For an example of this language see American Law Institute (n 24) 189 §230; Corbin (n 19) 5 §625.
[31] Corbin (n 19) 5 §625.
[32] Williston (n 27) 1308 §677.
[33] *School Facility Management Ltd v Governing Body of Christ the King College* [2020] EWHC 1118 (Comm) [421]. See Wilmot-Smith (n 18) 432–34.

known with certainty to exist at the time of contracting or events that in the ordinary course of things are certain to occur. It follows that 'the mere passage of time, as to which there is no uncertainty, is not a condition and a duty is unconditional if nothing but the passage of time is necessary to give rise to a duty of performance'.[34] In a similar vein, an obligation to perform 'if the sun rises tomorrow' would be treated as absolute and unconditional—this is an event which can be treated as certain to occur.

1.24 On this approach, an obligation to pay a sum of money in thirty days would not be described as subject to a condition that thirty days has passed.[35] Of course, this does not mean that the immediate duty of performance arises before thirty days has passed. In this sense, what we might call a 'temporal' delay, is similar to a condition in that until the time has passed there is no immediate duty to perform. The only difference is that the passage of time is certain, and conditions are concerned with uncertain events. But this distinction is the one that best accords with both the judicial and the ordinary usage of the word 'condition' and for this reason it is maintained in this book. It is also one of ancient provenance: classical Roman law drew a distinction between *condicio* (a condition), where the occurrence of a future event was uncertain, and *dies* (a time clause), where the occurrence of the future event was certain to occur.[36]

Conditions precedent, conditions subsequent, and concurrent conditions

1.25 Conditions are often divided up into 'conditions precedent' and 'conditions subsequent'.[37] The words 'precedent' and 'subsequent' 'express [a] relationship in time' between two things.[38] We know that the first of these is the uncertain fact or event that constitutes the condition. The second, as outlined above, is the immediate duty of performance. 'Precedent' and 'subsequent' therefore express a relationship between the uncertain fact or event and the immediate duty of performance.

[34] American Law Institute (n 24) 161 §224 comment (b).

[35] Corbin (n 19) 7 §626.

[36] Reinhard Zimmermann, *The Law of Obligations: Roman Foundations of the Civilian Tradition* (OUP 1996) 741; JAC Thomas, *Textbook of Roman Law* (reprint edn, Philip McDonald 2013) 249–55. For *dies*, when the event occurred did not need to be certain (eg when A dies), only that it was certain to occur eventually. A distinction was drawn between *dies certus*, where it was known when the event would occur, and *dies incertus quando*, where it was unknown when the event would occur, but it was inevitable that it would: Zimmerman (n 36) 741; Thomas (n 36) 250.

[37] As we shall see, there is a third category of 'concurrent conditions', but these are just a particular type of mutual conditions precedent.

[38] Corbin (n 19) 15 §628.

Where a fact must exist or an event must occur before an immediate duty of performance will arise, it can be referred to as a condition precedent.[39] Thus Corbin, adopting a similar definition to that used here, once said: 'Conditions precedent . . . are those facts and events, occurring subsequently to the making of a valid contract, that must exist or occur before there is a right to immediate performance'.[40] As an example, a seller's obligation to deliver goods may be subject to a condition precedent that the buyer open a confirmed letter of credit.[41] The seller's immediate duty to deliver the goods will not arise, absent waiver, unless the buyer opens a confirmed letter of credit. **1.26**

By contrast, where the existence of a fact or the occurrence of an event after the immediate duty of performance has arisen causes that duty to be extinguished, it can be referred to as a condition subsequent.[42] 'Such conditions are very rare'[43] (or more accurately, discussed very rarely) in cases dealing with the discharge of contractual obligations but, as we will see in Chapter 9, they may be able to explain several instances of restitution for failure of condition. Nonetheless, even in the discharge context obvious examples can be given. If a contract provides for a buyer of goods to return them upon the occurrence of particular events or if particular facts exist, ordinarily there will be an immediate duty to pay upon receiving the goods (unless credit has been given), but this immediate duty can be extinguished upon returning the goods.[44] **1.27**

It should be noted that insofar as conditions subsequent are uncertain facts or events that extinguish an immediate duty of performance, technically it can be said that in such cases the party is discharged for the fulfilment of the condition rather than its failure. But it is possible to express conditions subsequent in the form that the continued existence of an immediate duty to perform is subject to a condition that an uncertain fact not exist or an uncertain event not occur. And on this view, there is a failure of the condition whenever the fact exists or the event occurs. **1.28**

The third category of conditions—concurrent conditions—are in fact a subset of conditions precedent that arose due to the need to deal with cases of simultaneous performance, such as contracts for the conveyance of title to **1.29**

[39] Williston (n 27) 1284 §666a.
[40] Corbin (n 19) 16 §628.
[41] See *Trans Trust SPRL v Danubian Trading Co Ltd* [1952] 2 QB 297, 304 at [1.32] below.
[42] Corbin (n 19) 17 §628.
[43] Williston (n 27) 1286 §667.
[44] ibid.

land. In such cases it was recognised that there would be a 'stalemate'[45] if actual performance of each party's obligation was a condition precedent to the other's obligation. Thus, from early times it was recognised that in such cases it was sufficient 'if one party was ready, and offered, to perform his part'.[46] Accordingly, where the parties' obligations are concurrently conditional, each party's obligation to perform is conditional upon the other party being ready, willing, and able to perform, rather than prior performance itself.[47]

1.30 Seen in this light, it can be seen why concurrent conditions are in fact simply mutual conditions precedent; 'concurrent' here refers not to the relationship between the uncertain fact or event and the immediate duty of performance but to the idea that the actual performances are intended to be concurrent. The relevant condition precedent is simply that each party is ready, willing, and able to perform, not that each actually perform. Indeed, it has been said that '[c]oncurrent condition is an elliptical expression for a condition precedent where performances are due at the same time'.[48] In the foundational case, *Boone v Eyre*,[49] Lord Mansfield himself spoke of 'mutual conditions, the one precedent to the other'.

Non-promissory conditions

1.31 Strictly speaking all conditions are non-promissory. This is because a condition is simply an uncertain fact or event upon which the existence of an immediate duty to perform depends. A condition is distinct from a promise (a duty). But where a condition is an uncertain fact or event that neither party has guaranteed or promised exists or will occur, it can be referred to as a 'non-promissory' condition.[50] Such conditions, sometimes referred to as 'contingent conditions',[51] operate only to prevent performance of an obligation falling

[45] JW Carter and C Hodgekiss, 'Conditions and Warranties: Forebears and Descendants' (1977) 8 Sydney Law Review 31, 35.

[46] *Kingston v Preston* (1773) 2 Doug 689, 691; 99 ER 437, 438.

[47] See Corbin (n 19) 19 §629.

[48] American Law Institute, *Restatement of the Law of Contracts* (American Law Institute Publishers 1932) 363 §251, comment (a), quoted in Corbin (n 19) 19 §629 fn 21.

[49] (1777) 1 H BL 273n, 126 ER 160n. See also Williston (n 27) 1285 §666 ('Concurrent conditions, then, do not differ from conditions precedent in the relation of time which the happening of the condition bears to liability on the contract. They are, indeed, mutual conditions precedent.').

[50] '[A] term may simply lay down a condition of one party's liability without implying also a promise to perform the condition': Reynolds, 'Discharge of Contract by Breach' (n 1) 547.

[51] See, eg, Jack Beatson, Andrew Burrows, and John Cartwright, *Anson's Law of Contract* (31st edn, OUP 2020) 148; Peel (n 23) 70 [2-105]; Mindy Chen-Wishart, 'The Agreement' in Hugh Beale (ed), *Chitty on Contracts*, vol 1 (35th edn, Sweet & Maxwell 2023) 317, 425–26 [4-196]. This has a long pedigree: see MD Chalmers, *The Sale of Goods Act, 1893, including The Factors Acts, 1889 & 1890* (William Clowes and Sons Ltd 1894) 165.

due or to extinguish an existing immediate duty of performance—the non-occurrence or non-fulfilment of such conditions, not also being a breach of duty, does not give rise to an action for breach.[52]

It was noted above that conditions qualify obligations to perform under a contract. It has on occasion been suggested, however, that in some cases the effect of the non-occurrence or non-fulfilment of a non-promissory condition is to 'prevent the formation of any immediately binding contract'.[53] Thus in *Trans Trust SPRL v Danubian Trading Co Ltd*,[54] Denning LJ considered a term of the contract that the buyer should open a confirmed credit in favour of the seller and said: **1.32**

> What is the legal position of such a stipulation? Sometimes it is a condition precedent to the formation of a contract, that is, it is a condition which must be fulfilled before any contract is concluded at all. In those cases the stipulation 'subject to the opening of a credit' is rather like a stipulation 'subject to contract.' If no credit is provided, there is no contract between the parties.

However, the analogy between these two ('subject to the opening of a credit' and 'subject to contract') is imperfect,[55] for in the case of a non-promissory condition that the buyer open a letter of credit, the condition qualifies the parties' obligations of performance. Its non-occurrence prevents such obligations from falling due, but there is no doubt that there is a valid contract: 'The fact that no liability on either side can arise until the happening of a condition does not, however, make the validity of the contract depend upon its happening.... each is irrevocably bound by a contract from the outset.'[56] By contrast, in the case of a stipulation 'subject to contract' there is no condition upon which the existence of the parties' immediate duties of performance depend—there is simply 'neither offer nor acceptance, and no contract is formed'.[57] **1.33**

A 'case often cited'[58] for the proposition that the non-occurrence of a condition can in some cases prevent a contract from being formed is *Pym v Campbell*.[59] **1.34**

[52] JL Montrose, 'Conditions and Promises' (1960) 23 Modern Law Review 434, 485; Reynolds, 'Discharge of Contract by Breach' (n 1) 547.
[53] Beatson, Burrows, and Cartwright (n 51) 148.
[54] [1952] 2 QB 297, 304.
[55] Ewan McKendrick, 'Express Terms' in Hugh Beale (ed), *Chitty on Contracts* (33rd edn, Sweet & Maxwell 2018) vol 1 1013, 1027 [13-028] fn 115 (this footnote appears not to have been repeated in the later editions); Reynolds, 'Warranty, Condition and Fundamental Term' (n 1) 536.
[56] Williston (n 27) 1283–84 §666.
[57] Reynolds, 'Warranty, Condition and Fundamental Term' (n 1) 536. See also Stoljar (n 20) 490.
[58] Reynolds, 'Warranty, Condition and Fundamental Term' (n 1) 536.
[59] (1856) 6 El & Bl 370, 119 ER 903; cited for this proposition in Beatson, Burrows, and Cartwright (n 51) 148.

The plaintiff, in the course of negotiations to sell to the defendants a three-eighth share in an invention, signed a written document purporting to be an agreement for the sale of the share in the invention. Despite being absolute and unconditional on its face, the oral understanding of the parties was that its operation should be conditional upon the approval of the invention by a particular third party. The third party did not approve. On an action by the plaintiff for the price, Lord Campbell CJ, Erle, and Crompton JJ held that there was 'never any agreement at all'.[60]

1.35 As various commentators have observed, this surely is to introduce conceptual confusion. For it seems that in a case like *Pym v Campbell* there was an agreement—the parties had agreed upon all essential terms—but the majority of the obligations it created were conditional upon the approval by the third party.[61] Moreover, as suggested by Professor Samuel Stoljar, 'it must be perfectly clear that there was in fact a contract; for had the plaintiff tried to revoke his offer before the third party's approval, he would have been guilty of an anticipatory breach'.[62]

1.36 The reason the distinction between 'no agreement' and 'an agreement that created conditional obligations' mattered in *Pym v Campbell* is because of the argument that the parol evidence rule would not admit evidence of an oral agreement that contradicted the terms of the written agreement. Erle J said: 'The distinction in point of law is that evidence to vary the terms of an agreement in writing is not admissible, but evidence to shew that there is not an agreement at all is admissible.'[63] In light of this, *Pym v Campbell* is probably better understood as 'a striking example of yet another exception to the parol evidence rule'.[64]

1.37 Conditions to the formation of a contract are sometimes referred to as 'external conditions' in contrast to 'internal conditions', which are conditions that qualify obligations to perform.[65] In this book, 'condition' will only be used in

[60] *Pym v Campbell* (1856) 6 El & Bl 370, 373; 119 ER 903, 904 (Erle J).

[61] As argued by Arthur Corbin, 'Conditions in the Law of Contract' (1919) 8 Yale Law Journal 739, 766–67; Stoljar (n 20) 492; Corbin (n 19) 111 §649; Smith, 'Contracts—Mistake, Frustration and Implied Terms' (n 2) 410. See also Reynolds, 'Warranty, Condition and Fundamental Term' (n 1) 537, albeit equivocal on which view is correct.

[62] Stoljar (n 20) 492. See the similar argument in Smith, 'Contracts—Mistake, Frustration and Implied Terms' (n 2) 410 ('The seller was surely bound to give [the third party] the opportunity to inspect the invention. He would have been in breach of an implied term of the agreement if he had refused to do so or if he had sold the invention to a [different person] before [the third party] had had a reasonable opportunity to inspect it.').

[63] *Pym v Campbell* (1856) 6 El & Bl 370, 374; 119 ER 903, 905.

[64] Stoljar (n 20) 492. See also Corbin (n 61) 766–67.

[65] See the discussion in Stoljar (n 20) 489–92.

the latter sense. Indeed, insofar as external conditions are said to be 'all those operative facts without which a contract can neither exist nor survive',[66] they are only conditions of a contract in the same sense that offer and acceptance are 'conditions' of contract formation. The conditions with which we are concerned are those which qualify obligations to perform, not the existence of the contract itself.

Promissory conditions

As noted above, all conditions, strictly speaking, are non-promissory. But sometimes a term of a contract may have a 'double operation'[67] and create both a duty and a condition. As Scrutton LJ explained in *Westacott v Hahn*,[68] '[a] condition precedent is a limitation or qualification of another term of a contract, while it may also be itself a term of a contract whose breach gives a cause of action'.[69] In such cases, where the same term in the contract creates both a promise and a condition, it may conveniently be labelled a 'promissory condition'.[70] **1.38**

The key point about promissory conditions is that the promise (duty) and the condition are completely co-extensive and, because of this, breach of the duty will always cause the condition to fail. To give an example, if A promises to deliver goods to B that correspond with the description, A's duty is to deliver goods that correspond with the description, and performance of that duty exactly is the condition of B's obligation to pay the price. Hence the label 'promissory condition'—the promise (duty) and condition are co-extensive. **1.39**

The distinction between promises and conditions

A recurring theme throughout this book is that the nature of discharge following breach, frustration, and common mistake has been obscured in English law by a failure to draw a distinction between promises (duties) and conditions.[71] Professor Samuel Williston, commenting on the conflation of the two concepts in English contract law books, once wrote: 'The difference between **1.40**

[66] ibid 489.

[67] Corbin (n 61) 745; Corbin (n 19) 28 §633.

[68] [1918] 1 KB 495, 513.

[69] Note, however, that here Scrutton LJ appears to be using the word 'term' synonymous with 'duty' or 'promise'. There is no reason why a condition could not be expressly stated in the contract, and therefore a 'term', even though it is non-promissory.

[70] Corbin (n 61) 745; Corbin (n 19) 28 §633.

[71] See Williston (n 27) 1282–83 §665; Arthur Corbin, 'Supervening Impossibility of Performing Conditions Precedent' (1922) 22 Columbia Law Review 421, 423; Corbin (n 19) 25–36 §633–34; Montrose (n 52) 484–85.

conditions and promises is so radical in its consequence that there is no excuse for a nomenclature which fails to recognize the distinction.'[72]

1.41 The distinction is important because while a breach of duty always gives rise to an action for damages, it does not necessarily discharge a party from their obligation to perform.[73] This is because discharge on the failure of condition model depends not upon a breach of duty, but upon the failure of a condition. Indeed, it is not even necessary for there to be a breach of duty for a condition to fail. In cases of frustration or common mistake, there is no breach of duty, only relevant failures of conditions.

1.42 An example can be given to illustrate the point. Suppose that on 1 January C contracts with D for the use of a music hall for a week at the end of the month and promises to pay £100.[74] Then consider the following three scenarios:

1. On 10 January, D burns the music hall down.
2. On 10 January, the music hall is struck by lightning and burns down.
3. On 1 January, an hour before the contract is signed, the music hall is struck by lightning and burns down.

1.43 According to modern orthodoxy, English law has three distinct doctrines to deal with each of these three scenarios:

1. In the first scenario, C is given a power to terminate either on the basis that D has breached a 'condition', any breach of which automatically gives rise to a power to terminate,[75] or on the basis that D has breached an 'innominate term', the effect of which has been to deprive C of substantially the whole benefit of the contract.[76]
2. In the second scenario, the parties are discharged by the 'doctrine' of frustration.[77]
3. In the third, the contract is said to be 'void' for common mistake.[78]

1.44 By contrast, on the failure of condition model put forward in this book, the reason C is discharged is the same in each case. The effect of the music hall

[72] Williston (n 27) 1282 §665.
[73] Sir William R Anson, *Principles of the English Law of Contract* (1st edn, Clarendon Press 1879) 266.
[74] This example is taken from seminars in the University of Oxford Commercial Remedies BCL/MJur course run by Professor Robert Stevens and is itself adapted from *Taylor v Caldwell* (1863) 3 B & S 826, 122 ER 309.
[75] See, eg, *Photo Production Ltd v Securicor Transport Ltd* [1980] AC 827, 849.
[76] *Hongkong Fir Shipping Co Ltd v Kawasaki Kisen Kaisha Ltd* [1962] 2 QB 26, 66.
[77] *Taylor v Caldwell* (1863) 3 B & S 826, 122 ER 309.
[78] *Bell v Lever Brothers Ltd* [1932] AC 161.

burning down is that C has been deprived of substantially the whole benefit of the contract. The substantial-benefit condition has failed.[79] In the first scenario, it failed due to a breach of duty by D. The only relevance of this, however, is that this breach of duty also gives rise to an action for damages. It is still the failure of the condition that discharges C.

In the second and third scenarios, this condition failed without a breach of duty. But from the perspective of C's obligation, the result is the same: '[C] has not got what [they] bargained for and need not perform.'[80] Note, however, that D is not discharged for the same reason. D is discharged either because they expressly excepted such events from the scope of their contractual duty[81] or because D's obligation to perform was implicitly conditional upon it being possible to perform.[82] **1.45**

When seen in this light, the relationship between these three instances becomes clear. The only relevant difference between the first scenario on the one hand and the second and third scenarios on the other is the existence of a breach of duty. Had D's promise to perform been absolute insofar as the existence of the music hall was concerned, then there would be no difference between the three scenarios.[83] And in all three scenarios C would still be discharged from their obligation to perform on account of the failure of the substantial-benefit condition unless C had also promised to perform absolutely.[84] **1.46**

As for the second and third scenarios, the difference here is only a matter of timing.[85] If the obligations of the parties are conditional, then whether the contract never imposes any obligations upon the parties (common mistake) or whether it does but some or all are subsequently discharged (frustration) is simply a matter of when the fact ceases to exist or the event can no longer occur. The short point is that these are not three distinct and unrelated doctrines. Each is an instance of failure of condition. **1.47**

This is not the only benefit of drawing the distinction between promises and conditions. Even in the case of promissory conditions, the distinction remains **1.48**

[79] See Chapter 3.
[80] Samuel Williston, *A Treatise on the Law of Contracts* (Walter HE Jaeger ed, 3rd edn, Baker, Voorhis & Co Inc 1962) vol 6, 131–32 §838.
[81] See, eg, *Jackson v Union Marine Insurance Co Ltd* (1874) LR 10 CP 125. See further [3.24]–[3.35] and [6.31]–[6.35].
[82] See, eg, *Taylor v Caldwell* (1863) 3 B & S 826, 122 ER 309. See [6.5]–[6.23].
[83] See, eg, *Taylor v Caldwell* (1863) 3 B & S 826, 833; 122 ER 309, 312; *McRae v Commonwealth Disposals Commission* (1951) 84 CLR 377.
[84] See [6.73] and [7.73]–[7.74].
[85] See the discussion at [7.96]–[7.99].

vital. It allows us to see that in cases involving breach of a 'promissory condition' (more accurately, the breach of a promise the performance of which is a condition), what discharges one party from their obligation to perform is not the breach of duty, but the non-occurrence of the condition of that party's obligation. Unfortunately, English law lost sight of this distinction when it began talking about 'breach of a condition'.[86] Strictly speaking a condition cannot be breached; only a duty can be breached.[87]

1.49 Moreover, as we will see when discussing the substantial-benefit condition in Chapter 3, this is a condition which can fail in both cases involving breach and cases not involving breach. The reason it can do so is that, unlike promissory conditions, the substantial-benefit condition is not completely co-extensive with any particular duty. This means that the same duty can be breached in a way that does and in a way that does not cause the substantial-benefit condition to fail. And the substantial-benefit condition can fail in cases where there is no breach at all. This can only be seen, however, when a clear distinction is made between promises (duties) and conditions.

The meaning of 'discharge' and 'failure of condition'

1.50 In order to understand the sense in which 'discharge' and 'failure of condition' are used in this book, it is necessary to discuss the two possible effects of the non-occurrence of a condition precedent (or concurrent condition): 'The first effect always follows and the second often does.'[88] First, in all cases, unless the condition is waived, the non-occurrence of a condition will prevent the performance of the obligation from becoming due—ie it will prevent the immediate duty of performance from arising.[89] Where the condition might still occur, this is often referred to as the 'suspension' of the duty (although note that, in truth, the immediate duty of performance has not arisen in the first place). In these cases, the subsequent occurrence of the condition will cause the immediate duty of performance to arise.

1.51 Secondly, in some cases where the condition can no longer occur,[90] the condition can be said to have 'failed'—the performance of the obligation can never

[86] See [2.38].
[87] Corbin, 'Supervening Impossibility of Performing Conditions Precedent' (n 71) 423.
[88] See American Law Institute (n 24) 165 §225 comment (a).
[89] ibid.
[90] The condition may be unable to occur because it is impossible for it to do so (eg in a contract for the delivery of goods where delivery is the condition precedent to payment and the goods have been

become due unless the condition is waived. In such cases, the party who was to perform the obligation is permanently 'discharged' for failure of the condition.[91] This is what is meant in this book when it is said that one party is discharged from their obligation to perform on account of the failure of a condition. 'Discharge' is reserved for cases where the condition has failed and so can no longer occur.

The above applies to conditions precedent and concurrent conditions. In the **1.52**
case of conditions subsequent, 'discharged' is used to refer to situations where an immediate duty of performance has arisen but is extinguished due to the occurrence of the event. Subject to the qualification at [1.28] above, this can also be referred to as discharge for failure of condition. It is simply a matter as to how one expresses a condition subsequent.

Further, although this book is concerned with the discharge of parties from **1.53**
their contractual obligations for reasons other than the performance of those obligations, something should be said about cases of 'discharge by performance'. When discharge is used in connection with performance, it means that the immediate duty of performance has fallen due, remains in existence, but the obliged party has complied with their general obligation by performing. Importantly, performance does not make the immediate duty of performance disappear; it simply means the party has complied with it (and the more general obligation to perform). The party is discharged from their contractual obligation because the obligation no longer requires anything from that party.

When discharge is used in connection with failure of condition, it means that **1.54**
the immediate duty of performance either has not fallen due or has fallen due but has subsequently been extinguished. In these cases, the obliged party does not comply with any immediate duty of performance—as no such duty exists—but they do nonetheless comply with their more general obligation to perform by *not* doing anything. As Dr Anthony Shea explained, in such cases, the obliged party 'refers to the terms of the contract, and upholds them, and relies upon them to say that he is not bound to go on with his performance. By doing nothing, he performs his promises'.[92] And so similar to cases of discharge by performance, the party here is discharged from their contractual obligation

destroyed) or because in some circumstances, namely the doctrine of anticipatory breach, one party says that they will not perform (renunciation) and the law permits the other party to hold the renouncing party to their word that they will not perform: see Chapter 8.

[91] This is the language used in the second restatement: American Law Institute (n 24) 165 §225.
[92] Shea, 'Discharge from Performance of Contracts by Failure of Condition' (n 1) 625.

on account of the failure of a condition because, due to that failure, the obligation no longer requires anything from that party, now or in the future.

1.55 The language of 'discharge' for failure of condition admittedly is not perfect. But despite its imperfections, it is the most convenient and economical way of expressing the effect of a failure of condition—ie that one party need not perform. It is also the language used in the American Law Institute's *Restatement of the Law Second: Contracts 2d*[93] to describe the effect of the non-occurrence of a condition (where it can no longer occur), and it has a long pedigree in English law. In the first edition of *Anson's Law of Contract*, published in 1879, for example, Sir William Anson described 'discharge' in the context of breach as 'the right to consider oneself exonerated from any further performance under the contract'.[94]

Why It Matters

1.56 The final part of this chapter considers why any of this matters. A simple answer would be that the claims made in this book matter because they illuminate the relationships between seemingly disparate areas of contract law—discharge following breach, frustration, and common mistake—and provide a coherent and compelling explanation of each as well as how they relate to each other. A more sophisticated answer is that this book makes distinct contributions on a theoretical, analytical, and practical level. It also has implications for other areas of law, such as the law of restitution.

1.57 First, on a theoretical level, this book explains that each of these instances of discharge is a product of the parties' agreement and therefore justified by that agreement.[95] The reason that a party is discharged from their obligation to perform in the instances of discharge considered in this book is that their promise, objectively construed, was not absolute but conditional: 'He claims only that he agreed to perform in X circumstances, not in Y circumstances, and that he is under no liability to perform, X not having occurred.'[96] In this sense, the party arguing for discharge relies upon the scope of their promise to justify a refusal to perform.[97]

[93] American Law Institute (n 24) 165 §225.
[94] Anson (n 73) 266.
[95] See in the context of discharge following breach: Reynolds, 'Discharge of Contract by Breach' (n 1) 542.
[96] Shea, 'Discharge from Performance of Contracts by Failure of Condition' (n 1) 625.
[97] ibid.

This theoretical contribution is particularly important in the context of discharge following breach because the justification for this phenomenon—in contrast with the justification for frustration and common mistake—has, 'for the most part, been ignored'.[98] Even in the context of frustration and common mistake, this book offers a compelling defence of the view that these are simply instances of the failure of (usually implied) conditions and not distinct doctrines in their own right. 1.58

Next, on an analytical level, this book also demonstrates that there is a 'synallagma' or 'mutuality' at the heart of contracting, which explains why it is that parties are usually taken to have intended their performances to be conditional upon receiving counter-performance.[99] It is not just the parties' mutual promises that are linked, but often their rights and duties, and consequently their performances too. As Professor Francis Dawson has explained about contracts of sale: 1.59

> It was one of the achievements of the early common lawyers that they recognised that in a bilateral contract parties enter into contracts in order to secure the performance of the return promise rather than bargain for a lawsuit and they were therefore prepared to find that in contracts of sale, the parties' promises of payment and delivery were implicitly conditioned on the concurrent tender of performance by the counterparty.[100]

Indeed, as we will see in Chapter 2, discharge following breach is deeply connected with the idea that in bilateral contracts the mutual promises of the parties are either 'independent' and unconditional or, as is more common, 'dependent' and therefore conditional.[101] In this sense, there is a principle of 'reciprocity'[102] in English contract law, which manifests in this particular context in the law relating to conditions. 1.60

Thirdly, from a practical perspective, this book has significant implications for how the rules of discharge actually work. Most importantly, this book claims 1.61

[98] Wilmot-Smith (n 4) 312. See also Reynolds, 'Warranty, Condition and Fundamental Term' (n 1) 550. Notable exceptions include: Wilmot-Smith (n 4); Christopher Langley and Rebecca Loveridge, 'Termination as a Response to Unjust Enrichment' [2012] Lloyd's Maritime and Commercial Law Quarterly 65.

[99] Andrew Hutchison, 'Reciprocity in Contract Law' (2013) 24 Stellenbosch Law Review 3, 3, 12–13.

[100] Francis Dawson, 'Readiness and Willingness Under the Contractual Remedies Act' (2017) 23 New Zealand Business Law Quarterly 61, 65–66.

[101] See Reynolds, 'Discharge of Contract by Breach' (n 1) 542 ('It has long been clear that at common law such discharge is based on the interdependence of promises: hence the civilian term "synallagmatic," used from time to time by Lord Diplock, is useful in the explanation of the rules.').

[102] Hutchison (n 99) 12.

that in cases involving breach it is not necessary in all cases for the innocent party to exercise a power to terminate in order to be discharged from their obligation to perform. This is because the innocent party is discharged immediately following the failure of a condition unless they choose to waive the condition. Modern orthodoxy, which tends to only focus on the issue of discharge following the exercise of a power to terminate and neglects the failure of condition model, instead suggests that the innocent party remains bound to perform and is discharged if, and only if, they exercise the power to terminate. In many cases, the consequences of these two different starting points will be the same. But the two models can pull apart. In *Bank of Nova Scotia v Hellenic Mutual War Risks Association (Bermuda) Ltd (The Good Luck)*,[103] for example, the House of Lords held that the 'effect of a breach of a promissory warranty is to discharge the insurer from liability as from the date of the breach'[104] even though there has been no election to terminate the contract. This case has always been difficult to explain on the orthodox approach, particularly because promissory warranties are understood to operate in the same way as promissory conditions.[105] But it makes perfect sense on a failure of condition model. How to reconcile these two approaches is discussed in Chapter 2.

1.62 Another practical implication of the failure of condition model is that it can help solve the puzzle as to whether and how an express contractual power to terminate can be distinguished from termination at law, especially given their different effects in relation to damages for the loss of the bargain.[106] As we will see in Chapter 2,[107] the current state of the law, which denies loss of bargain damages for termination pursuant to an express power but awards them for termination for 'breach of a condition',[108] is difficult to defend on the power to terminate model. On the failure of condition model, however, there is a clear difference between discharge following breach and pursuant to an express termination clause. For discharge following breach, failure of a condition results in the innocent party being discharged from their obligation to perform unless they waive the condition. For termination pursuant to an express power, the failure of performance does not of itself discharge the innocent party, but gives

[103] [1992] 1 AC 233. See further discussion at [2.117].
[104] ibid 263.
[105] *Behn v Burness* (1863) 3 B & S 751, 753; 122 ER 281, 282.
[106] Edwin Peel, 'The Termination Paradox' [2013] Lloyd's Maritime and Commercial Law Quarterly 519, 522–25; Wilmot-Smith (n 4) 323–324; Edwin Peel, 'Loss of Bargain Damages' [2020] Lloyd's Maritime and Commercial Law Quarterly 442.
[107] See [2.118]–[2.133].
[108] Compare *Financings Ltd v Baldock* [1963] 2 QB 104 with *Lombard North Central plc v Butterworth* [1987] QB 527.

that party a power—in the sense of a capacity to change legal relations[109]—to terminate the parties' contractual obligations. Unless the innocent party is already discharged as a result of a failure of condition, it will be their act in exercising the express power to terminate that causes the loss of the bargain, not the defaulting party's breach.

Finally, as we will see in Chapter 9, the arguments set out in this book may also have implications for how we understand restitution for failure of condition in the law of unjust enrichment. In particular, this book explains why restitution for failure of condition does not contradict the law of contract in cases where there is an underlying valid contract and that contract, at first glance, appears to entitle the defendant to receive the performance in question. It is generally thought that a claim in restitution cannot 'override a valid and subsisting legal obligation of the claimant to confer the benefit on the defendant'.[110] The answer given is that the conflict between restitution and contract in these cases is more apparent than real. This is because where one party performs pursuant to an apparent obligation to do so and subsequently discovers that a condition precedent to that obligation had not been fulfilled there was, as it turns out, simply no immediate duty to perform. Moreover, obligations to perform in advance are often subject to a condition subsequent extinguishing the immediate duty of performance if the agreed exchange is not received. The effect of a condition failing is to create a localised absence of basis. **1.63**

Conclusion

This chapter has armed the reader with an overview of the book, an explanation of the key concepts, and a sense of why any of it matters. In the succeeding chapters, the aim is to prove these claims by reference to history, authority, and principle. We begin first, in Chapter 2, with promissory conditions. **1.64**

[109] Hohfeld (n 25) 44–45.

[110] *Dargamo Holdings Ltd v Avonwick Holdings Ltd* [2022] 1 All ER (Comm) 1244, 1261–62 [70]. See also *Kleinwort Benson Ltd v Lincoln City Council* [1999] 2 AC 349, 408; *Fairfield Sentry Ltd (in liq) v Migani* [2014] UKPC 9 [18]; *DD Growth Premium 2X Fund (in official liquidation) v RMF Market Neutral Strategies (Master) Ltd* [2017] UKPC 36 [62]; *Bank of New York Mellon (International) Ltd v Cine-UK Ltd; London Trocadero (2015) LLP v Picturehouse Cinemas Ltd* [2022] EWCA Civ 1021 [144]–[146].

2

Promissory Conditions*

Introduction

Lawyers are commonly told that in contract law a 'promissory condition', in its technical sense, is a contractual term the breach of which gives rise to a power to terminate.[1] Breach of such a term does not prevent performance by the other party from falling due,[2] but it does give the innocent party the ability to terminate the contract and henceforth discharge both parties from their unperformed obligations. The precise justification for this power to terminate remains unsettled,[3] but its existence is rarely questioned. This is the 'power to terminate' model of discharge of contractual obligations. 2.1

However, conditions were not always thought of in this way.[4] Traditionally, to say that a term of the contract was a 'promissory condition' was simultaneously to say (i) that one party had promised that some fact existed or that some event 2.2

* This chapter is a substantially re-worked version of an earlier article: Jordan English, 'The Nature of "Promissory Conditions"' (2021) 137 Law Quarterly Review 630. I am grateful to Thomson Reuters (Professional) UK Ltd for giving me permission to reproduce parts of it here.

[1] Edwin Peel, *The Law of Contract* (15th edn, Sweet & Maxwell 2020) 981 [18-043]; Ewan McKendrick, *Contract Law: Text, Cases, and Materials* (9th edn, OUP 2020) 742; Andrew Burrows, *A Restatement of the English Law of Contract* (2nd edn, OUP 2020) 118; Ewan McKendrick, 'Termination for Breach' in Hugh Beale (ed), *Chitty on Contracts* (35th edn, Sweet & Maxwell 2023) vol 1 2133, 2139–40 [28-016]; Mindy Chen-Wishart, *Contract Law* (7th edn, OUP 2022) 509.

[2] See, eg, Frederick Wilmot-Smith, 'Termination after Breach' (2018) 134 Law Quarterly Review 307, 308.

[3] ibid 311–12. See also Christopher Langley and Rebecca Loveridge, 'Termination as a Response to Unjust Enrichment' [2012] Lloyd's Maritime and Commercial Law Quarterly 65.

[4] See *Hurst v Bryk* [2002] 1 AC 185, 193–94; *Allianz Australia Insurance Ltd v Delor Vue Apartments CTS 39788* (2022) 277 CLR 445, 474 [48].

Discharge of Contractual Obligations. Jordan English, Oxford University Press. © Jordan English 2025.
DOI: 10.1093/9780198906704.003.0002

would occur, and (ii) that the fulfilment or performance of that promise was a condition of the other party's obligation to perform. The effect of one party 'breaching'[5] a promissory condition was that a fact or event that was the condition of the innocent party's obligation to perform either did not exist or had not occurred. The innocent party was therefore discharged immediately unless they chose to waive the condition.[6] This is the 'failure of condition' model of discharge of contractual obligations.

2.3 This way of thinking about conditions has its origins in an approach that saw mutual promises as either dependent on, or independent of, performance by the other party. But on most accounts, the law has moved on.[7] Today, the language of 'promissory conditions' is said to obscure two distinct concepts: (i) a 'condition' in the sense of an uncertain fact or event upon which the existence of an immediate duty of performance depends; and (ii) a 'condition' in the sense of an essential term the breach of which gives rise to a power to terminate.[8] On this account, it is possible for a term to be a condition in the second sense without being a condition in the first sense.[9] But the modern emphasis has undoubtedly been on the second sense of the word, with it often being taken for granted that a term is not a condition in the first sense.

2.4 The purpose of this chapter is threefold. First, it seeks to explain how the modern law arrived at the position that there is a distinction between a condition and a condition precedent (or concurrent condition), even when both terms are used in their promissory sense. It argues that, historically, there was no distinction between a promissory condition and a promissory condition precedent (or concurrent condition), but through a series of missteps and loose language the law has inadvertently come to recognise such a distinction. And although this modern position was arrived at largely by accident, it has since received significant judicial and academic support.

2.5 The second purpose of this chapter is to identify the problems that have arisen as a result of the departure from the traditional understanding of promissory conditions. The chapter argues that not only is the co-existence of the power to terminate model and the failure of condition model conceptually awkward, the power to terminate model has also given rise to a number of problems that

[5] An unfortunate, but ingrained, misuse of language: see [2.38].
[6] *Bentsen v Taylor, Sons & Co* [1893] 2 QB 274.
[7] See, eg, Wilmot-Smith (n 2) 307–08.
[8] GH Treitel, '"Conditions" and "Conditions Precedent"' (1990) 106 Law Quarterly Review 185, 185.
[9] ibid 188.

do not arise on the failure of condition model. Another consequence of this departure is that English law has lost sight of the relationship between discharge following a breach and discharge in cases of so-called frustration and common mistake. As this book explains, all three of these are explicable as instances of discharge for failure of condition. The power to terminate model disrupts that unity and has created questions that simply do not arise on the traditional approach.

The third and final purpose of this chapter is to propose a way forward. It is now too late to turn back the tide on the power to terminate model, but that does not mean that modern lawyers should not still be asking the same questions that were used to resolve contractual disputes for hundreds of years. In particular, in a case involving discharge following breach and non-compliance with a promissory condition, the *first* question should be whether the performance of that duty was a condition of the other party's obligation to perform—ie whether the parties' obligations were conditional. It is only after this question has been asked that it should be asked, *secondly*, whether the breach of this particular duty gave rise to a power to terminate because it was a 'condition' (viz an essential term). Currently, too much emphasis is placed on the second question and not enough, if any, is placed on the first. But as this chapter shows, if both questions are asked in their proper sequence, in many cases 'termination' would simply retire from view. **2.6**

The History of Promissory Conditions

Independent and dependent promises

In order to understand the traditional notion of a promissory condition, it is necessary to understand the old law of independent and dependent promises.[10] The issue of distinguishing between the two arose where one party brought an action against the other for non-performance. If mutual promises were *independent*, then one party could sue for non-performance of the counterparty's promise without having to plead and prove performance of their own promise.[11] In such cases, the parties' obligations to perform were **2.7**

[10] See generally, SJ Stoljar, 'Dependent and Independent Promises: A Study in the History of Contract' (1957) 2 Sydney Law Review 217; JW Carter and C Hodgekiss, 'Conditions and Warranties: Forebears and Descendants' (1977) 8 Sydney Law Review 31.

[11] See the notes to *Pordage v Cole* (1669) 1 Wms Saund 319, 320; 85 ER 449, 451. See further, Carter and Hodgekiss (n 10) 32.

unconditional. However, if mutual promises were *dependent*, then, in order to succeed, a party suing the other for non-performance had to plead and prove the performance of their own promise[12] or, in some cases, that they were at least ready, willing, and able to perform.[13] In these cases, the parties' obligations to perform were conditional.

2.8 At a very early stage in the law's development, it was the case that 'in the absence of an expressly stated condition, mutual promises were held to be independent of each other and unconditional'.[14] The justice of this was thought to be that each party had bargained for the other's promise (as opposed to their performance) and if either party wished to limit the scope of their obligation to perform then they could do so by express words.[15] Two cases that illustrate both sides of this coin are *Nichols v Raynbred*[16] and *Brocas's Case*.[17] In *Nichols v Raynbred*, the plaintiff promised to deliver to the defendant a cow in consideration for which the defendant promised to pay him fifty shillings. It was held in an action for assumpsit that the plaintiff did not need to plead the delivery of the cow in order to maintain the suit because 'it is promise for promise'.[18] The parties' respective promises were independent. By contrast in *Brocas's Case*, the lord of a manor covenanted to convey the freehold to his copyholder and 'in consideration for the same performed' the copyholder covenanted to pay a sum of money. It was held that because of this expressly stated condition the copyholder was not obliged to pay the sum before the conveyance was made. The Court said the position would have been different if the words had been '[i]n consideration of the said covenant to be performed', for then the copyholder would have been bound to pay, and to rely only on the covenant for his remedy.[19]

2.9 This approach was taken in connection with 'all kinds of bilateral contracts'.[20] But a side effect of it was that whether promises were dependent or

[12] See n 11.
[13] See JW Carter and Wayne Courtney, '"Ready and Willing to Perform": Discharge for Breach and Damages' [2020] Lloyd's Maritime and Commercial Law Quarterly 251, 252–55.
[14] Arthur Corbin, *Corbin on Contracts: A Comprehensive Treatise on the Rules of Contract Law* (West Publishing Co 1960) vol 3A, 136 §654. See also Stoljar (n 10) 219; Carter and Hodgekiss (n 10) 33.
[15] Corbin (n 14) 136 §654.
[16] (1614) Hob 88, 80 ER 238.
[17] (1587) 3 Leo 219, 74 ER 644.
[18] *Nichols v Raynbred* (1614) Hob 88, 88; 80 ER 238, 238.
[19] ibid.
[20] Corbin (n 14) 170 §661. See, eg, *Bettisworth v Campion* (1608) Yel 133, 80 ER 90; *Holder v Taylor* (1614) 1 Roll Abr 518; *The Spanish Ambassador v Gifford* (1615) 1 Rolle 336, 81 ER 526; *Caton v Dixon* (1639) 1 Roll Abr 415, pl 8; *Vivian v Shipping* (1634) Cro Car 384, 79 ER 935; *Bragg v Nightingale* (1649) 1 Roll Abr 416 pl 15; *Ware v Chappel* (1649) Sty 186, 82 ER 663; *Gibbons v Prewde* (1657) Hardres 102, 145 ER 402. A number of these cases are collected and translated in CC Langdell, *A Selection of Cases*

independent turned on fine distinctions, such as whether the words 'pro'[21] or 'for said cause'[22] were used. As Serjeant Williams put it, decisions were made on 'artificial and subtle distinctions, without regarding the intent and meaning of the parties'.[23]

The seventeenth century, and in particular, the decision in *Pordage v Cole*,[24] saw a shift in focus away from the technical words used by the parties and, in this sense, marked a 'turning-point in contractual history'.[25] The defendant covenanted to give to the plaintiff '£775 for all his lands' with 'the money to be paid before Midsummer, 1668'.[26] The plaintiff subsequently brought an action for the price.[27] The defendant resisted it on the grounds that the plaintiff did not plead that he had conveyed, or tendered a conveyance, of the title to the lands. The defendant argued 'that the word ["for"] made a condition in things executory'[28]—that the technical formula made the obligations dependent. The Court disagreed, holding that it was the intention of the parties that each should have a mutual remedy against the other on the covenant. The promises were therefore independent. **2.10**

The effect of *Pordage v Cole* was 'to upset the basic legal tenets which had been current for over a century'[29] and to focus on the question of 'what construction would best serve the intention of the parties'.[30] Thus a year later, in *Hunlocke v Blacklowe*,[31] the Court rejected the argument that the words '[i]n consideration of the performance thereof'[32] amounted to a condition precedent because 'such a construction would entirely defeat the intention of the parties'.[33] Similarly, in *Peeters v Opie*,[34] although consistent with the old cases, the plaintiff agreed to build a house and the defendant had agreed to pay the **2.11**

on the Law of Contracts with a Summary of the Topics Covered by the Cases (2nd edn, Little, Brown, and Company 1879) Part II, 619–25.

[21] *Pordage v Cole* (1669) 1 Wms Saund 319, 320; 85 ER 449, 450.
[22] See the notes to *Pordage v Cole* (1669) 1 Wms Saund 319, 320; 85 ER 449, 451, referring to *Anon* (1500) Y B 15 Hen VII 10 pl 17. See also Carter and Hodgekiss (n 10) 33; Stoljar (n 10) 219–20.
[23] In his notes to Sir Edmund Saunders' report of *Pordage v Cole* (1669) 1 Wms Saund 319, 320; 85 ER 449, 451.
[24] *Pordage v Cole* (1669) 1 Wms Saund 319, 85 ER 449.
[25] Stoljar (n 10) 229; Carter and Hodgekiss (n 10) 33.
[26] *Pordage v Cole* (1669) 1 Wms Saund 319, 320; 85 ER 449, 450.
[27] Less five shillings paid as a deposit.
[28] *Pordage v Cole* (1669) 1 Wms Saund 319, 320; 85 ER 449, 450.
[29] Stoljar (n 10) 229.
[30] Carter and Hodgekiss (n 10) 33.
[31] (1670) 2 Wms Saund 156, 85 ER 893.
[32] *Hunlocke v Blacklowe* (1670) 2 Wms Saund 156, 156; 85 ER 893, 895.
[33] ibid 157; 896.
[34] (1671) 2 Wms Saund 350, 85 ER 1144.

plaintiff 'for his labour'.[35] Saunders, for the defendant, had argued that 'the party who is to pay the money does not intend to pay it unless the work be performed'.[36] Chief Justice Hale agreed and held that 'the words *for his labour* make a condition precedent, so that the plaintiff ought of necessity to have shewn the work done, or at least that he was hindered from doing it by the plaintiff, before he can demand the money'.[37] Implicit in Saunders' argument was the early recognition by common lawyers that 'in a bilateral contract parties enter into contracts in order to secure the performance of the return promise rather than bargain for a lawsuit'.[38] In other words, they often bargain for performance of the promise, rather than for just the promise itself.

2.12 By the beginning of the eighteenth century, it was clear that whether promises were dependent or independent was to be determined by the proper construction of the contract.[39] It was these developments that allowed Lord Mansfield in *Kingston v Preston*[40] to say that 'the depend[e]nce, or independ[e]nce, of covenants was to be collected from the evident sense and meaning of the parties' as opposed to the technical words they had used. The decision is also important due to Lord Mansfield's statement that there are three kinds of covenants:

(1) independent covenants, 'where either party may recover damages from the other, . . . and where it is no excuse for the defendant, to allege a breach of the covenants on the part of the plaintiff';
(2) dependent covenants, 'in which the performance of one depends on the prior performance of another'; and
(3) covenants 'which are mutual conditions, to be performed at the same time', where 'if one party was ready, and offered, to perform his part' they may 'maintain an action for the default of the other'.[41]

2.13 Lord Mansfield's judgment proved enormously influential, and provided 'a basis for the modern law'.[42] Lord Mansfield's third category was what we have referred to as 'concurrent conditions'.[43] Where both performances were to

[35] ibid.
[36] ibid 351; 1145.
[37] ibid 352; 1146.
[38] Francis Dawson, 'Readiness and Willingness Under the Contractual Remedies Act' (2017) 23 New Zealand Business Law Quarterly 61, 65. See also n 36 referring to Saunders' argument in *Peeters v Opie* (1671) 2 Wms Saund 350, 351; 85 ER 1144, 1145.
[39] See, eg, *Thorp v Thorp* (1702) 12 Mod 455, 460; 88 ER 1448, 1451.
[40] (1773) 2 Doug 689, 691; 99 ER 437, 438.
[41] *Kingston v Preston* (1773) 2 Doug 689, 690–91; 99 ER 437, 437–38.
[42] Francis Dawson, 'Metaphors and Anticipatory Breach of Contract' (1981) 40 Cambridge Law Journal 83, 88.
[43] See [1.29]–[1.30].

occur at the same time, the actual performance of each obligation could not be a condition precedent to the other obligation, for there would be an obvious 'stalemate'.[44] In *Jones v Barkley*,[45] Lord Mansfield (with whom Willes and Ashhurst JJ agreed) said that in such cases '[t]he party must shew he was ready; but, if the other stops him on the ground of an intention not to perform his part, it is not necessary for the first to go farther, and do a nugatory act.'[46] Justice Buller similarly observed that 'where something is to be performed by each party at the same time, he who was ready, and offered to do his part, may sue the other for not performing his.'[47]

The decided cases so far all appear to have dealt with problems relating to non-performance in executory contracts.[48] But what would happen in a case involving a partly executed contract? Could one party refuse to perform their obligations because what the defaulting party had done was compliant with some of that party's obligations but not all of them? This question was raised and answered in *Boone v Eyre*.[49] The plaintiff conveyed to the defendant the equity of redemption of a plantation in the West Indies, together with title to the slaves upon it, in consideration of £500 and an annuity of £160 per annum for his life. The plaintiff covenanted (i) that he had good title to the plantation, (ii) that he was lawfully possessed of the slaves, and (iii) that the defendant would quietly enjoy. When the defendant failed to pay the annuity, the plaintiff sued. The defendant pleaded by way of defence that the plaintiff was not lawfully possessed of the slaves on the plantation. On a demurrer, the Court gave judgment for the plaintiff, Lord Mansfield saying: **2.14**

> The distinction is very clear; where mutual covenants go to the whole of the consideration on both sides, they are mutual conditions, the one precedent to the other: but where they go only to a part, where a breach may be paid for in damages, there the defendant has a remedy on his covenant, and shall not plead it as a condition precedent. If this plea were to be allowed, any one [slave] not being the property of the plaintiff would bar the action.[50]

[44] Carter and Hodgekiss (n 10) 35.

[45] (1781) 2 Doug 684, 694; 99 ER 434, 440.

[46] This passage has been construed as being about concurrent conditions: Carter and Hodgekiss (n 10) 34. But counsel in the case advanced two arguments, one based on concurrent conditions and the other based on waiver. Unfortunately, the Court did not make it clear which argument it was accepting: Dawson (n 42) 91. The passage may therefore equally be about waiver as discussed at [5.44]–[5.47].

[47] *Jones v Barkley* (1781) 2 Doug 684, 695; 99 ER 434, 440.

[48] Carter and Hodgekiss (n 10) 34.

[49] (1777) 1 H BL 273n, 126 ER 160n.

[50] ibid 273n; 160n.

2.15 As we shall see in Chapter 3, there are at least three different interpretations of this passage each of which has offspring in the modern law.[51] For present purposes, the effect of Lord Mansfield's decision was that the plaintiff's failure to fulfil the promise that he was lawfully possessed of the slaves did not discharge the defendant from his obligation to pay the annuity because the fulfilment of this promise was not a condition precedent to that obligation. On this interpretation, the significance of *Boone v Eyre* is that it demonstrated the need in cases where some but not all of A's promises had been performed or fulfilled to determine which of A's obligations were conditions precedent to B's obligations and which of A's obligation were not. This, as we shall see, formed the basis of the modern orthodox distinction between conditions and warranties.

2.16 In the nineteenth century courts continued to build upon the approach in *Kingston v Preston* as developed in *Boone v Eyre*. In *Ritchie v Atkinson*,[52] the plaintiff master of a ship agreed with the defendant freighter to carry a cargo of clean hemp and iron. The plaintiff only delivered a little more than half of the quantity of hemp stipulated. The issue was whether delivery of a complete cargo was a condition precedent to payment. The plaintiff argued that he was entitled to recover a proportion of the freight. The Court (Lord Ellenborough CJ, Grose, Le Blanc, and Bayley JJ) agreed, holding that the delivery of a complete cargo was not a condition precedent to payment, in particular, because it was to be paid for by the ton. Similarly, in *Davidson v Gwynne*,[53] the same members of the Court—relying upon *Boone v Eyre* and *Ritchie v Atkinson*—held that the performance of a stipulation to sail with the first convoy was not a condition precedent. Lord Ellenborough CJ said that it was 'useless to go over the same subject again, which has been so often discussed of late'.[54] He said:

> The principle laid down in *Boone v Eyre* has been recognized in all the subsequent cases, that unless the non-performance alleged in breach of the contract goes to the whole root and consideration of it, the covenant broken is not to be considered as a condition precedent, but as a distinct covenant, for the breach of which the party injured may be compensated in damages.[55]

2.17 The same approach can be seen in *Glaholm v Hays*.[56] A clause in a charterparty stated that the vessel was 'to sail from England on or before the 4th day of

[51] See [3.3]–[3.7].
[52] (1808) 10 East 295, 103 ER 787.
[53] (1810) 12 East 381, 104 ER 149.
[54] ibid 389; 152.
[55] ibid.
[56] (1841) 2 Man & G 257, 133 ER 743.

February next'. On an action by the shipowners against the defendant freighters for breach of their obligation to load the vessel with cargo, the freighters pleaded by way of defence that the vessel had not sailed from England on or before 4 February. The Court ultimately found for the defendants and held that the fulfilment of this obligation was a condition precedent to the defendants' obligation to load the vessel with cargo.

Tindal CJ, delivering the judgment of the Court, did speak of the defendants being 'at liberty to throw up the charter'[57] or 'at liberty to abandon the contract'[58] following non-compliance with the condition precedent. It has been suggested that the Chief Justice here was no longer speaking of the dependency or independency of promises but simply 'distinguishing between breaches giving the right to terminate and those conferring only a right to damages'.[59] Dr John Stannard and Dr David Capper refer to *Glaholm v Hays* as a 'landmark case'[60] in the 'story . . . of how we got from using *condition* to mean something on which one party's contractual performance was dependent or conditional upon, to the concept of promissory condition'.[61] But on closer examination, this case is not the landmark that the learned authors suggest it is. In addition to stating expressly 'that construing the words as a *condition precedent*, will carry into effect the intention of the parties, with more certainty', Tindal CJ also said that 'the obligation of the contract itself shall be made to depend upon the actual performance of the stipulation'.[62] **2.18**

Even as late as the mid-nineteenth century, the approach based upon the dependency or independency of promises continued to be applied. Thus in *Ellen v Topp*,[63] the plaintiff brought an action on an indenture against the father of an apprentice who had absented himself from the plaintiff's service. The plaintiff had stipulated in the indenture that he was an 'an auctioneer, appraiser and corn-factor', but he subsequently relinquished the trade of corn-factor, following which the apprentice left. The father argued that '[t]he exercise of the trades, or rather the non-abandonment of any one of them . . . [was] a condition precedent to the service of the apprentice'.[64] Chief Baron Pollock agreed. After noting that the argument was founded on the rules laid **2.19**

[57] ibid 265; 746.
[58] ibid 266; 746.
[59] John Stannard and David Capper, *Termination for Breach of Contract* (2nd edn, OUP 2020) 34–35 [2.08].
[60] ibid.
[61] ibid 32 [2.02] (emphasis in original).
[62] *Glaholm v Hays* (1841) 2 Man & G 257, 267–68; 133 ER 743, 747 (emphasis added).
[63] (1851) 6 Ex 424, 155 ER 609.
[64] ibid 430; 612.

down in *Boone v Eyre*, Pollock CB said: 'To this particular covenant to serve, the relative duty to teach seems to us to be directly a condition precedent'.[65]

The Common Law Procedure Act 1852: a shift in emphasis

2.20 In the mid-nineteenth century, however, a shift in emphasis occurred. Until 1852, a plaintiff who brought an action for non-performance had to assert and prove that they had complied with all the conditions precedent to the defendant's obligation.[66] This required the plaintiff to identify, at their own risk, which facts or events were conditions, irrespective of whether they were express or implied.[67] The Common Law Procedure Act 1852 changed this. In particular, s 57 provided:

> It shall be lawful for the Plaintiff or Defendant in any Action to aver Performance of Conditions precedent generally, and the opposite Party shall not deny such Averment generally, but shall specify in his Pleading the Condition or Conditions precedent the Performance of which he intends to contest.

2.21 The effect of this section was to make a general allegation of the performance of all conditions by the plaintiff sufficient.[68] The defendant then had to specify which condition they alleged had not been performed. The section was an effort 'to remedy the evils of allowing the decision of substantial rights to turn on the niceties of pleading'.[69]

2.22 Importantly, s 57 did not change the substantive legal relations of the parties.[70] The underlying position remained the same, and the ultimate burden of proof still remained on the plaintiff.[71] However, the Act did change the emphasis. Whereas previously a plaintiff had to say 'I have complied with conditions X, Y, and Z of the defendant's obligation', a plaintiff could now simply say 'I have complied with all conditions of the defendant's obligation'. The defendant

[65] ibid 442; 616.

[66] Samuel Williston, 'Fashions in Law with Illustrations from the Law of Contracts' (1942) 21 Texas Law Review 119, 128; Dawson (n 42) 89 fn 27.

[67] Williston (n 66) 128; Dawson (n 42) 89 fn 27.

[68] Until 1999 when the rules lapsed, RSC Ord 18, r 7(4) went further and implied an allegation of the performance or occurrence of all conditions precedent into the plaintiff's claim.

[69] Williston (n 66) 128.

[70] ibid 129; Dawson (n 42) 89 fn 27.

[71] *Bentsen v Taylor, Sons & Co* [1893] 2 QB 274, 283; *Jefferson v Paskell* [1916] 1 KB 57. See also Williston (n 66) 129; Dawson (n 42) 89 fn 27.

then had to say 'the plaintiff has broken this key stipulation, the performance of which was a condition precedent to my obligation'. As a result, the focus shifted to the particular term or promise that the defendant alleged had been breached.[72]

Unfortunately, this shift in emphasis, combined with loose language, led judges to begin to speak of conditions (rather than covenants or promises) being 'breached'. An example is *Graves v Legg*.[73] The plaintiff contracted to sell to the defendant 300 to 350 bales of white-washed fleece wool. A term of the contract provided that 'the names of the vessels to be declared as soon as the wools were shipped'. The defendant did not accept the wools and the plaintiff sued. Parke B (for the Court), after noting that the declaration had averred the performance of conditions precedent generally in accordance with s 57, said that 'the defendant proceeds in this plea to specify this condition of declaring the names of the vessels, as one on the breach of which he insists'.[74] **2.23**

Nonetheless, the Common Law Procedure Act did not change the contemporary understanding of promissory conditions. An illustrative case is *Bettini v Gye*.[75] The plaintiff singer was engaged by the defendant to perform at his theatre. The plaintiff agreed to be in London at least six days before the commencement of his engagement, but only arrived two days before his engagement. The defendant refused to accept the plaintiff's services and the plaintiff sued the defendant for not doing so, alleging a breach of contract. The plaintiff pleaded that he had complied with conditions precedent generally[76] but the defendant relied on the fact that the plaintiff had not been in London six days before commencement. On a demurrer, the plaintiff argued that attendance six days before commencement was not a condition precedent.[77] The Court ultimately agreed. Blackburn J said that the question was whether the plaintiff's failure to arrive six days prior 'justified the defendant in refusing to proceed with the engagement, and fulfil his, the defendant's part'.[78] He said the answer to this question: **2.24**

> depends on whether this part of the contract is a condition precedent to the defendant's liability, or only an independent agreement, a breach of which

[72] Dawson (n 42) 89 fn 27.
[73] (1854) 9 Ex 709, 156 ER 304.
[74] ibid 715–16; 306.
[75] (1876) 1 QBD 183.
[76] ibid 185.
[77] ibid 186.
[78] ibid 187.

will not justify a repudiation of the contract, but will only be a cause of action for a compensation in damages.[79]

2.25 The language here of a breach which may 'justify a repudiation of the contract'[80] might be taken to suggest that the claimant needs to 'repudiate' or 'terminate' before they are discharged. But it is clear from the context that this is not so. Indeed, Blackburn J spoke of a condition precedent 'to the defendant's liability' and contrasted this with an independent agreement. Moreover, immediately after this passage, Blackburn J noted that the 'numerous cases on the subject' were collected in Williams' notes to Saunders' report of *Pordage v Cole*,[81] which spoke in terms of the dependency or independency of promises—that is the language of conditions. Blackburn J must have been using 'repudiate' merely in the sense of the defendant refusing to perform his side of the bargain.

Waiver of condition: the next step

2.26 An important nineteenth-century case is *Bentsen v Taylor, Sons & Co.*[82] A clause in a charterparty described a ship as 'now sailed or about to sail' from a particular port. It was known to both parties that the ship was not in fact ready to sail from that port and it did not do so until sometime later. After the ship had failed to sail, the defendant charterers wrote to the plaintiff shipowner's brokers advising of their 'intention to load under protest, claiming damages for freight and increased insurance'.[83] The defendants ultimately refused to load the ship, following which the plaintiff brought an action for the freight due under the charterparty. The issue was whether the performance of the clause was a condition precedent to the defendants' liability to pay freight. The Court of Appeal (Lord Esher MR, Bowen, and Kay LJJ) held that (i) the clause was a condition precedent not a 'mere warranty',[84] (ii) it had not been complied with, but (iii) the defendants had by their correspondence waived the condition and as such they were liable for the freight,[85] subject to their own ability to bring a claim for damages.

[79] ibid.
[80] This language was also used in the earlier case of *Behn v Burness* (1863) 3 B & S 751, 754; 122 ER 281, 283.
[81] (1669) 1 Wms Saund 319, 320; 85 ER 449, 451.
[82] [1893] 2 QB 274.
[83] ibid 276.
[84] ibid 284.
[85] For the difficulties with the fact that this was a claim for the freight (ie the agreed sum), see [5.31]–[5.32].

In reaching the conclusion that the condition had been waived, Lord Esher MR and Bowen LJ expressed themselves in different ways.[86] Bowen LJ said: 2.27

> In order to succeed, the plaintiff must shew, either that he has performed the condition precedent, the onus being on him, or that the defendants have excused the performance of the condition, and we have to consider whether the plaintiff has sustained that burthen, so that no reasonable man could doubt that there has been a waiver of the condition or an excuse of its performance.[87]

Bowen LJ held that the defendants 'did not intend to rely upon that as a failure of a condition precedent, but only as a breach of warranty'.[88]

Lord Esher MR said: 2.28

> She did not sail till nearly a month afterwards, and there was a breach of the condition. The defendants had then a right to treat the contract as at an end, or they could, if they chose, treat it as still subsisting. But, if they intended to treat the contract as at an end, *it was their duty so to exercise their right* as not to lead the plaintiff to believe that he was still bound by the contract.[89]

These two different ways of expressing the conclusion reached in the case are important. On Bowen LJ's approach, where one party fails to comply with a condition precedent to the other's obligation, the other party is discharged from their obligation to perform but can, notwithstanding, waive the condition by continuing to render or accept performance. In such a case, the innocent party will no longer be discharged from their obligation and so will be required to perform. As Lord Chelmsford said in *Roberts v Brett*,[90] a party who, when faced with non-performance of a condition precedent, 'allows the other side to go on and perform the subsequent stipulations, has waived his right to insist upon the unperformed condition precedent'. 2.29

By contrast, on one reading of Lord Esher MR's judgment, while the defendants had a 'right' to treat the contract as at an end, they needed to exercise that 2.30

[86] Kay LJ delivered a short judgment in which he opined that the words amounted to a condition, rather than to a 'mere warranty'. However, his Lordship said 'it is not really necessary to decide the point, for, if there was a condition precedent, I have no doubt as to the waiver': *Bentsen v Taylor, Sons & Co* [1893] 2 QB 274, 284.

[87] ibid 283.

[88] ibid 284.

[89] ibid 279 (emphasis added).

[90] (1865) 11 HL Cas 337, 358; 11 ER 1363, 1371.

right. This would mean that unless and until the right 'to treat the contract as at an end' is exercised, the innocent party remains bound. Moreover, the innocent party's failure to exercise that right could, in some circumstances, preclude them from later doing so on the basis that the right had been lost.

2.31 The difference between these two views is not a matter of semantics and indeed is at the heart of the dispute in this chapter. It is submitted, particularly in light of the history canvassed thus far, that to the extent that the judgment of Lord Esher MR might be interpreted differently, the judgment of Bowen LJ is more reflective of the understanding at the time. The better view is that the relevant parts of Lord Esher MR's judgment were simply loose language. He cannot have intended 'without so much as a backward glance, let alone an express acknowledgement of the *volte face*'[91] to depart from the understanding of the nature of promissory conditions and their relation to discharge which had developed over the past 300 years and had been expressly applied not twenty years before in *Bettini v Gye*.[92] Nor would the issue have arisen in *Bentsen v Taylor*—the defendants had, by their positive conduct, indicated that they did not intend to rely upon the failure of the condition precedent. They had therefore waived the condition.

2.32 *Bentsen v Taylor*, however, is important for another reason. That is, it may help us understand why modern lawyers, academics, and judges have come to think of the innocent party as having to 'elect to terminate' in order to bring about a discharge of their obligations to perform. In particular, the risk that the innocent party's inactivity may be found to be a waiver of the condition means that in many cases, practically speaking, he 'will be well advised to notify the other party that he treats himself as discharged'.[93] But as Charles Morison observed in 1916, 'such notice is not required for the purpose of completing a rescission, but only for the purpose of negativing waiver'.[94] It is only a small (mis)step to go from this proposition to the proposition that the innocent party must take steps to terminate. A misreading of *Bentsen v Taylor* is arguably the birthplace of the modern 'election theory' of termination.[95]

[91] To borrow a phrase from Keith Mason, 'Strong Coherence, Strong Fusion, Continuing Categorical Confusion: The High Court's Latest Contributions to the Law of Restitution' (2014) 39 Australian Bar Review 284, 318.

[92] (1876) 1 QBD 183.

[93] Dawson (n 42) 90.

[94] Charles Bruce Morison, *Rescission of Contracts, A Treatise on the Principles Governing the Rescission, Discharge, Avoidance and Dissolution of Contracts* (Stevens & Haynes 1916) 18.

[95] I am grateful to Professor Francis Dawson for pointing this out.

Sale of Goods Act 1893

The Sale of Goods Act 1893, which came into force on 1 January 1894,[96] has also been identified as one possible cause of the shift from 'promissory condition' as traditionally understood to 'condition' in the sense of an essential term the breach of which gives rise to a power to terminate.[97] The Act famously contrasted 'conditions' with 'warranties'. Section 11(1)(b) relevantly provided: **2.33**

> Whether a stipulation in a contract of sale is a condition, the breach of which may give rise to a right to treat the contract as repudiated, or a warranty, the breach of which may give rise to a claim for damages but not a right to reject the goods and treat the contract as repudiated, depends in each case on the construction of the contract. A stipulation may be a condition, though called a warranty in the contract . . .

However, the Sale of Goods Act 1893 was '[a]n Act for codifying the law relating to the Sale of Goods'. As Vaughan Williams LJ observed in *Wallis, Son & Wells v Pratt & Haynes*,[98] it 'simply enact[ed] the law already established by the cases cited'. Likewise, it is clear that the draftsman of the Act, Sir Mackenzie Chalmers, did not intend to change the law. In his 1894 commentary to the Act, he wrote: **2.34**

> The Act throughout, so far as it relates to England, draws a distinction between the terms 'condition' and 'warranty'. This distinction has often been insisted on, but seldom observed by judges and text writers. As used in the Act, 'condition' is the equivalent to the old term 'dependent covenant,' while 'warranty' is equivalent to the old term 'independent covenant.'[99]

It has been argued that Chalmers' 'use of the term "condition" was a misuse of the term "condition precedent"',[100] and that '[f]undamentally, Chalmers . . . failed to distinguish promises from conditions'.[101] The most serious charge levelled at Chalmers is that he 'simply misunderstood the previous law on this subject'.[102] These criticisms are largely unfair. While it is true that the word **2.35**

[96] See Sale of Goods Act 1893, s 63. The Act was, however, given Royal Assent on 20 February 1894.
[97] Wilmot-Smith (n 2) 308 fn 10.
[98] [1910] 2 KB 1003, 1010.
[99] MD Chalmers, *The Sale of Goods Act, 1893, including The Factors Acts, 1889 & 1890* (William Clowes and Sons Ltd 1894) 24. See also his discussion of the term 'warranty': 168.
[100] Carter and Hodgekiss (n 10) 43.
[101] ibid 44.
[102] Stannard and Capper (n 59) 37 [2.11].

'condition' confusingly was being used to refer to both the condition and the promise, Chalmers was acutely aware of this. In an appendix to his commentary, he explained:

> The term 'condition' as applied to contracts appears to mean indifferently (a) an uncertain event on the happening of which the obligation of the contract is to depend, and (b) the stipulation in the contract making its obligation depend on the happening of such event. Though the Act uses the term condition, it does not define it. The definition belongs to the general law of contract.[103]

While there are undoubtedly problems with using the same word to refer to these two different concepts, judges were already doing this prior to the Sale of Goods Act 1893. At most, Chalmers can be criticised for perpetuating this confusing use of language. A fairer criticism is found in the fifth edition of *Benjamin on Sale*:

> It would have been, in the Editors' opinion, better to have used the word 'promises' in the Code in referring to conditions to be performed by the seller, with an independent statement that the performance of these promises is a condition precedent to the buyer's liability.[104]

2.36 As for Chalmers' use of the word 'warranty', this might be criticised because a warranty (in the sense of a guarantee)[105] can also amount to a condition precedent and many cases, especially in the insurance context, had used the word in that sense.[106] But Chalmers made clear that, when used in the Act, it was not being used in that sense; it was being used to denote an independent stipulation.[107] Moreover, this was not new. Indeed, in cases such as *Bentsen v Taylor*,[108] the language of condition precedent was contrasted with a 'mere warranty'. The inference to be drawn is that by the time of the Act, the language of 'warranty' had come to denote an independent promise. Sir William Anson, for example, writing some fifteen years before the Act came into force, made precisely this distinction when contrasting 'subsidiary

[103] Chalmers (n 99) 164.

[104] Walter Charles Alan Ker and Arthur Reginald Butterworth, *A Treatise on the Law of Sale of Personal Property with references to the American Decisions and to the French Code and Civil Law* (5th edn, Sweet & Maxwell 1906) 557–58 fn 6.

[105] See Chalmers (n 99) 169.

[106] *Behn v Burness* (1863) 3 B & S 751, 753; 122 ER 281, 282.

[107] Chalmers (n 99) 168.

[108] [1893] 2 QB 274.

promises, or *warranties*' with '*conditions* or terms on which the right to performance depends'.[109]

State of the law at the end of the nineteenth century

At least until the end of the nineteenth century, the word 'condition', even when used in its promissory sense, bore its natural meaning: one party's obligation to perform was conditional. However, by the end of the nineteenth century, the word 'condition' had begun to be used to refer to the term itself (ie the promise). Strictly speaking, however, it was (and still is when condition is used in this sense) the performance of A's promise that was a condition precedent to (or concurrent condition of) B's obligation.[110] As Professor Robert Bradgate noted, the words 'condition precedent' were simply 'a shorthand to describe a term whose *performance* is a condition precedent to the other party's obligation to perform. To describe such a term as a 'condition' is merely a further contraction'.[111] **2.37**

One problem with this approach, however, is that it led parties and courts to start talking about 'breach of a condition'. The potential for confusion was that, logically speaking, one cannot breach a condition if 'condition' is understood to refer to an uncertain fact or event upon which the existence of one party's immediate duty of performance depends. Professor Arthur Corbin noted this when he said: **2.38**

> [I]n many cases it is said that there has been a 'breach of the condition' by the defendant (clearly a misuse of the word condition). The defendant has in fact committed a breach, but it is a breach of *duty*, not a breach of condition.[112]

The use of this language by English lawyers was criticised, particularly by American writers,[113] but it was not because promissory conditions were not **2.39**

[109] Sir William R Anson, *Principles of the English Law of Contract* (1st edn, Clarendon Press 1879) 284 (emphasis in original). The use of the term in this way possibly originates from *Chanter v Hopkins* (1838) 4 M & W 399, 150 ER 1484: see Anthony Beck, 'The Doctrine of Substantial Performance: Conditions and Conditions Precedent' (1975) 38 Modern Law Review 413, 420.

[110] Robert Bradgate, 'Termination for Breach' in John Birds, Robert Bradgate, and Charlotte Villiers (eds), *Termination of Contracts* (Wiley Chancery 1995) 17, 40. See also Carter and Hodgekiss (n 10) 38.

[111] Bradgate (n 110) 42 (emphasis in original).

[112] Arthur Corbin, 'Supervening Impossibility of Performing Conditions Precedent' (1922) 22 Columbia Law Review 421, 423.

[113] ibid. See, eg, Samuel Williston, *The Law of Contracts* (Baker, Voorhis & Co 1921) vol 2, 1282–83 §665. See also JL Montrose, 'Conditions and Promises' (1960) 23 Modern Law Review 434, 434–35; FMB Reynolds, 'Discharge of Contract by Breach' (1982) 97 Law Quarterly Review 541, 542.

conditions in the strict sense. The problem was that the language of condition failed to distinguish between the condition and the promise; it simply referred to both.[114]

The immediate aftermath of the Sale of Goods Act

2.40 We have seen that the Sale of Goods Act 1893 did not set out to change the nature of promissory conditions. Nonetheless, did the subsequent interpretation of the Act cause our understanding to change? The short answer is that it did not. However, one early case which, if read out of context, might suggest the contrary is the decision of the Court of Appeal in *Wallis, Son & Wells v Pratt & Haynes*,[115] specifically, the dissenting judgment of Fletcher Moulton LJ, which was unanimously adopted on appeal to the House of Lords.[116]

2.41 The defendants sold seed by sample to the plaintiffs. The relevant description on the back of the sale note described the seeds as 'common English sainfoin'. As it turned out, neither the sample nor the seed sold was common English sainfoin. A term on the back of the note provided: 'Sellers give no warranty express or implied as to the growth, description, or any other matters'. The Court of Appeal held that although it was a condition precedent that the goods match the description, as the plaintiffs had accepted and resold the seed they could only treat it as a warranty entitling them to damages.[117] However, the majority of the Court also held that the defendants had excluded any such liability by excluding their liability for breach of any warranty. This latter aspect of the decision was overturned on appeal to the House of Lords. The important passage for present purposes is from the dissenting judgment of Fletcher Moulton LJ in the Court of Appeal in which he contrasted obligations described as 'conditions' with obligations described as 'warranties' and said:

> Both classes are equally obligations under the contract, and the breach of any one of them entitles the other party to damages. But in the case of the former class he has the alternative of treating the contract as being completely broken

[114] FMB Reynolds, 'Warranty, Condition and Fundamental Term' (1963) 79 Law Quarterly Review 534, 536.

[115] [1910] 2 KB 1003.

[116] *Wallis, Son & Wells v Pratt & Haynes* [1911] AC 394.

[117] Relying upon s 11(1)(c) of Sale of Goods Act 1893 and the cases from which the section was derived.

> by the non-performance and (*if he takes the proper steps*) he can refuse to perform any of the obligations resting upon himself and sue the other party for a total failure to perform the contract.[118]

The reference to 'if he takes the proper steps' appears, at first glance, to be a reference to taking steps in order to bring about a discharge. However, a proper reading of Fletcher Moulton LJ's judgment reveals that this is not the case. Rather, he was referring to the need to take proper steps to reject the goods, so as not to be barred from relying on the condition (ie so as to negate any waiver). This instance of waiver was found in s 11(1)(c) of the Sale of Goods Act 1893,[119] which provided: **2.42**

> Where a contract of sale is not severable, and the buyer has accepted the goods, or part thereof . . . the breach of any condition to be fulfilled by the seller can only be treated as a breach of warranty, and not as a ground for rejecting the goods and treating the contract as repudiated . . .

The section was based in part on Serjeant Williams' observations of *Boone v Eyre*.[120] We have already seen the first interpretation of that decision, namely, that fulfilment of the promise that the plaintiff had good title to all the slaves was not a condition precedent. The second interpretation, which assumes that fulfilment of the promise was a condition precedent, arose from Serjeant Williams' comment that: **2.43**

> where a person has received a *part* of the consideration for which he entered into the agreement, it would be unjust that because he had not had the *whole*, he should therefore be permitted to enjoy that part without either paying or doing any thing for it.[121]

Prior to the Sale of Goods Act, the cases had interpreted this comment as giving rise to a rule that where a party received the 'whole or any substantial part of the consideration for the promise on his part' that party could no longer rely upon the non-performance of the condition precedent.[122] In *Ellen v Topp*,[123] Pollock CB adopted the rule, although observed that it was 'remarkable' that a contract could be construed 'ex post facto' and that 'that which is a condition precedent when the deed is executed may cease to be so by the **2.44**

118 *Wallis Son & Wells v Pratt & Haynes* [1910] 2 KB 1003, 1010 (emphasis added).
119 See now Sale of Goods Act 1979, s 11(4).
120 *Pordage v Cole* (1669) 1 Wms Saund 319, 320; 85 ER 449, 453.
121 ibid (emphasis in original).
122 *Behn v Burness* (1863) 3 B & S 751, 755; 122 ER 281, 283.
123 (1851) 6 Ex 424, 155 ER 609.

subsequent conduct of the covenantee in accepting less'.[124] However, subsequent cases explained that it was not a case of construing the contract ex post facto (so that what was a condition precedent was no longer so), but rather one where, because of the party's conduct, they could no longer rely upon the non-performance of a condition precedent.[125] In short, it appears to have been an instance of waiver.[126]

2.45 It is clear then that, notwithstanding the fact that a failure of a condition precedent by a seller would discharge the buyer from their obligation to pay the price, they must reject the goods in order to avoid being barred from relying upon the condition. And Fletcher Moulton LJ made exactly this point in *Wallis* when he said:

> But in the case of a breach of a condition he has the option of another and higher remedy, namely, that of treating the contract as repudiated. But, as I have said, he must act promptly if he desires to avail himself of this higher remedy, and in s. 11, sub-s. 1 (c), two cases are given in which he will be deemed as a matter of law to have elected to content himself with his right to damages.[127]

In other words, the simple point Fletcher Moulton LJ was making was that, in this context, the buyer needs to take steps so as to avoid accepting, and receiving the benefit of, the goods, and therefore to avoid being barred from relying upon the condition precedent. He was not suggesting that the nature of conditions had changed; indeed he said exactly the opposite, noting that 'the Act adopts the well-settled law that existed at the date when it was passed'.[128]

Heyman v Darwins Ltd

2.46 We have seen that so far the two major contributions to the modern view that there is a distinction between a condition in the sense of an essential term and a condition in the sense of a condition precedent or concurrent condition were (i) loose language, deriving from the shift in emphasis brought about by the Common Law Procedure Act 1852, which led judges and lawyers to begin speaking about conditions being 'breached', and (ii) the decision in *Bentsen*

[124] *Ellen v Topp* (1851) 6 Ex 424, 441; 155 ER 609, 616. This suggestion was viewed 'with repugnance' by Lord Shaw in *Wallis, Son & Wells v Pratt & Haynes* [1911] AC 394, 400.

[125] *Graves v Legg* (1854) 9 Ex 709, 717; 156 ER 304, 307; *Behn v Burness* (1863) 3 B & S 751, 755; 122 ER 281, 283.

[126] Morison (n 94) 100–05; Beck (n 109) 418–19.

[127] *Wallis, Son & Wells v Pratt & Haynes* [1910] 2 KB 1003, 1013.

[128] ibid.

v Taylor, and specifically, the misstep flowing from the practical steps that often need to be taken in order to negate any suggestion of waiver of the condition. The third major contribution to the modern orthodoxy that following 'breach of a condition' the innocent party is given a power to terminate is the decision in *Heyman v Darwins Ltd*.[129] That case, however, had nothing to do with conditions (promissory or otherwise). It was concerned with the effects of a 'repudiation'.

The word 'repudiation' can be used in three senses: **2.47**

1. It can refer to a 'renunciation',[130] namely, where one party 'evinces an intention no longer to be bound by the contract . . . or shows that he intends to fulfil the contract only in a manner substantially inconsistent with his obligations and not in any other way'.[131] This is a form of anticipatory breach.
2. It may also refer to circumstances where one party disables themselves from performing.[132] This is another form of anticipatory breach.
3. Finally, sometimes the language of 'repudiation' or 'repudiatory breach' is used to refer to cases of actual breaches of duty, where that breach of duty gives rise to a discharging event.[133] But this latter use generally should be avoided for it only obscures the true ground of discharge.[134]

Heyman v Darwins Ltd was concerned with a repudiation in the first sense—ie a renunciation. The appellants, who were selling agents of the respondent steel manufacturers, alleged that following a dispute about remittance of moneys due under their contract, the respondents had 'repudiated and/or evinced an intention not to perform'.[135] They commenced an action in the High Court. The respondents sought for the action to be stayed on the basis that there was an arbitration clause in the contract and the dispute fell within its scope. The House of Lords agreed with this argument. However, in responding to 'the **2.48**

[129] [1942] AC 356.

[130] ibid 397. See also *Koompahtoo Local Aboriginal Land Council v Sanpine Pty Ltd* (2007) 233 CLR 115, 135 [44].

[131] *Shevill v Builders Licensing Board* (1982) 149 CLR 620, 625–26. See also *Heyman v Darwins Ltd* [1942] AC 356, 379; *Progressive Mailing House Pty Ltd v Tabali Pty Ltd* (1985) 157 CLR 17, 33, 40; *Laurinda Pty Ltd v Capalaba Park Shopping Centre Pty Ltd* (1989) 166 CLR 623, 634, 643; *Koompahtoo Local Aboriginal Land Council v Sanpine Pty Ltd* (2007) 233 CLR 115, 135 [44].

[132] *Universal Cargo Carriers Corp v Citati* [1957] 2 QB 401, 436–38.

[133] *Heyman v Darwins Ltd* [1942] AC 356, 397. See also *Koompahtoo Local Aboriginal Land Council v Sanpine Pty Ltd* (2007) 233 CLR 115, 135–36 [44].

[134] See generally JW Carter, Wayne Courtney and Gregory Tolhurst, 'The Detrimental Impact of "Repudiatory Breach" on Discharge for Breach of Contract' (2020) 4 Journal of Business Law 287; JW Carter, *Carter's Breach of Contract* (2nd edn, Hart 2018) 289 [7-07].

[135] *Heyman v Darwins Ltd* [1942] AC 356, 358.

view that an agreement is automatically terminated if one party "repudiates" it',[136] various members of the House of Lords made statements that if not confined to circumstances involving repudiation (in the sense of renunciation), would suggest that a person must always 'accept' a breach (ie exercise a power to terminate) before they can be discharged from their obligation to perform. Viscount Simon LC, for example, said:

> [T]he other party may rescind the contract, or (as it is sometimes expressed) 'accept the repudiation'... But repudiation by one party standing alone does not terminate the contract. It takes two to end it, by repudiation, on the one side, and acceptance of the repudiation, on the other.[137]

2.49 The proposition that in order for a repudiation (renunciation) to operate as a discharging event it must be 'accepted'[138] is undoubtedly correct. An 'acceptance' is required because a statement by one party *in advance* of performance that they will not perform, on its own, does not discharge the other party from their obligation to perform. To quote the time-honoured phrase of Asquith LJ in *Howard v Pickford Tool Co Ltd*,[139] 'An unaccepted repudiation is a thing writ in water and of no value to anybody: it confers no legal rights of any sort or kind.'[140] Anticipatory breach is considered in more detail in Chapter 8.

2.50 But the language of 'repudiation', as already outlined, can be used in different senses. In *Heyman v Darwins Ltd*, Lord Porter said that '[a]ll these acts [actual failure of performance, renunciation, and disablement] may be compendiously described as repudiation, though that expression is more particularly used of renunciation before the time for performance has arrived'.[141] This is a recipe for confusion: 'repudiation' in one sense involves an actual breach but in another sense (renunciation or disablement) it is a form of anticipatory

[136] ibid 361.

[137] ibid. The only qualification to add is that of Lord Porter, who said: 'To say that the contract is rescinded or has come to an end or has ceased to exist may in individual cases convey the truth with sufficient accuracy, but the fuller expression that the injured party is thereby absolved from future performance of his obligations under the contract is a more exact description of the position. Strictly speaking, to say that on acceptance of the renunciation of a contract the contract is rescinded is incorrect': ibid 399.

[138] For criticism of this language, see JC Smith, 'Anticipatory Breach of Contract' in E Lomnicka and C Morse (eds), *Contemporary Issues in Commercial Law: Essays in Honour of AG Guest* (Sweet & Maxwell 1997) 175, 184–88.

[139] [1951] 1 KB 417, 421.

[140] See also ibid 420–21 (Evershed MR); *Golding v London & Edinburgh Insurance Co Ltd* (1932) 43 Ll L Rep 487, 488. It should, however, be noted that this statement, unqualified, is misleading: Sir Michael Mustill, 'Anticipatory Breach of Contract: The Common Law at Work' in *Butterworth Lectures 1989–90* (Butterworths 1990) 61–62. See further [5.37]–[5.97].

[141] *Heyman v Darwins Ltd* [1942] AC 356, 397.

breach. The situation is also made more complex because sometimes the conduct to infer a renunciation of future obligations is in fact the way in which a present obligation is breached.[142]

All of this appears to have led to a situation where although *Heyman v Darwins Ltd* was a decision concerned with repudiation in the sense of renunciation (ie anticipatory breach), the statements in it were taken by some to be applicable to discharge following actual breach. Earlier textbook writers had drawn a distinction between the rules applicable to each form of discharge,[143] but post-*Heyman v Darwins Ltd* statements relying upon the case for propositions about discharge following actual breach could be found. Geoffrey Cheshire and Cecil Fifoot, for example, wrote the following, in reliance upon the case: **2.51**

> It must be observed, however, that a contract cannot be terminated unilaterally. Therefore, if one party commits a breach sufficiently serious to constitute a discharge, this does not automatically abrogate the mutual obligations, but merely gives the other party an option either to ignore the breach and to insist upon performance when due, or to accept the repudiation and treat himself as free from further liability.[144]

This was undoubtedly a mistake, but it can be seen how this thinking would come to influence the modern lawyer's understanding of the nature of promissory conditions. When combined with the loose language referring to 'breaches of conditions' and the misstep from the practical steps needed to negate any allegation of waiver, the assumption of modern lawyers that a 'condition' is simply an essential term the breach of which does not of itself discharge either party but gives the innocent party a power to terminate, becomes easier to understand. It is a misstep that has been contributed to by applying rules about the need for an acceptance of a repudiation in the sense of renunciation (a form of anticipatory breach) to situations involving discharge following actual breach (so-called repudiatory breach).[145] It must be stressed, however, that *Heyman v Darwins Ltd* itself said nothing about the nature of promissory conditions. **2.52**

[142] *Suisse Atlantic Société d'Armement Maritime SA v NV Rotterdamsche Kolen Centrale* [1967] 1 AC 361, 435. See also McKendrick, 'Termination for Breach' (n 1) 2003 [27–039]; Peel (n 1) 978 [18-038]; Mustill (n 140) 55–56; *Koompahtoo Local Aboriginal Land Council v Sanpine Pty Ltd* (2007) 233 CLR 115, 135 [44].

[143] A good example is Morison (n 94) 8.

[144] GC Cheshire and CHS Fifoot, *The Law of Contract* (5th edn, Butterworth & Co 1960) 491.

[145] Similar statements to those found in *Heyman v Darwins Ltd* [1942] AC 356 can be found in *Hirji Mulji v Cheong Yue Steamship Co Ltd* [1926] AC 497, 509–10.

Hongkong Fir

2.53 Another candidate for the shift in thinking about promissory conditions is *Hongkong Fir Shipping Co Ltd v Kawasaki Kisen Kaisha Ltd*.[146] In that case, the claimant shipowners chartered the *Hongkong Fir* to the defendants. By clause 1 of the charterparty, the owners contracted to deliver the vessel 'she being in every way fitted for ordinary cargo service' (the 'seaworthiness obligation'). The vessel sailed from Liverpool to Osaka but there were insufficient members of the engine room to maintain the vessel's old machinery and the chief engineer was a drunk, both of which caused serious breakdowns. Sometime after the vessel arrived in Osaka, the charterers renounced their obligations under the charterparty. The owners brought an action for wrongful repudiation. The charterers in their defence alleged that the owners had breached the seaworthiness obligation, the performance of which they argued was a condition of the contract, or, alternatively, the charterparty was 'frustrated' by reason of the breakdowns, repairs, and delay. The Court of Appeal (Sellers, Upjohn, and Diplock LJJ) held that the seaworthiness obligation was not a condition and that the delays caused by the breakdowns and repairs were not so great as to 'frustrate' the commercial purpose of the charterparty. Our focus here is on the first aspect; the second aspect is discussed in detail in Chapter 3.[147]

2.54 In explaining why the seaworthiness obligation (or its performance) was not a condition, Sellers LJ said:

> It would be unthinkable that all the relatively trivial matters which have been held to be unseaworthiness could be regarded as conditions of the contract or conditions precedent to a charterer's liability and justify in themselves a cancellation or refusal to perform on the part of the charterer.[148]

2.55 It is possible here that Sellers LJ was drawing a distinction between two different concepts. The first is that of a 'condition', which justifies a 'cancellation'. The second is that of a 'condition precedent', which justifies a 'refusal to perform'. However, in the remainder of his judgment this distinction (if it were intended to be one) disappeared in favour of the latter concept. Indeed, in the dispositive part of his judgment, Sellers LJ stated: '[I]t is not open to the

[146] [1962] 2 QB 26.
[147] See [3.49]–[3.75].
[148] *Hongkong Fir Shipping Co Ltd v Kawasaki Kisen Kaisha Ltd* [1962] 2 QB 26, 56.

charterers to rely on the obligation of seaworthiness as a condition precedent to the obligation on the charterers to pay freight or hire.'[149]

Upjohn LJ's judgment is even clearer. He said: **2.56**

> A condition, or a condition precedent, to give it its proper title under the old system of pleading, was a condition performance of which had to be averred by the plaintiff in the declaration in order to establish his claim against the defendant.[150]

Upjohn LJ then went on to say that 'the stipulation as to seaworthiness is not a condition in the strict sense'.[151] At no point did he consider whether the seaworthiness obligation was a condition in any other sense.

2.57 As for Diplock LJ's judgment, his central point was that it was an event, rather than the breach itself, which relieved one party of their obligations under the contract.[152] Speaking of 'conditions precedent', he said that 'the non-performance by one party of an undertaking of this class was an event which excused the other party from the performance of his corresponding undertaking'.[153] Furthermore, after referring to a number of the cases discussed above, Diplock LJ observed:

> The fact that the emphasis in the earlier cases was upon the breach by one party to the contract of his contractual undertakings, for this was the commonest circumstance in which the question arose, tended to obscure the fact that it was really the event resulting from the breach which relieved the other party of further performance of his obligations . . .[154]

Subject to the qualification that, strictly speaking, it is the non-occurrence of an event which discharges the innocent party, this is consistent with the history of promissory conditions as traditionally understood.

2.58 Diplock LJ, however, sought to go further than the observation that it is an event that discharges the party. He said that '[t]he test whether the event relied

[149] ibid 58 (emphasis added).
[150] ibid 63.
[151] ibid 64.
[152] A point made in Donal Nolan, '*Hongkong Fir Shipping Co Ltd v Kawasaki Kisen Kaisha Ltd, The Hongkong Fir* (1961)' in Charles Mitchell and Paul Mitchell (eds), *Landmark Cases in the Law of Contract* (Hart Publishing 2008) 269, 286.
[153] *Hongkong Fir Shipping Co Ltd v Kawasaki Kisen Kaisha Ltd* [1962] 2 QB 26, 67.
[154] ibid 68.

upon has this consequence is the same whether the event is the result of the other party's breach of contract or not'.[155] He expressed it thus:

> [D]oes the occurrence of the event deprive the party who has further undertakings still to perform of substantially the whole benefit which it was the intention of the parties as expressed in the contract that he should obtain as the consideration for performing those undertakings?[156]

2.59 In this, Diplock LJ sought to identify a single event the occurrence of which discharges a party from their obligation to perform both in cases of breach and frustration.[157] The purpose of this was to explain why the so-called condition/warranty dichotomy was non-exhaustive: in relation to some terms, 'all that can be predicated is that some breaches will and others will not give rise to [such] an event'.[158] And in seeking to bring conditions into this framework, Diplock LJ said that a condition was a term:

> of which it can be predicated that every breach of such an undertaking must give rise to an event which will deprive the party not in default of substantially the whole benefit which it was intended that he should obtain from the contract.[159]

2.60 As a preliminary matter, we can note that this definition was not 'entirely correct'.[160] As Lord Roskill explained in *Bunge Corp, New York v Tradax Export SA, Panama*:[161]

> [I]t is beyond question that there are many cases in the books where terms, the breach of which do not deprive the innocent party of substantially the whole of the benefit which he was intended to receive from the contract, were nonetheless held to be conditions.

And in *Photo Production Ltd v Securicor Transport Ltd*,[162] Lord Diplock (as he had then become) retreated from it by separating out conditions as terms which the parties have simply agreed that any breach 'irrespective of the gravity of the event' shall entitle the other to be discharged.

155 ibid 69.
156 ibid 66.
157 ibid 69.
158 ibid 70.
159 ibid 69.
160 Sir Guenter Treitel, *Some Landmarks of Twentieth Century Contract Law* (OUP 2002) 116.
161 [1981] 1 WLR 711, 724.
162 [1980] AC 827, 849.

2.61 But more importantly, and unlike the other two members of the court in *Hongkong Fir*, Diplock LJ appears to have departed from the traditional understanding in two respects. First, by focusing on a single event that would discharge a party from their obligation to perform, Diplock LJ appears to have thought that, today, the discharge of that party could be explained in terms of a rule of law and need not be explained, as it historically was explained, in terms of agreed conditions. Thus, speaking of the tendency to describe cases of 'frustration' and cases of discharge following breach of a warranty[163] as resting upon an implied condition, he said:

> [I]t does not clarify, but on the contrary obscures, the modern principle of law where such an event *has* occurred as a result of a breach of an express stipulation in the contract, to continue to add the now unnecessary colophon 'Therefore it was an implied *condition* of the contract that a particular kind of breach of an express *warranty* should not occur.' The common law evolves not merely by breeding new principles but also, when they are fully grown, by burying their progenitors.[164]

2.62 Secondly, Diplock LJ did subsequently speak of 'an event which relieves the charterer of further performance of his undertakings *if he so elects*'[165] and he referred to 'where one party to a contract relies upon a breach by the other party as giving him a right to *elect* to rescind the contract'.[166]

2.63 The judgment of Diplock LJ in *Hongkong Fir* then does mark another shift towards the modern view that breach of a condition gives rise to a power to terminate. But Diplock LJ is the only judge to have expressed himself in that way and his proposed way of bringing promissory conditions into his new framework was later abandoned. As we saw above, he later accepted that 'breaches of conditions' did not need to deprive one party of substantially the whole benefit of the contract to operate as a discharging event. In *Hongkong Fir*, he certainly drew no clear distinction between 'conditions precedent' and 'promissory conditions'. And his judgment still contains a crucial insight for the traditional view, namely, that it is not the breach of a promise that discharges the innocent party from their obligation to perform but the (non-)occurrence of

[163] This is not how most lawyers would use the term 'warranty' today, but see [3.67] and the text accompanying n 152 in that section.

[164] *Hongkong Fir Shipping Co Ltd v Kawasaki Kisen Kaisha Ltd* [1962] 2 QB 26, 71 (emphasis in original).

[165] ibid (emphasis added).

[166] ibid 72 (emphasis added).

an event. That is consistent with the traditional understanding of promissory conditions.

2.64 In sum, when read as a whole, the judgments in *Hongkong Fir* give little support to the suggestion that a 'promissory condition' had anything other than its historical meaning. As Lord Wilberforce later recorded in *L Schuler AG v Wickman Machine Tool Sales Ltd*,[167] '[n]othing in the judgments [in *Hongkong Fir*] as I read them cast any doubt upon the meaning or effect of 'condition' where that word is technically used' and the 'development of the term through 19th-century cases . . . to the present time' was not reversed by *Hongkong Fir*.

A definitive shift

2.65 Although there were some exceptions and a degree of confusion, the position up to and including the decision in *Hongkong Fir* appears to have been that there was no difference between a 'condition precedent' and a 'condition' when used in their promissory sense. This understanding was also maintained by at least some academics. Indeed in 1963, Professor Francis Reynolds referred to the account given by Diplock LJ in the *Hongkong Fir* of the development of conditions, and said:

> The result was, and is, that where A breaks a promise forming substantially the whole of the consideration, B can repudiate the contract, because A is unable to prove the condition precedent to B's liability, viz., that he himself has performed or is ready to do so, and thus cannot successfully sue B for non-performance.
>
> In such a case it is the *performance* of A's promise that is the condition of B's liability. The modern usage, however, refers to the *promise* going to the whole of the consideration, breach of which would release B, as being a condition. Thus the way in which the law reached the position that a party injured by serious breach could repudiate leaves traces in the name given to the type of promise, breach of which will release the other party.[168]

2.66 One inescapable truth, however, is that a number of cases in the second half of the twentieth century spoke about the innocent party having an 'election'

[167] [1974] AC 235, 262.

[168] Reynolds (n 114) 535 (emphasis in original, citations omitted). See also Kenneth William Wedderburn, *Sutton and Shannon on Contracts* (6th edn, London Butterworths 1963) 277–78.

following breach of a condition.[169] Thus, in *The Mihalis Angelos*[170] Lord Denning MR said the innocent party was 'entitled, at his election, to treat himself as discharged from any further performance'. Megaw LJ similarly spoke of a condition in the sense that 'when it has been broken, the other party can, if he wishes, by intimation to the party in breach, elect to be released from performance of his further obligations under the contract'.[171] It is this period that marks the definitive shift from the failure of condition model of promissory conditions to the power to terminate model.

2.67 But even in this period, the position was not always entirely clear. In the Court of Appeal in *Wickman Machine Tool Sales Ltd v L Schuler AG*,[172] for example, Lord Denning MR contrasted a 'condition' in the sense of 'a prerequisite to the very existence of the agreement' with a 'condition' in the sense of a 'prerequisite to the right to recover on the agreement' and a condition the breach of which:

> gives the other party a right to be quit of his future obligations and to sue for damages: unless he, by his conduct, waives the condition, in which case he is bound to perform his future obligations, but can sue for the damages he has suffered.[173]

2.68 It is not entirely clear what distinction Lord Denning MR was seeking to draw. It is possible in respect of the latter two senses that he was only intending to distinguish between a non-promissory condition and a promissory one. To add to the confusion, in discussing the latter, Lord Denning MR noted that this 'use of the word "condition" goes back at least to 1841 in *Glaholm v Hays*'.[174] As we have noted above, this was a case about the dependency of promises. He also observed that this use 'was given statutory sanction by Parliament in the Sale of Goods Act 1893 and by the House of Lords in *Wallis, Son & Wells v Pratt & Haynes*',[175] which again suggests no distinction between a promissory condition precedent and a promissory condition. But by the time *Wickman v L Schuler* had reached the House of Lords, Lord Reid felt able to say that a

[169] See, eg, *Maredelanto Compania Naviera SA v Bergbau-Handel GmbH (The Mihalis Angelos)* [1971] 1 QB 164, 193 (Lord Denning MR), 205 (Megaw LJ); *L Schuler AG v Wickman Machine Tool Sales Ltd* [1974] AC 235, 251 (Lord Reid), 265 (Lord Simon), 271 (Lord Kilbrandon), but cf 259 (Lord Morris), 262 (Lord Wilberforce, dissenting on the facts); *Photo Production Ltd v Securicor Transport Ltd* [1980] AC 827, 849 (Lord Diplock), but cf 844 (Lord Wilberforce).

[170] [1971] 1 QB 164, 193.

[171] ibid 205.

[172] [1972] 1 WLR 840, 851.

[173] ibid.

[174] ibid.

[175] ibid.

condition is 'a term the breach of which by one party gives to the other an option either to terminate the contract or to let the contract proceed and, if he so desires, sue for damages for the breach'.[176]

2.69 To add to the confusion, the traditional understanding of promissory conditions then resurfaced in *Cehave NV v Bremer Handelsgesellschaft mbH (The Hansa Nord)*.[177] In that case, Lord Denning MR traced the development of the law from *Pordage v Cole* to *Hongkong Fir*. He did not refer to termination or rescission but instead spoke of 'a "condition" strictly so called, in which any breach entitled the other to be discharged from further performance'[178] and later 'a condition strictly so called, that is, a stipulation such that, for any breach of it, the other party is entitled to treat himself as discharged'.[179]

2.70 By the 1980s, however, the language of 'election' appears to have taken hold. In *Photo Production Ltd v Securicor Ltd*,[180] Lord Diplock famously stated that a breach of a condition 'entitle[s] the other party to elect to put an end to all primary obligations of both parties remaining unperformed'.[181] But even in this case Lord Wilberforce (with whom Lords Salmon, Keith, and Scarman agreed) spoke in different terms. He said that 'when in the context of a breach of contract one speaks of "termination," what is meant is no more than that the innocent party or, in some cases, both parties, are excused from further performance'[182] and that expressions such as 'discharge, rescission, [and] termination' simply refer to 'situations where a breach has been committed by one party of such a character as to entitle the other party to refuse further performance'.[183] This is at least consistent with the traditional understanding of promissory conditions.

2.71 The fact that the traditional understanding was being obscured by loose language was observed by Professor Francis Dawson in 1981. He explained how traditionally 'because the defaulting party could not enforce the contract [upon the failure of a condition], the innocent party could treat himself as excused from further performance'.[184] He added:

[176] *L Schuler AG v Wickman Machine Tool Sales Ltd* [1974] AC 235, 251. See also 265 (Lord Simon), 271 (Lord Kilbrandon), but cf 259 (Lord Morris), 262 (Lord Wilberforce; dissenting on the facts).
[177] [1976] QB 44.
[178] ibid 59.
[179] ibid 60.
[180] [1980] AC 827.
[181] ibid 849.
[182] ibid 844.
[183] ibid.
[184] Dawson (n 42) 89.

> Although this is all that is meant when a modern lawyer says that the innocent party is entitled to bring the contract to an end, it is often said that the innocent party is in addition required to elect to bring the contract to an end and to communicate that election if he is to be excused from further performance on a repudiation. Strictly speaking this is not the position ... 'he need do nothing except refrain from performing or receiving performance until he is sued.'[185]

It was also around this time that Dr Anthony Shea wrote an important article in which he argued that 'the reason that the party not in breach is excused from performance by reason of the other party's breach is *failure of condition*.'[186] In particular, he argued that '[f]ailure of condition ... may occur in cases in which there is a breach, but is distinct from the breach in the sense that the promisee is discharged not by the breach but by the *event* which is or may be a consequence of the breach.'[187] The approach taken by Shea is consistent with the traditional understanding of promissory conditions. **2.72**

The final decision to mention is the decision in *Bunge Corp, New York v Tradax Export SA, Panama*.[188] The issue in that case was whether a clause requiring the buyers to give at least fifteen days' notice of the ship's readiness to load the goods was a 'strict condition' or an 'innominate' or 'intermediate' term.[189] The House of Lords held that the clause was a condition. Lord Roskill, who delivered the leading speech, said: **2.73**

> [W]hen a term has to be performed by one party as a condition precedent to the ability of the other party to perform another term, especially an essential term such as the nomination of a single loading port, the term as to time for the performance of the former obligation will in general fall to be treated as a condition.[190]

Professor Michael Bridge, writing shortly after *Bunge v Tradax*, identified the possibility that a term may be a 'condition' in the modern sense of a term the breach of which gives rise to a power to terminate but not also in the traditional sense. He wrote that it was 'hard to see any logical reason why this should not be possible' but noted that such an analysis, while not inconsistent **2.74**

[185] ibid 89–90 (citations omitted).
[186] AM Shea, 'Discharge from Performance of Contracts by Failure of Condition' (1979) 42 Modern Law Review 623, 623 (emphasis in original).
[187] ibid 624 (emphasis in original, citations omitted).
[188] [1981] 1 WLR 711.
[189] ibid 714.
[190] ibid 729.

with *Bunge v Tradax*, had not been considered by the House of Lords or Court of Appeal.[191]

Summary of the position so far

2.75 It should now be clear that historically no distinction was drawn between the concept of a 'condition' and a 'condition precedent' (or 'concurrent condition') when both these terms were used in their promissory sense. By the latter half of the twentieth century, however, a number of cases began to speak of a breach of a condition as giving rise to a power or election to terminate. This would suggest that a condition is not something that upon its failure discharges the innocent party (subject to waiver), but simply an important term the breach of which gives rise to a power to terminate. But as we have seen, while the modern position did slowly emerge, a number of the cases were either ambiguous or confused. The confusion was attributable to three factors: (i) loose language, prompted by the shift in emphasis caused by the Common Law Procedure Act, when speaking about 'conditions', such as describing conditions (as opposed to duties) as capable of being breached; (ii) a misunderstanding of the traditional failure of condition model, flowing from the practical steps that often need to be taken in order to negate any suggestion of waiver of the condition;[192] and (iii) the tendency post-*Heyman v Darwins Ltd* to apply statements about needing to 'accept' a repudiation made in the context of renunciation, ie anticipatory breach, to cases of actual breach. Indeed, it appears that the modern position—that breach of a condition gives rise to a power to terminate—has been arrived at largely by accident.

Treitel on 'Conditions' and 'Conditions Precedent'

2.76 Although the modern conception of a promissory condition was initially arrived at by accident, in the latter half of the twentieth century it gained a number of powerful supporters. Judicially that support has come from the likes of Lord Diplock who, as we saw in the previous section, spoke of the innocent party having an election to terminate. Academically, the greatest support for this new conception came from the late Sir Guenter Treitel, who

[191] Michael G Bridge, 'Discharge for Breach of the Contract of Sale of Goods' (1983) 28 McGill Law Journal 867, 904.

[192] See the discussion of *Bentsen v Taylor, Sons & Co* [1893] 2 QB 274 at [2.26]–[2.32].

has been described by Lord Burrows as '*the* world authority on the English law of contract in all its glory'.[193] Treitel famously argued that 'the concept of promissory condition is used in two senses': the first relates to the *order* of performance and the second relates to the *conformity* of the performance rendered with that promised.[194] He said that when speaking of the order of performance 'condition precedent' was to be contrasted with 'concurrent condition' and 'independent covenant'.[195] But when speaking of the conformity of performance, 'condition' was to be contrasted with 'warranty' (and 'intermediate term' or 'innominate term').[196] Treitel was well aware that historically this distinction had not been drawn. Indeed, he noted that 'references to "condition precedent" were formerly common in discussions of the condition-warranty distinction'.[197] But he argued that today such references in discussions of the condition-warranty distinction were less common and moreover:

> they are misleading in that 'condition precedent' (when used in relation to the order of performance) refers to an *event* (ie the *performance* of one party's obligation) while 'condition' (when used in relation to the conformity of performance) refers to a *term* of the contract (or to the *content* of one party's obligation).[198]

There is an initial issue with this passage in that there is no reason why a condition could not be expressly stated in the contract and therefore a 'term'. But more fundamentally, this passage, which has appeared in all subsequent editions of *Treitel on Contract*, casts significant doubt on the utility of the failure of condition model and may have contributed to the prominence of the power to terminate model of promissory conditions in modern academic and judicial discourse. In this section, therefore, we consider a number of issues. First, is there a distinction between the order of performance and the conformity of performance? Secondly, can the examples given by Treitel and others be explained on the traditional basis? And finally, did the decision in *State Trading Corp of India Ltd v M Golodetz Ltd*,[199] on which Treitel principally relied, in fact support the distinction he sought to draw? **2.77**

[193] Andrew Burrows, 'Professor Sir Guenter Treitel (1928–2019)' in James Goudkamp and Donal Nolan (eds), *Scholars of Contract Law* (Hart Publishing 2022) 277, 277.
[194] Treitel (n 8) 185.
[195] ibid 185–86.
[196] ibid.
[197] ibid 186.
[198] ibid (emphasis in original).
[199] [1989] 2 Lloyd's Rep 277.

Is there a distinction between order and conformity?

2.78 At the heart of Treitel's argument is the idea that the concept of a 'condition precedent' is concerned with the order of performance, while the concept of a 'condition' is concerned with the conformity of the performance rendered with that promised. It is submitted that while seemingly intuitive, this bright-line distinction between order and conformity is a false one to draw. The flaw lies in the assumption that the cases said to be concerned with the order of performance are not concerned with conformity.

2.79 It was noted earlier that, prior to the decision in *Boone v Eyre*,[200] the reported cases had all dealt with problems relating to non-performance in executory contracts.[201] *Boone v Eyre*, however, was not concerned with a case where the defaulting party had completely failed to perform all of their promises, but rather with a case where the defaulting party had performed only some of their promises. This has led some to argue, in line with the distinction Treitel sought to draw, that the cases pre-*Boone v Eyre* 'had been dealing with the problems posed by the proper order of performance',[202] whereas *Boone v Eyre* was dealing with 'the problem posed by defective performance by a party of [their] obligations under a contract'.[203] While in a loose sense this is true, there are a number of problems with this supposed distinction between 'order' and 'conformity'.

2.80 First, although *Boone v Eyre* can be described as a case of 'defective performance' or a case about 'conformity', it is not true to say that the earlier cases were not concerned with conformity. After all, failing to perform any of one's obligations is the most extreme form of non-conformity—the failure to render any promised performance.

2.81 Secondly, the language of 'defective performance' is often used to suggest that one party has performed, but simply performed badly. But as Professor Edwin Peel notes, '[t]he phrase "defective performance" arguably contains an element of self-contradiction, in the sense that a person who promises to do one thing does not perform if he does another'.[204] To establish a breach of contract, one party cannot simply allege that the other performed badly. One needs to point to a particular promise that was not performed, whether express or implied. Understood in this way, cases of so-called 'defective performance' are really

200 (1777) 1 H BL 273n, 126 ER 160n.
201 See [2.14].
202 Carter and Hodgekiss (n 10) 34.
203 ibid.
204 Peel (n 1) 932 [17-056].

cases in which one party has performed some of their obligations but failed to perform all of them.

Take the example of building a house. A general promise to build a house is comprised, at a lower level of abstraction, of several distinct promises (to build the house, to exercise reasonable care, that the house will be of a certain size or shape, or of reasonably quality, and so on), and once this is appreciated, it becomes clear that many cases of defective performance are really cases, like *Boone v Eyre*, in which some, but not all, of the party's promises have been performed. As Sir William Anson put it: 'The promise is in fact regarded as a number of promises to do a number of similar acts, and a breach of one of these does not discharge the promisee.'[205] For the purposes of discharge following failure of a 'promissory condition'—as opposed to discharge following failure of the 'substantial-benefit condition', which is dealt with in Chapter 3—the question then becomes whether performance of the particular obligation the promisor has failed to perform was a condition precedent (or concurrent condition) the failure of which will discharge the other party.[206] **2.82**

Finally, the reasoning in *Boone v Eyre* was a logical extension of the principles which had hitherto been applied to the so-called 'order of performance' cases. If the performance or fulfilment by A of A's promises is, at least in some circumstances, a condition precedent to B's obligation(s) to perform, then the question must arise as to which of A's promises are such that their performance or fulfilment are conditions precedent to B's obligation(s). The previous cases had not had to consider this issue because, on the state of the pleadings, the plaintiff had totally failed to perform. **2.83**

Can the examples given be explained?

A number of examples have been given to explain the apparent distinction between the two senses of a 'promissory condition'. All these examples are explicable on the traditional understanding. **2.84**

Example 1: sale of goods by sample

One example given by Treitel was the seller of goods by sample who agrees to give credit: **2.85**

[205] Anson (n 109) 278.

[206] See also discussion at [2.88]–[2.93].

> A seller of goods by sample who has agreed to give credit may deliver the goods before being paid and so perform a 'condition precedent,' but if the goods turn out not to correspond with the sample he will be in breach of 'condition.'[207]

On Treitel's analysis, the obligation to deliver the goods is a 'condition precedent', while the obligation that the goods correspond with the description is a 'condition'. Accordingly, it is possible to perform the condition precedent while at the same time being in breach of a condition.

2.86 However, this is to misdescribe the relevant condition(s). The condition precedent to the buyer's obligation to pay is that the seller deliver goods that correspond with the sample. Alternatively (although it amounts to the same thing), it can be said that there are two conditions precedent to the seller's obligation to pay: (i) that the buyer deliver the goods; and (ii) that the goods correspond with the sample. In any case, the effect is the same: if the seller delivers goods that do not correspond with the sample, then they have not performed a condition precedent to the buyer's obligation to pay.

2.87 Of course, practically speaking, the buyer will need to take steps to reject the goods in order to negate any suggestion of waiver of the condition. This rule, found in s 11(4) of the Sale of Goods Act 1979,[208] was discussed above.[209] But this does not detract from the fact that (absent waiver) the buyer's obligation to pay simply never fell due because delivery of goods that correspond with the sample was a condition precedent to that obligation.

Example 2: 'defective' building work

2.88 Professor Ewan McKendrick has also given the example of a builder who carries out building work but does so 'defectively':

> [A] builder may enter into a contract with a householder to carry out some building work. Payment is to be made on completion of the work. Completion of the work is a condition precedent to the obligation of the householder to pay for the work. . . . But suppose that the builder completes the work defectively. In such a case the builder may have breached a promissory condition of the contract but here the condition relates not to the order of performance but to the quality of that performance.[210]

[207] GH Treitel, *The Law of Contract* (8th edn, Sweet & Maxwell 1991) 690. See also Peel (n 1) 982 [18-044].
[208] Originally Sale of Goods Act 1893, s 11(1)(c).
[209] See [2.42]–[2.45].
[210] McKendrick, *Contract Law: Text, Cases, and Materials* (n 1) 743.

It is first necessary to clarify that it is not completion of the work simpliciter that is a condition precedent to the obligation to pay but rather 'substantial completion' or 'substantial performance' of the work: 'something less than full and exact performance of that duty'.[211] This is not the same thing as a promissory condition with which we have been concerned hitherto. As we will see in Chapter 3, this is an example of the substantial-benefit condition.[212] Unlike in the case of a promissory condition, in this case the condition and the duty are not identical. The promise or duty of the builder is to perform the contract exactly—it is no defence to an action for damages that he 'substantially performed'.[213] But the condition of the householder's duty to pay is 'substantial performance' by the builder—it is not exact performance. In *Hoenig v Isaacs*,[214] Denning LJ implicitly recognised this point when he said '[t]he promise to complete the work is, therefore, construed as a term of the contract, but not as a condition'. **2.89**

Putting aside this clarification, the core problem with this example is that whether the term that is breached is a 'condition', in the modern sense of an essential term the breach of which gives rise to a power to terminate, would appear to have no legal significance on these facts. It has no impact here on the measure of damages. In both cases the builder will still have breached their contractual duty. The only live issue is whether the non-performance of the promise discharges the householder from their obligation to pay. And, on the assumption that the builder substantially completed the work but 'breached a condition', the power to terminate is simply irrelevant. This is because, unless performance of that promise is also a condition precedent, the builder's right to payment will have already accrued and the householder's subsequent termination—on the orthodox approach—can only operate for the future and would not divest the builder of rights 'which have already been unconditionally acquired'.[215] **2.90**

The only relevant question in this example then is which of the several distinct promises comprised in the general promise to build a house are promissory conditions in the traditional sense. It is possible that the agreement between the parties may have made the householder's obligation to pay conditional upon the performance by the builder of all of their promises. This is sometimes **2.91**

[211] Corbin (n 14) 315 §702. See, eg, *Hoenig v Isaacs* [1952] 2 All ER 176.
[212] See [3.42]–[3.48].
[213] Corbin (n 14) 315–16 §702.
[214] [1952] 2 All ER 176, 180–81.
[215] *Johnson v Agnew* [1980] AC 367, 396, quoting *McDonald v Dennys Lascelles Ltd* (1933) 48 CLR 457, 476–77.

referred to by the suggestion that 'entire performance [is] a condition precedent to payment'.[216] But 'courts lean against a construction of the contract which would deprive the contractor of any payment at all simply because there are some defects or omissions';[217] the 'fulfilment of every term is not necessarily a condition precedent in a contract for a lump sum'.[218]

2.92 The more likely position is that the obligation of the householder will be conditional upon performance by the builder of some of their promises, namely, those that are promissory conditions. Suppose that the builder completes the work, but, in breach of contract, paints the house grey instead of white. If the obligation to paint the house white is not a promissory condition in the traditional sense, then the householder will be required to pay for the work (although they will be able to set up a cross-claim for damages). This is because the builder has performed all conditions precedent to payment.

2.93 Now suppose that both parties knew that it was essential to the householder that the house be white, and the parties had described the obligation to paint the house white as a 'condition'. Subject to arguments about labelling,[219] the effect of this would be to make it a condition precedent to the householder's obligation to pay that the builder paint the house white.[220] If the builder were to fail to paint the house white, they would commit a breach of contract but additionally the non-compliance with the condition would mean that an event which was the condition of the householder's obligation to pay had not occurred. If the builder refused to, or could not, cure the defect, the condition would fail. The householder would therefore be discharged from their obligation to pay.

Example 3: failure to tender the price

2.94 Another example given by Treitel was that of a buyer of goods who fails to tender the price on time:

> [I]f A, a buyer of goods, fails to perform the concurrent condition of paying or tendering the price, the seller, B, is prima facie justified in refusing to deliver; but it again does not follow that B is, merely on account of the failure,

[216] *Hoenig v Isaacs* [1952] 2 All ER 176, 180 (Denning LJ).
[217] ibid (Denning LJ).
[218] ibid 178 (Somervell LJ).
[219] *L Schuler AG v Wickman Machine Tool Sales Ltd* [1974] AC 235.
[220] No doubt it is unlikely that the parties would have made this agreement but, as Blackburn J explained in *Bettini v Gye* (1876) 1 QBD 183, 187, '[p]arties may think some matter, apparently of very little importance, essential; and if they sufficient express an intention to make the literal fulfilment of such a thing a condition precedent, it will be one'.

> entitled to rescind the contract: he may, for example, still be bound to deliver if A tenders the price on the day after that fixed by the contract.[221]

Treitel was correct to note that A's failure to tender the price will mean that B's obligation to deliver the goods does not fall due. He was also correct to note that in some cases, though not all, A's subsequent tender of the price, even if late, will cause B to come under an immediate duty to deliver the goods. However, by resorting to the power to terminate model, Treitel failed to distinguish between situations where the condition simply has not yet occurred and situations where the condition has failed because it can no longer occur. This distinction was explained in Chapter 1.[222] Nor did Treitel acknowledge that there may be more than one type of condition in play. To understand this, it is necessary to distinguish between two situations: where 'time is of the essence' and where it is not. **2.95**

Where time is of the essence, what is really meant is that B's obligation to deliver the goods is conditional upon A paying or tendering the price at the specified time[223]—this is a promissory condition. If A is ten minutes late in tendering the purchase price, the condition has failed and B is discharged.[224] A cannot unwind the clock and comply with the condition, whose time for compliance has now passed, though of course B can waive the condition, in which case B will be required to deliver the goods. The condition of B's obligation to deliver the goods was not simply that A tender the price, but that A tender the price at the specified time. Whether this is expressed as two concurrent conditions or one does not change the analysis. The condition fails at the time at which it can no longer occur, which was when A failed to tender the price on the day fixed by the contract. **2.96**

Where time is not of the essence, the position is more complex. Here, the failure of A to tender the price will operate to suspend B's duty, but it may not bring about a permanent discharge. Whether or not the failure to tender the price does operate as a permanent discharge of B's obligation to deliver the goods depends upon 'two matters which . . . have often been confused in the case law'.[225] **2.97**

[221] GH Treitel, *The Law of Contract* (7th edn, Sweet & Maxwell 1987) 581. See now Peel (n 1) 912 [17-024].
[222] See [1.50]–[1.51].
[223] Corbin (n 14) 137 §654 fn 4.
[224] *Union Eagle Ltd v Golden Achievement Ltd* [1997] AC 514.
[225] *Urban 1 (Blonk Street) Ltd v Ayres* [2014] 1 WLR 756, 767 [44(7)].

2.98 The first is that the delay by A may be 'such as in all the circumstances to deprive the other party of substantially the benefit it was intended he or she should obtain from the contract'.[226] In such circumstances, the delay will bring about a permanent discharge of B's obligation to deliver the goods. This is because B's obligation to deliver, in addition to being conditional upon A tendering the price, is conditional upon such performance as gives B substantially the whole benefit of the contract.[227] There are thus two conditions in play. And while A may seek to satisfy the former condition by tendering the price, A's delay has been such that the latter condition has failed and can no longer occur. The result is that B is discharged from their obligation to perform unless the condition is waived.

2.99 Secondly, the circumstances of A's delay in tendering the price may be such as to indicate that A can no longer perform due to disablement or that A has demonstrated an intention not to fulfil the contract, or to do so in a manner substantially inconsistent with A's obligations (renunciation).[228] In such a case, B is discharged from the duty to deliver the goods (following 'acceptance' in the latter case) in accordance with the doctrine of anticipatory breach. This is discussed in Chapter 8.

2.100 In sum, the examples given lend no support to the supposed distinction between 'conditions' and 'conditions precedent'. Each example fails to identify accurately the condition(s) upon which the innocent party might seek to rely. And each example is explicable on the traditional understanding, indicating that there is no need for the concept of a condition in the modern sense of an essential term, breach of which gives rise to a power to terminate.

The decision in *Golodetz*

2.101 Treitel also claimed that support for the distinction between the two senses of 'promissory condition' was provided by the decision of the Court of Appeal in *Golodetz*.[229] He had in his previous work drawn the distinction between 'conditions' and 'conditions precedent',[230] but the decision in *Golodetz* prompted

[226] ibid.
[227] *United Scientific Holdings Ltd v Burnley Borough Council* [1978] AC 904, 928.
[228] *Urban 1 (Blonk Street) Ltd v Ayres* [2014] 1 WLR 756, 768 [44(7)]; *Federal Commerce & Navigation Co Ltd Respondents v Molena Alpha Inc* [1979] AC 757, 778–79. See also the authorities in n 131 of this chapter.
[229] *State Trading Corp of India Ltd v M Golodetz Ltd* [1989] 2 Lloyd's Rep 277.
[230] Treitel (n 221) 581.

Treitel to write a new section in his text on the 'Nature of the distinction'[231] in which he argued that '[m]odern authority accordingly recognises the distinction between the two concepts'.[232] That section, and the authority relied upon—*Golodetz*—remains substantially unaltered by the current author of that text today.[233]

The dispute in *Golodetz* arose out of a contract for the sale of 12,600 tonnes of sugar on 11 December 1985. Payment was to be made by an irrevocable letter of credit which was to be opened by the buyers within seven days of the conclusion of the contract (18 December). The sellers agreed to give (i) a performance bond guarantee immediately after conclusion of the contract, and (ii) a 'counter-trade' guarantee, within seven days of the conclusion of the contract (also 18 December). The buyers failed to open the letter of credit by 18 December. The sellers had opened the performance bond guarantee, but had failed to open the counter-trade guarantee. **2.102**

The sellers treated the buyers' failure to open the letter of credit as a breach which had the effect of discharging them from their obligation to perform and claimed damages equal to the price of the sugar. The buyers in turn claimed the sellers' failure to provide the counter-trade guarantee by 18 December excused the buyers' breach in failing to open the letter of credit—an obligation that was admitted to be a 'condition'.[234] The buyers also counter-claimed for damages. **2.103**

Two issues were said to arise. First, whether the sellers' obligation to provide a counter-trade guarantee was in the nature of a 'condition'. Secondly, if it were, whether 'this excused [the buyers'] breach in failing to open the letter of credit'.[235] The Court of Appeal found in favour of the sellers on both issues. On the first issue, Kerr LJ (with whom Lloyd and Butler-Sloss LJJ agreed) said that he could see no basis for concluding that the sellers' obligation 'had the character of a condition, let alone of a condition precedent to [the buyers'] obligation'.[236] While Kerr LJ did appear to distinguish between 'conditions' and 'conditions precedent', because the sellers' obligation was neither any possible distinction between them did not, strictly speaking, arise. **2.104**

231 Treitel (n 207) 690–91.
232 ibid 690.
233 Peel (n 1) 982–83 [18-044].
234 *State Trading Corp of India Ltd v M Golodetz Ltd* [1989] 2 Lloyd's Rep 277, 279.
235 ibid.
236 ibid 284.

2.105 Although the second issue did not arise, Kerr LJ was of the view that, even if both parties had been in 'breach of a condition', this made no difference. He said:

> If A is entitled to treat B as having wrongfully repudiated the contract between them and does so, then it does not avail B to point to A's past breaches of contract, whatever their nature. . . . B would have to show that A, being in breach of an obligation in the nature of a condition precedent, was therefore not entitled to rely on B's breach as repudiation. . . . But this is not the position here. . . . Since both obligations are (assumedly) in the nature of conditions, both parties had an equal right, so long as the other party's obligation remained unperformed, to treat the other party as having wrongfully repudiated.[237]

2.106 These obiter comments undoubtedly support Treitel's view and demonstrate the change in thinking that had occurred over the second half of the twentieth century. On the assumption that both obligations were in the nature of a 'condition' breach of which gives rise to a power to terminate, the buyers' defence could only have succeeded if performance of the obligation to open the counter-trade guarantee were also a 'condition precedent'. As Treitel explained, 'it was not enough for [the buyers] to establish that the sellers were merely in breach of "condition" '.[238]

2.107 But these comments are difficult to reconcile with the earlier House of Lords decision in *Bremer Vulkan Schiffbau und Maschinenfabrik v South India Shipping Corp Ltd*.[239] The plaintiffs, who were respondents to an arbitration, sought an injunction to restrain the defendants from continuing with the arbitration. The plaintiffs argued that the defendants, by their 'inordinate and inexcusable' delay in prosecuting the claim, had committed a breach of the arbitration agreement entitling the plaintiffs to terminate. Lord Diplock (with whom Lords Edmund-Davies and Russell agreed) was of the view that it was a 'necessary implication' from the arbitration agreement 'that both parties . . . [were] under a mutual obligation to one another to join in applying to the arbitrator for appropriate directions to put an end to the delay'.[240] However, in allowing the appeal, and holding that no injunction ought to be granted, Lord Diplock said:

> [B]oth claimant and respondent were in my view in breach of their contractual obligations to one another; and neither can rely upon the other's breach

237 ibid 286.
238 Treitel (n 8) 191.
239 [1981] AC 909.
240 ibid 986.

> as giving him a right to treat the primary obligations of each to continue with the reference as brought to an end. Respondents in private arbitrations are not entitled to let sleeping dogs lie and then complain that they did not bark.[241]

In *Golodetz*, Kerr LJ made no reference to *Bremer Vulkan*.[242] Treitel noted this point and observed 'the difficulty of squaring this assumption' in *Golodetz*—that 'where both parties are in breach of condition, *both* can rescind'—'with the reasoning of the *Bremer Vulkan* case'.[243] **2.108**

Ultimately, Treitel argued that 'logic and policy favour the assumption made in [*Golodetz*]'.[244] Certainly, on the assumption that the concept of a 'condition' is distinct from a 'condition precedent', logic would favour the result in *Golodetz*. But if there were no distinction, then logic would favour the result in *Bremer Vulkan*. As for policy, it might be said that allowing either party to terminate promotes certainty, but against this are other considerations.[245] First, the 'orthodox rule is that only the terminating party is entitled to damages for future performance lost due to the termination of the contract' (ie damages for the 'loss of the bargain').[246] If, as *Golodetz* suggests, each is given a power to terminate for the other's breach of a promissory condition, 'there may be in some situations a race to terminate the contract, the winner being an accident of fate'.[247] A savvy commercial party may even terminate simply for the 'strategic advantage of denying the *other* party . . . the right to terminate and claim damages for the loss of the bargain'.[248] **2.109**

Admittedly, this concern may be overstated. When it comes to the assessment of damages, in a case like the above the party prima facie liable to pay loss of bargain damages should be able to reduce their liability by proving that had the other party not terminated then they would have terminated for the other party's breach. The obiter comments in *Flame SA v Glory Wealth Shipping Pte Ltd*[249] support this conclusion. But this would not overcome the problem in a case where one party has 'affirmed' the contract: 'if only one of the parties **2.110**

[241] ibid 987–88.
[242] cf the decision at first instance where it was distinguished on the basis that the obligations in *Golodetz* were not 'concurrent, or dependent, or complementary' as they were in *Bremer Vulkan*: *State Trading Corp of India Ltd v M Golodetz Ltd* [1988] 2 Lloyd's Rep 182, 189 (Evans J).
[243] Treitel (n 8) 190 (emphasis in original).
[244] ibid.
[245] See generally Wayne Courtney, 'Termination of Contract by a Party in Breach' (2008) 3 Journal of Business Law 226, 243–44.
[246] ibid 243 (citations omitted).
[247] ibid 243–44.
[248] ibid 244 (emphasis in original).
[249] [2014] QB 1080.

affirms the contract, the other then presumably may still terminate and claim loss of bargain damages.'[250] In such a case, the party who has affirmed and is now liable to pay loss of bargain damages is unable to say that they would have terminated the contract. The result in *Golodetz* therefore still provides a perverse incentive to terminate or remain inactive so as to avoid the risk of being the only one to have affirmed and therefore being vulnerable to the other party terminating and claiming loss of bargain damages in any event.

2.111 As a matter of precedent, the answer is clear.[251] The ratio in *Golodetz* is that the sellers' obligation to open the counter-trade guarantee was not a condition. The ratio in *Bremer Vulkan* is that where both parties have committed a so-called 'repudiatory breach'[252]—whether because the breach is a 'breach of a condition' or a breach which deprives the other party of substantially the whole benefit of the contract[253]—neither can terminate. But these contrasting decisions show the confusing state that had emerged at the end of the twentieth century, and highlight at least some of the issues that have arisen from the adoption of the power to terminate model of promissory conditions.

Problems with Departing from the Traditional Understanding

2.112 Whatever the position may be with respect to the twentieth century, it needs to be conceded that the authorities in the twenty-first century assume that a condition is an essential term the breach of which gives rise to a power to terminate.[254] The penultimate part of this chapter therefore considers the problems that have arisen as a consequence of the departure from the traditional understanding of the nature of promissory conditions.

Conceptually awkward

2.113 The first difficulty is that the existence of both models is 'conceptually awkward'.[255] To be clear, there is no logical incompatibility between the two

[250] Courtney (n 245) 244.
[251] ibid 234.
[252] For criticism of this language, see n 134.
[253] The case did not make clear which it was.
[254] See, eg, *Spar Shipping AS v Grand China Logistics Holding (Group) Co Ltd* [2017] 4 All ER 124, 130 [16].
[255] Bridge (n 191) 904 fn 191.

approaches. It is possible for a legal system to have both the concept of a 'promissory condition' in the traditional sense, and a 'condition' in the sense of an essential term the breach of which gives rise to a power to terminate. But the conceptual awkwardness arises from the difficulty in seeking to differentiate between discharge for the failure of a condition and the termination of contractual obligations following breach.[256] This problem is exacerbated by the fact that English law appears to have the same test for determining whether an obligation is a 'condition' breach of which gives rise to a power to terminate and for determining whether performance of an obligation is a 'condition precedent'. Outside of cases where the parties have expressly agreed that a particular obligation is a 'condition', the court must consider whether the parties have expressed an intention 'by necessary implication from the nature, purpose and circumstances of the contract'.[257] And, as Lord Roskill observed in *Bunge v Tradax*,[258] the 'basic and long standing rules for determining whether a particular term in a contact is or is not a condition . . . are enshrined in the oft quoted judgment of Bowen LJ in *Bentsen v Taylor, Sons & Co*', where he said:

> There is no way of deciding that question except by looking at the contract in the light of the surrounding circumstances, and then making up one's mind whether the intention of the parties, as gathered from the instrument itself, will best be carried out by treating the promise as a warranty sounding only in damages, or as a condition precedent by the failure to perform which the other party is relieved of [their] liability.[259]

This passage has been described as 'well known'[260] and 'well recognised'[261] **2.114** and is quoted in *Chitty on Contracts*[262] for the purpose of determining whether a term is a condition (viz an essential term). The problem for the power to terminate model is that Bowen LJ was speaking of 'conditions precedent' in the traditional sense, not of the modern 'condition'. In explaining why he had 'no hesitation in saying' that he believed the 'now sailed or . . . about to sail' phrase

[256] ibid. Bridge referred to the difficulty in distinguishing between the 'suspension and the termination of a contract' but the same point applies mutatis mutandis.

[257] *State Trading Corp of India Ltd v M Golodetz Ltd* [1989] 2 Lloyd's Rep 277, 282. See also McKendrick, 'Termination for Breach' (n 1) 1989 [27–019].

[258] *Bunge Corp, New York v Tradax Export SA, Panama* [1981] 1 WLR 711, 725.

[259] *Bentsen v Taylor, Sons & Co* [1893] 2 QB 274, 281.

[260] *Bunge Corp, New York v Tradax Export SA, Panama* [1981] 1 WLR 711, 725; *State Trading Corp of India Ltd v M Golodetz Ltd* [1989] 2 Lloyd's Rep 277, 282.

[261] *Hongkong Fir Shipping Co Ltd v Kawasaki Kisen Kaisha Ltd* [1962] 2 QB 26, 60.

[262] McKendrick, 'Termination for Breach' (n 1) 1989 [27–019].

to be a 'condition precedent', he said: 'It is a representation the accuracy of which is made a condition precedent, though I do not doubt that the fulfilment of a promise may be equally made a condition precedent.'[263] There can be no doubt that Bowen LJ here is speaking of a 'condition precedent' in the sense of a representation or promise, the truth or fulfilment of which qualifies the other party's obligation to perform.

2.115 This surely creates conceptual confusion and overlap. It means that the same obligation (or its performance) is both a 'condition' and a 'condition precedent'. And this being the case, numerous questions arise. When, if at all, is it necessary to terminate if one is already discharged from the obligation to perform? Is it possible to waive the condition precedent but still terminate for breach of the condition? These complex questions would never have arisen if the law had not mistakenly developed the concept of a condition as a term the breach of which gives rise to a power to terminate.

Can a party themselves in breach terminate for the other party's serious breach?

2.116 The second problem was noted above when discussing *Golodetz*. In particular, the power to terminate model has given rise to conflicting answers to a 'deceptively simple' question: 'can A at law terminate the contract for B's serious breach or repudiation, if A is, at the same time, in breach of the contract?'[264] This issue is 'not yet authoritatively settled'.[265] *Golodetz* would suggest the answer is yes, while *Bremer Vulkan* would suggest the answer is no. On the failure of condition model, the answer is clear: if A has breached a promise the performance of which is condition precedent (a promissory condition) or the non-performance of which deprives B of substantially the whole benefit of the contract (the substantial-benefit condition) then, absent waiver of the condition, B's subsequent conduct is not a breach. If A and B's relevant promises are concurrent conditions, then neither party is in breach while the other party is not performing.

[263] *Bentsen v Taylor, Sons & Co* [1893] 2 QB 274, 283.
[264] Courtney (n 245) 226 (citations omitted).
[265] ibid 244.

Promissory warranties in insurance contracts

Thirdly, the power to terminate model has had a difficult time explaining the traditional effect of 'promissory warranties' in insurance contracts.[266] It has long been the case that in insurance contracts a 'promissory warranty' is synonymous with a 'promissory condition'.[267] What, then, is the position if an insured breaches a 'promissory warranty' and before the insurer exercises the supposed power to terminate, an insurable event occurs? Is the insurer liable to pay? On the power to terminate model, it would seem that unless and until the insurer terminates the contract, they are bound to perform. Yet in *Bank of Nova Scotia v Hellenic Mutual War Risks Association (Bermuda) Ltd (The Good Luck)*,[268] the House of Lords held that the 'effect of a breach of a promissory warranty [was] to discharge the insurer from liability as from the date of the breach'[269] even though there had been no election to terminate the contract. Although the decision was concerned with the wording of s 33(3) of the Marine Insurance Act 1906, the wording of that section merely gave effect to the position at law that predated it.[270] On the power to terminate model, this case has to be put down as an exception—unique to insurance contracts—to the general rule that both parties are bound to perform unless and until the power to terminate is exercised.[271] On the traditional failure of condition model, however, this represents the general rule, not an exception to it.[272] There is a law of contract, not a law of contracts. **2.117**

Solving the 'loss of bargain' damages puzzle

A fourth problem is that the power to terminate model has given rise to one of the 'most intractable'[273] issues within the law of contract. That is, whether and how the exercise of an express contractual power to terminate can be distinguished from termination at law, particularly in light of the apparently conflicting decisions in *Financings Ltd v Baldock*[274] and *Lombard North Central plc v Butterworth*,[275] **2.118**

[266] See JW Carter, 'Discharge as the Basis for Termination for Breach of Contract' (2012) 128 Law Quarterly Review 283, 294.
[267] *Behn v Burness* (1863) 3 B & S 751, 753; 122 ER 281, 282.
[268] [1992] 1 AC 233.
[269] ibid 263.
[270] See the authorities cited in argument: ibid 238.
[271] Peel (n 1) 961–62 [18-008].
[272] The law has now been amended by the Insurance Act 2015. See Peel (n 1) 962–63 [18-009].
[273] Wilmot-Smith (n 2) 323.
[274] [1963] 2 QB 104.
[275] [1987] QB 527.

concerning the availability of loss of bargain damages.[276] As will be seen, this conflict can be resolved on the failure of condition model.

2.119 In *Financings Ltd v Baldock*, Mr Baldock entered into a vehicle hire-purchase agreement with Financings Ltd. The agreement expressly provided that if he should fail to pay any instalment within ten days of it falling due, Financings could terminate the hiring. Although Mr Baldock paid the first instalment, he failed to pay the next two instalments, with the result that Financings exercised its express power to terminate. The Court of Appeal (Lord Denning MR, Upjohn, and Diplock LJJ) held that, there being no repudiation of the obligation to pay future rentals, the company was not entitled to damages for loss of the bargain and, moreover, that a minimum payment clause, which entitled the company to two-thirds of the total hiring cost, was a penalty. Lord Denning MR said:

> [I]f there is no repudiation, and simply, as here, a failure to pay one or two instalments (the failure not going to the root of the contract and only giving a right to terminate by virtue of an express stipulation in the contract), the owners can only recover the instalments in arrear, with interest, and nothing else: for there was no other breach in existence at the termination of the hiring.[277]

2.120 In *Lombard North Central plc v Butterworth*, Mr Butterworth entered into a lease agreement for a computer with the plaintiff finance company. Although he made the first two payments, he struggled to make the subsequent payments. This caused Lombard to give notice of termination under the contract and to retake possession of the computer pursuant to the contract's express terms. However, this time a clause in the contract described punctual payment of each rental instalment as being 'of the essence' of the agreement. The Court of Appeal (Mustill, Nicholls, and Lawton LJJ) held that the effect of this 'time of the essence' clause was to make punctual payment a 'condition', with the result that following termination the plaintiff was 'entitled to claim damages for loss of the whole transaction'.[278]

2.121 The apparent inconsistency between these two cases is that in *Financings* the plaintiff was unable to recover loss of bargain damages, yet in *Lombard*

[276] See generally Edwin Peel, 'Loss of Bargain Damages' [2020] Lloyd's Maritime and Commercial Law Quarterly 449; Wilmot-Smith (n 2) 323–24; Edwin Peel, 'The Termination Paradox' [2013] Lloyd's Maritime and Commercial Law Quarterly 519, 522–25.

[277] *Financings Ltd v Baldock* [1963] 2 QB 104, 113.

[278] *Lombard North Central plc v Butterworth* [1987] QB 527, 546.

the plaintiff was able to recover loss of bargain damages simply by making punctual payment a condition. In neither case did the defendant's conduct amount to a repudiation (in the sense of a renunciation) of his contractual obligations. Nicholls LJ, despite feeling bound to reach this result in *Lombard*, felt 'considerable dissatisfaction' with it because in his view the difference between this case and *Financings* was 'one of drafting form, and wholly without substance'.[279]

The problem is exacerbated by the fact that, on the power to terminate model, 'the best justification of the power to terminate following breach of a promissory condition is almost certainly agreement-based'.[280] This is the same justification for termination pursuant to an express termination clause. And at least in cases where the breach does not deprive one party of substantially the whole benefit of the bargain: **2.122**

> there seems to be no principled distinction between the breach of promissory condition case and the express termination case: in both situations the claimant is given a power to terminate following a trivial breach; in both situations, the justification of the power to terminate is the parties' agreement.[281]

Attempts to reconcile these cases on the orthodox approach have usually led to suggestions that one of them is wrongly decided. It has been argued, first, that loss of bargain damages should only be available where the breach deprives the innocent party of substantially the whole benefit of the bargain and that they should not be available merely because an obligation has been designated a condition.[282] On this view, *Lombard* is wrongly decided. **2.123**

A second argument is that loss of bargain damages should be available both where there has been a breach of condition and following termination after breach pursuant to an express termination power.[283] On this view, *Financings* is wrongly decided. **2.124**

A third argument, advanced by Professor Edwin Peel, is that the current state of the law is correct.[284] As he says: **2.125**

[279] ibid. See also 540 (Mustill LJ).

[280] Wilmot-Smith (n 2) 324.

[281] ibid.

[282] GH Treitel, 'Damages on Rescission for Breach of Contract' [1987] Lloyd's Maritime and Commercial Law Quarterly 143. See also Peel, 'Loss of Bargain Damages' (n 276) 458–59; ibid 324–25.

[283] Brian R Opeskin, 'Damages for Breach of Contract Terminated Under Express Terms' (1990) 106 Law Quarterly Review 293. See also Peel, 'Loss of Bargain Damages' (n 276) 459–61.

[284] Peel, 'Loss of Bargain Damages' (n 276) 449.

> [T]he justification for treating contractual termination and termination for breach of condition differently is simply: *that is what the parties have agreed.* In the case of a contractual power, the parties have agreed only that the contract may be terminated for the breach, or breaches, identified. Where the parties have agreed that a term is a condition, they have agreed that the contract may be terminated if the term is breached *and* that the claimant may recover loss of bargain damages.[285]

2.126 Of course, the immediate difficulty with this view is that in *Financings* the minimum payment clause, which expressly conferred a right to lost future rentals, was held to amount to a penalty. And in *Lombard* the same view was expressed about the validity of a similar clause insofar as it applied to the case where there had been no breach of a condition.[286] Why should a clause which achieves recovery of lost future rentals indirectly (by designating it as a condition) be enforceable, but a clause which, in effect, achieves it directly (by expressly stating so) be unenforceable? Peel's response is that the law on penalties has changed following the decision of the Supreme Court in *Cavendish Square Holding BV v Makdessi*[287] and that, applying the current test for what amounts to a penalty, such clauses should no longer be regarded as penalties today.[288]

2.127 This is a clever argument and perhaps the best one available on the power to terminate model. But it stands or falls on the success of the penalty argument. If, consistent with these cases, a court were to find that such express agreements to confer loss of bargain damages are penalties, then the argument falls away.

2.128 On the traditional failure of condition model, however, the different results in *Financings* and *Lombard* are explicable on the basis that there is a very significant difference in the nature of discharge following breach and pursuant to an express termination clause, even though both are based upon the parties' agreement. The difference, flowing from the different starting point of each, is that for discharge following breach, failure of a condition results in the innocent party being discharged immediately unless they waive the condition. By contrast, for termination pursuant to an express power, the failure of performance does not of itself discharge the innocent party, but gives that party a power—in the sense of a capacity to change legal relations[289]—to terminate the

[285] ibid 461 (emphasis in original).
[286] *Lombard North Central plc v Butterworth* [1987] QB 527, 541–43.
[287] [2016] AC 1172.
[288] Peel, 'Loss of Bargain Damages' (n 276) 468–71.
[289] Wesley Newcomb Hohfeld, 'Some Fundamental Legal Conceptions as Applied in Judicial Reasoning' (1913) 23 Yale Law Journal 16, 44–45.

parties' contractual obligations. But unless and until it is exercised, both parties remain bound to perform.

This means that in cases where the defendant has breached a duty the performance of which is a condition to the innocent party's obligation to perform, 'the claimant has *in fact* lost [their] bargain'[290] as a result of the defendant's breach and loss of bargain damages ought to be payable. The effect of the defendant's breach is that a condition has failed and the claimant is discharged from their obligation to perform. The only sense in which it could be said that the claimant caused the loss of the bargain is by refusing to waive the condition and continue to perform and insist upon performance. By contrast, in cases where the claimant terminates pursuant to an express power, unless that claimant is already discharged for failure of a condition, it will be their act in exercising the express power to terminate that causes the loss of the bargain, not the defendant's breach. Loss of bargain damages therefore should not be payable. **2.129**

This does mean, however, that *Phones 4U Ltd (in administration) v EE Ltd*[291] is wrongly decided on this view. The claimant in that case, Phones 4U, was a phone retailer and had contracted with the defendant, EE—a mobile network operator—to sell its mobile phone contracts to customers. Phones 4U ran into financial difficulties and on 15 September 2014, appointed administrators. It was common ground that this was not a breach of contract. However, on 17 September, EE wrote to Phones 4U terminating the contract, relying specifically on an express termination power contained in the contract that permitted termination upon the appointment of an administrator. EE then sought loss of bargain damages. **2.130**

In an application for summary judgment by Phones 4U to dismiss EE's claim, EE argued that despite relying on the express termination power, Phones 4U had committed an earlier breach of contract that would have entitled it to terminate at common law. Assuming this to be correct for the purposes of the summary judgment application, the question was whether EE's reliance on the express termination power, which could be triggered without a breach of contract, defeated any claim for loss of bargain damages based upon the extant breach that did give rise to a common law power to terminate. Mr Justice Andrew Baker held that it did. He said that the loss of bargain damages claim required 'EE to show that the contract was terminated by its exercise of *its* **2.131**

[290] Peel, 'Loss of Bargain Damages' (n 276) 451 (emphasis in original).
[291] [2018] 2 All ER (Comm) 315.

common law right to terminate for that breach'.[292] Because EE had relied upon the express termination clause which was independent of a breach of contract, its claim could not succeed.

2.132 The decision in *Phones 4U* is clearly inconsistent with the view that has been put forward above. On the failure of condition model, assuming that Phones 4U had breached a duty the performance of which was a condition to EE's obligation to perform, or breached a duty in a way which caused the substantial-benefit condition to fail,[293] EE was already discharged from its obligation to perform and had lost the bargain due to Phones 4U's breach. The fact that EE had exercised an express contractual power was not the reason for the loss of the bargain.

2.133 The problem with *Phones 4U* is that it treats the exercise of a common law power to terminate as a necessary condition of the loss of bargain damages claim. This creates problems even on the orthodox view. It means that a party faced with a serious breach who seeks to terminate cannot rely upon a clearly expressed clause that does not depend upon breach to bring about a discharge of the parties' contractual obligations lest they risk forgoing their claim to damages. More problematically, it means that a party's claim for damages for an actual, established, breach depends upon the fortuity of what they wrote in their letter terminating the contract and whether they referred to an express clause. Even on the orthodox view, the question of damages and discharge should be separated. If a party has two levers they can pull to bring about a discharge, the fact that they pull lever A instead of lever B—without more[294]—should not make a material difference to the outcome so far as damages is concerned.

The relation to other instances of discharge

2.134 Finally, perhaps the most fundamental problem caused by the departure from the traditional understanding of promissory conditions is that it has caused judges, lawyers, and academics to lose sight of the basis of discharge of contractual obligations more generally. As this book demonstrates, discharge

[292] *Phones 4U Ltd (in administration) v EE Ltd* [2018] 2 All ER (Comm) 315, 346 [117] (emphasis added).
[293] See Chapter 3.
[294] As for cases involving the 'something more', see Peel, 'The Termination Paradox' (n 276) 526–37 and the cases there discussed.

following breach (on the traditional model), cases of 'frustration', and cases of 'common mistake' are all instances of discharge for failure of condition. To repeat the claim, where a party breaches a duty, the performance of which is a condition (a promissory condition) the innocent party is discharged because the condition fails. A party may also breach other duties, the precise performance of which is not a condition, in a way that causes the 'substantial-benefit' condition to fail. The same concept—failure of condition—also explains the apparent doctrines of frustration and common mistake. That is how these doctrines were traditionally understood.[295] The key difference is that in these cases the condition fails without a breach of duty—that is because there is an important distinction between the promise and the condition.[296]

A Way Forward

As the previous section has shown, there are serious problems with the power to terminate model of discharge of contractual obligations and the dual concepts of a 'promissory condition' in the traditional sense and a 'condition' in the sense of an essential term the breach of which gives rise to a power to terminate. But the power to terminate model is so ingrained in modern orthodoxy that absent a wholesale abandonment of the last fifty years of jurisprudence, it is unlikely to be going anywhere any time soon. This section, pragmatically, accepts that position—it is now probably too late to turn back the tide. But this does not mean that we cannot learn anything from the past. The fact that for hundreds of years contractual disputes were resolved by asking whether the obligations of one or both parties to a contract were conditional is significant. It suggests that *before* asking whether a term that has been breached is a 'condition' giving rise to a power to terminate, there is an anterior question that must be asked: was the performance of that duty a condition of the other party's obligation to perform in the traditional sense? In other words, were the parties' obligations to perform conditional, such that the non-performance by one discharged the other? It is only after this first question has been asked, that it should be asked whether breach of this particular duty gives rise to a power to terminate because it is a 'condition' (viz an essential term). **2.135**

[295] See Chapters 6 and 7.
[296] See [1.40]–[1.49].

Two questions, not one

2.136 England and Wales is not the only jurisdiction to face the difficulty of reconciling the power to terminate model with the traditional failure of condition model. Other jurisdictions, such as New Zealand, have unequivocally adopted the power to terminate model. But what is significant about the experience of that jurisdiction is that courts there have attempted 'to refine the [power to terminate] model to achieve results which are more consistent with practical and just outcomes of contractual disputes'.[297] In particular, they have drawn a distinction:

> between an obligation being discharged because the contract has been cancelled as a result of a breach, and an obligation never having become due because it was subject to a condition precedent and the event on which the promise was conditioned has not occurred.[298]

2.137 The context for this is that in New Zealand the power to terminate model was expressly adopted in the Contractual Remedies Act 1979.[299] The relevant provisions of that Act, which have since been incorporated into the Contract and Commercial Law Act 2017, took effect in place of the rules of the common law governing the circumstances in which a party could treat a contract as discharged for repudiation or breach.[300] Under the Act, where one party has (i) repudiated the contract,[301] (ii) breached an 'essential term' of the contract,[302] or (iii) breached a term of the contract, the effect of which is to deny the innocent party of substantially the benefit of the contract,[303] the innocent party is given a power to 'cancel' (ie terminate) the contract. The cancellation does not take effect until it is made known to the other party[304] or, in limited cases, where communication with the other party is not practicable, until the innocent party evinces an intention to cancel the contract.[305] The effect of 'cancellation' is to discharge the parties from their obligations to perform prospectively[306]

[297] Dawson (n 38) 64.
[298] ibid (citation omitted).
[299] ibid 61; Francis Dawson, 'Essential Terms and Condition Precedent' (2017) 133 Law Quarterly Review 183, 183.
[300] Contractual Remedies Act 1979 (NZ) (CRA), s 7(1); Contract and Commercial Law Act 2017 (CCL), s 40(1).
[301] CRA, s 7(2); CCL, s 36.
[302] CRA, ss 7(3)(b) and 7(4)(a); CCL, ss 37(1)(b) and 37(2)(a).
[303] CRA, ss 7(3)(b) and 7(4)(b); CCL, ss 37(1)(b) and 37(2)(b).
[304] CRA, s 8(1)(a); CCL, s 41(1)(a).
[305] CRA, s 8(1)(b); CCL, s 41(1)(b).
[306] CRA, s 8(3); CCL, s 42(1).

without affecting the right of either party to claim damages.[307] The power to cancel is lost if, with full knowledge of the breach, the innocent party affirms the contract.[308]

Yet despite Parliament having adopted the power to terminate model, the New Zealand Supreme Court has, on no less than five[309] occasions: **2.138**

> resolved contractual disputes involving nonperformance of contractual obligations by reference to reasoning based on readiness and willingness and failure of or waiver of a condition precedent rather than by reference to the discharge of a contractual obligation consequent on the cancellation of the contract. In each of the recent cases the Supreme Court has made use of an analysis based on failure of condition to provide a qualification to the idea that the discharge of a contract obligation only occurs on the cancellation of the contract after an election to accept the repudiation.[310]

One such case is *Kumar v Station Properties Ltd*.[311] The appellants, who were investors, entered into an agreement with the respondent to purchase units in an apartment development in Queenstown. The agreement was entered into on the understanding that the appellants would simply underwrite the units and would not be required to purchase the units until such time as the development could be on-sold to a third party who would manage the development as serviced apartments. By the time the development was substantially completed in 2008, however, the Global Financial Crisis had struck, and the respondent was unable to find a purchaser for the development. The respondent then attempted to settle the purchase transactions with the appellants, all of whom refused. Importantly, only one of the appellants had purported to cancel his agreement. The other appellants refused to settle after which the respondent purported to cancel the purchase agreements for the appellants' repudiation. The respondent then sought to claim damages for breach of contract. **2.139**

The Supreme Court, by a majority, held that the respondent was in breach of essential terms of the contract: namely, an obligation to provide a furniture package for each apartment and an obligation to arrange a management agreement for the whole of the development. In addition to giving the appellants **2.140**

[307] CRA, s 8(4); CCL, s 42(3).
[308] CRA, s 7(5); CCL, s 38.
[309] *Bahramitash v Kumar* [2006] 1 NZLR 577; *Property Ventures Investments Ltd v Regalwood Holdings Ltd* [2010] 3 NZLR 231; *Ingram v Patcroft Properties Ltd* [2011] 3 NZLR 433; *Kumar v Station Properties Ltd* [2016] 1 NZLR 99; *Kawarau Village Holdings Ltd v Ho* [2018] 1 NZLR 378.
[310] Dawson (n 38) 64 (citation omitted). See also Dawson (n 299) 187.
[311] [2016] 1 NZLR 99.

a power to cancel the contract, the Court held that this breach relieved them of the requirement to settle the purchase transactions. In other words, the respondent's failure to perform justified the appellants' subsequent refusals to perform. This was the case even though only one of the appellants had purported to formally 'cancel' his agreement. Arnold J (also delivering the reasons of Elias CJ, McGrath, and Glazebrook JJ) said:

> [E]ven if the appellants did not formally cancel their agreements at this point, they were not obliged to perform when [the respondent] called for settlement. . . . [The respondent] had made it clear that it would not be able to meet its essential contractual obligations of providing furniture packages and a management agreement. In those circumstances, it was not entitled to call for settlement on the basis that it was ready, willing and able to complete. On the face of it, the appellants were entitled to refuse to perform . . .[312]

2.141 One reason for this was that the parties' obligations were 'mutually dependent and concurrent'.[313] As Dawson has explained, the appellants could not justify their non-performance by maintaining that they had validly cancelled the contract for breach, but they could say that they were not in breach of their obligation to pay the price on the basis that:

> [their] obligation to pay only arose if the vendor was ready and willing to perform its part of the contract, which in this instance consisted not only of completing the apartment and providing title, but also furnishing it as promised and offering a manager for the entire complex.[314]

The appellants were therefore not required to pay simply because their obligation had not fallen due.

2.142 Drawing this distinction between discharge for failure of condition and discharge following the exercise of a power to terminate clearly represents the best way forward on the modern law. In a case involving discharge following breach and non-compliance with a promissory 'condition', the *first* question should be whether the performance of that duty was a condition of the other party's obligation to perform—ie whether the parties' obligations were conditional.

[312] ibid 131 [94].

[313] ibid. See also *Property Ventures Investments Ltd v Regalwood Holdings Ltd* [2010] 3 NZLR 231, 264 [82], quoting *Foran v Wight* (1989) 168 CLR 385, 417. The other reason was that a party in breach of an essential term is unable to cancel the contract for the innocent party's subsequent non-performance on the basis that the party in breach was repudiating the contract. See *Ingram v Patcroft Properties Ltd* [2011] 3 NZLR 433, 443–47 [31]–[41]; *Kawarau Village Holdings Ltd v Ho* [2018] 1 NZLR 378, 410 [108].

[314] Dawson (n 38) 75.

It is only after this question has been asked that it should be asked, *secondly*, whether breach of this particular duty gave rise to a power to terminate because it was a 'condition' (viz an essential term). Currently, too much emphasis is placed on the second question and not enough, if any, is placed on the first.[315] But as the experience of jurisdictions like New Zealand shows, if both questions are asked in their proper sequence, in many cases 'termination' would simply retire from view.

Not subject to the vices of the automatic discharge theory

The way forward proposed in this section is not subject to the vices that have led to the rejection of the 'automatic discharge theory' on the power to terminate model. That is the theory, rejected in the authorities, by which 'a contract-breaker may in some circumstances by his breach unilaterally bring the contract to an end in law'.[316] In contrast, it is said that '[a] breach which justifies termination . . . does not automatically determine the contract'.[317] In *Geys v Société Générale*,[318] Lord Hope explained that the reason for this is that 'the party who is in the wrong should not be permitted to benefit from his own wrong',[319] and if he or she were able to unilaterally bring performance of the contract to an end, the defaulting party 'may well be tempted to play this to [their] advantage'.[320] The objection therefore is that 'the decision as to whether the contract is at an end is made beyond the control of the innocent party in all circumstances' whereas it should be 'for the innocent party to judge whether it is in [their] interests to keep the contract alive'.[321] **2.143**

While the failure of a condition operates to discharge the innocent party from their obligation to perform automatically, the decision as to whether to continue performing, or to insist upon performance, remains firmly in the hands of the innocent party. This is because by waiving the condition and continuing to render or accept performance, 'the promisee may, if he wishes, enforce the promises of the defaulter—he may insist that the defaulter perform his **2.144**

[315] A notable exception is the decision of the Court of Appeal in *Doherty v Fannigan Holdings Ltd* [2018] EWCA Civ 1615.
[316] *Decro-Wall International SA v Practitioners in Marketing Ltd* [1971] 1 WLR 361, 370. See also *Heyman v Darwins Ltd* [1942] AC 356, 36; *Geys v Société Générale* [2013] 1 AC 523.
[317] Peel (n 1) 957 [18–005].
[318] [2013] 1 AC 523.
[319] ibid 537 [18].
[320] ibid. See also 559–60 [93]–[94] (Lord Wilson).
[321] ibid 537 [19]. See also 559–60 [93]–[94] (Lord Wilson).

promises'.[322] Thus, it remains true to say, even on the traditional failure of condition model, that 'one party cannot unilaterally bring [their] own obligations to an end by breaking [their] contract'.[323]

Conclusion

2.145 This chapter has been concerned with the nature of promissory conditions. Modern orthodoxy suggests that the language of 'condition', even when used in its promissory sense, is used in two senses. In one sense, a promissory condition is a promise the fulfilment of which is a condition of the other party's obligation to perform. Where the condition fails, the other party is discharged from the obligation to perform unless they waive the condition. In another sense, a promissory condition is simply an essential term the breach of which does not prevent an immediate duty of counter-performance from arising but gives rise to a power to terminate. Unless and until the power is exercised, the innocent party remains bound to perform.

2.146 The aim of this chapter has been, first, to explain how the modern law reached the position that the phrase 'promissory condition' is used in two very different senses. It was argued that the modern orthodoxy that 'breach of a condition' gives rise to a power to terminate is ahistorical and has resulted from a series of missteps. The modern position is not one that has been arrived at after careful deliberation but rather largely by accident.

2.147 Secondly, this chapter sought to demonstrate a number of the problems that have arisen as a result of the departure from the traditional understanding of promissory conditions. It was argued that the existence of both models is conceptually awkward (albeit not logically incompatible) and the power to terminate model leads to a number of difficulties that do not arise on the failure of condition model. In particular, it has given conflicting answers to the question whether a party themselves in breach can terminate for the other party's serious breach, it has created difficulties in explaining how promissory warranties in insurance contracts work, and it struggles to explain the different effects of termination at law and termination pursuant to an express contractual power. Most worryingly of all, it has caused us to lose sight of the relationship between discharge following breach, frustration, and common mistake.

[322] Shea (n 186) 631.
[323] ibid.

Finally, accepting that a wholesale revival of the failure of condition model and consequent extinction of the power to terminate model is unlikely, this chapter sought to propose a coherent way forward. And here it was seen that the great insight of the traditional learning is that in cases involving breach and non-compliance with a potential 'promissory condition' there are *two* questions courts should be asking and not one: first, was the performance of the duty that has been breached a condition precedent to, or a concurrent condition of, the other party's obligation to perform; and secondly, is this particular term a 'condition' such that its breach gives rise to a power to terminate? But these questions must be asked in their proper sequence and appropriate emphasis must be placed on the first question. Doing so will not only provide a practical way to resolve contractual disputes, but it will render the power to terminate in many cases unnecessary. It would be a 'cry for the moon'[324] to insist that lawyers abandon the power to terminate model of promissory conditions, but we can at least attempt not to lose sight of the nature of the different concepts in play, their effects, and consequently how seemingly disparate areas of contract law—such as discharge following breach, frustration, and common mistake—fit together. 2.148

[324] *Photo Production Ltd v Securicor Transport Ltd* [1980] AC 827, 844.

3

The Substantial-Benefit Condition

Introduction

The previous chapter focused on promissory conditions in order to reveal a fundamental proposition about contract law, namely, that the reason an innocent party is discharged following breach is because of the failure of a condition. The purpose of this chapter is to demonstrate that the same proposition holds true for the discharge of parties from their contractual obligations following the breach of so-called 'innominate' or 'intermediate' terms. This is the form of discharge associated with the decision in *Hongkong Fir Shipping Co Ltd v Kawasaki Kisen Kaisha Ltd*.[1] The chapter argues that the best explanation of discharge in such cases is the failure of what is termed the 'substantial-benefit condition': the condition that renders one party's obligation to perform conditional upon that party receiving 'substantially the whole benefit which it was the intention of the parties as expressed in the contract that he [or she] should obtain as the consideration for performing those undertakings'.[2] **3.1**

As will be demonstrated in this chapter, although it is sometimes thought that this instance of discharge was 'invented' or 'discovered' in *Hongkong Fir*,[3] the **3.2**

[1] [1962] 2 QB 26.
[2] ibid 66.
[3] cf Sir Guenter Treitel, *Some Landmarks of Twentieth Century Contract Law* (OUP 2002) 113, who spoke of the 'invention, or perhaps more accurately the rediscovery' of this form of discharge (clearly being aware of the historical developments traced in this chapter).

Discharge of Contractual Obligations. Jordan English, Oxford University Press. © Jordan English 2025.
DOI: 10.1093/9780198906704.003.0003

substantial-benefit condition in fact significantly predates it,[4] and can be traced to the decision in *Boone v Eyre*[5] and the cases thereafter, where it ran under the label of 'failure of consideration' and, later, 'frustration'.[6] In the 150 years before *Hongkong Fir*, the substantial-benefit condition had been applied in cases involving breach and cases not involving breach, in the context of instalment contracts, and also in the context of the so-called doctrine of substantial performance. On closer inspection, *Hongkong Fir* was nothing more than an orthodox application of this long line of authorities that had in fact been applied only five years earlier in *Universal Cargo Carriers Corp v Citati*.[7] Moreover, as will be seen, the irony of the modern focus on the tripartite classification of conditions, warranties, and innominate terms is that it goes against the whole tenor of Diplock LJ's judgment in *Hongkong Fir*, which was to focus on the 'event' rather than the breach of duty itself. That focus is a symptom of larger disease in English contract law: the failure to distinguish the promise from the condition.[8] And, as this chapter shows, if this disease is left unchecked, we will lose much of the insight which is to be gained from this long line of authorities, including its relation to other instances of discharge that do not involve breach, such as the so-called doctrine of frustration.[9]

The Origin of the Substantial-Benefit Condition

Three interpretations of *Boone v Eyre*

3.3 It will be recalled from Chapter 2 that in *Boone v Eyre* the plaintiff conveyed to the defendant the equity of redemption of a plantation in the West Indies as well as the titles to the slaves who worked upon it in consideration of £500 and an annuity of £160 per annum. The defendant failed to pay the annuity and resisted the action by the plaintiff for non-payment by pleading that the plaintiff

[4] A point made in Donal Nolan, '*Hongkong Fir Shipping Co Ltd v Kawasaki Kisen Kaisha Ltd, The Hongkong Fir* (1961)' in Charles Mitchell and Paul Mitchell (eds), *Landmark Cases in the Law of Contract* (Hart Publishing 2008) 269.

[5] (1777) 1 H BL 273n, 126 ER 160n. See David Harvey Peek, 'The History of Conditions in the English Law of Contract' (LLM thesis, University of Tasmania 1976) 204; Michael G Bridge, 'Discharge for Breach of the Contract of Sale of Goods' (1983) 28 McGill Law Journal 867, 927.

[6] Roy Granville McElroy, *Impossibility of Performance: A Treatise on the Law of Supervening Impossibility of Performance of Contract, Failure of Consideration, and Frustration* (Glanville L Williams ed, CUP 1941) 122. See also *Hongkong Fir Shipping Co Ltd v Kawasaki Kisen Kaisha Ltd* [1962] 2 QB 26, 48 (counsel for the shipowners).

[7] [1957] 2 QB 401.

[8] See [1.40]–[1.49].

[9] See Chapter 6.

was not lawfully possessed of the slaves. Lord Mansfield, giving judgment for the plaintiff, said:

> The distinction is very clear, where mutual covenants go to the whole of the consideration on both sides, they are mutual conditions, the one precedent to the other. But where they go only to a part, where a breach may be paid for in damages, there the defendant has a remedy on his covenant, and shall not plead it as a condition precedent. If this plea were to be allowed, any one [slave] not being the property of the plaintiff would bar the action.[10]

This statement, which is the entirety of the reported reasoning, has formed the foundation of much of the modern law on the discharge of parties from their contractual obligations. The irony is that the statement itself gave rise to at least three different interpretations, the veracity of which are difficult to ascertain due in part to the fact that 'the words quoted above are probably the words of the reporter or commentator and not the words of Lord Mansfield'.[11] Each of these three interpretations, however, has given birth to its own line of authority and the offspring are now firmly rooted in the modern law. **3.4**

The first interpretation formed the bedrock of the argument advanced in the previous chapter about the nature of promissory conditions. On that interpretation, the plaintiff's failure to fulfil the promise that he was lawfully possessed of the slaves did not discharge the defendant from his obligation to pay the annuity because the fulfilment of this promise was not, on a proper construction of the contract, a condition precedent to that obligation. On this view, Lord Mansfield was concerned with the construction of the contract,[12] and whether performance of a particular promise exactly was a condition precedent to the other party's obligation. This interpretation, and the line of authorities following it, formed the basis for the modern law of promissory conditions. **3.5**

The second interpretation was also touched upon in Chapter 2 in discussing the rule now found in s 11(4) of the Sale of Goods Act 1979.[13] On that interpretation of *Boone v Eyre*, although the performance of the covenant to convey title to the slaves was a condition precedent, the defendant's conduct in accepting title to some of the slaves and the conveyance of the equity of **3.6**

[10] *Boone v Eyre* (1777) 1 H BL 273n, 273n; 126 ER 160n, 160n.

[11] Arthur Corbin, *Corbin on Contracts: A Comprehensive Treatise on the Rules of Contract Law* (West Publishing Co 1960) vol 3A, 158 §659 fn 26. A point made in JW Carter and C Hodgekiss, 'Conditions and Warranties: Forebears and Descendants' (1977) 8 Sydney Law Review 31, 35 fn 24.

[12] Anthony Beck, 'The Doctrine of Substantial Performance: Conditions and Conditions Precedent' (1975) 38 Modern Law Review 413, 416; Carter and Hodgekiss (n 11) 35.

[13] See originally Sale of Goods Act 1893, s 11(1)(c).

redemption precluded him from relying upon the condition.[14] While its basis was initially unclear, with some cases suggesting that which was originally a condition precedent somehow ceased to be so,[15] later cases quickly established that it was, in fact, simply an instance of waiver.[16] Waiver of conditions is discussed in Chapters 4 and 5.

3.7 The third interpretation, which is our focus, was that Lord Mansfield was focusing on 'the nature of the breach'[17] and 'arguing that if the breach of contract was minor it would be unreasonable to allow this to be a bar to recovery'.[18] On this view, Lord Mansfield was concerned with the effect of the breach and whether this caused a failure of consideration, ie deprived one party of substantially the whole benefit of the contract. Thus, in *Davidson v Gwynne*,[19] a case which appears to be based on the first interpretation,[20] but has been referred to in the context of the third,[21] Lord Ellenborough CJ said:

> The principle laid down in *Boone v Eyre* has been recognized in all the subsequent cases, that unless the non-performance alleged in breach of the contract goes to the whole root and consideration of it, the covenant broken is not to be considered as a condition precedent, but as a distinct covenant, for the breach of which the party injured may be compensated in damages.[22]

Two separate questions

3.8 As the quote above illustrates, the cases post-*Boone v Eyre* did not always draw a clear distinction between the first and third interpretations and appeared sometimes to meld them together. This has led some to argue that Lord Mansfield was stating that 'the nature of the breach as a matter of law could alter what at the outset was intended to be a condition precedent'.[23] And putting the same proposition the other way around, Sir William Anson once suggested

[14] *Ellen v Topp* (1851) 6 Ex 424, 441–42; 155 ER 609, 616; *Graves v Legg* (1854) 9 Ex 709, 717; 156 ER 304, 307; *Behn v Burness* (1863) 3 B & S 751, 755; 122 ER 281, 283; *Wallis, Son & Wells v Pratt & Haynes* [1910] 2 KB 1003, 1013; [1911] AC 394, 400.

[15] See, eg, *Ellen v Topp* (1851) 6 Ex 424, 441–42; 155 ER 609, 616.

[16] Charles Bruce Morison, *Rescission of Contracts, A Treatise on the Principles Governing the Rescission, Discharge, Avoidance and Dissolution of Contracts* (Stevens & Haynes 1916) 100–05; Beck (n 12) 418–19.

[17] Beck (n 12) 416.

[18] Carter and Hodgekiss (n 11) 35 (emphasis removed, citations omitted).

[19] (1810) 12 East 381, 104 ER 149.

[20] See the discussion of this case at [2.16].

[21] See, eg, *MacAndrew v Chapple* (1866) LR 1 CP 643, 648.

[22] *Davidson v Gwynne* (1810) 12 East 381, 389; 104 ER 149, 152.

[23] Beck (n 12) 416.

that '[i]t is possible therefore that a promise which is independent, so that a partial breach does not affect the contract, may, if wholly broken, change its character and become a condition'.[24]

That this language has been used by the courts cannot be doubted. However, an analysis of the cases demonstrates that there were in fact two separate questions being asked: (i) was performance of the precise covenant alleged to have been breached a condition; and (ii) if not, were the effects of the alleged breach such as to deprive the other party of substantially the whole benefit of the contract? The precise order in which these questions are asked does not matter as much as the fact that two separate questions are being asked. That this is the case is readily illustrated by three nineteenth-century cases which considered both questions: *Havelock v Geddes*,[25] *Tarrabochia v Hickie*,[26] and *MacAndrew v Chapple*.[27] **3.9**

In *Havelock v Geddes*, the plaintiff owner of a ship covenanted in a charterparty that the ship would be 'made tight, staunch, and strong' and would be 'well and sufficiently equipped, manned, and fitted' for a voyage of twelve months. Almost eleven months into the voyage, the ship caught fire and was lost. The plaintiff sued for unpaid freight alleging that the defendant had not paid the third instalment of freight due at the end of ten calendar months. The defendant charterers in their defence said that the ship was not sufficiently tight, staunch, and strong etc and argued that because the performance of this covenant 'was a condition precedent and was not performed, they [were] not liable to pay any thing'.[28] The defendants' argument was rejected and judgment given for the plaintiff. **3.10**

Lord Ellenborough CJ thought that it was clear, as a matter of construction, that performance of the covenant was not a condition precedent. In words which would be picked up over 150 years later in *Hongkong Fir*[29] and repeated by law students in tutorials and seminars ever since, he said: **3.11**

> [T]o be sure, if this were a condition precedent, the neglect of putting a single nail for a single moment after the ship ought to have been made tight, staunch, [etc] would be a breach of the condition, and a defence to the whole of the plaintiff's demand.[30]

[24] Sir William R Anson, *Principles of the English Law of Contract* (1st edn, Clarendon Press 1879) 293.
[25] (1809) 10 East 555, 103 ER 886.
[26] (1856) 1 H & N 183, 156 ER 1168.
[27] (1866) LR 1 CP 643.
[28] *Havelock v Geddes* (1809) 10 East 555, 563; 103 ER 886, 889.
[29] *Hongkong Fir Shipping Co Ltd v Kawasaki Kisen Kaisha Ltd* [1962] 2 QB 26, 58, 62.
[30] *Havelock v Geddes* (1809) 10 East 555, 563; 103 ER 886, 889.

However, after referring to the rule in *Boone v Eyre*, Lord Ellenborough CJ went on to identify an alternative basis upon which it might have been said that the defendant was discharged. He said:

> Had the plaintiff's neglect here precluded the defendants from making any use of the vessel, it would have gone to the whole consideration, and might have been insisted upon as an entire bar; because the consideration for the defendants to pay the freight would then have failed in toto; but as the defendants have had some use of the vessel, notwithstanding the plaintiff's neglect, the plaintiff's covenant is to be considered as going to a part only; the consideration has not wholly failed; and the covenant cannot be looked upon as having raised a condition precedent . . .[31]

3.12 The second case that illustrates this distinction is *Tarrabochia v Hickie*. On 22 April 1854, the plaintiff entered into a charterparty with the defendant, under which the plaintiff covenanted that his ship was 'tight, staunch, and strong, and every way fitted for the voyage' and that it would sail 'with all convenient speed' to Cardiff to load a cargo of coal from the defendant. Owing to a series of delays and weather conditions, the ship did not set sail until 19 May 1854, and did not arrive in Cardiff until 16 August 1854, at which point the defendant refused to load. The plaintiff sued the defendant for damages for breach.

3.13 At trial, a verdict was returned for the defendant on the basis of the jury's finding that the ship was not 'not tight, staunch, or strong' and that it 'did not with all convenient speed, or in a reasonable time, sail and proceed to Cardiff'. This was so even though the jury had answered the judge's second question—'whether the object of the voyage was thereby frustrated'—in the negative. But the Court of Exchequer (Pollock CB, Martin B, and Bramwell B) set aside this verdict and found for the plaintiff. Pollock CB said:

> The first plea alleges that the vessel was not tight, staunch, or strong, and that by 'reason thereof the object of the charter-party and of the voyage was wholly frustrated.' The latter is a material allegation, and the jury have found it in the negative. The question then is, whether the fact of the vessel not being tight, staunch, or strong, is a condition precedent to the performance by the defendant of his contract. I think not.[32]

[31] ibid 564; 890.
[32] *Tarrabochia v Hickie* (1856) 1 H & N 183, 186; 156 ER 1168, 1170.

Again, this illustrates that there were two questions being considered. The jury had rejected any suggestion that the effects of the breach were to deprive the defendant of substantially the whole benefit of the contract or 'wholly frustrate' the voyage. The only question then was whether the parties had made precise performance of the relevant covenants conditions precedent, which the Court held they had not. **3.14**

The third and final case that illustrates this distinction is *MacAndrew v Chapple.* The plaintiff owners of a ship agreed with the defendants that the ship, 'being tight, staunch, and strong, and every way fitted for the voyage', should proceed 'with all convenient speed' to Alexandria to load a cargo of cotton and return to London or Liverpool. The ship deviated to unload cargo at various ports causing it to be a few days late. The defendants refused to load at Alexandria and the master of the vessel had to obtain cargo elsewhere, obtaining only a small freight. The plaintiffs sued for damages for the defendants' alleged breach in refusing to load the ship. **3.15**

The issue for the Court of Common Pleas was whether the plaintiffs' delay was sufficient for the defendants to refuse to load at Alexandria. As Mellish QC argued for the plaintiffs, the defendants could only show this if the stipulation that the ship proceed with all convenient speed was a 'condition precedent to the duty of the charterer to provide a cargo' or, as '[s]ome of the cases indeed seem[ed] to shew', was 'broken to such an extent as entirely to frustrate the object of the voyage'.[33] The Court (Erle CJ, Willes, Byles, and Montague Smith JJ) gave judgment for the plaintiffs, holding that the deviation was not an answer to the action. **3.16**

Demonstrating once again that these are two distinct issues, three out of four of the justices (Erle CJ, Byles, and Montague Smith JJ) expressly stated that it was unnecessary to consider whether the whole object of the voyage had been frustrated because it was admitted that the present case was not such a case.[34] Instead, each based their judgment on whether precise performance of the term was a condition precedent. Erle CJ said: **3.17**

> The present case turns only on the construction of the charterparty; and I think the clause in question amounts to a stipulation for the breach of which the remedy is by cross action, and not to a condition precedent. It is

[33] *MacAndrew v Chapple* (1866) LR 1 CP 643, 645–46. Mellish QC also refers to the stipulation that the ship be 'tight, staunch, and strong, and every way fitted for the voyage' (some repairs were carried out before the voyage took place), but the judgments appear to focus only on the delay.

[34] ibid 647 (Erle CJ), 648 (Byles J), 649 (Montague Smith J). Willes J did consider the issue: see 648.

> unnecessary to go into the cases which have been cited with reference to the doctrine that where the whole object of the voyage has been frustrated there is an answer to the action, as it is admitted that such was not the case in the present instance.[35]

3.18 In sum, while the language did not always make it clear, courts were asking two different questions: first, whether precise performance of the term broken was a condition (a promissory condition); and secondly, whether the breach that had in fact occurred had deprived the other party of substantially the whole benefit of the contract (the substantial-benefit condition).

The Substantial-Benefit Condition Applied

3.19 As will be seen in this section, the substantial-benefit condition has been applied in several different contexts. It has been applied in cases involving breach, in cases not involving breach, in the context of instalment contracts, and in connection with the so-called doctrine of substantial performance.

Cases involving breach

3.20 Throughout the nineteenth century, in addition to the cases mentioned above, the substantial-benefit condition was applied and developed in a number of cases involving breach. In *Freeman v Taylor*,[36] for example, the plaintiff shipowner agreed to proceed to the Cape of Good Hope to deliver goods there and then to proceed 'with all convenient speed' to Bombay to load cargo of cotton from the defendant's agents. But, upon arriving at the Cape, the plaintiff delayed his departure by eight days and instead of proceeding directly to Bombay, proceeded via Mauritius, which caused the ship to arrive six or seven weeks later than it would have if it had sailed direct. The defendant's agents refused to load the ship. The plaintiff sought damages for the defendant's failure to load. At trial, Tindal CJ directed the jury that an ordinary deviation would not have entitled the defendant to refuse to load, but:

> if the deviation was so long and unreasonable that, in the ordinary course of mercantile concerns, it might be said to have put an end to the whole object

[35] ibid 647.
[36] (1831) 8 Bing 124, 131 ER 348.

> the freighter had in view in chartering the ship, in that case the contract might be considered at an end . . . [37]

The jury found for the defendant, following which the plaintiff sought to set aside the verdict. Tindal CJ refused and said that the jury had found that 'the deviation was of such a nature and description as to deprive the freighter of the benefit of the contract'.[38] The defendant was therefore under no obligation to provide a cargo. **3.21**

Similarly, in *Stanton v Richardson*,[39] the owner of a ship had agreed to sail to Manila in order to fulfil orders to load a cargo of sugar in bags, hemp, and/or measurement goods at nearby ports. The ship did in fact load a cargo of 'wet sugar' at Iloilo, but a very large quantity of moisture drained from the cargo and by the time the full cargo had been loaded molasses (viscous product from the sugar) had accumulated in the ship's hold. Although the pumps on the ship were of a usual kind for a vessel of that size, they were insufficient to deal with the drainage. As a result, the cargo was unloaded at Iloilo, following which the charterer refused to provide another cargo. Cross-actions for damages were brought by both parties. **3.22**

The Court of Common Pleas (Bovill CJ, Byles, and Brett JJ) ultimately found for the charterer, who it held was under no obligation to provide a cargo. Bovill CJ referred to Lord Ellenborough CJ's statement of the principle in *Havelock v Geddes*[40] and said: 'It appears to me, therefore, in the present case, that the object of the voyage being frustrated, the charterer was not bound to load a cargo.'[41] The Court also found that the owner was in breach because he was bound to supply a vessel fit to carry the cargo that the charterer had undertaken to put on board. The judgment was affirmed on appeal.[42] **3.23**

Cases not involving breach

The cases above were all concerned with instances of breach. It is perhaps this feature which has contributed to the lack of a clear distinction between the **3.24**

[37] ibid 132; 351–52.
[38] ibid 138; 354.
[39] (1872) LR 7 CP 421.
[40] See text to n 31.
[41] *Stanton v Richardson* (1872) LR 7 CP 421, 432–33. See also 437 (Brett J).
[42] *Stanton v Richardson* (1874) LR 9 CP 390.

breach of duty and the failure of the condition.[43] However, two cases decided in the 1870s show that the distinction between the two remains of vital importance: *Jackson v Union Marine Insurance Co Ltd*[44] and *Poussard v Spiers*.[45] This is because it is possible for the substantial-benefit condition to fail in circumstances which do not amount to a breach of duty. The failure to notice this has led to much confusion about the relationship between discharge following breach and the so-called doctrine of frustration.[46]

3.25 In *Jackson v Union Marine Insurance Co Ltd*,[47] the plaintiff owner of a vessel agreed to proceed from Liverpool to Newport with all possible dispatch—'dangers and accidents of navigation'[48] excepted—in order to collect a cargo of iron rails for delivery to San Francisco. The rails were needed in San Francisco for the construction of a railway. The vessel set sail from Liverpool on 2 January 1872, but ran aground on 3 January[49] and had to be taken to a place of safety on 18 February. In the meantime, however, the charterer had, on 16 February, renounced their obligations under the charterparty and chartered another ship to carry the rails, while refusing to pay freight. The plaintiff's ship was later sold by auction and at the time of trial, on 16 August 1872, was still being repaired.

3.26 The plaintiff sought to recover his loss of freight on an insurance policy which insured against loss of freight 'by perils of the sea'.[50] The defendant insurers denied liability on the basis that any loss suffered was not caused by the perils insured against, but rather the wrongful refusal of the charterer.[51] The plaintiff, however, argued that upon the damage being caused to the ship, the charterer was no longer obliged to provide any cargo, with the result that the right to earn the freight was lost as an immediate consequence of the peril insured against.[52] The issue thus turned upon whether the damage to the ship was an event which discharged the charterer from its obligation to provide a cargo.

3.27 At trial, the jury found that the time necessary for repairing the vessel was 'so long as to put an end in a commercial sense to the commercial speculation

[43] Diplock LJ made a similar point in *Hongkong Fir Shipping Co Ltd v Kawasaki Kisen Kaisha Ltd* [1962] 2 QB 26, 68.
[44] (1874) LR 10 CP 125.
[45] (1876) 1 QBD 410.
[46] See [3.76]–[3.78] and generally Chapter 6.
[47] (1874) LR 10 CP 125.
[48] *Jackson v Union Marine Insurance Co Ltd* (1873) LR 8 CP 572, 572.
[49] *Jackson v Union Marine Insurance Co Ltd* (1874) LR 10 CP 125, 126. The first instance decision actually says it was on 4 January: ibid, 575.
[50] *Jackson v Union Marine Insurance Co Ltd* (1873) LR 8 CP 572, 577.
[51] ibid 576.
[52] ibid 577.

entered upon by the ship-owner and the charterers'.[53] Nonetheless, the trial judge found in favour of the defendants on the basis that the plaintiff had 'a right to repair his ship, however long it might take'[54] and to insist that the charterers provide a cargo. The loss, therefore, had been caused by the charterer's (wrongful) refusal to supply a cargo and not by the perils of the sea. However, when the matter was heard again in the Court of Common Pleas, and on appeal to the Court of Exchequer Chamber, judgment was given for the plaintiff and it was held that the charterer was discharged.

The primary judgment in the Court of Exchequer Chamber was given by Bramwell B (with whom Blackburn, Mellor, Amphlett, and Lush JJ agreed; Cleasby B dissenting). There are three points worth making about this judgment. The first, as noted by Dr Roy McElroy and Professor Glanville Williams, is that unfortunately, 'the expression "failure of consideration" [which is synonymous with failure of the substantial-benefit condition] is not used. Otherwise the ground of decision might have been made clearer'.[55] Instead, Bramwell B spoke of implying a condition precedent that the ship should arrive in Newport in time for the voyage, or alternatively, within a reasonable time.[56] On the latter, Bramwell B said that '[w]here no time is named for the doing of anything, the law attaches a reasonable time' and here the charterer was discharged 'because the implied condition to arrive in a reasonable time was not performed'.[57] **3.28**

This had the unfortunate consequence that 'the ground of decision itself has been misunderstood'.[58] However, as we shall see below, that failure of consideration (which is synonymous with failure of the substantial-benefit condition) is the true ground of the decision is made clear in the judgment of Blackburn J in *Poussard v Spiers*, where the eminent judge, who was also a member of the Court in both cases, discusses *Jackson v Union Marine Insurance Co Ltd*. **3.29**

The second point is that throughout the judgment, Bramwell B made tolerably clear that there was a distinction between the promise and the condition. He said: **3.30**

[53] ibid 573.
[54] ibid 575.
[55] McElroy (n 6) 137.
[56] *Jackson v Union Marine Insurance Co Ltd* (1874) LR 10 CP 125, 143–44.
[57] ibid 144. It should be noted that the implication of this specific condition here by Bramwell B was subsequently criticised by Diplock LJ in *Hongkong Fir Shipping Co Ltd v Kawasaki Kisen Kaisha Ltd* [1962] 2 QB 26, 70–71. Moreover, that the relevant condition is *not* a reasonable time was made abundantly clear in both *Universal Cargo Carriers Corp v Citati* [1957] 2 QB 401 and *Honkgong Fir*.
[58] McElroy (n 6) 136.

> The shipowner, in the case put, expressly agrees to use all possible dispatch: that is not a condition precedent; the sole remedy for and right consequent on the breach of it is an action. He also impliedly agrees that the ship shall arrive in time for the voyage: that *is* a condition precedent as well as an agreement; and its non-performance not only gives the charterer a cause of action, but also releases him. Of course, if these stipulations, owing to excepted perils, are not performed, there is no cause of action, but there is the same release of the charterer.[59]

3.31 Moreover, in discussing the effect of the 'excepted perils' clause,[60] Bramwell B said:

> Suppose it was not there, and not implied, the shipowner would be subject to an action for not arriving in a reasonable time, and the charterers would be discharged. . . . The words are there. What is their effect? I think this: they excuse the shipowner, but give him no right. The charterer has no cause of action, but is released from the charter. When I say *he* is, I think *both* are.[61]

Bramwell B was thus making clear that the only relevance of the 'excepted perils' clause was as to whether the owner was in breach. It had no impact on the question of discharge because the only matter relevant to that question was the failure of the condition, and whether the excepted perils clause was there or not the charterer would be discharged.[62]

3.32 The third point, which arises from the last sentence of the quote extracted immediately above, is that despite initial appearances, it is clear from the other parts of his judgment that Bramwell B was not suggesting that both parties were discharged for the same reason.[63] For now, it suffices to note that the charterer was discharged because the ship did not 'arrive in time for the voyage'; the 'implied condition' had failed. The owner on the other hand was discharged because he made his duty expressly conditional upon the excepted perils not taking place.[64] As McElroy has noted, '[h]ad there been no express exception

[59] *Jackson v Union Marine Insurance Co Ltd* (1874) LR 10 CP 125, 143 (emphasis in original).

[60] Throughout his judgment, Bramwell B speaks of 'perils of the seas' which appears to be the words from the insurance policy and not the charterparty. 'It was immaterial which exception was spoken of since both covered the event which happened': McElroy (n 6) 135 fn 3.

[61] ibid 144 (emphasis in original).

[62] See also Sir Michael Mustill, 'Anticipatory Breach of Contract: The Common Law at Work' in *Butterworth Lectures 1989–90* (Butterworths 1990) 57–58.

[63] McElroy (n 6) 138–39. cf Arnold D McNair, 'Frustration of Contract by War' (1940) 56 Law Quarterly Review 173, 182 fn 40; Arnold D McNair, *Legal Effects of War* (CUP 1920) 82.

[64] See *Jackson v Union Marine Insurance Co Ltd* (1874) LR 10 CP 125, 144.

it can hardly be doubted that the shipowner would *not* have been excused'.[65] The only difference between this case and the cases considered in the previous sub-section applying the substantial-benefit condition is that here there was no breach of duty.

3.33 The second case to illustrate the application of the substantial-benefit condition in a case not involving breach is *Poussard v Spiers*,[66] which was decided some sixteen months later. The defendant's manager had made a contract with the plaintiff's wife,[67] Madame Poussard, for her to sing and play in an opera at the defendant's theatre. Madame Poussard fell ill and was unable to attend the final week of rehearsals, or to perform on the opening night and the first three days of the following week. The defendant in the meantime had hired a replacement. Madame Poussard recovered and sought to tender her services, which the defendant refused to accept. The plaintiff brought an action for wrongful dismissal. The Court (Blackburn, Quain, and Field JJ) held that 'the failure on the plaintiff's part went to the root of the matter and discharged the defendants'.[68] Blackburn J observed:

> This inability having been occasioned by sickness was not any breach of contract by the plaintiff, and no action can lie against him for the failure thus occasioned. But the damage to the defendants and *the consequent failure of consideration* is just as great as if it had been occasioned by the plaintiff's fault, instead of the wife's misfortune. The analogy is complete between this case and that of... *Jackson v Union Marine Insurance Co*.[69]

3.34 It is clear from this passage that Blackburn J saw *Poussard v Spiers* as directly analogous to *Jackson v Union Marine Insurance Co Ltd*. The plaintiff was not in breach of any contractual duty due to Madame Poussard falling ill—her obligation to perform was conditional upon it being possible to do so[70]—but this was irrelevant to the question whether the substantial-benefit condition had failed. That is because the defendant was discharged by the failure of condition, not any breach of duty. Indeed, the analogy could not have been more perfect, because in *Jackson v Union Marine Insurance Co Ltd*, when explaining

[65] McElroy (n 6) 139 (emphasis in original, editorial footnote omitted).
[66] (1876) 1 QBD 410.
[67] The husband was the plaintiff due to the old doctrine of 'coverture', abolished by the Married Women's Property Act 1882, pursuant to which upon marriage the husband and wife were treated as a single entity, the husband subsuming the rights of the wife.
[68] *Poussard v Spiers* (1876) 1 QBD 410, 415.
[69] ibid 414 (emphasis added).
[70] See [6.5]–[6.23].

that the 'excepted perils' clause prevented the shipowner's non-performance from being a breach but did not affect the discharge of the charterer, Bramwell B had said, in almost prophetic terms:

> Thus, A enters the service of B, and is ill and cannot perform his work. No action will lie against him; but B may hire a fresh servant, and not wait his recovery, if his illness would put an end, in a business sense, to their business engagement, and would frustrate the object of that engagement: a short illness would not suffice, if consistent with the object they had in view.[71]

3.35 Both these cases therefore show that while the failure of the substantial-benefit condition might be brought about as a result of a breach of duty, it can also occur where there is no breach of duty at all. In neither case is the defendant discharged for breach; the defendant is discharged for the failure of a condition.[72]

Instalment contracts

3.36 The substantial-benefit condition has also been applied in the context of instalment contracts.[73] The reason that this has not always been clear is two-fold. First, cases involving instalment contracts will often involve promissory conditions as well. Secondly, in such cases, renunciation in the sense of anticipatory breach has not been delineated clearly from failure of the substantial-benefit condition. An example of the conflation between the two concepts can be seen in *Freeth v Burr*,[74] where Lord Coleridge CJ said that '[w]here by the non-delivery of part of the thing contracted for the whole object of the contract is frustrated, the party making default renounces on his part all the obligations of the contract.'

3.37 A case which illustrates this overlap is *Mersey Steel and Iron Co Ltd v Naylor, Benzon & Co.*[75] The respondents agreed to buy from the appellant company 5,000 tons of steel, to be delivered in batches of 1,000 tons per month, commencing January 1881. Two deliveries were made in January and February,

[71] *Jackson v Union Marine Insurance Co Ltd* (1874) LR 10 CP 125, 145.

[72] See, eg, AM Shea, 'Discharge from Performance of Contracts by Failure of Condition' (1979) 42 Modern Law Review 623, 624.

[73] Nolan (n 4) 275–76.

[74] (1874) LR 9 CP 208, 214, cited with approval in *Maple Flock Co Ltd v Universal Furniture Products (Wembley) Ltd* [1934] 1 KB 148, 155.

[75] (1884) 9 App Cas 434.

but each fell short. The total amount shipped was around half of one instalment. Shortly before payment for these deliveries was due, a petition to wind up the company was presented. The buyers were advised, incorrectly, that they could not without leave of the Court pay the company pending the petition, upon which they asked the company to obtain a court order sanctioning their payment. The company treated this as a refusal to pay. The company was subsequently wound up and the liquidator refused to make any further deliveries, instead commencing an action to recover the price of what had been delivered. The buyers admitted that the amounts were due, but counter-claimed for damages for non-delivery. The company argued that the non-payment had operated to discharge the company from its obligation to deliver.

The House of Lords, affirming the decision of the Court of Appeal, found in favour of the buyers. Lord Selborne LC rejected the argument of the company that payment for one instalment was a condition precedent to each subsequent instalment.[76] Instead, the Lord Chancellor said that the relevant question was whether there was conduct that 'amounts to a renunciation, to an absolute refusal to perform the contract',[77] relying upon *Freeth v Burr*.[78] Ultimately, he refused to ascribe to the buyers conduct 'the character of a renunciation of the contract',[79] on the basis that the buyers were seeking to fulfil the contract. **3.38**

Lord Blackburn delivered a concurring speech. He agreed that the case did not fall within the principle in *Freeth v Burr*, which he identified as being based upon the same principle as *Hochster v De La Tour*,[80] namely renunciation in the sense of anticipatory breach.[81] Having dismissed that argument, Lord Blackburn then went on to say: **3.39**

> The rule of law, as I always understood it, is that where there is a contract . . . if you see that the failure to perform one part of it goes to the root of the contract, goes to the foundation of the whole, it is a good defence to say, 'I am not going on to perform my part of it when that which is the root of the whole and the substantial consideration for my performance is defeated by your misconduct.'[82]

[76] ibid 439.
[77] ibid.
[78] (1874) LR 9 CP 208, 214.
[79] *Mersey Steel and Iron Co Ltd v Naylor, Benzon & Co* (1884) 9 App Cas 434, 441.
[80] (1853) 2 El & Bl 678, 118 ER 922.
[81] *Mersey Steel and Iron Co Ltd v Naylor, Benzon & Co* (1884) 9 App Cas 434, 443.
[82] ibid 443–44.

Lord Blackburn was here relying upon failure of consideration reasoning.[83] Ultimately he held that the breach was not one that went to the root of the contract.[84]

3.40 Unfortunately, subsequent cases have not distinguished between these two different ideas (renunciation and failure of the substantial-benefit condition). Thus, in the leading decision of *Maple Flock Co Ltd v Universal Furniture Products (Wembley) Ltd*,[85] which was concerned with defects found in instalments delivered, the Court of Appeal (Lord Hewart CJ, Lord Wright, and Slesser LJ) quoted the test for renunciation set out by Lord Selborne LC in *Mersey Steel*, but then, relying upon Lord Coleridge CJ in *Freeth v Burr*,[86] said the question was 'the relation in fact of the default to the whole purpose of the contract'.[87] Indeed, the test posited by the Court of Appeal appears to conflate the two ideas. The Court said that the following must be considered: 'first, the ratio quantitatively which the breach bears to the contract as a whole, and secondly the degree of probability or improbability that such a breach will be repeated'.[88]

3.41 It is submitted that in order to make sense of the law, a proper understanding of the conditions at play is needed. Subject always to the proper construction of the contract, the following general rules might be stated. First, in a contract for the sale of goods by instalments, delivery of each instalment is likely to be a promissory condition to payment for that instalment. Equally, it is a condition of the buyer's obligation to accept delivery, and hence to pay, that they receive substantially the whole benefit of that instalment.[89] Secondly, it is possible that if the performance rendered by one party is such as to deprive the buyer of substantially the whole benefit of the contract, the buyer can be discharged from the obligation to accept delivery of all instalments of the goods. An example of this might be where the subsequent instalments are rendered otiose without the prior instalments, such as a contract for the delivery in instalments of parts to build a machine. This, however, is likely to be an exceptional case,

[83] Nolan (n 4) 276 fn 39. See also Carter and Hodgekiss (n 11) 41.

[84] The approach in *Mersey Steel* based upon renunciation subsequently found expression in the Sale of Goods Act 1893, s 31(2) (now the Sale of Goods Act 1979, s 31(2)), despite apparently being based on the quote from Lord Blackburn, which was concerned with failure of consideration; see MD Chalmers, *The Sale of Goods Act, 1893, including The Factors Acts, 1889 & 1890* (William Clowes and Sons Ltd 1894) 64.

[85] *Maple Flock Co Ltd v Universal Furniture Products (Wembley) Ltd* [1934] 1 KB 148.

[86] (1874) LR 9 CP 208, 214.

[87] *Maple Flock Co Ltd v Universal Furniture Products (Wembley) Ltd* [1934] 1 KB 148, 156.

[88] ibid 157.

[89] See the authorities referred to in JW Carter, GJ Tolhurst, and Elisabeth Peden, 'Developing the Intermediate Term Concept' (2006) 22 Journal of Contract Law 268, 279–81. See further Corbin (n 11) 332 §708.

particularly where performance has already commenced. Thirdly, the conduct of one party, in line with *Mersey Steel* and *Maple Flock*, may be such as to indicate an intention not to perform in the future or an inability to do so—these are cases of renunciation or disablement and are forms of anticipatory breach.[90] The risk of confusion arises because, as we noted in Chapter 2, sometimes the conduct to infer a renunciation of future obligations is in fact the way in which a present obligation is breached.[91] The key to removing the confusion is to distinguish between actual non-performance and merely anticipated non-performance.[92]

The doctrine of substantial performance

The substantial-benefit condition has also travelled under another name: the so-called doctrine of substantial performance. This apparent doctrine, which 'has been chiefly applied to building contracts',[93] was explained in the following way by Geoffrey Cheshire and Cecil Fifoot: 3.42

> According to this doctrine, which dates back to Lord Mansfield's judgment in *Boone v Eyre* in 1779, if there has been substantial though not perhaps an exact and literal performance by the promisor, the promisee cannot treat himself [or herself] as discharged.[94]

Despite the fact that it traces its lineage to the same decision, it appears to have gone largely unnoticed that the substantial performance 'doctrine' is simply an instance of the substantial-benefit condition.[95] In every case where it is said to apply, the question is whether the promisee has received substantially the whole benefit that it was intended they should obtain from the contract. To ask whether the promisor has 'substantially performed' is simply another way of expressing the question. 3.43

That this is the case is illustrated by the well-known decision in *Hoenig v Isaacs*.[96] 3.44
The plaintiff had been hired to decorate and furnish the defendant's flat. The

[90] See Chapter 8.
[91] See [2.50] and the text accompanying n 142 in that section.
[92] ibid.
[93] Edwin W Patterson, 'Constructive Conditions in Contracts' (1942) 42 Columbia Law Review 903, 927. See also FMB Reynolds, 'Discharge of Contract by Breach' (1982) 97 Law Quarterly Review 541, 543.
[94] GC Cheshire and CHS Fifoot, *The Law of Contract* (5th edn, Butterworth & Co 1960) 447 (citation omitted).
[95] cf Beck (n 12).
[96] [1952] 2 All ER 176.

contract price was £750 to be paid 'net cash, as the work proceeds; and balance on completion'.[97] The defendant paid £400 but refused to pay the balance of £350 on the ground that the work was done defectively. It was found that a door of a wardrobe required replacing and that a bookshelf was too short and would need to be remade, thus requiring additional alterations to the bookcase. The plaintiff brought an action for the balance of the price. The Court of Appeal (Somervell, Denning, and Romer LJJ) held that the plaintiff was entitled to recover the balance of the contract price, subject to a counter-claim for damages.

3.45 The issue, simply put, was what constituted the condition precedent to payment.[98] The defendant argued that the contract was an 'entire contract', meaning, in this context, that full and exact performance of the promise to decorate the flat was required before the obligation to pay fell due. This argument was rejected.

3.46 Somervell LJ expressly referred to *Boone v Eyre* for '[t]he principle that fulfilment of every term is not necessarily a condition precedent in a contract for a lump sum'.[99] He said that 'if there was a substantial compliance with the contract' then 'the price must be paid subject to set-off or counterclaim'.[100] Denning LJ was also of the view that because the contract was 'substantially performed' the plaintiff was entitled to recover.[101] He said:

> [T]he first question is whether, on the true construction of the contract, entire performance was a condition precedent to payment. . . . When a contract provides for a specific sum to be paid on completion of specified work, the courts lean against a construction of the contract which would deprive the contractor of any payment at all simply because there are some defects or omissions. The promise to complete the work is, therefore, construed as a term of the contract, but not as a condition. It is not every breach of that term which absolves the employer from [their] promise to pay the price, but only a breach which goes to the root of the contract, such as an abandonment of the work when it is only half done. Unless the breach does go to the root of the matter, the employer cannot resist payment of the price.[102]

[97] ibid 177.
[98] ibid 180.
[99] ibid 178.
[100] ibid 179.
[101] ibid 181.
[102] ibid 180–81.

3.47 Denning LJ's judgment is particularly instructive because it proceeds in the same two stages we have seen at [3.8]–[3.18] above. First, it asks whether performance of the promise to decorate the flat exactly was a condition precedent to payment (ie a promissory condition). Secondly, it asks, notwithstanding, whether the breach is such as to go to the 'root of the contract'. And this question was answered in the negative by Denning LJ stating that the plaintiff had 'substantially performed'. The question is simply another way of asking whether the substantial-benefit condition has failed, and it is part of the same two-stage analysis that judges had been engaging in at this stage for over 140 years.[103]

3.48 When seen in this light, it also becomes apparent that there is no 'doctrine' of substantial performance, insofar as this suggests the existence of a rule that a condition will be taken to have been satisfied if it is 'substantially performed'. Nor, to state the obvious, is it a defence to an action for breach of duty for the promisor to say that they have 'substantially performed'.[104] The so-called 'doctrine' of substantial performance is simply a matter of ascertaining the relevant conditions precedent to payment. It would therefore be a mistake to say that there will be no failure of a condition 'where the condition is substantially performed'.[105] Conditions are binary. They are either performed or they are not. The true position in cases where substantial performance will enliven the duty to pay is that '"substantial performance" *is* the condition—the fact that must exist before payment is due'.[106]

The Decision in *Hongkong Fir*

3.49 As the previous section has shown, the substantial-benefit condition, though famously associated with the decision in *Hongkong Fir*, significantly predates it, and has been applied in a range of different contexts. Indeed, while it has been said that *Hongkong Fir* represents 'the most important judicial contribution to English contract law in the past century',[107] its importance is not in establishing new principles, but in shedding 'a new light on old and accepted principles'.[108]

[103] See, eg, the discussion of *Havelock v Geddes* (1809) 10 East 555, 103 ER 886 at [3.10]–[3.11] above.
[104] Corbin (n 11) 315–16 §702.
[105] Frederick Wilmot-Smith, 'Reconsidering "Total" Failure' (2013) 72 Cambridge Law Journal 414, 428.
[106] Corbin (n 11) 314 §701 (emphasis in original).
[107] Treitel (n 3) 113.
[108] *Bunge Corp, New York v Tradax Export SA, Panama* [1981] 1 WLR 711, 719. Nolan skilfully advances this very claim: Nolan (n 4).

The authorities before *Hongkong Fir*

3.50 In the first half of the twentieth century, the substantial-benefit condition 'flourished'[109] in cases where there was no breach. But in cases where there was a breach the focus on promissory conditions appears to have taken centre stage.[110] Nonetheless, the substantial-benefit condition did not fall completely into disuse and, in addition to the 'substantial performance' cases discussed above, a number of cases continued to apply it.[111]

3.51 The most important is the decision in *Universal Cargo Carriers Corp v Citati*.[112] A ship had been chartered to load a quantity of scrap iron at Basrah for carriage to Buenos Aires. The ship arrived at Basrah in due course but the charterer failed to nominate an effective shipper or loading berth, and failed to provide a cargo. Three days before the lay-days had expired, the shipowners rechartered the vessel to another party and the issue, on a special case from the arbitrator, was whether they were entitled to do so. A large part of the case focused on renunciation and disablement (both forms of anticipatory breach), and on these issues it was held that on the findings of the arbitrator, it had not been shown that the charterer had evinced an intention not to perform the charterparty (renunciation), but that the matter should be remitted to the arbitrator to determine whether the charterer was 'willing and able to perform the charterparty within such time as would not have frustrated the commercial object of the adventure' (disablement).[113]

3.52 On the issue of actual breach, the Court first considered whether any of the breaches by the charterer were of 'a condition of the charterparty as distinct from a warranty'.[114] The Court held that none of them was a condition.[115] But secondly, the Court went on to say that the delay could not go on indefinitely, and that '[w]hen the delay becomes so prolonged that the breach assumes a character so grave as to go to the root of the contract, the aggrieved party is entitled to rescind'.[116]

109 Nolan (n 4) 275.
110 ibid.
111 See, eg, *Inverkip Steamship Co Ltd v Bunge & Co* [1917] 2 KB 193; *Aerial Advertising Co v Batchelors Peas Ltd* [1938] 2 All ER 788; *Universal Cargo Carriers Corp v Citati* [1957] 2 QB 401. See also Nolan (n 4) 275–76.
112 [1957] 2 QB 401.
113 ibid 455.
114 ibid 429.
115 ibid.
116 ibid 430.

On this second inquiry, an issue arose as to 'the yardstick by which this length of delay [was] to be measured'.[117] Counsel for the owners, Mr Ashton Roskill QC,[118] had argued that the yardstick was not one of 'frustration', but rather a 'reasonable time'.[119] The Court rejected this argument and held that the former had been 'settled as the correct one by a long line of authorities'[120]—specifically, the authorities discussed earlier in this chapter. And as the arbitrator had found that the delay when the owners rechartered the vessel had not become so long as to frustrate the object of the voyage, this ground of discharge could not be relied upon. **3.53**

Importantly, this two-staged approach to discharge is exactly the same analysis we have seen in earlier sections of this chapter. Indeed, the Court made the astute observation that the term 'frustration' 'was in use in relation to breach of contract well before the doctrine was declared in 1870 or thereabouts'.[121] And in terms which make it clear that the Court was talking about failure of consideration (ie failure of the substantial-benefit condition), it said: **3.54**

> To bring a contract to an end by breach of warranty[122] there had to be a failure of consideration, that is to say, the breach had to be such as to *deprive the plaintiff in effect of the benefit of his [or her] contract.* Various metaphors came into use for describing the character of such a breach, such as 'going to the whole root and consideration of the contract' and 'frustrating the object of the voyage'.[123]

It is perhaps surprising that this decision, albeit only a decision at first instance, has not been given more attention on the issue of discharge following actual breach. As will be seen in the next subsection, the case itself formed the basis of the arguments advanced in *Hongkong Fir* and clearly formed an important part of each justice's reasoning.[124] Indeed, aside from further exposition of the substantial-benefit condition, it is difficult to see what, if anything, the judgments in *Hongkong Fir* added to the explanation given in *Universal Cargo Carriers*. Nonetheless, there can be no doubting that the decision in *Hongkong* **3.55**

[117] ibid.

[118] Not to be confused with his younger brother Eustace Roskill, who later became Lord Roskill, and who coincidentally was the arbitrator in the case.

[119] See, eg, *Universal Cargo Carriers Corp v Citati* [1957] 2 QB 401, 417.

[120] ibid 430.

[121] ibid.

[122] This is not how most lawyers would use the term 'warranty' today, but see the text accompanying n 152 below.

[123] *Universal Cargo Carriers Corp v Citati* [1957] 2 QB 401, 431 (emphasis added).

[124] *Hongkong Fir Shipping Co Ltd v Kawasaki Kisen Kaisha Ltd* [1962] 2 QB 26, 61 (Sellers LJ), 65 (Upjohn LJ), 69 (Diplock LJ).

Fir, especially the judgment of Diplock LJ, has been by far the most influential and, consequently, it has been said (inaccurately) that the 'credit for this invention or discovery belongs to Diplock LJ'.[125]

Hongkong Fir

3.56 The facts of *Hongkong Fir* were summarised in the previous chapter, but bear repeating. The claimant shipowners chartered the *Hongkong Fir* to the defendants for a period of twenty-four months. By clause 1 of the charterparty, the owners contracted to deliver the vessel 'she being in every way fitted for ordinary cargo service' (the 'seaworthiness obligation'). On 13 February 1957, the vessel sailed from Liverpool to Osaka, but there were insufficient members of the engine room to maintain the vessel's old machinery, and the chief engineer was a drunk, both of which led to serious breakdowns. Almost fourteen and a half weeks later, on 25 May, the vessel reached Osaka, where it was discovered that the main engine and auxiliaries were in a damaged state and needed repairs. A further fifteen weeks were required to make the vessel ready for sea. On 6 June 1957, the charterers renounced their obligations under the charterparty. The owners brought an action seeking damages for the charterers' (alleged) wrongful repudiation. The charterers in their defence argued that the owners had breached the seaworthiness obligation, the performance of which they argued was 'a condition precedent to the charterer[s'] liability under the charterparty'[126] or, alternatively, that the charterparty was frustrated by reason of the breakdowns, repairs and delay.

3.57 At first instance, Salmon J held that the owners were in breach of the seaworthiness obligation,[127] but that its performance was not a condition.[128] This meant that the charterers could not succeed 'unless the delay in making the vessel seaworthy was or appeared likely at the date of the repudiation to be so great as to frustrate the commercial purpose of the charter'.[129] Advancing the argument that he had made unsuccessfully in *Universal Cargo Carriers*, counsel for the charterers, Mr Roskill QC, again argued that it was enough if the delay was unreasonable, and that it was not necessary in cases of breach for the delay

125 Treitel (n 3) 113.
126 *Hongkong Fir Shipping Co Ltd v Kawasaki Kisen Kaisha Ltd* [1962] 2 QB 26, 35.
127 ibid 34.
128 ibid 38.
129 ibid.

to amount to 'frustration'.[130] Salmon J rejected this submission, and ultimately concluded that the charterparty had not been 'frustrated'.[131]

3.58 The charterers then appealed to the Court of Appeal and ran the exact same arguments that had been put before Salmon J. In particular, contrary to the picture often painted of *Hongkong Fir* (which suggests that it invented or rediscovered this form of discharge), there was no doubt whatsoever that a party could be discharged in circumstances where the term breached (here, the seaworthiness obligation) was not a 'promissory condition'. The argument advanced on behalf of the charterers was simply that the standard by which the delay was to be measured was an 'unreasonable delay from the point of view of the charterers' rather than 'such delay as is necessary to frustrate the contract'.[132]

3.59 The Court of Appeal (Sellers, Upjohn, and Diplock LJJ) dismissed the charterers' appeal, holding that the charterers had not been entitled to renounce their obligations under the charterparty because (i) performance of the seaworthiness obligation was not a condition, and (ii) the delays caused by the breakdowns and repairs were not so great as to frustrate the commercial purpose of the charterparty (expressly rejecting Mr Roskill QC's submission that it was enough if the delay was unreasonable).

3.60 Sellers LJ specifically stated that the charterers would be discharged if the delay were 'so long in fact, or likely to be so long in reasonable anticipation, that the commercial purpose of the contract would be frustrated'.[133] Moreover, he noted that the argument as to the standard by which the delay was to be measured was a 'similar argument' to that which Mr Roskill QC had advanced in *Universal Cargo Carriers*[134] and, for the reasons given by the Court in that case, Sellers LJ rejected it.[135]

3.61 Upjohn LJ also rejected this argument, stating that '[the judge in *Universal Cargo Carriers*] came to clearly the right conclusion after an exhaustive review of the authorities'.[136] Upjohn LJ thought that it would be 'wrong to introduce the idea that the innocent party can treat the contract as at an end for delays which ... fall short of a frustration of the contract',[137] and stated that 'the

[130] ibid.
[131] ibid 40.
[132] ibid 41.
[133] ibid 57.
[134] ibid 61.
[135] ibid 60–61.
[136] ibid 65.
[137] ibid.

question to be answered is, does the breach of the stipulation go so much to the root of the contract that it makes further commercial performance of the contract impossible, or in other words is the whole contract frustrated?'[138]

3.62 Turning to Diplock LJ's judgment, as we noted in Chapter 2, his central point was that it was an event rather than the breach itself, which relieved one party of his or her undertakings under the contract. He said:

> The test whether an event has this effect or not has been stated in a number of metaphors all of which I think amount to the same thing: does the occurrence of the event deprive the party who has further undertakings still to perform of substantially the whole benefit which it was the intention of the parties as expressed in the contract that he [or she] should obtain as the consideration for performing those undertakings?[139]

Diplock LJ's statement of the test is an apt way of describing the substantial-benefit condition—each party's obligation to perform is conditional upon that party receiving substantially the whole benefit of the contract.[140]

3.63 Unsurprisingly, Diplock LJ also expressly rejected the argument that a different test ought to be applied in cases of discharge following breach and in cases of so-called 'frustration', stating that '[t]he test . . . is the same whether the event is the result of the other party's breach of contract or not, as [was] pointed out in *Universal Cargo Carriers*'.[141] Diplock LJ said that the 'fallacy' in Mr Roskill QC's argument stemmed from 'a failure to view the cases in their historical context'.[142] After referring to a number of those cases, he said:

> The fact that the emphasis in the earlier cases was upon the breach by one party . . . tended to obscure the fact that it was really the event resulting from the breach which relieved the other party of further performance of [their] obligations. . . . It was not, however, until *Jackson v Union Marine Insurance Co Ltd* that it was recognised that it was the happening of the event and not the fact that the event was the result of a breach by one party of [their] contractual obligations that relieved the other party from further performance of [their] obligations.[143]

[138] ibid 64.
[139] ibid 66.
[140] See also Reynolds (n 93) 542.
[141] *Hongkong Fir Shipping Co Ltd v Kawasaki Kisen Kaisha Ltd* [1962] 2 QB 26, 69.
[142] ibid 66.
[143] ibid 68.

This is substantially the claim that has been put forward in this chapter. And it is submitted that the reason it has been so difficult to see is because of the failure to distinguish between the promise, the breach of which gives rise to an action for damages, and the condition, the failure of which operates as a discharge.

It is for this reason that Diplock LJ was correct when he went on to say there are 'many contractual undertakings of a more complex character which cannot be categorised as being "conditions" or "warranties"'[144] breach of which will always or never give rise to a discharge, and that: **3.64**

> [o]f such undertakings all that can be predicated is that some breaches will and others will not give rise to an event which will deprive the party not in default of substantially the whole benefit which it was intended that [they] should obtain from the contract . . .[145]

This is because where exact performance of a contractual term is not a condition, not every breach of that term (ie not every breach of duty) will cause the substantial-benefit condition to fail. A breach will only do so where its effect is to deprive the other party of substantially the whole benefit of the contract and thus cause the substantial-benefit condition to fail.

In sum, a number of points can be taken away from the decision in *Hongkong Fir*. First, far from being 'revolutionary'[146] it appears to have been little more than an orthodox application of a long line of authorities stemming back to *Boone v Eyre*.[147] Secondly, while Diplock LJ has been credited with the 'invention' or 'rediscovery' of this form of discharge, it seems that the credit should really be given to *Universal Cargo Carriers*, which formed the primary basis of much of the argument in *Hongkong Fir*. Indeed, it was not even in dispute that this second form of discharge existed in *Hongkong Fir*; the issue on appeal was only as to the standard or yardstick to be applied. Finally, the decision is readily explicable on the basis that while performance of the seaworthiness obligation exactly was not a 'condition' (ie not a promissory condition), the obligations of the charterers were nevertheless subject to the substantial-benefit condition.[148] **3.65**

[144] ibid 70.
[145] ibid.
[146] Tony Weir, 'Contract—The Buyer's Right to Reject Defective Goods' (1976) 35 Cambridge Law Journal 33, 35.
[147] An argument made in Nolan (n 4).
[148] Reynolds (n 93) 542.

And despite there being a clear breach of the seaworthiness obligation, the substantial-benefit condition simply had not failed on the facts.

The 'intermediate' or 'innominate' term

3.66 It follows from the above that the decision in *Hongkong Fir* is perfectly explicable on a failure of condition model. Unfortunately, it seems that despite Diplock LJ's insistence that the question of discharge could not be answered solely by reference to a priori classification of contractual terms, the decision in *Hongkong Fir* is said to have 'given birth'[149] to a brand-new type of term: the 'intermediate' term or 'innominate' term. This third category of contractual term now sits alongside 'conditions' and 'warranties'.[150]

3.67 But as Professor Donal Nolan has observed, to suggest that Diplock LJ introduced a third category of term 'seems rather a simplistic way of encapsulating the very sophisticated analysis which [Diplock LJ's judgment] presents'.[151] The whole point of Diplock LJ's judgment was to move away from the so-called classification of terms. The classification of terms for this purpose is also, as this chapter has shown, completely ahistorical. No prior case had considered the need to classify the term when considering the application of the substantial-benefit condition. Indeed, in *Universal Cargo Carriers*, when discussing this form of discharge, the Court said that '[t]o bring a contract to an end by *breach of warranty* there had to be a failure of consideration'.[152] And even after *Hongkong Fir*, there were doubts expressed as to whether any so-called third term had been created.[153]

3.68 The tendency to focus on the classification of terms is all the more surprising when it is recognised that Diplock LJ himself at no point mentioned 'innominate' or 'intermediate' terms and never adopted the terminology post-*Hongkong Fir*.[154] The first reported reference in a case appears to be the

149 Carter, Tolhurst, and Peden (n 89) 268.
150 See, eg, Edwin Peel, *The Law of Contract* (15th edn, Sweet & Maxwell 2020) 989–91 [18-052]–[18-054]; Jack Beatson, Andrew Burrows, and John Cartwright, *Anson's Law of Contract* (31st edn, OUP 2020) 151–53; Ewan McKendrick, 'Termination for Breach' in Hugh Beale (ed), *Chitty on Contracts* (35th edn, Sweet & Maxwell 2023) vol 1 2133, 2156 [28-041]; Andrew Burrows, *A Restatement of the English Law of Contract* (2nd edn, OUP 2020) 118–19.
151 Nolan (n 4) 286.
152 *Universal Cargo Carriers Corp v Citati* [1957] 2 QB 401, 431 (emphasis added).
153 *Cehave NV v Bremer Handelsgesellschaft mbH (The Hansa Nord)* [1976] QB 44, 84.
154 Carter, Tolhurst, and Peden (n 89) 271.

judgment of Stephenson LJ in the Court of Appeal *Wickman Machine Tool Sales Ltd v L Schuler AG*,[155] where he referred to '*Anson's* "innominate term" '.[156]

One difficulty this has caused is that, as all students of contract law will know, it now means that there is a debate as to whether there is a continued need for three categories of terms: (i) 'conditions', any breach of which will give rise to a power to terminate; (ii) 'intermediate terms', some breaches of which will give rise to a power to terminate; and (iii) 'warranties', no breaches of which will give rise to a power to terminate.[157] The doubt relates to the continued need for a third category of 'warranty' on the basis that it is difficult to imagine any obligation in a contract that could not somehow be breached in a way so as to deprive one party of substantially the whole benefit of the contract. **3.69**

This debate only arises because of the assumption that a 'power to terminate' arises in response to certain kinds of breaches of certain kinds of terms. This thinking in turn has only arisen because, as we saw in Chapter 2, English lawyers began to refer to stipulations, the performance of which was a condition, as 'conditions' themselves.[158] A 'warranty' was then used simply to refer to everything else, but crucially it did not need to carry the implication that no breach of a warranty could ever give rise to a discharging event.[159] On the approach put forward in this book, the tripartite classification of terms misses the whole point that it is not the breach of a particular term or duty that discharges one party from his or her obligation to perform, but the failure of the condition. The key focus is always upon ascertaining the conditions of each party's obligation to perform. There is no significance in how a term or duty is classified. **3.70**

In other words, the problem with the continued insistence that it is necessary to classify the terms of a contract as either conditions, warranties, or innominate terms in order to answer questions about discharge, is that it again blinds us to the distinction between the promise and the condition. Two examples illustrate the point and the difficulties that arise on the now-orthodox approach. **3.71**

First, suppose that in a charterparty to collect a cargo of perishable goods, multiple promises are breached: the ship does not proceed to the loading port with **3.72**

155 [1972] 1 WLR 840, 860.

156 Noted in *Spar Shipping AS v Grand China Logistics Holding (Group) Co Ltd* [2017] 4 All ER 124, 131 [19]. The expression is said to have originated in the academic literature in MP Furmston, 'The Classification of Contractual Terms' (1962) 25 Modern Law Review 584. See Carter, Tolhurst, and Peden (n 89) 271 fn 19.

157 See, eg, Peel (n 150) 990 [18-053].

158 Reynolds (n 93) 542.

159 See ibid 548–49.

all convenient speed;[160] the owner then delays in leaving on time;[161] the owner deviates slightly on the way to the end-destination;[162] and finally, due to the unseaworthiness of the ship it requires repairs on the way and is even further delayed.[163] Suppose further that the combined effect of all these delays is that the goods perish, depriving the charterer of substantially the whole benefit of the contract, but no breach on its own would have been sufficient to cause this outcome. If each of these obligations is to be classified as an 'innominate term', then it seems that no individual breach of any innominate term has deprived the innocent party of substantially the whole benefit of the contract. But once we separate the promise and the condition, we can see that the short answer is that there can be multiple breaches of duty, the combined effect of which is to cause the substantial-benefit condition to fail.[164]

3.73 Secondly, what happens if a delay that deprives one party of substantially the whole benefit of the contract is partly due to a breach and partly due to an excepted peril (ie an event that is not a breach of any duty)? Again, if a 'power to terminate' arises in response to certain kinds of breaches of 'innominate terms', this too looks difficult to resolve. The breach of the duty has not, on its own, deprived the other party of substantially the whole benefit of the contract—only the combined effect of the breach and the excepted peril has done so. But on the model put forward here, whether the failure of condition is caused by a breach of duty or not is irrelevant to the question of discharge: the condition has failed, and the party need not perform. Indeed, this was the view taken in *Nitrate Corp of Chile Ltd v Pansuiza Compania de Navegacion SA (The Hermosa)*,[165] where Mustill J correctly stated that 'it is the consequences of the events, not their origins, which matter'.[166]

3.74 An approach which focuses on the classifications of terms, rather than the identification of conditions, struggles with these issues. This is because the distinction between promises and conditions, which this book focuses on, is fundamental.

[160] *Tarrabochia v Hickie* (1856) 1 H & N 183, 156 ER 1168; *MacAndrew v Chapple* (1866) LR 1 CP 643.
[161] *Freeman v Taylor* (1831) 8 Bing 124, 131 ER 348.
[162] ibid.
[163] *Hongkong Fir Shipping Co Ltd v Kawasaki Kisen Kaisha Ltd* [1962] 2 QB 26.
[164] Reynolds (n 93) 548.
[165] [1980] 1 Lloyd's Rep 638, 649. cf *The Hermosa* [1982] 1 Lloyd's Rep 570, 580. The decision was affirmed on appeal.
[166] *The Hermosa* [1980] 1 Lloyd's Rep 638, 649.

To be fair to the modern approach, more recent cases have suggested that there is a presumption that 'a term is innominate unless a contrary intention is made clear'.[167] To some extent then, the modern law focuses slightly more on the consequences of the breach rather than classifying the nature of term. But this poses three problems. First, to focus on the consequences of the breach only ignores the anterior question whether the performance of the broken promise precisely is a condition of the other party's obligation to perform (a promissory condition). Secondly, on the current orthodox approach in England, notwithstanding this slight shift in emphasis towards the consequences of a breach, significant cases still turn upon whether a term, properly construed, is a condition or an innominate term.[168] Thus, English law still focuses on the a priori classification of terms rather than the identification of the relevant conditions. Thirdly, even if there is a strong presumption that a term is innominate, the key point, which cannot be emphasised enough, is that the innocent party is discharged not for the breach of an innominate term, but for the failure of the substantial-benefit condition. 3.75

The Substantial-Benefit Condition and Frustration

This failure to distinguish promises from conditions has also obscured the relationship between the substantial-benefit condition and the doctrine of frustration. Nolan has described the failure to notice this as 'remarkable', pointing out that 'Diplock LJ could not have asserted more clearly the consistency of the rules governing discharge by frustration and discharge for breach'.[169] Indeed, what is more remarkable is that the authors who have noticed the link reject it or seek to 'play it down'.[170] Professor Andrew Burrows (as his Lordship then was), for example, noted that in *Hongkong Fir* 'the judges used the language, or the analogy, of frustration' but he suggested that '[i]t is misleading to draw too close a link between the two'.[171] Similarly, Professor Hugh Beale has written: 'whatever may be said in theory, in practice it is doubtful whether 3.76

[167] *Spar Shipping AS v Grand China Logistics Holding (Group) Co Ltd* [2017] 4 All ER 124, 154 [93(viii)]. See also *Silverburn Shipping (IoM) Ltd v Ark Shipping Co LLC* [2019] 2 Lloyd's Rep 603, 616 [81].

[168] See, eg, *Spar Shipping AS v Grand China Logistics Holding (Group) Co Ltd* [2017] 4 All ER 124, 154.

[169] Nolan (n 4) 286. See also 295–96.

[170] Ewan McKendrick, 'Innominate Terms Revisited' in Louise Gullifer and Stefan Vogenauer (eds), *English and European Perspectives on Contract and Commercial Law: Essays in Honour of Hugh Beale* (Hart Publishing 2014) 183, 191.

[171] Andrew Burrows, *A Casebook on Contract* (7th edn, Hart Publishing 2020) 361.

the same degree of seriousness is required when one party has failed to perform as when it is alleged that supervening circumstances have frustrated the contract.'[172]

3.77 It should be clear by now that the claim in this chapter is precisely to the opposite effect: it would be misleading not to draw the link. Cases such as *Jackson v Union Marine Insurance Co Ltd* and *Poussard v Spiers* make clear that the substantial-benefit condition can fail even in cases where there is no breach of duty. Moreover, *Hongkong Fir* is direct authority against Burrows' contention—the judgments expressly rejected the proposition, which was the primary ground of appeal, that a different test ought to be applied in cases of discharge following breach and in cases of frustration. The argument that the two are not the same, to borrow Diplock LJ's words, makes the same 'fallacy' as the 'contention that a different test is applicable when the event occurs as a result of the default of one party from that applicable in cases of frustration', namely, 'a failure to view the cases in their historical context'.[173] More recent authorities have accepted that the 'test whether the breach has deprived the injured party of "substantially the whole benefit" of the contract . . . is the same test as that applicable to frustration'.[174]

3.78 There is, however, a very limited sense in which we must be careful in assimilating the substantial-benefit condition with the doctrine of frustration. It will be seen in Chapter 5 that cases said to fall within the ambit of 'frustration' in fact involve the failure of several different conditions commonly found in contracts, only one of which is the substantial-benefit condition. The simple point for present purposes is that the failure to distinguish between the promise and the condition obscures the relationship between these different instances of discharge.

Conclusion

3.79 The purpose of this chapter has been to demonstrate that discharge following breach of a so-called 'innominate' or 'intermediate' term is explicable in terms of failure of the substantial-benefit condition. In the older cases, the substantial-benefit condition ran under the label of 'failure of consideration'

[172] Hugh Beale, *Remedies for Breach of Contract* (Sweet & Maxwell 1980) 45.
[173] *Hongkong Fir Shipping Co Ltd v Kawasaki Kisen Kaisha Ltd* [1962] 2 QB 26, 66.
[174] *Ampurius Nu Homes Holdings Ltd v Telford Homes (Creekside) Ltd* [2013] 4 All ER 377, 393 [48]. See the discussion in McKendrick (n 170) 190–91.

and 'frustration' but, as we have seen, it has also travelled under other names such as the so-called doctrine of substantial performance. For over 150 years before *Hongkong Fir*, the substantial-benefit condition was applied alongside promissory conditions. On closer inspection, it becomes apparent that the judgments in *Hongkong Fir* added very little to what had gone before. But what has occurred since *Hongkong Fir*, under the guise of the 'innominate' or 'intermediate' term concept, is a renewed focus upon the a priori classification of terms. The problem is that this focus runs the risk of obscuring the very point to be gleaned from that case, namely, that it is the failure of the condition (the 'event' in Diplock LJ's language) that discharges the innocent party, and not the breach of duty. Once we see this, not only does this instance of discharge itself become clearer, but so too do other instances of discharge, such as cases said to fall within the doctrine of frustration.

4
Waiver of Conditions I—Election and Estoppel

Introduction

The core claim in this book is that the failure of a condition operates to discharge a party from their obligation to perform unless they waive (or have waived) the condition. The next two chapters therefore consider the circumstances in which conditions can be waived. The focus of this chapter is on the waiver of conditions by election and the waiver of conditions by estoppel. Chapter 5 then considers waiver of conditions by prevention of fulfilment and waiver of conditions on a repudiation. **4.1**

The first part of this chapter defines what is meant by the language of 'waiver'. It explains that to say that a condition is waived it to say that one party has given up or lost their ability to insist upon the performance or fulfilment of a condition as a requirement for their obligation to fall due (ie for the immediate duty of performance to exist). This is, at least in theory, distinct from a variation of the contract. **4.2**

The second part then discusses waiver by election. It shows that there are a number of cases that have applied the principle that a party who is entitled to rely upon a condition but who, in the face of non-compliance with the condition, continues to perform or allows the other side to go on and perform will be held to have waived the condition. However, as seen in Chapter 2, in the second half of the twentieth century, thinking in relation to discharge of **4.3**

Discharge of Contractual Obligations. Jordan English, Oxford University Press. © Jordan English 2025.
DOI: 10.1093/9780198906704.003.0004

contractual obligations changed. What had previously been seen as discharge for failure of a condition became discharge following the exercise of a power to terminate, and what had previously been seen as waiver of conditions became the affirmation of the contract. The problem with this shift in thinking is that it seems to have led courts to assume that the finality associated with waiver by election is applicable only to the loss of the power to terminate. The tendency has then been to assume that all instances of waiver of conditions are aspects of the law of estoppel, requiring some detrimental reliance before a waiver is treated as irrevocable.

4.4 The third part explores waiver of conditions by estoppel. Despite earlier cases having treated waiver of conditions as its own phenomenon, from around the 1950s, a number of cases began to treat particular instances of waiver of conditions as instances of estoppel (promissory estoppel in particular). This part records that trend and the particular influence of Lord Denning in this area.

4.5 The modern tendency to subsume cases of waiver of conditions into the doctrine of promissory estoppel has not been altogether satisfactory. The fourth and final part of this chapter therefore asks whether the law should continue to treat waiver of conditions as part of the law of promissory estoppel. The conclusion reached is that some instances of waiver of conditions can be treated as instances of promissory estoppel so long as (i) a clear distinction is drawn between waiver of conditions by election and waiver of conditions by estoppel, and (ii) it is borne in mind that waiver of conditions by estoppel is only one circumstance in which conditions can be waived. There exist also the doctrine of waiver of conditions by acceptance—applied in the sale of goods context—and the doctrines of waiver of conditions by prevention of fulfilment and on a repudiation—considered in the next chapter—none of which can convincingly be seen as part of the law of promissory estoppel. There is thus an intelligible body of law concerned with waiver of conditions that is broader than 'waiver by election' and 'waiver by estoppel'. While some cases of waiver of conditions can be seen as instances of waiver by election, and some cases can be seen as instances of waiver by estoppel, some cases fit into neither category.

Waiver Defined

4.6 Professor Samuel Stoljar once observed that 'waiver has had far too little recognition in our contract books' and that this 'neglect has also led to much misunderstanding'.[1] Part of the reason for the neglect is no doubt that '[i]n contract law, waiver is used in different senses which can cause confusion'.[2] If the concept is to be of any use in this book, it is necessary to specify the sense in which it is being used.

At its core, waiver is concerned with the forgoing or the giving-up of a power, right, or privilege.[3] This is the meaning adopted in this chapter. But even this simple definition is apt to mislead. This is because while it is often said that one waives duties or conditions, in contract law (and elsewhere in private law) the underlying duty or condition, strictly speaking, is not what is waived. What is waived is the ability to insist on the performance of the duty or the fulfilment of the condition. Thus, in this chapter, the phrase 'waiver of conditions' is a loose expression. To say that a condition is waived is not to say that the condition is struck out of the contract, but rather to say that one party has foregone or given up their 'right to insist upon the unperformed condition precedent as an answer to the action'.[4] **4.7**

It is this feature of waiver that, in theory, distinguishes waiver from a variation of the contract.[5] In contrast with waiver, a variation of the contract does alter the primary rights and duties of the parties. And for a variation to be effective, there must be an agreement and, on current orthodoxy, consideration.[6] The difficulty is that, in practice, the distinction between variation and waiver may be fine, for in the context of waiver of conditions the practical effect of waiver will be to enlarge the scope of one party's primary obligation to perform.[7] **4.8**

The more difficult question is the extent to which waiver is distinct from the doctrine of promissory estoppel.[8] Indeed, the explanation given above—that the underlying right or condition is not waived, but rather the ability to rely upon that right or condition is waived—is practically indistinguishable from **4.9**

[1] Samuel J Stoljar, 'The Modification of Contracts' (1957) 35 Canadian Bar Review 485, 489 fn 12.

[2] Robert Stevens, 'Not Waiving but Drowning' in Andrew Dyson, James Goudkamp, and Frederick Wilmot-Smith (eds), *Defences in Contract* (Hart Publishing 2017) 125, 127 (footnote omitted). See the various meanings identified in Samuel Williston, *The Law of Contracts* (Baker, Voorhis & Co 1921) vol 2, 1311–14 §679.

[3] Stoljar (n 1) 489–90.

[4] *Roberts v Brett* (1865) 11 HL Cas 337, 357; 11 ER 1363, 1371.

[5] Stevens (n 2) 126.

[6] *MWB Business Exchange Centres Ltd v Rock Advertising Ltd* [2017] QB 604; [2019] AC 119, 131 [18].

[7] Arthur Corbin, *Corbin on Contracts: A Comprehensive Treatise on the Rules of Contract Law* (West Publishing Co 1960) vol 3A, 480 §752.

[8] To avoid confusion as between the various forms of estoppel that have arisen in equity, this chapter will only use the term 'promissory estoppel', as opposed to 'equitable estoppel' which is often used to refer simply to 'promissory estoppel'.

the effect of promissory estoppel. It is perhaps for this reason that it is sometimes said that waiver and promissory estoppel are 'really two ways of saying exactly the same thing'.[9]

4.10 No attempt is made in this chapter to deny that the effects of waiving a condition are the same as those of promissory estoppel. But, as will be seen, to ask whether waiver is simply an instance of promissory estoppel in many ways puts the cart before the horse. Indeed, the doctrine of waiver of conditions significantly predates promissory estoppel, and only in the 1950s, in a series of cases decided by Lord Denning,[10] was an attempt made to subsume some (but not all) instances of waiver of conditions into promissory estoppel. For the reasons given in this chapter, the integration has not been wholly successful and, in any event, leaves a number of instances of waiver of conditions outside the scope of promissory estoppel. So long as promissory estoppel continues to be seen as a unified doctrine with uniform rules,[11] it seems that any further integration of waiver of conditions into promissory estoppel will be neither possible nor desirable. Indeed, it might be better to put the question the other way around: is promissory estoppel in this context simply an instance of waiver?[12]

4.11 Another important clarification is that, even in this context, the language of 'waiver' can be used in two senses. The first is to refer to a statement or conduct that represents (expressly or implicitly) that a person is not relying upon a condition, such as where one party allows the other to continue to perform in the face of known non-compliance with a condition. The second is to refer to the conclusion that, on a set of given facts, the ability to rely on the condition has been lost. The two will not always coincide. For example, sometimes it will be possible for someone who has represented that they will not rely upon a condition to subsequently retract the representation and rely upon the condition in an action for non-performance.[13] It is sometimes said in such cases that the person has 'retracted the waiver'. Inversely, in some cases, a person will be held to have waived a condition even though no representation was made that they would not rely upon it.[14] To avoid confusion, the term 'waiver' will

[9] *Prosper Homes Ltd v Hambros Bank Executor & Trustee Co Ltd* (1980) 39 P & CR 395, 401, quoted in Edwin Peel, *The Law of Contract* (15th edn, Sweet & Maxwell 2020) 130 [3-091]. See also *Woodhouse AC Israel Cocoa Ltd SA v Nigerian Produce Marketing Co Ltd* [1972] AC 741, 762.

[10] See [4.31]–[4.39].

[11] cf Ben McFarlane, 'Understanding Equitable Estoppel: From Metaphors to Better Laws' (2013) 66 Current Legal Problems 267; Ben McFarlane, 'Promissory Estoppel and Debts' in Andrew Burrows and Edwin Peel (eds), *Contract Formation and Parties* (OUP 2010) 115.

[12] See [4.42].

[13] See, eg, *Charles Rickards Ltd v Oppenhaim* [1950] 1 KB 616, discussed at [4.32]–[4.34].

[14] See Chapter 5.

be used principally in the second sense identified at the beginning of this paragraph. Although it might be argued that 'waiver' here is doing no more than expressing a conclusion (that the ability to rely on the condition is lost), using waiver in this sense has the benefit of allowing us to employ the language used in the cases themselves.

Waiver of Conditions by Election

Affirmation as waiver of a condition

As earlier chapters explained, where one party fails to comply with a condition, the counterparty's immediate duty of performance will either not fall due or, if it has fallen due, be extinguished. In this sense, the counterparty is 'discharged' from their obligation to perform.[15] But 'the necessity of performing the condition precedent may be *waived* by the party in whose favour it is stipulated, either expressly or tacitly, by inference from [their] acts or conduct'.[16] And in this connection, there is a well-established principle that a party who is entitled to rely on a condition, but who, in the face of non-compliance with the condition, continues to perform or allows the other side to go on and perform, will be held to have waived the condition.[17] This principle—insofar as it applies in the context of discharge following breach—has today, on the orthodox approach, come to be known as the 'affirmation' of the contract or 'waiver by election'. In *Allianz Australia Insurance Ltd v Delor Vue Apartments CTS 39788*,[18] a majority of the High Court of Australia (Kiefel CJ, Edelman, Steward, and Gleeson JJ) recognised this history when they said: **4.12**

> Historically, an election by affirmation of a contractual term arose in circumstances in which the performance of an obligation by one party was seen as a condition precedent to the existence of an obligation of the other party.... If the condition precedent failed, the counterparty could, nevertheless, affirm the corresponding obligation.

[15] See [1.50]–[1.55].

[16] Walter Charles Alan Ker and Arthur Reginald Butterworth, *A Treatise on the Law of Sale of Personal Property with references to the American Decisions and to the French Code and Civil Law* (5th edn, Sweet & Maxwell 1906) 563 (emphasis in original).

[17] ibid; Corbin (n 7) 497 §755.

[18] (2022) 277 CLR 445, 472 [41] (citations omitted).

4.13 Traditionally, the leading case was *Bentsen v Taylor, Sons & Co*,[19] the facts of which were discussed in Chapter 2.[20] It will be recalled that, notwithstanding the fact the condition that the ship was 'now sailed or about to sail' had not been fulfilled, the defendant charterers' conduct in advising the plaintiff shipowners of their intention to load meant that they had waived the condition and were therefore liable on the contract. Bowen LJ said that the question was whether 'the condition precedent had been waived by the defendants'.[21] In other words, '[d]id the defendants lead the plaintiff to believe that they intended to treat the misdescription as a breach of contract only, and not as a failure to perform a condition precedent?'[22] Importantly, while the waiver of the condition meant that the charterers could not treat themselves as discharged, it did not deprive them of their right to damages:[23] '[w]aiver of the condition does not release the other party from his promise'.[24]

4.14 Earlier cases took a similar approach. In *Alexander v Gardner*,[25] the plaintiff sold to the defendants a quantity of butter, which was to be shipped to London in October 1833—this being a condition precedent to the defendant's obligation to perform—and paid for within two months of landing. The butter was not in fact shipped until November 1833. This fact had been communicated to the defendants who had at first refused to abide by the contract, but then shortly thereafter abandoned their objection and accepted the invoice and bill of lading. In December 1833, the butter was lost by shipwreck. A small quantity arrived in a damaged state and the defendants refused to pay. It was held that the plaintiffs could recover the price of the butter.[26] Tindal CJ said:

> If the Defendants had in the first instance repudiated the bargain on that ground [ie that the goods were shipped late], it is true that no action would have lain against them. But it is found by the jury that they waived the objection . . . if the party waives the condition he is in the same situation as if it had never existed.[27]

[19] [1893] 2 QB 274.
[20] See [2.26]–[2.32].
[21] *Bentsen v Taylor, Sons & Co* [1893] 2 QB 274, 283.
[22] ibid 284.
[23] ibid 279.
[24] JL Montrose, 'Conditions, Warranties, and other Contractual Terms' (1937) 15 Canadian Bar Review 309, 326.
[25] (1835) 1 Bing NC 671, 131 ER 1276.
[26] The Court held that the arrival of the goods was not a condition precedent to the defendant's obligation to pay: ibid 677; 1278.
[27] ibid.

In *Ollive v Booker*,[28] the issue, similar to *Bentsen v Taylor* albeit different in the ultimate result, was whether a statement in a charterparty that described the vessel as 'now at sea, having sailed three weeks ago' was a mere representation or a warranty (in the sense of a guarantee), and if so, whether its performance was a condition precedent to the defendant's obligation to load. The defendant, upon learning that the vessel had not sailed until some later time, had refused to load any cargo. Parke B held that the statement was a warranty and that its performance was a condition precedent. He then went on to say: **4.15**

> This being a condition precedent, and not performed, the defendant was not bound to load the vessel. If he had loaded her, the breach of the condition would have been waived, and he would have been liable for the full freight.[29]

Even before *Bentsen v Taylor* was decided, this principle had been approved of in the House of Lords. In *Roberts v Brett*,[30] Lord Chelmsford said: **4.16**

> I have no difficulty in saying that . . . [a] party who may avail [themselves] of the non-performance of the condition precedent, but who allows the other side to go on and perform the subsequent stipulations, has waived [their] right to insist upon the unperformed condition precedent as an answer to the action.

The cases post-*Bentsen v Taylor* also continued to apply the principle of waiver of conditions in similar contexts. In *Panoutsos v Raymond Hadley Corp of New York*,[31] the defendant sellers entered into a contract to sell 4,000 tons of flour to the plaintiff buyers. The contract provided that 'each shipment shall be deemed a separate contract' and payment was to be 'by confirmed bankers' credit'. Credit was opened in favour of the buyers in respect of the full shipment of 4,000 tons, but because the credit was not irrevocable it was not a confirmed bankers' credit. Despite this, the sellers made five shipments of flour in partial fulfilment of the contract and were duly paid. However, the sellers subsequently purported to cancel the balance of the contract on the ground that the buyer had failed to perform the condition as to payment by confirmed banker's credit. **4.17**

At first instance, Bailhache J held that 'the sellers must be taken to have waived the performance of the condition, that the buyer was entitled to reasonable **4.18**

[28] (1847) 1 Ex 416, 154 ER 177.
[29] ibid 423; 180.
[30] (1865) 11 HL Cas 337, 357; 11 ER 1363, 1371.
[31] [1917] 2 KB 473.

notice [of the sellers' intention to insist upon its performance], and that such notice had not in fact been given'.[32] On appeal, Viscount Reading CJ (with whom Lord Cozens-Hardy MR and Scrutton LJ agreed) was of the same view and thought that Bowen LJ's judgment in *Bentsen v Taylor* 'applie[d] exactly to the present case'.[33]

4.19 This same principle was applied in *Hartley v Hymans*,[34] a case in which a buyer of goods sought to rely upon the seller's late deliveries to justify his refusal to accept the balance of the goods due under the contract. While deliveries had not commenced on time and the buyer had protested this delay, he had nonetheless continued to press for delivery, and the buyer had in fact obtained seven further deliveries after the initial late delivery. McCardie J was of the view that the buyer 'had undoubtedly waived the condition . . . inasmuch as . . . he demanded and received deliveries under the contract'.[35] While confusingly basing his decision in favour of the seller on three grounds, McCardie J held, on one of those grounds, that the buyer was 'debarred by the doctrine of waiver from asserting that an original condition precedent [was] still operative and binding'.[36]

4.20 The same approach had also been applied in the context of insurance contracts. In *Ayrey v British Legal and United Provident Assurance Co Ltd*,[37] the proposal form for a life insurance policy contained a clause providing that if any false information were provided 'the policy to be granted in pursuance of the above proposal shall be absolutely void'.[38] The assured stated his occupation to be that of a fisherman (which was true) but he omitted to state on the form that he was also a member of the Royal Naval Reserve Service and he was expecting to be called up for the purpose of being employed in minesweeping. On the date he signed the proposal form, he had received orders to report for service, which he duly did. The plaintiff executrix had asked the defendant whether, in light of the fact that the assured had been employed to engage in minesweeping and had not disclosed this on the form, any insurance money would be paid. The defendant in turn informed the plaintiff that the insurance money would be paid notwithstanding the omission on the form. The plaintiff thereupon

[32] ibid 477.
[33] ibid 478.
[34] [1920] 3 KB 475.
[35] ibid 487.
[36] ibid 495.
[37] [1918] 1 KB 136.
[38] ibid 137. Note that '[s]uch a provision as this seldom means what it appears to say. Generally, what is meant is that the duty of one of the parties shall be conditional': Corbin (n 7) 517 §761.

continued to pay the premiums for two years. The deceased drowned at sea and although it was not known how he had drowned, he had not in fact been engaged in minesweeping or any other dangerous form of work.

It was held that by continuing to receive the premiums with knowledge of the material facts, 'the company must be taken to have waived any objection to the validity of the policy founded upon that omission'.[39] While treating the issue as one of estoppel, Atkin J said that '[t]he true principle to be invoked is best stated in the judgment of Bowen LJ in *Bentsen v Taylor*'.[40] **4.21**

Affirmation as loss of power to terminate

As we saw in Chapter 2, during the course of the twentieth century, the orthodox understanding of discharge following breach changed such that a condition came to be seen simply as an important term breach of which gives rise to a power to terminate. Unless and until that power was exercised, the innocent party remained bound to perform. What had previously been seen as discharge for failure of a condition became a power to terminate, and what had previously been seen as waiver of the condition became the affirmation of the contract. **4.22**

The leading case on affirmation in this context is *Motor Oil Hellas (Corinth) Refineries SA v Shipping Corp of India (The Kanchenjunga)*.[41] The charterers of a vessel had ordered it to load a cargo of oil at Kharg Island, Iran. The vessel arrived and provided a notice of readiness to load, but a few days later an air raid occurred as part of the Gulf War. The master had sailed away to safety and the owners thereupon called on the charterers to nominate an alternative safe port. The charterers insisted that the vessel proceed to Kharg Island. The owners accordingly instructed the master of the vessel to load at Kharg Island, but he refused due to safety concerns. It was found that Kharg Island, at its time of nomination, was not a prospectively safe port and that the owners were entitled to reject it as a valid nomination.[42] Lord Goff, delivering the leading speech in the House of Lords, however, held that the owners had 'elected not to reject the charterers' nomination', and so must be taken 'to have waived their right to do so or to call for another nomination'.[43] The owners therefore would **4.23**

[39] *Ayrey v British Legal and United Provident Assurance Co Ltd* [1918] 1 KB 136, 140.
[40] ibid 142.
[41] [1990] 1 Lloyd's Rep 391.
[42] ibid 397.
[43] ibid 400.

have been liable for damages for breach had they not been protected by a 'war clause' in the charterparty.

4.24 *The Kanchenjunga*, strictly speaking, was concerned with the 'right to reject' rather than the 'power to terminate' (which, on the orthodox approach, are not the same thing).[44] Nonetheless, Lord Goff said that the 'same principles apply'.[45] He said:

> [W]e are concerned with an election which may arise in the context of a binding contract, when a state of affairs comes into existence in which one party becomes entitled, either under the terms of the contract or by the general law, to exercise a right, and he has to decide whether or not to do so. . . . [I]f he does not [make a decision], the time may come when the law takes the decision out of his hands, either by holding him to have elected not to exercise the right which has become available to him, or sometimes by holding him to have elected to exercise it.[46]

4.25 When this is applied to the modern-orthodox understanding of discharge following breach we get the following propositions:

(1) 'breach of a condition'[47] gives the innocent party a power to terminate;
(2) the innocent party must elect to exercise that power;
(3) if the innocent party instead elects to affirm the contract, they are 'thereby waiving or abandoning [their] right to terminate it'.[48]

4.26 It is sometimes suggested that the election is between inconsistent rights,[49] namely, the 'power to terminate' and the 'right to affirm'. But this is not straightforward even on the orthodox approach. This is because on the orthodox view there is only one 'right' (in the broadest sense of that term),

[44] For example, in instalment contracts, on the orthodox approach, a defect in the goods delivered as part of one instalment will entitle the buyer to 'reject' that instalment, but it may not entitle the buyer to 'terminate' the contractual obligations of the parties. In a similar fashion on the orthodox approach, a failure to comply with a 'condition' (viz an essential term) may not give rise to the power to terminate, but only a right to reject with the seller having a chance to 'cure' any defective performance: Michael Bridge (ed), *Benjamin's Sale of Goods* (12th edn, Sweet & Maxwell 2023) 633–34 [12-029].

[45] *The Kanchenjunga* [1990] 1 Lloyd's Rep 391, 399.

[46] ibid 398.

[47] For reasons already explained, a loose and inaccurate phrase: [2.38].

[48] *The Kanchenjunga* [1990] 1 Lloyd's Rep 391, 398.

[49] *Kammins Ballrooms Co Ltd v Zenith Investments (Torquay) Ltd* [1971] AC 850, 883; *Allianz Australia Insurance Ltd v Delor Vue Apartments CTS 39788* (2022) 277 CLR 445, 471 [38]. See also William Day, 'Variation and Waiver' in William Day and Sarah Worthington (eds), *Challenging Private Law: Lord Sumption on the Supreme Court* (Hart Publishing 2020) 25, 41; Ewan McKendrick, 'Termination for Breach' in Hugh Beale (ed), *Chitty on Contracts* (35th edn, Sweet & Maxwell 2023) vol 1 2133, 2173 [28-060]; Jack Beatson, Andrew Burrows, and John Cartwright, *Anson's Law of Contract* (31st edn, OUP 2020) 461 fn 54.

namely, the power to terminate. The choice appears instead to be between inconsistent courses of action. The so-called right to affirm is simply a label to describe the choice made *not* to exercise the power to terminate—it has no normative content other than that it results in the innocent party losing the power to terminate. To put it another way, the only effect of choosing not to terminate (or to affirm) is that the innocent party is then 'said to have waived his right to terminate'.[50] That is why the principle is sometimes referred to as 'waiver by election'.[51]

As we have already seen,[52] the main difference between modern orthodoxy and the failure of condition model put forward in this book is the starting point: on the failure of condition model, the innocent party is discharged immediately following the failure of a condition, unless they choose to waive the condition. By contrast, on the power to terminate model, the innocent party is discharged if, and only if, they exercise the power to terminate. But this very large and important difference aside, the two approaches unsurprisingly have similar features. **4.27**

First, '[a]n important characteristic of affirmation is that it bars only the injured party's right to terminate: it does not deprive [them] of [their] right to damages for breach'.[53] That is self-evidently true for waiver of a condition, which does not operate to waive the duty.[54] **4.28**

Secondly, even the failure of condition model can be expressed in terms of an 'election' in the same way as the power to terminate model if it must be. So it could be said that following the failure of a condition the party who is entitled to rely upon that condition has a choice: they can choose to rely upon the condition and treat themselves as discharged, or they can choose not to rely upon the condition, and waive it (eg by continuing to render or receive performance). The key point is that by 'affirming' the contract, the innocent party loses the ability to rely upon the condition. The only difference is the position in the interim before the innocent party has definitively made any such choice. On the approach being put forward here, the innocent party is discharged unless and until they decide to waive the condition. While that is the reverse of the orthodox approach—which states that both parties are bound unless and **4.29**

[50] Peel (n 9) 1014 [18-089].
[51] McKendrick (n 49) 2173 [28-060]. See also *Allianz Australia Insurance Ltd v Delor Vue Apartments CTS 39788* (2022) 277 CLR 445, 471 [39].
[52] See [1.61].
[53] Peel (n 9) 1015 [18-091].
[54] See [4.7].

until the power to terminate is exercised—that does not change the essential point that both approaches provide the party with a choice: on the orthodox approach, to exercise the power to terminate or not and, on the failure of condition model, to waive the condition or not.

4.30 The true difficulty with the modern shift in thinking from waiver of conditions to affirmation as the loss of the power to terminate, however, is that it has led courts to assume that the finality associated with waiver by election—namely, that statements or conduct amounting to waiver by election are irrevocable—is applicable only to the loss of the power to terminate. The tendency has then been to assume that all instances of waiver of conditions are aspects of the law of estoppel, requiring some detrimental reliance before a waiver is treated as irrevocable. As the next section explains, not only is this distinction ahistorical, but it leads to some results that are difficult to justify in principle.

Waiver of Conditions by Estoppel

4.31 The earlier cases typically had not characterised waiver of conditions as being concerned with estoppel, and certainly not as part of promissory estoppel, which was yet to be 'rescued from oblivion'[55] by *Central London Property Trust Ltd v High Trees House Ltd*.[56] For example, there is no mention of estoppel in *Bentsen v Taylor* or in *Panoutsos v Raymond Hadley Corp*, which had purported to follow *Bentsen v Taylor*. Some cases did, however, notice the similarities. In *Hartley v Hymans*,[57] McCardie J gave three grounds for his decision, one of which was waiver and another of which was that, 'in so far as estoppel differs from waiver', 'the defendant [was] estopped from saying that the period for delivery expired' at the end of November.

4.32 Following the decision in *High Trees*, however, Lord Denning set out to rationalise the law on waiver of conditions as being a principle within the law of promissory estoppel (waiver by estoppel). The earliest case is *Charles Rickards Ltd v Oppenhaim*.[58] The defendant contracted with the plaintiff motor-car traders for a body to be built on a Rolls Royce Silver Wraith chassis that he had ordered. The work was to take six or seven months, making the time for delivery,

[55] *WJ Alan & Co Ltd v El Nasr Export and Import Co* [1972] 2 QB 189, 212.
[56] [1947] 1 KB 130.
[57] [1920] 3 KB 475, 495.
[58] [1950] 1 KB 616.

at the latest, 20 March 1948. The work was not completed on time, but the defendant continued to press for delivery. On 29 June, the defendant wrote to the coachbuilders telling them that he would not be able to accept delivery after 25 July, when he had planned to take the car abroad on a holiday. The car was completed on 18 October, but the defendant refused to accept delivery.

At first instance, Finnemore J held that time was of the essence of the contract and therefore it was a condition that the car should be delivered within seven months. And while the defendant initially had waived that condition,[59] the defendant, by his letter of 29 June, had reinstated his right to rely upon that condition, on terms specifying a reasonable time for completion.[60] The defendant was therefore entitled to refuse to accept delivery; he had not waived the condition. **4.33**

An appeal from this decision was dismissed by the Court of Appeal (Denning, Singleton, and Bucknill LJJ). But Denning LJ considered what the situation would have been if the defendant had simply waived the condition and not written the 29 June letter specifying a reasonable time for completion. He said: **4.34**

> If the defendant, as he did, led the plaintiffs to believe that he would not insist on the stipulation as to time, and that, if they carried out the work, he would accept it, and they did it, he could not afterwards set up the stipulation as to the time against them.... It is a kind of estoppel. By his conduct he evinced an intention to affect their legal relations. He made, in effect, a promise not to insist on his strict legal rights. That promise was intended to be acted on, and was in fact acted on. He cannot afterwards go back on it.... It is a particular application of the principle which I endeavoured to state in *Central London Property Trust Ld v High Trees House Ld*.[61]

Lord Denning thus sought to bring waiver of conditions within the newfound doctrine of promissory estoppel.

Lord Denning set out his views again in *Plasticmoda Societa per Azioni v Davidsons (Manchester) Ltd*.[62] The defendant sellers entered into a contract to sell to the plaintiff buyers 100 tons of cable strippings to be paid for by a confirmed letter of credit. The sellers sought to deny liability for failing **4.35**

[59] 'Waived' here being used in the sense of having represented by conduct that he would not rely upon the condition: see [4.11].
[60] *Charles Rickards Ltd v Oppenhaim* [1950] 1 KB 616, 619.
[61] ibid 623.
[62] [1952] 1 Lloyd's Rep 527.

to deliver the goods on the basis that the letter of credit for 100 tons had never been opened. The Court of Appeal accepted that the stipulation for credit was 'a condition precedent to the obligation of the seller[s] to ship the goods, and that condition precedent was not fulfilled'.[63] But the Court held that the condition had been waived because the 'the seller[s], by [their] conduct, led the buyer[s] to believe that [they] would not insist on the credit being established until the seller[s] had told the buyer[s] that the goods were ready'.[64] The sellers were therefore liable. Singleton LJ said that the sellers' conduct 'was of the nature of a waiver of the condition precedent'.[65] But Denning LJ, although agreeing with Singleton LJ, said that it fell within the 'broad principle of "fair dealing and justice"',[66] which is now known as promissory estoppel.[67]

4.36 Only a few years later, Lord Denning (now Master of the Rolls) applied the same approach in *Barrett Bros (Taxis) Ltd v Davies*[68] to hold that an insurance company had waived a condition precedent that the insured inform the insurer as soon as possible in writing of any accident and of any notice of intended prosecution he received. After referring to the 'principle of waiver'[69] from *Plasticmoda Societa*, he said: 'By not asking for the documents, they as good as said they did not want them. So he did not send them. I do not think they should be allowed now to complain of not receiving them. I think they waived the condition.'[70]

4.37 Not all cases followed Lord Denning wholeheartedly in this explanation. In *Enrico Furst & Co v WE Fischer Ltd*,[71] Diplock J was similarly faced with an action for non-delivery in which the defendant sellers sought to rely upon the fact that the buyers had not opened a conforming letter of credit. He accepted that 'the defendants waived their right to insist upon the credit complying strictly with the contract'[72] and said that it was a 'classic case of waiver, indistinguishable, indeed (without going into any more esoteric argument), from the decision in *Panoutsos v Raymond Hadley Corporation*'.[73] While noting what Lord Denning had said in *Charles Rickards Ltd v Oppenhaim* about waiver being an instance of promissory estoppel, Diplock J said that he 'prefer[red] to say that,

[63] ibid 538.
[64] ibid.
[65] ibid 536.
[66] ibid 538.
[67] ibid 539.
[68] [1966] 1 WLR 1334.
[69] ibid 1339.
[70] ibid.
[71] [1960] 2 Lloyd's Rep 340.
[72] ibid 348.
[73] ibid.

in relation to sale of goods, it was a particular application of [s] 11(1)(a) of the [Sale of Goods Act 1893]'.[74] Section 11(1)(a) provided that:

> Where a contract of sale is subject to any condition to be fulfilled by the seller, the buyer may waive the condition, or may elect to treat the breach of such condition as a breach of warranty, and not as a ground for treating the contract as repudiated.[75]

Lord Denning was evidently unperturbed by the fact that Diplock J in *Enrico Furst* had refrained from considering whether waiver was an instance of promissory estoppel because in *WJ Alan & Co Ltd v El Nasr Export and Import Co*,[76] Lord Denning said: **4.38**

> In *Enrico Furst*, Diplock J said it was a 'classic case of waiver.' I agree with him. It is an instance of the general principle which was first enunciated by Lord Cairns LC in *Hughes v Metropolitan Railway Co*, . . . and rescued from oblivion by *Central London Property Trust Ltd v High Trees House Ltd*. . . . The principle is much wider than waiver itself: but waiver is a good instance of its application.

The influence of Lord Denning can also be seen in leading contract texts today, which write that '[t]his type of waiver does not exist as a separate principle but is in fact an application of the principle of equitable estoppel deriving from the classic statement of Lord Cairns in *Hughes v Metropolitan Ry Co*'.[77] 'Deriving from' is an interesting choice of wording here given that, as we have seen, the cases considered in this section were, in fact, derived from *Panoutsos v Raymond Hadley Corp*, which in turn was derived from *Bentsen v Taylor*, a case that today would be seen as 'affirmation' or 'waiver by election'. Nonetheless, it shows that Lord Denning appears, by fiat, to have subsumed part of the law of waiver of conditions within the doctrine of promissory estoppel. **4.39**

Should Waiver of Conditions be Understood as Part of the Law of Estoppel?

It is clear that there are certain benefits to understanding waiver of conditions as part of the law of promissory estoppel. First, analytically, waiver of conditions **4.40**

[74] ibid 350.
[75] See now Sale of Goods Act 1979, s 11(2).
[76] [1972] 2 QB 189, 212 (citations omitted).
[77] McKendrick (n 49) 2173–74 [28-060].

operates in the same way as promissory estoppel.[78] As was explained above, to say that a condition is 'waived' is not to say that the condition is struck out of the contract, but rather to say that one party has waived their 'right to insist upon the unperformed condition precedent as an answer to the action'.[79]

4.41 Secondly, it allows us to treat together the cases in which conditions have been waived and the cases in which it has been held that a duty can be waived. In this regard, a number of cases have relied indifferently on (i) the common law doctrine of forbearance,[80] (ii) the decision in *Panoutsos v Raymond Hadley Corp*, or (iii) a doctrine of 'total waiver',[81] to hold that the parties can, in some circumstances at least, waive duties (not just conditions).[82] These appear to be cases in which courts have been willing to hold that the acceptance by one party of a substitute performance, which does not strictly comply with the terms of the contract, is sufficient to discharge the duty.[83] Again, due to the influence of Lord Denning,[84] these cases today would be understood as part of the law of promissory estoppel.[85] Indeed, it has been observed by Professor Ben McFarlane, that this principle—acceptance of a substitute performance—is the same principle that was 'recognized by Denning J in what has become the foundation of the modern law of promissory estoppel: his "brilliant obiter dictum" in *Central London Property Trust Ltd v High Trees House Ltd*'.[86]

4.42 Thirdly, treating waiver of conditions as part of the law of promissory estoppel assists not only in explaining waiver but also promissory estoppel itself.

[78] *Allianz Australia Insurance Ltd v Delor Vue Apartments CTS 39788* (2022) 277 CLR 445, 501–02 [137].

[79] *Roberts v Brett* (1865) 11 HL Cas 337, 357; 11 ER 1363, 1371.

[80] See generally, AJ Phipps, 'Resurrecting the Doctrine of Common Law Forbearance' (2007) 123 Law Quarterly Review 286; Beatson, Burrows, and Cartwright (n 49) 461; Day (n 49) 38–40; Peel (n 9) 115 [3-069].

[81] See Peel (n 9) 1015 [18-093].

[82] See, eg, *Tankexpress A/S v Compagnie Financière Belge des Petroles SA* [1949] AC 76, 98, 103–04; *WJ Alan & Co Ltd v El Nasr Export and Import Co* [1972] 2 QB 189, 212–13; *Toepfer v Warinco AG* [1978] 2 Lloyd's Rep 569, 576–77 (although the claim ultimately failed: see 577–78); *Bottiglieri di Navigazione SpA v Cosco Qingdao Ocean Shipping Co (The Bunga Saga Lima)* [2005] 2 Lloyd's Rep 1, 11 [30]–[31].

[83] See generally, McFarlane, 'Promissory Estoppel and Debts' (n 11) 116–22; McFarlane, 'Understanding Equitable Estoppel' (n 11) 281–82.

[84] *WJ Alan & Co Ltd v El Nasr Export and Import Co* [1972] 2 QB 189, 212–13.

[85] On forbearance, see Andrew Burrows, *A Restatement of the English Law of Contract* (2nd edn, OUP 2020) 79–80 ('in practice largely, if not entirely, subsumed by promissory estoppel'). On *Panoutsos v Raymond Hadley Corp of New York* [1917] 2 KB 473, see ibid. On 'total waiver', see Peel (n 9) 1015 [18-093] ('[a]nother type of estoppel').

[86] McFarlane, 'Understanding Equitable Estoppel' (n 11) 281 (citations omitted). See also McFarlane, 'Promissory Estoppel and Debts' (n 11) 118.

Professor Robert Stevens has argued that the law of 'promissory estoppel' is simply an 'equitable extension of the doctrine of waiver'.[87] And when understood in this way certain of its features become readily explicable: (i) that promissory estoppel is a 'shield not a sword' (this is because to rely upon a waiver by one party is not to assert the creation of new rights); (ii) that there must be a pre-existing relationship (this is because there must be pre-existing rights to waive); and (iii) that in some circumstances the doctrine only 'suspends' rights rather than precluding all reliance on them (this is because sometimes a statement amounting to a waiver can be revoked).[88]

The line between waiver by election and waiver by estoppel

However, it is also clear that subsuming part of the law of waiver of conditions into promissory estoppel has created a number of difficulties. One is that, although waiver of conditions can be understood as part of the law of promissory estoppel, it is still necessary to draw a clear line between 'waiver by election' and 'waiver by estoppel', particularly because statements or conduct amounting to waiver by election are said to be irrevocable—on account of the principle of finality—whereas statements or conduct in the context of waiver by estoppel are capable of being retracted provided there has not been detrimental reliance.[89] **4.43**

This issue is particularly acute in the context of insurance contracts. In *Kosmar Villa Holidays plc v Trustees of Syndicate 1243*,[90] for example, the question for the Court of Appeal was as follows: where the insured fails to comply with a condition precedent to the insurer's obligation to pay out on a claim,[91] but the insurer nonetheless begins to deal with the claim, is the appropriate principle to apply 'waiver by election' or 'waiver by estoppel'? A number of cases had traditionally adopted a 'waiver by election' approach to non-compliance with conditions precedent, such as *Ayrey v British Legal* considered above.[92] But in *Kosmar Villa Holidays*, Rix LJ (with whom Jacob LJ and Forbes J agreed) held that the doctrine of 'waiver by election' was 'ill-fitting in these circumstances, **4.44**

[87] Stevens (n 2) 131.
[88] ibid 131–32.
[89] See generally Peel (n 9) 1016 [18-094].
[90] [2008] 2 All ER (Comm) 14.
[91] That the insured 'immediately' notify the insurer of the occurrence of any injury.
[92] *Allianz Australia Insurance Ltd v Delor Vue Apartments CTS 39788* (2022) 277 CLR 445, 473–74 [46]. See also *Craine v Colonial Mutual Fire Insurance Co Ltd* (1920) 28 CLR 305.

and unneeded' for waiver by estoppel would give the insured 'all the protection that he needs'.[93]

4.45 A majority of the High Court of Australia has even suggested, albeit without deciding the point,[94] that the doctrine of waiver by election should no longer apply at all to conditions precedent. In *Allianz Australia Insurance Ltd v Delor Vue Apartments CTS 39788*,[95] after acknowledging that historically in insurance contracts there had been 'liberal recognition of irrevocable affirmation following failure of any condition precedent', Kiefel CJ, Edelman, Steward, and Gleeson JJ questioned whether such an approach would 'cohere with the common law in its modern state'.[96] They said:

> If a contractual term is today properly interpreted as a condition precedent to counter-performance, it is strongly arguable that upon the failure of such a condition precedent a party's decision to affirm its obligation of counter-performance will generally only be irrevocable after detrimental reliance by the other party.[97]

4.46 But this is a position which, if the law is to take it, needs to be justified. Why should the finality associated with waiver by election—namely, that statements or conduct amounting to waiver by election are irrevocable—be applicable only to the loss of powers, such as the power to terminate? Why should a party be permitted to blow hot and cold when it comes to waiver of conditions but not when it comes to the loss of the power to terminate? No good reason, other than that it is commonly assumed that the doctrine of election only applies to the latter, has been given.

4.47 The difficult question that remains is how the line might be drawn between waiver of conditions by election and waiver of conditions by estoppel. Unfortunately, courts have not quite grappled with how to draw the line between these cases because it appears to have been assumed that 'waiver by election' refers only to the loss of a power to terminate by the affirmation of the contract. Once it is appreciated that a number of cases said to be concerned with affirmation and waiver by election, such as *Bentsen v Taylor*, were actually concerned with waiver of conditions, the distinction between these cases and

[93] *Kosmar Villa Holidays plc v Trustees of Syndicate 1243* [2008] 2 All ER (Comm) 14, 36 [70]. It was held in any event that the communications were equivocal: 39–40 [79]. See also *Lexington Insurance Co v Multinacional de Seguros SA* [2009] 1 All ER (Comm) 35, 47–51 [52]–[68].

[94] *Allianz Australia Insurance Ltd v Delor Vue Apartments CTS 39788* (2022) 277 CLR 445, 477 [55].

[95] (2022) 277 CLR 445.

[96] ibid 473–74 [46].

[97] ibid 474 [47] (citation omitted).

cases said to involve waiver of conditions by estoppel becomes much more difficult to draw.

One suggestion would be to say that waiver by election applies where the condition has already failed, and the party entitled to rely upon the condition represents by words or conduct that they will not so rely. The fact that such a waiver is final could be justified by the need for 'finality in commercial transactions'[98] which negatives 'any liberty to blow hot and cold in commercial conduct'.[99] Waiver by estoppel would then apply where the condition is still capable of being fulfilled.[100] In such cases, the party waiving the condition should be entitled to retract the waiver on the giving of reasonable notice, unless (i) it is no longer possible for the other party to comply with the condition, in which case it becomes, in essence, a case of waiver by election, or (ii) where complying with the condition will now cause prejudice to the other party. But this is only a tentative suggestion. Courts need to grapple with the distinction between waiver of conditions by election and by estoppel. **4.48**

Not all instances of waiver are instances of estoppel: waiver of conditions by acceptance

A further reason for caution when treating waiver of conditions as part of the law of promissory estoppel is that, even putting to one side cases of waiver by election, the various instances of waiver of conditions are not uniform and do not all fall within promissory estoppel. One such instance of waiver of conditions occurs in sale of goods cases in which it is said that by accepting the goods the buyer waives any unperformed conditions of their obligation to pay the price. The key difference between this instance of waiver and the instances of waiver considered in the previous two sections is that it can apply even though the party accepting the benefit of performance is unaware that the condition has not been fulfilled and even though the other party may not have relied upon any representation by the person waiving the condition.[101] As we shall see, the attempt made by Lord Denning in *Panchaud Freres SA v Etablissements* **4.49**

[98] *BP Exploration Co (Libya) Ltd v Hunt (No 2)* [1979] 1 WLR 783, 811. Note that Robert Goff J was discussing the instance of waiver considered at [4.49]–[4.54]. However, a similar idea arguably applies here.

[99] *Panchaud Freres SA v Etablissements General Grain Co* [1970] 1 Lloyd's Rep 53, 59.

[100] See, eg, *Barrett Bros (Taxis) Ltd v Davies* [1966] 1 WLR 1334. It is worth noting that it was conceded that when the insured received the letter waiving the condition, the insured would still have been in time to comply: at 1334.

[101] Peel (n 9) 1022 [18-106].

General Grain Co[102] to analyse it as a case of estoppel by conduct has generally been met with scepticism.[103]

4.50 The rule on waiver of conditions by acceptance is now found in s 11(4) of the Sale of Goods Act 1979.[104] As was explained in earlier chapters,[105] it is derived from a line of cases at common law interpreting *Boone v Eyre*.[106] Thus in *Graves v Legg*,[107] Parke B said:

> The defendants, therefore, have a right to object to fulfil the contract on their part, as the plaintiff did not fulfil his, though they could no longer object to the plaintiff's non-performance, had they afterwards taken any benefit under the contract.

4.51 This principle was subsequently extended in *Panchaud Freres*[108] to the acceptance of shipping documents. In that case, buyers under a cif contract had received shipping documents, including a bill of lading and a certificate of quality, the latter of which stated that the goods had been shipped late. The buyers nonetheless took up the documents and paid for them. They subsequently rejected the goods on the ground of their quality and description, but when these grounds were held in an arbitration to be inadequate, they sought, on an arbitration appeal, to rely on the late shipment. It was held that they were precluded from complaining of the late shipment or of any defect in the bill of lading.

4.52 Lord Denning MR sought to characterise this case as one of estoppel by conduct, stating that:

> If a man, who is entitled to reject goods on a certain ground, so conducts himself as to lead the other to believe that he is not relying on that ground, then he cannot afterwards set it up as a ground of rejection, when it would be unfair or unjust to allow him so to do.[109]

[102] [1970] 1 Lloyd's Rep 53, 57.
[103] See, eg, McKendrick (n 49) 2171–73 [28-059].
[104] See originally s 11(1)(c) of the Sale of Goods Act 1893.
[105] See [2.42]–[2.45] and [3.6].
[106] *Ellen v Topp* (1851) 6 Ex 424, 441–42; 155 ER 609, 61; *Graves v Legg* (1854) 9 Ex 709, 717; 156 ER 304, 307; *Behn v Burness* (1863) 3 B & S 751, 755; 122 ER 281, 283; *Wallis, Son & Wells v Pratt & Haynes* [1910] 2 KB 1003, 1013; [1911] AC 394, 400. See Charles Bruce Morison, *Rescission of Contracts, A Treatise on the Principles Governing the Rescission, Discharge, Avoidance and Dissolution of Contracts* (Stevens & Haynes 1916) 100–05; Anthony Beck, 'The Doctrine of Substantial Performance: Conditions and Conditions Precedent' (1975) 38 Modern Law Review 413, 418–19.
[107] (1854) 9 Ex 709, 718; 156 ER 304, 307. See also Beck (n 106) 418.
[108] *Panchaud Freres SA v Etablissements General Grain Co* [1970] 1 Lloyd's Rep 53.
[109] ibid 57.

He thought that this was the case even if the buyer had no knowledge of the non-compliance with the condition, 'for the simple reason that he had the full opportunity of finding out from the contract documents what the real date of shipment was'.[110]

4.53 One 'difficulty with the estoppel analysis is that there does not appear to have been any reliance by the sellers on any representation which was made by the buyers when they took up the documents'.[111] By contrast, Winn LJ thought that it was impossible to say that there was 'anything which, within the scope of the doctrine as hitherto enunciated, could be described as an estoppel or a quasi estoppel'.[112] He said:

> [W]hat one has here is something perhaps in our law not yet wholly developed as a separate doctrine—which is more in the nature of a requirement of fair conduct—a criterion of what is fair conduct between the parties. There may be an inchoate doctrine stemming from the manifest convenience of consistency in pragmatic affairs, negativing any liberty to blow hot and cold in commercial conduct.[113]

4.54 In *BP Exploration Co (Libya) Ltd v Hunt (No 2)*,[114] Robert Goff J similarly rejected any estoppel analysis. Instead, he said that '[t]he decision stems from the need for finality in commercial transactions, as does the doctrine of acceptance in contracts for the sale of goods'.[115] In brief, this is another instance of waiver that falls outside of waiver by election and waiver by estoppel.

4.55 The next chapter explores two further instances of waiver that are also not clearly based on estoppel: (i) waiver of conditions by prevention of fulfilment; and (ii) waiver of conditions on a repudiation. The first of these is at present treated wholly separately from estoppel. As for the second, it will be seen that in an attempt to explain the absolving effects of an unaccepted repudiation, courts have confusingly rejected waiver of conditions only to introduce a 'quite new kind of estoppel'[116] to reach the same result.[117] In sum, some instances of

[110] ibid.
[111] McKendrick (n 49) 2172 [28-059]. See also *BP Exploration Co (Libya) Ltd v Hunt (No 2)* [1979] 1 WLR 783, 811.
[112] *Panchaud Freres SA v Etablissements General Grain Co* [1970] 1 Lloyd's Rep 53, 59.
[113] ibid.
[114] [1979] 1 WLR 783.
[115] ibid 811. For a discussion of the competing interpretations of this case, see Sean Wilken and Karim Ghaly, *The Law of Waiver, Variation and Estoppel* (3rd edn, OUP 2012) 308–12 [13.07]–[13.15].
[116] Sir Michael Mustill, 'Anticipatory Breach of Contract: The Common Law at Work' in *Butterworth Lectures 1989–90* (Butterworths 1990) 68.
[117] *Fercometal SARL v Mediterranean Shipping Co SA (The Simona)* [1989] AC 788, 805. See [5.85]–[5.95].

waiver of conditions can be understood as part of promissory estoppel, so long as it is borne in mind that waiver by estoppel is not the only instance in which conditions can be waived.

Conclusion

4.56 This chapter has explained the various instances in which conditions can be waived. It was seen that, despite being supported by centuries of authority, much of the law in this area has been either doubted or subsumed within the doctrine of promissory estoppel. This latter approach has not been altogether satisfactory. First, it has led to the implicit assumption that the finality associated with waiver by election is only applicable to the loss of the power to terminate and not to waiver of conditions. Secondly, it is overinclusive. In particular, it is misleading to suggest that all instances of waiver can be understood either as waiver by election or waiver by estoppel. Two clear exceptions are the doctrine of waiver by acceptance applied in the sale of goods context, which was explored in this chapter, and the doctrine of waiver of conditions by prevention of fulfilment, considered in the next. A further potential exception is the waiver of conditions on a repudiation, but as we will see, the story there is more complicated.

5

Waiver of Conditions II—Prevention and Repudiation

Introduction

This chapter considers waiver of conditions by prevention of fulfilment and waiver of conditions on a repudiation. The former instance of waiver operates where one party prevents the performance or the fulfilment of a condition. Its basis is that a party who wrongfully causes the failure of a condition ought not to be able to benefit from their wrong by turning around and relying on the unperformed or unfulfilled condition as an answer to an action.[1] The latter instance of waiver traditionally arose on a repudiation by a promisor—that is where the promisor disabled themselves from performing or renounced their obligation to perform. The basis of this form of waiver was that the law does not require a party to do anything that is vain or useless, such as complying with a condition to the obligation of a party who is repudiating that very same obligation. But continuing the trend from the previous chapter, it will be seen that this latter instance of waiver has since been rejected in English law in order to introduce a 'quite new kind of estoppel'.[2] **5.1**

In exploring these forms of waiver, two further points will be seen in this chapter. The first arises in the context of waiver of conditions by prevention **5.2**

[1] cf *King Crude Carriers SA v Ridgebury November LLC* [2025] 1 All ER 179, 202–03 [81], linking it to 'the presumed contractual intention of the parties'.

[2] Sir Michael Mustill, 'Anticipatory Breach of Contract: The Common Law at Work' in *Butterworth Lectures 1989–90* (Butterworths 1990) 68.

Discharge of Contractual Obligations. Jordan English, Oxford University Press. © Jordan English 2025.
DOI: 10.1093/9780198906704.003.0005

and the decision of the House of Lords in *Mackay v Dick*.[3] Importantly, this chapter claims that there is a distinction between the principle of 'waiver of conditions', which English law does recognise, and the 'fictional fulfilment' of conditions, which English law, at least until very recently,[4] did not recognise. Waiver only precludes a person from relying upon a condition—it does not deem that condition to have been fulfilled. The difference is more than mere semantics.

5.3 The second key point, which assumes importance both in the context of waiver of conditions by prevention and waiver of conditions on a repudiation, is that not all conditions can be waived for all purposes. In particular, a condition cannot be waived for the purpose of an action for the price if the performance of the condition is the consideration for the promise it qualifies.[5] This is because of the rule in *Laird v Pim*,[6] discussed later in this chapter, that no action for the price can be brought unless the consideration has become executed.

Waiver of Conditions by Prevention

5.4 A general principle, subject to limitations to be discussed, is that a person who prevents the performance or fulfilment of a condition will be held to have waived that condition.[7] This principle is longstanding. As the editors of the fifth edition of *Benjamin on Sale* recorded:

> As long ago as 1787, Ashhurst J, in delivering the opinion of the King's Bench in *Hotham v East India Company*, said that it was evident from common sense, and therefore needed no authority to prove it, that if the performance of a condition precedent had been rendered impossible by the neglect or default of the defendant, 'it is equal to performance.'[8]

[3] (1881) 6 App Cas 251.

[4] *King Crude Carriers SA v Ridgebury November LLC* [2025] 1 All ER 179.

[5] CC Langdell, *A Selection of Cases on the Law of Contracts with a Summary of the Topics Covered by the Cases* (2nd edn, Little Brown, and Co 1879) Part II, 1087 ('[T]he performance of the condition is the *quid pro quo* of the covenant or promise'). See also Arthur Corbin, *Corbin on Contracts: A Comprehensive Treatise on the Rules of Contract Law* (West Publishing Co 1960) vol 3A, 486 §753 ('material part of the agreed equivalent of the promise'); American Law Institute, *Restatement of the Law Second: Contracts 2d* (American Law Institute Publishers 1981) 217 §84(1)(a), 218 comment (c) ('a material part of the agreed exchange for the performance of the duty'). However, note that the American texts put the threshold too low by referring to a 'material part'. This is not consistent with the position in English law: see [5.52]–[5.63].

[6] (1841) 7 M & W 474, 151 ER 852.

[7] *Hotham v The East India Company* (1787) 1 Term Rep 638, 99 ER 1295; *Mackay v Dick* (1881) 6 App Cas 251. See also Langdell (n 5) 1083.

[8] Walter Charles Alan Ker and Arthur Reginald Butterworth, *A Treatise on the Law of Sale of Personal Property with references to the American Decisions and to the French Code and Civil Law* (5th edn, Sweet

Despite being longstanding, the authorities on this principle are not clear and there is doubt both as to the existence of this principle and as to its scope.[9] Indeed, in *Nautica Marine Ltd v Trafigura Trading LLC (The Leonidas)*,[10] Foxton J said that '[t]he precise status of the . . . rule is one which may well merit exploration by a higher court on a future occasion'. **5.5**

This doubt is due to two matters. The first can be seen in the words 'it is equal to performance' in the quote above. This might suggest that the rule is concerned with the 'fictional fulfilment' of conditions, a doctrine found in some civilian legal systems,[11] rather than the common law doctrine of waiver of conditions. As this section argues, the English authorities have been correct to reject, in the majority of cases,[12] any principle of the fictional fulfilment of conditions, but that does not mean that there is not a principle of waiver of conditions by prevention of fulfilment. The distinction between the two is explained below and, as will be seen, it is not merely a matter of semantics. The second matter is a failure to appreciate the limits on which conditions can be waived. As will be shown, not all conditions can be waived, at least not for all purposes; if they could, it would lead to some undesirable outcomes. In particular, it is not possible to waive a condition for the purpose of an action for the price if the performance of the condition is the consideration for the promise it qualifies. Once both of these matters are appreciated, the objections to the principle of waiver of conditions by prevention fall away. **5.6**

Mackay v Dick: waiver or fictional fulfilment?

While earlier cases established this general principle in English law,[13] the leading case—*Mackay v Dick*[14]—was in fact a Scottish appeal to the House **5.7**

& Maxwell 1906) 563 (citations omitted). See also Arthur Corbin, 'Conditions in the Law of Contact' (1919) 28 Yale Law Journal 739, 757; Corbin (n 5) 540 §767.

[9] Edwin Peel, *The Law of Contract* (15th edn, Sweet & Maxwell 2020) 74 [2-112]. See also Robert Stevens, *The Laws of Restitution* (OUP 2023) 122–23.

[10] [2021] 1 All ER (Comm) 1157, 1187 [105]. See also *King Crude Carriers SA v Ridgebury November LLC* [2024] 2 Lloyd's Rep 115, 130 [94].

[11] German Burgerliches Gesetzbuch, s 162(1); French Code Civil, Art 1304-3.

[12] cf *King Crude Carriers SA v Ridgebury November LLC* [2025] 1 All ER 179, which is discussed in detail at [5.23]–[5.36].

[13] See, eg, *Hotham v The East India Company* (1787) 1 Term Rep 638, 99 ER 1295; *Giles v Giles* (1846) 9 QB 164, 115 ER 1237. *Inchbald v Western Neilgherry Coffee, Tea, and Cinchona Plantation Co Ltd* (1864) 17 CB (NS) 733, 144 ER 293 is also sometimes cited in support, but on a proper examination of the case, it was not concerned with waiver of conditions but the breach of a duty not to prevent performance. The plaintiff did not recover the action for the agreed sum, but rather a lesser amount by way of damages: see *Thompson v ASDA-MFI Group plc* [1988] 1 Ch 241, 251–52.

[14] (1881) 6 App Cas 251.

of Lords. Indeed, as we shall see, the confusion over the applicability of this case in English law might stem from the different ways in which the Scottish lawyer (Lord Watson), who favoured a principle of fictional fulfilment, and the English lawyer (Lord Blackburn) who, on one view, favoured a principle of waiver, expressed themselves. The important question for present purposes is whether either approach forms part of English law.

5.8 The appellant, Mr Mackay, was a railway contractor. He agreed to buy a steam excavator from the respondents and it was a condition of the obligation to accept and pay for the machine that the machine would, upon fairly being tested, dig and fill 350 cubic yards of clay, or other soft substances, within a day. The machine was tested at one of the appellant's sites but by the time it was tested the circumstances had entirely changed so that the machine could not be fairly tested. The machine failed to dig and fill the guaranteed quantity. The appellant refused to provide another opportunity to conduct the test and asked the respondents to remove the machine. The House of Lords held that, even though the machine had not passed a test, because the appellant had prevented a fair test from taking place, the appellant was liable to pay the price. Two speeches were delivered by Lord Blackburn and Lord Watson. Lord Selborne LC agreed with both.

5.9 Lord Blackburn first explained that there was an implied duty on the part of the appellant not to prevent the fulfilment of the condition.[15] Subsequent cases have relied upon this for the proposition that if one party prevents the other from fulfilling a condition they may be liable in damages for breach of an implied duty that they not prevent fulfilment of the condition.[16] But more importantly for present purposes, in explaining why the appellant was liable for the price, Lord Blackburn said:

> [T]he [appellant] having had the machine delivered to him, was by his contract to keep it, unless on a fair test according to the contract it failed to do the stipulated quantity of work, in which case he would be entitled to call on the [respondents] to remove it. And by his own default he can now never be in a position to call upon the [respondents] to take back the machine, on the ground that the test had not been satisfied, he must, as far as regards that, keep, and consequently pay for it.[17]

[15] ibid 263.

[16] See, eg, *Luxor (Eastbourne) Ltd v Cooper* [1941] AC 108; *Mona Oil Equipment & Supply Co Ltd v Rhodesia Railways Ltd* [1949] 2 All ER 1014; *Thompson v ASDA-MFI Group plc* [1988] 1 Ch 241; *Compagnie Noga d'Importation et d'Exportation SA v Abacha (No 3)* [2002] CLC 207; *King Crude Carriers SA v Ridgebury November LLC* [2025] 1 All ER 179, 187 [29].

[17] *Mackay v Dick* (1881) 6 App Cas 251, 264.

By contrast, Lord Watson spoke in terms of the 'fiction of fulfilment'. He said: **5.10**

> The Respondents were only entitled to receive payment of the price of the machine on the condition that it should be tried at a proper working face provided by the Appellant, and that on trial it should excavate a certain amount of clay or other soft substance within a given time. They have been thwarted in the attempt to fulfil that condition by the neglect or refusal of the Appellant to furnish the means of applying the stipulated test; and their failure being due to his fault, I am of opinion that . . . they must be taken to have fulfilled the condition.[18]

Lord Watson's approach is clear in adopting the fiction of fulfilment. But Lord Blackburn's approach is capable of two interpretations. On the first interpretation, Lord Blackburn construed the contract as involving not a condition precedent to the duty to accept and pay for the machine, but a condition subsequent the occurrence of which would extinguish the immediate duty to pay that had already fallen due.[19] That condition subsequent was of the form: if upon a fair test, the machine fails to dig the stipulated quantity, the price shall cease to be payable. And because a test would never take place, the condition subsequent would never occur and the price would remain payable. The immediate duty of performance had arisen and the appellant had 'prevented himself from escaping from the liability to pay'.[20] On this interpretation, no question of waiver arose. **5.11**

The second interpretation that has been proffered in the case law is that 'Lord Blackburn . . . favoured a principle of waiver'.[21] This is supported by a reference in his speech to a case decided in 1469 concerning the great bell of Mildenhall.[22] The defendant, a brazier, was sued on an indenture to recast the great bell of Mildenhall and make a new bell in harmony with the tone of the other bells in Mildenhall. It was a condition of the indenture that the bell be brought to the defendant's house, weighed, and put into the fire in the presence of the men of Mildenhall. The defendant pleaded that the bell was not **5.12**

[18] ibid 270.

[19] See *Mona Oil Equipment & Supply Co Ltd v Rhodesia Railways Ltd* [1949] 2 All ER 1014, 1017–18; *Colley v Overseas Exporters* [1921] 3 KB 302, 308; *King Crude Carriers SA v Ridgebury November LLC* [2025] 1 All ER 179, 187 [29], 191 [43]. See also Michael Bridge (ed), *Benjamin's Sale of Goods* (12th edn, Sweet & Maxwell 2023) 1152–53 [16-023].

[20] *Mona Oil Equipment & Supply Co Ltd v Rhodesia Railways Ltd* [1949] 2 All ER 1014, 1018.

[21] *Compagnie Noga d'Importation et d'Exportation SA v Abacha (No 3)* [2002] CLC 207, 232 [100]. See also *The Leonidas* [2021] 1 All ER (Comm) 1157, 1184–85 [96].

[22] (1469) YB Pas 9 Edw IV, fo 3b–4a, pl 13. See John James Raven, *The Church Bells of Suffolk* (Jarrold and Sons 1890) 47–50.

weighed nor put into the furnace according to the indenture. It was argued for the plaintiff, and the Court of Common Pleas agreed, that this was a bad plea because it was the defendant who ought to have weighed the bell and put it into the furnace. Moreover, and importantly for our purposes, Lord Blackburn in discussing this case said:

> [A] further point was mooted . . . that if the Defendant had put the bell in the fire, without seeing it weighed, he would have waived that which was but an incident, and been as much bound to fulfil that which was the substance of the contract, viz, to make a proper tenor, as if he had had it weighed. I mention this old case, decided in 1469, because it is on it that the different digests laying down the principle are all founded, and because I think it is obvious good sense and justice.[23]

In other words, if the defendant had prevented the condition from being fulfilled, he would be held to have waived the condition.

5.13 If Lord Blackburn is understood as having relied upon waiver it might be thought that there is no substantive difference between his approach and Lord Watson's approach: 'On either principle, the seller was entitled to his price.'[24] But there is an important difference between the fiction of fulfilment and the principle of waiver and it manifests in how each of their Lordships dealt with the appellant's alternative argument. That argument was that, despite the absence of a fair test as per the contract, the repeated failures of the machine, coupled with the other evidence, showed that the machine did not conform with the description in the contract and could not in substance have satisfied it.[25]

5.14 Lord Watson took the view that this argument was 'irrelevant' because, applying the fiction of fulfilment, 'the machine must be held to have satisfied the contract test'.[26] By contrast, Lord Blackburn thought that it was unnecessary to consider this argument, only because it had not been raised in any of the courts below.[27] He said that 'if such a defence had been raised on the record in this case, the Court of Session ought . . . to have found how much, if any, of the allegations were proved in fact'.[28]

[23] *Mackay v Dick* (1881) 6 App Cas 251, 263–64.
[24] *Compagnie Noga d'Importation et d'Exportation SA v Abacha (No 3)* [2002] CLC 207, 232 [100]. See also *King Crude Carriers SA v Ridgebury November LLC* [2025] 1 All ER 179, 185 [23], 202 [80].
[25] *Mackay v Dick* (1881) 6 App Cas 251, 265.
[26] ibid 271.
[27] ibid 265–66.
[28] ibid.

This difference in approach is important. Lord Blackburn's way of dealing with this alternative argument amounts to saying that, although the appellant had waived the condition of testing, this would not have prevented him from showing that the machine did not, in fact, conform to the contract and therefore that *another* condition to his liability to pay the price had not been fulfilled. In contrast to the fiction of fulfilment, waiver does not deem the condition to have been satisfied—it only precludes the defendant from relying on that condition. While this will in many cases produce the same result, *Mackay v Dick* is an example of a case where it would have produced a different result (had the argument been raised in time). **5.15**

Does either principle form part of English law?

Mackay v Dick is therefore capable of supporting either an approach based on the fictional fulfilment of conditions or an approach based upon the waiver of conditions. But as mentioned above, *Mackay v Dick* was a Scottish appeal. The question then arises whether either principle can be found in English law. **5.16**

Starting with the fiction of fulfilment, until recently this principle had largely been rejected in English law. Thus academics were able to say with confidence that the '[m]ore recent authorities rightly hold that such a doctrine of "fictional fulfilment" of a condition does not form part of English law'.[29] For example, in *Thompson v ASDA-MFI Group plc*,[30] Scott J stated that '[t]he principle expressed by Lord Watson in *Mackay v Dick* . . . is not, in my view, a principle of English law'. And in *Little v Courage Ltd*,[31] Millett LJ stated that '[t]he doctrine of fictional fulfilment of a condition precedent which is found in the civil law forms no part of English law.' **5.17**

More recently, in *King Crude Carriers SA v Ridgebury November LLC (The Agathonissos)*,[32] after a lengthy review of the authorities, Dias J said: **5.18**

> [T]he doctrine of deemed fulfilment does not form any part of English law. It is a doctrine derived from the civil law and in so far as it formed the basis

[29] Peel (n 9) 74 [2-112].
[30] [1988] 1 Ch 241, 266.
[31] (1995) 70 P & CR 469, 474.
[32] [2024] 2 Lloyd's Rep 115.

of Lord Watson's decision in *Mackay v Dick*, that was a Scottish case which is not binding on the English courts.[33]

However, when the matter reached the Court of Appeal the decision of Dias J was reversed.[34] The Court of Appeal held that 'the principle expressed by Lord Watson in *Mackay v Dick* is a principle of English law and applies to conditions precedent to the accrual of debts . . . with the result that non-fulfilment of the condition forms no defence to the claim in debt'.[35] However, as explained below when considering this decision in more detail, the Court expressly stated that it did not see any significant difference between 'deemed fulfilment' and 'waiver',[36] and at times the approach taken appears to be more indicative of waiver rather than deemed fulfilment.

5.19 By contrast, before *King Crude Carriers*, a number of cases had recognised the principle of waiver of conditions by prevention of fulfilment. In *Colley v Overseas Exporters*,[37] for example, McCardie J did not refer at all to Lord Watson and instead referred only to 'the principle indicated by Lord Blackburn' which 'operates to make a price payable which, apart from that principle, would not be payable',[38] adding that:

> Although, as I have said, *Mackay v Dick* turned on Scotch law yet I think that that principle is equally well settled in English law. It has frequently been asserted in well-known text books based on English law . . . This rule is recognized by the text books as embodied in English law, and has been widely applied by high tribunals as of obvious justice and convenience . . .[39]

5.20 Similarly, in *Tiberghien Draperie SaRL v Greenberg & Sons (Mantles) Ltd*,[40] the Court applied the principle from *Mackay v Dick* to hold that it was not open to buyers of cloth to rely upon the delivery of the goods to London as a condition precedent to payment when the goods had been delivered to Folkestone and prevented from arriving in London because the buyers refused to pay the customs duty. The Court expressly said that it was 'not open to [the buyers]

[33] Ibid 130 [95(i)]. cf at 131 [95(v)(c)] ('It may alternatively be possible to say that a party who fails to fulfil a condition precedent which he is obliged to perform, or prevents his counterparty from performing waives compliance with the condition.').
[34] *King Crude Carriers SA v Ridgebury November LLC* [2025] 1 All ER 179.
[35] ibid 197 [63]. See also at 202 [77].
[36] ibid 185 [23], 202 [80].
[37] *Colley v Overseas Exporters* [1921] 3 KB 302.
[38] ibid 308.
[39] ibid 308–09 (citations omitted).
[40] [1953] 2 Lloyd's Rep 739.

now to set up that condition, the non-fulfilment of that condition' because they had 'waiv[ed] delivery'.[41] As the Court of Appeal accepted in *King Crude Carriers*: the judge in *Tiberghien Draperie* 'was purporting to apply the principle in *Mackay v Dick*, albeit that he concluded that it amounted in effect to a form of waiver'.[42]

Finally, in *Compagnie Noga d'Importation et d'Exportation SA v Abacha (No 3)*,[43] Rix LJ observed that in *Mackay v Dick* 'Lord Blackburn appears to have favoured a principle of waiver, Lord Watson a principle of deemed fulfilment of the condition precedent' and, while expressly not deciding between them, said '[a] doctrine of waiver perhaps sounds more like the common law than a doctrine of deemed fulfilment'.[44] **5.21**

Doubts expressed about the principle

Despite the longstanding authority supporting the principle of waiver of conditions by prevention of fulfilment, doubts have been expressed about it, with some judges and academics even questioning the principle's existence. These doubts stem from two matters. The first is the failure to distinguish between waiver of conditions and the fiction of fulfilment. The second matter is a failure to appreciate the limits on which conditions can be waived. **5.22**

Failure to distinguish waiver of conditions from the fiction of fulfilment

As to the first, one reason for the difficulty in acceptance of this principle is that courts and commentators do not clearly distinguish between the principle of waiver of conditions by prevention of fulfilment and the principle of deemed fulfilment of conditions. In *King Crude Carriers*,[45] for example, Popplewell LJ said: **5.23**

> The authorities use a series of different epithets to describe how the principle takes effect. In some cases the language is that of deemed fulfilment of the condition ... In others it is that the condition is dispensed with ... In others it is the language of estoppel or quasi estoppel or waiver ... These, however, are merely descriptors of the effect of the principle ...

[41] ibid 744.
[42] *King Crude Carriers SA v Ridgebury November LLC* [2025] 1 All ER 179, 195 [56].
[43] [2002] CLC 207.
[44] ibid 232 [100], 233 [106].
[45] *King Crude Carriers SA v Ridgebury November LLC* [2025] 1 All ER 179, 202 [80].

5.24 In that case, the respondent buyers had entered into three contracts for the sale of second-hand oil tankers for a total price of US$49.4 million. Clause 2 of the contracts required the buyers to provide a 10 per cent deposit to be paid into an escrow account held by a deposit holder for the parties but only once the deposit holder had confirmed in writing to the parties that the account had been opened. By the same clause, the buyers were under an obligation to provide all necessary documentation to the deposit holder to enable the account to be opened. The buyers, in breach of this obligation, failed to provide the necessary documents and did not pay the deposits, totalling US$4.94 million. The sellers subsequently terminated the contracts both on the basis of an express termination power for non-payment of the deposits and at common law on the basis that the non-payment of the deposits was a 'repudiatory breach', which the sellers accepted. They then brought an action in debt seeking to recover the deposits, and argued that the deposits were due and owing on the basis that the condition precedent to the deposits falling due—namely, the opening of the accounts—had been prevented from being fulfilled by the buyers' breach of cl 2 and that, applying the principle in *Mackay v Dick*, 'the condition is treated as dispensed with or fulfilled, with the result that the debt accrues'.[46]

5.25 The Court of Appeal agreed with that argument. Popplewell LJ (with whom Nugee and Falk LJJ agreed) said:

> [A]lthough *Mackay v Dick* was a Scottish Appeal and Lord Watson's reasoning was based on Scottish law with civil law origins, it was reflective of English common law at the time. That is indeed how it has been treated in subsequent English law decisions which are either binding or persuasive.[47]

5.26 While Popplewell LJ expressly adopted Lord Watson's speech in *Mackay v Dick*, which was concerned with the fictional fulfilment of conditions and not the waiver of conditions, this was only because he saw Lord Blackburn's speech as being concerned only with a condition subsequent analysis and not waiver.[48] Moreover, Popplewell LJ appeared to attach no significance to the different formulations.[49] For example, at one point in the judgment, when discussing the distinction between 'the concept of deemed or fictional fulfilment' and the concept of being 'precluded from claiming that the condition has not

[46] ibid 181 [2].
[47] ibid 190 [41].
[48] ibid 187 [29], 191 [43].
[49] ibid 185 [23], 202 [80].

been fulfilled', he said that the 'difference in description of the effect of the principle is apparent in a number of the authorities but is irrelevant to the existence or scope of the principle itself'.[50] And when providing a concluding statement as to the principle from *Mackay v Dick*, he said:

> [The authorities] provide a consistent body of case-law, both persuasive and... binding on this court, for the principle contained in the reasoning of Lord Watson in *Mackay v Dick*, applicable as a matter of English law, that an obligor is not permitted to rely upon the non-fulfilment of a condition precedent to its debt obligation where it has caused such non-fulfilment by its own breach of contract...[51]

Thus, while Popplewell LJ expressly referred to Lord Watson's speech and therefore the fictional fulfilment of conditions, his formulation appeared more geared towards the principle of waiver. The language of not being 'permitted to rely upon the non-fulfilment of a condition precedent' is the language of waiver and not fictional fulfilment.

An example of the failure to distinguish between waiver of conditions and fictional fulfilment also comes from a common academic criticism of the decision in *Mackay v Dick*. Thus, Professor Edwin Peel, who is rightly critical of the fiction of fulfilment, writes in *Treitel on Contract*: **5.27**

> [I]n *Mackay v Dick* the buyer was held liable *for the price* ... In principle it seems wrong to hold him so liable, for such a result ignores the possibility that the machine might have failed to come up to the standard required by the contract, even if proper facilities for trial had been provided.[52]

The criticism that can be levelled at this passage is that it does not discuss the separate principle of waiver of conditions by prevention and how it may differ from fictional fulfilment. The distinction matters because the very argument raised in the passage was the argument addressed by both Law Lords in *Mackay v Dick*. As we saw at [5.13]–[5.15], Lord Blackburn, applying a principle of waiver, held that it was too late to raise the argument, but it appears that he would have agreed with it had it been raised and proved earlier. This is because, unlike the fiction of fulfilment, waiver does not deem the condition to have been fulfilled. It was only Lord Watson who, applying the fiction

[50] ibid 202 [76].
[51] ibid 202 [77].
[52] Peel (n 9) 74 [2-112].

of fulfilment, would have rejected this argument. As such, this criticism only applies to the fiction of fulfilment; it does not apply to the principle of waiver.

5.28 This criticism was also addressed by Popplewell LJ in *King Crude Carriers*. Noting the argument he said:

> I disagree. The argument supposes that the principle dispenses with the concept of causation, but it does not: the concept of a causative link is contained in the principle itself, namely that the obligor's conduct must have prevented the condition precedent being fulfilled. So in *Mackay v Dick*, for example, it would have been sufficient to prevent the principle applying had the buyer sought to plead and prove that the machine would in any event have failed the test at Carfin so that his failure to arrange it had no causative effect on the condition being unfulfilled. That was why the judgments focussed so closely on the procedural position which prevented the buyer from raising any such argument.[53]

5.29 There are two points that emerge from this response. First, as we have seen,[54] only Lord Blackburn, who applied a principle of waiver, focused on the procedural position preventing the buyers from raising this sort of argument because otherwise he thought it would have been valid. Lord Watson, who applied the fiction of fulfilment, took the view that this kind of argument was simply 'irrelevant'.[55] In this respect, the approach in *King Crude Carriers* therefore seems much closer in substance to the common law doctrine of waiver of conditions.

5.30 Secondly, even if adopting a fiction of fulfilment, the approach in *King Crude Carriers* is not the same as the approach taken by Lord Watson in *Mackay v Dick*. As just mentioned, Lord Watson thought the argument that the machine might not have satisfied the description in the contract was irrelevant. However, the approach in *King Crude Carriers* provides a further way to deal with the objection that the machine might otherwise have passed the test. If it can be shown that the test inevitably would have failed, then the principle of waiver or fictional fulfilment should not be able to be relied upon. This idea of causation, that the person must have actually been prevented from complying with the condition, is also consistent with a limitation on the scope of the principle of waiver of conditions on a repudiation that is discussed in the next section.[56]

[53] *King Crude Carriers SA v Ridgebury November LLC* [2025] 1 All ER 179, 204 [88].
[54] See [5.13]–[5.15].
[55] *Mackay v Dick* (1881) 6 App Cas 251, 271.
[56] See [5.65].

The limits on which conditions can be waived

The second matter that has caused doubt to be cast on the principle of waiver of conditions by prevention of fulfilment is a failure to appreciate the limits on which conditions can be waived. In particular, part of the reluctance to embrace this principle of waiver stems from an intuition that in some cases the principle would lead to 'extraordinary results'.[57] It would mean, for example, that a landowner is liable to a builder for the price if they prevent the builder from completing the work, that a buyer of goods who refuses to accept them is liable to pay for the goods even if title to the goods never passes,[58] and that a freighter is bound to pay freight if they refuse to load the cargo even though the effect of refusing to load a cargo is that the goods are never carried.[59] **5.31**

But that has not been the position in English law since the 1841 decision in *Laird v Pim*.[60] As will be argued at [5.52]–[5.63] below when discussing that case, the best understanding of that decision and its consequences is that the principle of waiver is subject to an important limitation: a condition cannot be waived for the purpose of an action for the price if the performance of the condition is the consideration for the promise it qualifies.[61] Unless the consideration has become executed, a party to a conditional contract involving dependent promises can only recover damages.[62] In *King Crude Carriers*, Popplewell LJ also noted this limit, although expressed it slightly differently, and said that the principle in *Mackay v Dick* only applies where the 'condition is not the performance of a principal obligation by the obligee nor one which it is necessary for the obligee to plead and prove as an [essential] ingredient of its cause of action.'[63] **5.32**

This limitation significantly reduces the scope of waiver of conditions by prevention of fulfilment and avoids the 'extraordinary results'[64] that might otherwise occur. For example, it explains why the principle did not apply in a case like *Colley v Overseas Exporters*,[65] in which goods were to be sold FOB **5.33**

[57] *Colley v Overseas Exporters* [1921] 3 KB 302, 311.
[58] ibid.
[59] In this respect there may be a difficulty with *Bentsen v Taylor, Sons & Co* [1893] 2 QB 274, where it appears that the action was for the price.
[60] (1841) 7 M & W 474, 151 ER 852.
[61] See text in n 5.
[62] Francis Dawson, 'Metaphors and Anticipatory Breach of Contract' (1981) 40 Cambridge Law Journal 83, 95–96. See also *Newmont Pty Ltd v Laverton Nickel NL* [1983] 1 NSWLR 181, 188.
[63] *King Crude Carriers SA v Ridgebury November LLC* [2025] 1 All ER 179, 202 [77]. See also at 204 [85]. Although the passage quoted does not use the word 'essential' this qualifier is made clear elsewhere: see at 198 [66].
[64] *Colley v Overseas Exporters* [1921] 3 KB 302, 311.
[65] [1921] 3 KB 302.

Liverpool. The seller sent the goods to the port at Liverpool but the buyers, in breach, failed to nominate an effective ship. Title to the goods would not pass until the goods have been put onboard the ship. McCardie J held that the principle in *Mackay v Dick* did not apply where title to goods had not passed. The best explanation for this case is that the consideration for the promise to pay—the transfer of title to the goods—had not been executed, and insofar as it formed a condition of the obligation to pay, it could not be waived for the purpose of an action for the price.

5.34 The limitation also explains why the principle of waiver of conditions by prevention of fulfilment did apply in a case like *Abacha (No 3)*,[66] where an obligation to pay a sum of money under a settlement agreement was conditional on that party's accounts being released from a freezing order, and the party had refused to cooperate in the implementation of the agreement, with the result that the freezing orders were not discharged. The consideration for the promise to pay—the settlement—had been executed, and the condition that was waived (ie discharge of the freezing orders) was not the consideration for the promise to pay.

5.35 This limitation appears to be a manifestation of the principle of 'mutuality' or 'reciprocity' that, as discussed in Chapter 1, is at the heart of contracting.[67] But it has also been explained as turning on the parties' intentions.[68] In *Newmont Pty Ltd v Laverton Nickel NL*,[69] the Privy Council said:

> [W]hether the performance of a condition precedent is excused where a party has prevented its performance must depend on the nature of the condition and the circumstances of the case. In some cases the nature and purposes of the condition will themselves be sufficient to indicate that the parties must have intended that the obligations which are expressed to be dependent on the fulfilment of the condition will come into existence only if the condition is fulfilled, and that it will not be enough that performance of the condition has been prevented by the wrongful act of one of the parties.[70]

5.36 To sum up: the principle of waiver of conditions by prevention of fulfilment is not the same as a principle of the fictional fulfilment of conditions. Insofar as

[66] *Compagnie Noga d'Importation et d'Exportation SA v Abacha (No 3)* [2002] CLC 207.
[67] See [1.59]–[1.60].
[68] *King Crude Carriers SA v Ridgebury November LLC* [2025] 1 All ER 179, 202–204 [81]–[86].
[69] [1983] 1 NSWLR 181, 188.
[70] See also Bridge (n 19) 1153 [16-023].

Lord Watson adopted the latter approach in *Mackay v Dick*, the better view is that this is not the law in England. On the other hand, the principle of waiver is well established and, provided that it is distinguished from the fictional fulfilment of conditions and the above limitation is kept in mind, it is entirely unobjectionable. As Lord Blackburn himself said, the principle rests on 'obvious good sense and justice'.[71]

Waiver of Conditions on a Repudiation

The final instance of waiver of conditions that will be considered in this book traditionally arose following the disablement of, or a renunciation by, a promisor (a 'repudiation'). 'Long before the doctrine of anticipatory breach of contract was developed',[72] the law took the position that: **5.37**

> a positive absolute refusal by one party to carry out the contract, or his conduct in incapacitating himself from performing his promise . . . dispenses the other party from the useless formality of tendering performance of the condition . . .[73]

The basis of the rule was that 'the law will not enforce any one to do a thing which will be vain and fruitless'.[74]

However, as we will see, this principle was never absolute and was limited in two important ways. The first limitation—which applies across all instances of waiver, but was developed in this context—is the limitation just mentioned that a condition cannot be waived for the purpose of an action for the price where performance of the condition is the consideration for the promise it qualifies. This is because of the rule in *Laird v Pim* that no action for the price can be brought unless the consideration has become executed. The second limitation is that the principle of waiver of conditions on a repudiation required the promisee actually to have been prevented (in a loose sense of prevention discussed below) from completing the contract by acting on the renunciation. If the plaintiff did not act upon the renunciation then, in principle, there was **5.38**

[71] *Mackay v Dick* (1881) 6 App Cas 251, 264.

[72] *Peter Turnbull & Co Pty Ltd v Mundus Trading Co (Australasia) Pty Ltd* (1954) 90 CLR 235, 246–47.

[73] Ker and Butterworth (n 8) 564.

[74] *Sir Anthony Main's Case* (1596) 5 Co Rep 20b, 21a; 77 ER 80, 81. See also Langdell (n 5) 1083–84; Ker and Butterworth (n 8) 564.

nothing to preclude the defendant from relying upon any conditions of their obligation if the plaintiff failed to perform.

5.39 Finally, in terms of the applicability of this principle in the modern law, while the doctrine of anticipatory breach has certainly reduced the scope of its application (or rather the need for it), as will be seen, in certain cases the principle of waiver of conditions on a repudiation still has an important role to play. Suppose that in a contract for the sale of land, the seller intimates to the buyer that they will not perform the contract on the date for completion. The buyer neither 'accepts' the repudiation nor 'affirms' the contract, but simply waits to see whether the seller will change their mind.[75] The repudiation is never retracted, the day for performance comes, and neither party tenders performance. Can the buyer sue the seller for not performing the contract when they themselves (on account of the fact that it would be useless to do so) did not perform the concurrent condition of tendering the purchase price? Applying the principle to be discussed in this section, the answer is 'yes'.[76]

5.40 Unfortunately, it will be shown at the end of this section that, due to a series of cases that extended the rule beyond its proper limits, this principle has been rejected in the modern law, but curiously, only to be reintroduced under a 'quite new kind of estoppel'.[77]

Disablement

5.41 A number of early cases held that disablement by a promisor operated as a waiver of the conditions of the obligation that they were unable to perform.[78] These cases were forerunners to the modern doctrine of anticipatory breach.[79] One of the earliest is *Sir Anthony Main's Case*.[80] Sir Anthony Main leased land to Scott for twenty-one years, and covenanted that at any time during the life

[75] See further [5.85]–[5.97].

[76] *Peter Turnbull & Co Pty Ltd v Mundus Trading Co (Australasia) Pty Ltd* (1954) 90 CLR 235, 251.

[77] Mustill (n 2) 68.

[78] *Sir Anthony Main's Case* (1596) 5 Co Rep 20b, 77 ER 80; *Bowdell v Parsons* (1808) 10 East 359, 103 ER 811; *Amory v Brodrick* (1822) 5 B & Ald 712, 106 ER 1351; *Ford v Tiley* (1827) 6 B & C 325, 108 ER 472; *Short v Stone* (1846) 8 QB 358, 115 ER 911; *Lovelock v Franklyn* (1846) 8 QB 371, 115 ER 916; *Caines v Smith* (1847) 15 M & W 189, 153 ER 816; *Sands v Clarke* (1849) 8 C B 751, 137 ER 703. See Stephen Martin Leake and Alfred Randall, *Principles of the Law of Contracts* (4th edn, Stevens and Sons 1902) 469–70.

[79] See generally, Mustill (n 2) 14–26; Paul Mitchell, '*Hochster v De La Tour* (1853)' in Charles Mitchell and Paul Mitchell (eds), *Landmark Cases in the Law of Contract* (Hart Publishing 2008) 135, 136–39.

[80] (1596) 5 Co Rep 20b, 77 ER 80.

of Scott, upon surrender of his lease, Sir Anthony would make a new lease for Scott's life, and bound himself to perform those covenants by a bond. In an action by Scott on that bond, Sir Anthony pleaded that Scott had not surrendered the lease. Scott replied that Sir Anthony had granted an eighty-year lease of the land to a third party. On a demurrer to this plea, it was held that Sir Anthony had breached the covenant and that a surrender of the lease was unnecessary because it would be 'vain to compel [Scott] to make a surrender to [Sir Anthony]'[81] when he had disabled himself from performing.

This principle was applied in a number of cases where a request by the plaintiff was a condition precedent to the defendant's obligation. In such cases, typically the defendant had disabled themselves from performing an obligation but sought to rely upon the fact that no request had been made by the plaintiff as a defence to an action for damages. The courts, however, held that disablement by a defendant dispensed with the need to make a request.[82] In *Caines v Smith*,[83] Pollock CB said: 'If a man were under a contract to deliver certain goods to another, and he had put it out of his power to do so by destroying them, it could not be necessary to request him to deliver them.' These cases showed that the claimant was dispensed from performing a condition where to do so would be in vain—in other words, the defendant's self-disablement operated as a waiver of the condition. **5.42**

Renunciation

An extension of the prevention principle?

In a similar vein, it had long been held that a 'renunciation . . . by one party dispenses with a condition to be performed in the meantime'.[84] Historically, these cases were seen as an extension of the prevention principle,[85] which was discussed at [5.4]–[5.36] above. But as we shall see, the loose approach taken in these cases to 'prevention' suggests that the principle underlying these cases is not really about prevention at all, but rather, as in the previous sub-section, not requiring parties to act in vain. **5.43**

[81] ibid 21a; 81.

[82] *Bowdell v Parsons* (1808) 10 East 359, 103 ER 811; *Amory v Brodrick* (1822) 5 B & Ald 712, 106 ER 1351; *Short v Stone* (1846) 8 QB 358, 115 ER 911; *Caines v Smith* (1847) 15 M & W 189, 153 ER 816.

[83] (1847) 15 M & W 189, 190; 153 ER 816, 817.

[84] *Hochster v De La Tour* (1853) 2 El & Bl 678, 694; 118 ER 922, 927–28.

[85] See, eg, *Peter Turnbull & Co Pty Ltd v Mundus Trading Co (Australasia) Pty Ltd* (1954) 90 CLR 235, 246–47.

5.44 The leading case is *Jones v Barkley*.[86] The plaintiffs were the assignees in bankruptcy of Gardiner. Gardiner was entitled to the equity of redemption of £1,490 of bank stock that he had mortgaged to Lane. The defendant, Barkley, agreed that in consideration of the plaintiffs assigning the equity of redemption to Lane, as well as executing a general release of all claims that they had against Lane, the defendant would pay the sum of £611. In an action for damages for non-performance of the agreement, the plaintiffs alleged that while they had offered to assign the equity of redemption and to execute a general release (they had even shown the defendant a draft release), the defendant had 'discharged the plaintiffs'[87] from doing so by refusing to execute it and, despite being requested to do so, had refused to pay the sum of £611. The defendant sought to defend the claim on the basis that the plaintiffs had never in fact executed the assignment or a general release. The plaintiff demurred to these pleas.

5.45 The plaintiffs advanced two distinct arguments. The first argument was advanced on the assumption that the execution of the assignment and release was a condition precedent, and not simply a concurrent condition where an offer to execute the assignment would have been sufficient on its own.[88] The plaintiffs argued that even if the tender of the draft release had not satisfied the condition precedent, the defendant had 'made it good by waver [sic], having discharged the plaintiffs from doing anything further'.[89] Counsel for the plaintiffs argued that 'it is a general principle, that he who prevents a thing from being done, shall not avail himself of the non-performance which he has occasioned.'[90] As explained in more detail below, 'prevent' here was being used in a loose sense. It was enough to prevent the plaintiffs from performing that the defendant had intimated that the defendant did not intend to perform their part.[91]

5.46 The second argument advanced by the plaintiffs was an argument that would be more familiar to modern lawyers. That argument was 'that there [was] no condition precedent',[92] but rather a concurrent condition, and therefore 'absolute performance by the plaintiff[s] was not necessary' and it was only necessary to plead that they were 'ready to assign the stock, and grant the release'.[93]

[86] (1781) 2 Doug 684, 99 ER 434.
[87] ibid 685; 434.
[88] ibid 688; 436.
[89] ibid. The language of 'discharge' here was being used in a special sense simply to mean that the act of the defendant was the reason that the contract was not further performed by the plaintiff: *Cort v Ambergate Railway Co* (1851) 17 QB 127, 145–46; 117 ER 1229, 1236.
[90] *Jones v Barkley* (1781) 2 Doug 684, 686; 99 ER 434, 435.
[91] See, eg, ibid 694; 440.
[92] ibid 688; 436.
[93] ibid 691; 438.

5.47 The Court of King's Bench (Lord Mansfield, Willes, Ashhurst, and Buller JJ) ultimately found for the plaintiffs. But the judgments given were not explicit as to which argument they were accepting.[94] Lord Mansfield said:

> Take it on the reason of the thing. The party must shew he was ready; but, if the other stops him on the ground of an intention not to perform his part, it is not necessary for the first to go farther, and do a nugatory act.[95]

The result has been that the judgment has been interpreted as illustrative of both how concurrent conditions work[96] and how waiver works. Our focus here, however, is on the principle of waiver.

5.48 This principle of waiver was applied in two further cases concerned with actions for damages, both of which held that a renunciation, so long as it was not withdrawn, had the effect of waiving the conditions of the promisor's obligation to perform.[97] In *Ripley v M'Clure*,[98] the defendant agreed to buy one third of a cargo of tea from the plaintiff on the arrival of the vessel with the cargo in Belfast. Before the arrival of the vessel the defendant wholly refused to perform the agreement. This renunciation had remained unretracted, albeit that it was not accepted by the plaintiff. The Court of Exchequer (affirmed on appeal) held that the refusal to perform, unretracted at the time of performance, operated as a waiver of the conditions to the defendant's liability. Parke B said:

> By an express refusal to comply with the conditions of the contract of purchase, the defendant must be understood to have said to the plaintiff, 'You need not take the trouble to deliver the cargo to me, when it arrives at Belfast, as purchaser, for I never will become such;' and this would be a waiver, at that time, of the delivery, and, if unretracted, would dispense with the actual delivery after arrival.[99]

5.49 The decision in *Cort v Ambergate Railway Co*[100] also demonstrates this principle[101] as well as the loose sense in which 'prevention' was used. The plaintiffs agreed to supply chairs to be used in the construction of a railway by the

[94] Dawson (n 62) 91.
[95] *Jones v Barkley* (1781) 2 Doug 684, 694; 99 ER 434, 440.
[96] See, eg, JW Carter and C Hodgekiss, 'Conditions and Warranties: Forebears and Descendants' (1977) 8 Sydney Law Review 31, 34, and [2.13].
[97] Leake and Randall (n 78) 619.
[98] (1849) 4 Ex 345, 154 ER 1245; affirmed on appeal (1850) 5 Ex 140, 155 ER 60.
[99] *Ripley v M'Clure* (1849) 4 Ex 345, 359–60; 154 ER 1245, 1251.
[100] (1851) 17 QB 127, 117 ER 1229.
[101] Langdell (n 5) 1084.

defendants. The agreement provided for the construction of the chairs according to certain specifications and for their delivery from time to time, the price being payable on delivery. After a number of chairs had been delivered under the agreement, the defendants' engineer told the plaintiffs not to make any more as the defendants had all that they needed and would not take any more—this renunciation was never retracted.[102] The plaintiffs brought an action against the defendants (after the date on which the chairs ought to have been received) for wrongfully refusing to accept the residue of the chairs agreed to be supplied. The defendants, among other things, argued that the plaintiffs could not show that they were ready, willing, and able to carry out the contract because they 'had not offered to deliver, nor had ever made, the residue of the chairs'.[103] The defendants—with an eye to this principle of waiver—also argued that they had not prevented the plaintiffs from supplying the residue since there had been no physical obstruction.

5.50 The Court of Queen's Bench rejected both these arguments and held that by refusing to accept the residue of the goods the defendant had 'prevented and discharged the plaintiff from manufacturing and delivering them'.[104] As for the defendants' argument that they had not physically prevented performance, Lord Campbell CJ said:

> It is contended that 'prevent' here must mean an obstruction by physical force; and, in answer to a question from the Court, we were told it would not be a preventing of the delivery of goods if the purchaser were to write, in a letter to the person who ought to supply them, 'Should you come to my house to deliver them, I will blow your brains out.' But may I not reasonably say that I was prevented from completing a contract by being desired not to complete it? Are there no means of preventing an act from being done, except physical force or brute violence?[105]

5.51 *Cort v Ambergate* thus adopted the 'looser approach to prevention'[106] that had prevailed in *Jones v Barkley*. It will be recalled there that Lord Mansfield spoke of the defendant stopping the plaintiff 'on the ground of an intention not to perform his part'.[107] In light of this, it might be queried to what extent these cases were really about 'prevention' at all. As Professor Paul Mitchell observed

[102] *Cort v Ambergate Railway Co* (1851) 17 QB 127, 148; 117 ER 1229, 1237.
[103] ibid 134; 1232.
[104] ibid 148; 1237.
[105] ibid 145; 1236.
[106] Mitchell (n 79) 142. See also 143.
[107] *Jones v Barkley* (1781) 2 Doug 684, 694; 99 ER 434, 440.

in relation to *Jones v Barkley*, '[t]his was not really prevention; rather, it was a good reason for the claimant to be excused from further performance'.[108] And when understood in this way, the underlying idea is the same as that underlying waiver of conditions following self-disablement: if a promisor indicates that they do not intend to perform, the law does not require the promisee to act in vain and perform the condition to the promisor's obligation. As Professor Christopher Columbus Langdell once said, 'the former cannot complain that the latter takes him at his word'.[109] The repudiating party would thus be held to have waived the condition.

The rule in *Laird v Pim* and the limits of waiver

The principle that a renunciation by a promisor, while unretracted, operated as a waiver of the conditions to the promisor's obligation was, however, qualified in its operation. An important limitation is that a condition cannot be waived for the purpose of an action for the price if the performance of the condition is the consideration for the promise it qualifies.[110] As this section argues, this is a result of the decision in *Laird v Pim*,[111] the effect of which is that no action for the price can be brought unless the consideration has become executed. **5.52**

The prospect of this limitation first arose due to the uncertainty surrounding the scope of *Jones v Barkley*.[112] Although *Jones v Barkley* was an action for damages, at trial the plaintiffs were awarded £611—the same amount as the price the defendant was to pay.[113] While all the cases discussed above were concerned with actions for damages, the question would soon arise as to whether this principle of waiver permitted a claimant to recover the price from the defendant, even if the consideration for the promise to pay had never been executed.[114] **5.53**

The question was considered in *Smith v Wilson*[115] in an action for the freight alleged to be due on a charterparty. The plaintiff had agreed to take the defendant's goods and deliver them to Monte Video and afterwards proceed back to Great Britain. The ship was, however, seized by persons unknown off **5.54**

[108] Mitchell (n 79) 142. Although cf Dawson (n 62) 96–97.
[109] Langdell (n 5) 1083–84.
[110] See text in n 5.
[111] (1841) 7 M & W 474, 151 ER 852.
[112] Mitchell (n 79) 144.
[113] For completeness, it is worth noting that the judgment given at trial was later nonsuited, for the agreement fell afoul of the Bankrupts Act 1731 (5 Geo 2 c 30), s 11: *Jones v Barkley* (1781) 2 Doug 684, 698; 99 ER 434, 444–45.
[114] Mitchell (n 79) 144.
[115] (1807) 8 East 437, 103 ER 410.

the coast of Africa. After a long time the ship was released back to the plaintiff, who repaired the ship and sought instructions. The defendant, however, refused to give any instructions in respect of the voyage and renounced their obligations under the charterparty. The plaintiff alleged that this 'discharged'[116] him from the further prosecution of the voyage and that he was therefore entitled to the freight. The Court of King's Bench rejected this argument and gave judgment for the defendant.

5.55 Lord Ellenborough CJ noted that the 'arrival and discharge at her destined port in Great Britain' was 'a condition precedent to the plaintiff's right to demand the [freight]'.[117] But the plaintiff relied on *Jones v Barkley* to argue 'that the plaintiff had acquired the right to the sums demanded as freight [etc], as completely as if the voyage had been performed'.[118] The Lord Chief Justice, however, distinguished *Jones v Barkley*. He said that in that case 'no contingency but the immediate death of the party tendering the act could have disappointed its performance' and that the party doing the act 'would have instantly acquired, without any further act . . . a full right by the terms of his contract to the duty demanded; which in that case was the payment . . . of a sum of money'.[119] In contrast, in the present case, 'if he had done all that he offered to do, and which the defendant discharged him from performing, still it would have amounted at most only to an endeavour on his part to prosecute and complete the voyage'.[120]

5.56 Lord Ellenborough CJ's reasons for distinguishing *Jones v Barkley* were not 'completely convincing'.[121] After all, the difference between the two cases appears to be a difference in degree, not a difference in kind. But regardless of whether it was a convincing basis upon which to distinguish *Jones v Barkley*, the decision in *Smith v Wilson* was an attempt to constrain the scope of the principle in *Jones v Barkley* so as to avoid permitting a party to recover the contract price in circumstances where the consideration for the promise to pay had remained unexecuted.

5.57 As stated above, however, the decision that is responsible for this limitation is *Laird v Pim*.[122] There is a certain irony in this because the case itself was

[116] In the sense referred to in n 89.
[117] *Smith v Wilson* (1807) 8 East 437, 442–43; 103 ER 410, 413.
[118] ibid 443; 413.
[119] ibid 444; 413.
[120] ibid 443–44; 413.
[121] Mitchell (n 79) 144.
[122] (1841) 7 M & W 474, 151 ER 852. In addition to the discussion below, see generally, Dawson (n 62) 93–96.

concerned with an action for damages. The plaintiff had agreed to sell to the defendants title to a parcel of land. The plaintiff alleged that he had offered to execute a conveyance and would have tendered a conveyance but the defendants had refused to proceed and, despite entering into possession, they 'did not nor would pay the plaintiff the said purchase-money'.[123] The plaintiff claimed as damages the full amount of the purchase money (£4,125) and interest thereon. The defendants pleaded that no conveyance had ever been made or executed, which they alleged was a condition precedent.[124] They argued therefore that they were under no immediate duty to pay the purchase price and that it could not be recovered as damages while the plaintiff still held title to the land. They also demurred generally to the plaintiff's claim.

At trial, Rolfe B held that the plaintiff could not recover the whole purchase price as damages and could only recover such damages as resulted from the breach, namely, £680 for interest on the purchase money and £70 for the value of brick clay that the defendants had taken from the plaintiff's land. The plaintiff then argued before the Court of Exchequer (Parke, Alderson, Gurney, and Rolfe BB) that the damages award should be increased by the amount of the purchase money on the basis that the plaintiff was entitled to the price. The Court rejected this argument. Parke B said: **5.58**

> The question is, how much worse is the plaintiff by . . . the loss of the purchase-money, in consequence of the non-performance of the contract? It is clear he cannot have the land and its value too. A party cannot recover the full value of a chattel, unless under circumstances which import that the property has passed to the defendant, as in the case of goods sold and delivered, where they have been absolutely parted with, and cannot be sold again.[125]

The second issue—whether the pleadings disclosed a cause of action at all—then arose upon the general demurrer. Here, the main question was the precise breach alleged by the plaintiff on the pleadings, and whether this entitled the plaintiff to succeed. The breach alleged was simply that the defendants 'did not nor would pay the plaintiff the said purchase-money'.[126] The defendants argued that if the breach assigned was non-payment of the purchase money—as opposed to, for example, a refusal to execute the conveyance—then they were not liable, for '[a] tender of the conveyance is not sufficient; it must be executed **5.59**

[123] *Laird v Pim* (1841) 7 M & W 474, 475; 151 ER 852, 853.
[124] No argument appears to have been made that tendering of the conveyance was a concurrent condition.
[125] *Laird v Pim* (1841) 7 M & W 474, 478; 151 ER 852, 854.
[126] ibid 475; 853.

before payment can be enforced'.[127] The plaintiff argued that '[t]he execution of a conveyance [was] not a condition precedent to the plaintiff's recovering in this action, and if it were, it ha[d] been waived by the defendants'.[128]

5.60 The Court found in favour of the plaintiff on this issue. Lord Abinger CB said that the breach was 'informally alleged' but 'the objection, as it arises on general demurrer, cannot prevail'.[129] On the issue of waiver, the Chief Baron added that 'the case of *Jones v Barkley* appears to be an express authority, and must govern the present case'.[130] Parke B expressed some doubt, but ultimately arrived at the same conclusion. He said:

> This declaration is certainly informally drawn, but I think it is sufficient on general demurrer, upon the principle laid down in *Jones v Barkley*. Upon the facts alleged in this declaration, the plaintiff is substantially in the same situation, for the purpose of recovering the money, as if all had been done on his part which he engaged to do. It does not follow that he shall recover the whole purchase-money, but he is in the same situation for the purpose of recovering damages for the non-payment of the price, as if all had been done by him.[131]

5.61 Although *Laird v Pim* was only an action for damages, it was axiomatic that Parke B's statements of principle must also apply to an action for the price itself (ie an action for the agreed sum). For if they did not apply to an action for the price, then there would be nothing to prevent a vendor from bringing an action for the price against the buyer, on the basis that the conditions to the obligation to pay had been waived, while also selling the title to the land to a third party. In other words, if these statements of principle did not apply to an action for the price, a vendor could obtain both the agreed sum from the buyer and substitute performance from a third party. The vendor would thus find themselves in a far better position than contractual performance ever could have produced—the vendor could have their cake and eat it too.[132] Consequently, since *Laird Pim*, the position has been 'that the price is only payable in return for an executed

[127] ibid 481; 855.
[128] ibid 478–79; 854.
[129] ibid 484; 856. A general demurrer takes the pleadings as generally sufficient but objects on a 'matter of *substance*'. A special demurrer objects to a 'matter of *form* only': Henry John Stephen, *A Treatise on the Principles of Pleading in Civil Actions* (Butterworth and Son 1824) 159 (emphasis in original).
[130] *Laird v Pim* (1841) 7 M & W 474, 484; 151 ER 852, 856.
[131] ibid 485; 857.
[132] A similar question might have arisen in *White and Carter (Councils) Ltd v McGregor* [1962] AC 413 had White and Carter (Councils) Ltd not actually gone ahead and performed by displaying the advertisements for the next three years and instead sought to claim the *price* while performing for a third party.

consideration'.[133] This is the 'rule . . . in *Laird v Pim*',[134] and it is now found in all kinds of contracts, not just contracts for the sale of title to land.[135]

The result of the rule in *Laird v Pim* is that there is an important limitation on waiver of conditions, namely, that a condition cannot be waived for the purpose of an action for the price if the performance of that condition is the consideration for the promise it qualifies. This is because, in such cases, to permit the promisee to recover on the principle of waiver of conditions on a repudiation, despite not fulfilling the condition, 'would be to permit him to keep the *quid pro quo*, and yet recover payment for it'.[136] And this is the very thing the rule in *Laird v Pim* prohibits. **5.62**

Importantly, this does not prevent the condition being waived for the purpose of an action for damages, albeit that consistently with Parke B's approach, the damages would be calculated taking into account the fact that the plaintiff has not had to provide the consideration. As Kitto J said in the High Court of Australia decision in *Peter Turnbull & Co Pty Ltd v Mundus Trading Co (Australasia) Pty Ltd*,[137] when discussing *Laird v Pim*: **5.63**

> [W]hat the defendants did by dispensing with the tender of a conveyance was not to make the price payable independently of such tender . . . but to entitle the plaintiff to treat their refusal to complete the purchase as a refusal after tender of a conveyance, *for the purpose only of recovering such damages* as the plaintiff had sustained by not getting the price in exchange for a conveyance.[138]

That is why in *Laird v Pim*, Parke B said that the vendor 'is in the same situation for the purpose of recovering damages for the non-payment of the price, as if all had been done by him'.[139]

The limited scope of the principle

While the limitation discussed in the previous sub-section related to the conditions that can be waived, the limitation discussed in this sub-section relates to the 'scope of the principle' of waiver of conditions on a repudiation.[140] In **5.64**

[133] Francis Dawson, 'Waiver of Conditions Precedent on a Repudiation' (1980) 96 Law Quarterly Review 239, 243 fn 25. See also Dawson (n 62) 95; *Colley v Overseas Exporters* [1921] 3 KB 302, 311.
[134] *Guardians of the East London Union v The Metropolitan Railway Co* (1869) LR 4 Ex 309, 310.
[135] *Colley v Overseas Exporters* [1921] 3 KB 302, 311. See the Sale of Goods Act 1979, s 49(1).
[136] Langdell (n 5) 1087.
[137] (1954) 90 CLR 235.
[138] ibid 253 (emphasis added). See also 252.
[139] *Laird v Pim* (1841) 7 M & W 474, 485; 151 ER 852, 857. cf the criticism of this view in Dawson (n 62) 94–95. Space does not permit a detailed discussion of the issue here.
[140] Dawson (n 133) 244.

particular, in this section we explore the problem caused by 'the notorious trio of cases':[141] *Braithwaite v Foreign Hardwood Co*,[142] *Taylor v Oakes, Roncoroni & Co*,[143] and *British and Beningtons Ltd v North Western Cachar Tea Co Ltd*.[144]

5.65 The difficulties have arisen due to the failure to appreciate that the old cases, which said that a renunciation operates as a waiver of the conditions of the renunciating party's obligation, gave the principle of waiver of conditions on a repudiation a limited scope.[145] As was demonstrated above, on one view, the earlier cases saw a renunciation by one party as preventing the other party from performing their side of the bargain. The principle of waiver therefore required the promisee actually to have been prevented (albeit in a loose sense) from completing the contract by acting on the renunciation.[146] Similarly, on the approach that this principle is simply recognition that the law does not require the promisee to act in vain and tender a useless performance:

> A waiver of a condition precedent arising from the defendant's repudiation did not entirely relieve the plaintiff from showing that he was ready and willing; the plaintiff was dispensed from the need to do that which the defendant had indicated would be pointless.[147]

5.66 The limited scope of the principle had two consequences. First, as Lord Campbell CJ said in *Cort v Ambergate*,[148] it meant that a plaintiff seeking to justify their non-performance of a condition on account of the defendant's renunciation had to show 'that the noncompletion of the contract was not the fault of the plaintiffs, and that they were disposed and able to complete it if it had not been renounced by the defendants.' The language of 'fault' here should not be taken to connote moral blameworthiness, but rather that the cause of the plaintiff not performing the condition was the defendant's renunciation and not some other factor.

5.67 Secondly, it meant that if a plaintiff did not rely upon the repudiation, and chose to tender performance in any event, they would not be absolved from complying with the conditions to the defendant's obligation for the purpose

[141] Mustill (n 2) 65. See generally, Bridge (n 19) 505–13 [9-012]–[9-019]; Ewan McKendrick, *Goode and McKendrick on Commercial Law* (6th edn, Penguin 2020) 472–75.
[142] [1905] 2 KB 543.
[143] (1922) 127 LT 267.
[144] [1923] AC 48.
[145] Dawson (n 133) 244.
[146] *Peter Turnbull & Co Pty Ltd v Mundus Trading Co (Australasia) Pty Ltd* (1954) 90 CLR 235, 247.
[147] *Foran v Wight* (1989) 168 CLR 385, 398 (Mason CJ), citing Dawson (n 133) 244–45.
[148] (1851) 17 QB 127, 144; 117 ER 1229, 1236. See also Dawson (n 133) 247.

of an actual tender of performance—the waiver only operated to the extent that the plaintiff acted upon the renunciation by not completing. If the plaintiff chose to perform in any event, but failed to comply with some condition to the defendant's obligation, there was nothing preventing the defendant from relying on the condition for the purpose of refusing a performance actually tendered. In such a case, the cause of the non-compliance with the condition was simply the plaintiff's defective performance.

However, in the trio of cases discussed below, these limitations were either not applied or confused, the result of which was to push the principle of waiver of conditions on a repudiation far beyond its proper limit. It was this expansion of the principle which ultimately led to its abandonment in the House of Lords decision in *Fercometal SARL v Mediterranean Shipping Co SA (The Simona)*.[149] **5.68**

The first decision in this trio is *Braithwaite's Case*.[150] The plaintiff seller made a contract with the defendant buyers for the sale of 100 tons of Honduras rosewood by instalments, cash being payable on presentation of a bill of lading. The buyers subsequently wrote to the seller's agent renouncing their liability under the contract and refusing to accept any wood under it. The ground on which they did so, as it turned out at trial, was insufficient. At the time the letter was received, the first shipment was already on its way. The seller's agents informed the buyers that they were ready to hand over the bill of lading,[151] but the buyers persisted in their refusal. The seller then sold the goods elsewhere. A second shipment was similarly refused by the buyers and sold elsewhere by the seller. **5.69**

The seller claimed damages for non-acceptance of the goods. The buyers sought to resist the claim in respect of the first shipment on the basis that the seller had not fulfilled the conditions on his part because—as they had discovered sometime later—a portion of the rosewood onboard the first shipment did not answer the description of quality in the contract, and therefore the buyers were entitled to reject the goods.[152] The Court of Appeal (Collins MR, Mathew, and Cozens-Hardy LJJ) found for the seller and held that the buyers' **5.70**

[149] *Fercometal SARL v Mediterranean Shipping Co SA (The Simona)* [1989] AC 788.

[150] *Braithwaite v Foreign Hardwood Co* [1905] 2 KB 543.

[151] There is an ambiguity as to whether the plaintiff's agents actually tendered the bill of lading or merely offered to tender it. The headnote appears to say the former, while Collins MR says the latter: see ibid 549. cf *Taylor v Oakes, Roncoroni & Co* (1922) 127 LT 267, 269 (Greer J) and 270–71 (Bankes LJ) with 271 (Scrutton LJ) and 272 (Atkin LJ).

[152] *Braithwaite v Foreign Hardwood Co* [1905] 2 KB 543, 546–47.

repudiation had operated to waive the condition that the plaintiff tender a conforming shipment. The buyers were therefore liable for breach.[153]

5.71 As for the measure of damages, the primary judge had allowed a reduction in damages in respect of the inferior quality. While not setting aside this order, Collins MR said:

> Logically, the damages should, I think, have been assessed upon the footing that the wood which the plaintiff was excused from delivering was up to the standard stipulated for in the contract, though it turns out that it in fact fell slightly short of the monetary value of wood quite up to that standard . . .[154]

5.72 The second decision in the trio is *Taylor v Oakes, Roncoroni and Co.*[155] Under two separate contracts the sellers agreed to sell to the buyers certain quantities of Scotch fur, deliveries to be made in monthly instalments. After certain deliveries had been made and accepted, the buyers stopped taking delivery of the goods and refused to accept further instalments. The buyers did not have any good reason for this at the time and did not offer any ground as justification. The sellers brought an action for damages and after the action had commenced, the buyers became aware that the goods that had been delivered did not comply with the contract description. They thereafter sought to rely upon this in their defence to the action.

5.73 Greer J found that the goods delivered had in fact failed to comply with the contract description in a way that would have entitled the buyers to reject. However, by accepting and paying for the goods, they were precluded from returning them (ie they had waived the condition) and were limited to an action for damages. Moreover, they were not entitled to support their repudiation in respect of the balance on the ground that 'the plaintiffs would in all probability, indeed as a practical certainty, have tendered goods which the defendants would, if they so chose, have been justified in refusing to accept'.[156] And for this latter conclusion, Greer J applied *Braithwaite's Case*. This conclusion was upheld in the Court of Appeal (Bankes, Scrutton, and Atkin LJJ).

5.74 The third and final decision is *British and Beningtons Ltd v North Western Cachar Tea Co Ltd.*[157] Pursuant to three separate contracts, the appellant buyers agreed to buy crops of tea from the respondents (three firms of tea

[153] ibid 551.
[154] ibid 552.
[155] (1922) 127 LT 267.
[156] ibid 269.
[157] [1923] AC 48.

growers in India). Delivery was to be made to a warehouse in London. In early 1920, ships carrying consignments of tea under the contracts had arrived in London but, due to congestion at that port, they were diverted to other ports throughout England and Scotland resulting in delay. In July 1920, the buyers renounced their obligation to accept the tea on the ground of delay but this reason was found at arbitration to be insufficient. The buyers were ordered to pay damages. On appeal before the House of Lords, the buyers argued that the contract required delivery in London and that due to the congestion the sellers were never ready and willing to deliver in London. The House of Lords found in favour of the sellers. Lord Atkinson held, applying *Braithwaite's Case*,[158] that the buyers' wrongful repudiation had dispensed with the need for the sellers to be ready, willing, and able, to deliver the tea in London.

Lord Sumner, who agreed in the result, rejected the suggestion that *Braithwaite's Case* had decided that 'when there has been a repudiation by one party on a given ground, and an acceptance of that repudiation by the other party, the former can no longer rely on any other ground for refusing to perform his obligations'.[159] He said 'the case as reported either does not lay down this proposition or, if it does so, is wrong'.[160] In particular, Lord Sumner said: **5.75**

> I do not see how the fact, that the buyers have wrongly said 'we treat this contract as being at an end, owing to your unreasonable delay in performance of it' obliges them, when that reason fails, to pay in full, if, at the very time of this repudiation, the sellers had become wholly and finally disabled from performing essential terms of the contract altogether. *Braithwaite's Case* says nothing, which affects the regular consequences, when it appears that at the time of breach the plaintiff is already disabled from doing his part at all.[161]

Ultimately, Lord Sumner did not think that this was a case of that kind (ie one of disablement). In particular, it had not been found that the sellers 'could not have forwarded the tea to London, or that the tea, when so forwarded, would not have been still such as the contract provided for'.[162] Lord Sumner's speech cast some doubt on *Braithwaite's Case*, but it did not appear to have overruled it.[163] **5.76**

[158] ibid 64–66.
[159] ibid 70.
[160] ibid.
[161] ibid 72.
[162] ibid.
[163] *Continental Contractors Ltd v Medway Oil & Storage Co Ltd* (1925) 23 Ll LR 124, 132.

5.77 Prior to being 'overshadowed'[164] by *The Simona*,[165] these three cases appeared to establish the following propositions:

(1) a repudiation by a defendant 'completely absolve[d]'[166] the plaintiff of the need to comply with the conditions to the defendant's obligation or to 'show any readiness and willingness to perform at all';[167]
(2) consequently, a defendant who repudiated for a bad reason was precluded from 'subsequently justifying the repudiation by showing that had the contract run its course a discharging breach would inevitably have occurred';[168] and
(3) as per the obiter statement of Collins MR in *Braithwaite's Case*, damages were to be assessed as if all the conditions to the defendant's obligation to perform in fact had been fulfilled.[169]

5.78 Each of these propositions was inaccurate. To take the first proposition, for the reasons discussed above, the scope of the principle of waiver of conditions on a repudiation was limited. It did not mean that the repudiating party waived the right to rely upon the condition for all purposes. The waiver was only operative insofar as the non-completion of the contract was the 'fault' of the repudiating party—ie because it had been acted on by the innocent party in circumstances where they otherwise would have been able to perform.

5.79 The second proposition—subject to one qualification below—was always doubtful, as the speech of Lord Sumner in *British and Beningtons* showed. In particular, if at the date of a purported repudiation, the other party had become wholly and finally disabled from performing the contract, then the repudiation was not wrongful because the 'repudiating' party was already discharged on account of the other's disability. This is the doctrine of anticipatory breach and the law in this respect was set out clearly in *Universal Cargo Carriers Corp v Citati*.[170] The waiver of conditions on a repudiation principle did not apply in such a case because, in the language of the old cases, the non-completion of the contract was not the 'fault' of the repudiating party—it was the 'fault' of (in the sense of 'caused by') the party who had disabled themselves from performance.

[164] Mustill (n 2) 65.
[165] *The Simona* [1989] AC 788.
[166] Dawson (n 133) 243.
[167] ibid.
[168] ibid.
[169] See also *Continental Contractors Ltd v Medway Oil & Storage Co Ltd* (1925) 23 Ll LR 124, 132–33 (Scrutton LJ).
[170] [1957] 2 QB 401, 445–46.

However, it is necessary to distinguish between two situations: **5.80**

(1) where the plaintiff was, at the time of the defendant's repudiation, wholly and finally disabled from performing; and
(2) where the plaintiff was not wholly and finally disabled from performing, but it can be shown that, but for the repudiation, they would in fact have tendered a defective performance.[171]

The difficulty arises because the line between the two can become blurred, as in the case where the non-conforming goods have already been shipped.[172] The doctrine of anticipatory breach applies only to the former. But in cases of the latter, it appears that the waiver of conditions on a repudiation principle might still operate so as to dispense the innocent party from the need to comply with any conditions. This would be subject to an argument of the kind that we saw in the previous section in relation to the principle of waiver of conditions by prevention of fulfilment—namely, that there is a requirement of causation and if not satisfied, the innocent party cannot rely upon the principle of waiver.[173]

Finally, the third proposition—that damages were to be assessed as if all the conditions to the defendant's obligation to perform had been fulfilled—appears to have flowed from a misunderstanding about the nature of waiver. If true, it would lead to the consequence, as Professor Francis Dawson noted, that: **5.81**

> if one party agrees to sell a quantity of cheese and it can be proved that he would only have tendered chalk, he recovers damages as if the chalk were cheese, if prior to the time for performance the other party is unfortunate enough to have repudiated and the seller alert enough to accept the repudiation.[174]

This is to attempt to introduce the fiction of fulfilment by the back door (and in circumstances where it is doubtful that even those systems that recognise the doctrine would seek to apply it). It has already been explained that English law should not recognise the doctrine of fictional fulfilment of conditions.[175] And the principle of waiver of conditions does not require a court to treat **5.82**

[171] In *Taylor v Oakes, Roncoroni & Co* (1922) 127 LT 267, 268–69, for example, Greer J at first instance said on the one hand that the 'the plaintiffs would in all probability, indeed as a practical certainty, have tendered goods which the defendants would … have been justified in refusing to accept', but on the other hand, that it was not clear 'that if the defendants had asked for a better compliance with the contracts, the plaintiffs might not have been able to improve' so as to comply.

[172] See, eg, *Braithwaite v Foreign Hardwood Co* [1905] 2 KB 543.

[173] See [5.28].

[174] Dawson (n 133) 243.

[175] See [5.22]–[5.36].

the condition as if it had been fulfilled; it only precludes the defendant from relying upon the condition as an answer to the action. If the defendant can show that the plaintiff would not in fact have performed at the due date, there is nothing in this principle of waiver that precludes this from being taken into account in the assessment of damages.

5.83 A case which is sometimes cited to support the result that damages should be assessed as if all relevant conditions and obligations had been fulfilled, even if this would not in fact have occurred, is the decision of the House of Lords in *Berger & Co Inc v Gill & Duffus SA*.[176] In that case the House of Lords held that the buyers' refusal to pay the contract price upon the presentation of conforming shipping documents was a repudiation which could not be justified by the fact that the goods still to be delivered under the contract would not have conformed to the contract description, thus justifying rejection. Insofar as the question of breach is concerned, this is undoubtedly right. This is because, as Lord Diplock explained, if a buyer were entitled to reject conforming shipping documents where it '*subsequently* turn[s] out that the actual goods shipped under the conforming documents did not in fact conform to the contract . . . [it] would destroy the very roots of the system by which international trade, particularly in commodities, is enabled to be financed'.[177]

5.84 But certain comments made by Lord Diplock in obiter appeared to suggest that when calculating damages, the quantum of liability would not be reduced on account of the fact that the goods which were yet to be delivered would not have conformed to the contract description, thus justifying a rejection.[178] But following the decision of the House of Lords in *The Golden Victory*[179] and the decision of Teare J in *Flame SA v Glory Wealth Shipping Pte Ltd*,[180] this appears to no longer be the position (and rightly so).[181] The assessment of damages will take into account what would, in fact, have occurred but for the breach.

The demise of waiver and the rise of promissory estoppel

5.85 The final decision that needs to be considered in this section is *The Simona*.[182] This decision is important for its interpretation of *Braithwaite's Case*, but also

[176] [1984] AC 382.
[177] ibid 392 (emphasis in original).
[178] See the discussion in *Flame SA v Glory Wealth Shipping Pte Ltd* [2014] QB 1080, 1098–100 [55]–[62].
[179] [2007] 2 AC 353.
[180] [2014] QB 1080.
[181] cf Edwin Peel, 'Desideratum or Principle: The "Compensatory Principle" Revisited' (2015) 131 Law Quarterly Review 29.
[182] *The Simona* [1989] AC 788.

for what it held about the nature of the principle of waiver of conditions on a repudiation. Continuing with what is now a familiar theme, the House of Lords appears to have subsumed the principle within promissory estoppel. But, for the reasons given below, the integration is not altogether satisfactory.

The Simona concerned a charterparty for the carriage of a cargo of steel. Clause 10 provided that if the vessel should not be ready to load on or before 9 July 1982, the charterers were to have the option of cancelling the charterparty. On 2 July, the owners requested an extension of the cancellation date. The charterers refused to grant this extension and purported to cancel the charterparty. It was common ground that this was premature and amounted to a repudiation. This repudiation, however, was not accepted by the owners who had, on 5 July, tendered a notice of readiness to load. That notice was, however, false as the vessel was not ready to load and indeed was still not ready by 9 July due to the owners' decision to load other cargo first. On 12 July, the charterers sent a further cancellation notice on the ground that the vessel was not ready to load. **5.86**

The owners claimed dead freight from the charterers. Relying on *Braithwaite's Case*, the owners argued that the non-readiness of the vessel was a condition precedent to the exercise by the charterers of the option to cancel but that the charterers, by their repudiation, had excused the owners from serving any notices or having the vessel ready to load.[183] In essence, the argument was that the charterers had lost their right to rely upon the condition as enlivening the power to cancel as a result of their prior unaccepted repudiation. **5.87**

The House of Lords held that the charterers had not lost the power to cancel the contract as a result of the prior unaccepted repudiation.[184] Lord Ackner said: **5.88**

> [T]he decision in *Braithwaite* . . . is not an authority for the proposition advanced by the appellants, alternatively if it is, then it is wrong. When A wrongfully repudiates his contractual obligations in anticipation of the time for their performance, he presents the innocent party B with two choices. He may either affirm the contract by treating it as still in force or he may treat it as finally and conclusively discharged. There is no third choice, as a sort of via media, to affirm the contract and yet to be absolved from tendering further performance unless and until A gives reasonable notice that he is once again able and willing to perform.[185]

[183] ibid 791.
[184] ibid 801.
[185] ibid 805.

5.89 At the outset, it should be said that the result in the case is clearly correct. The principle of waiver of conditions on a repudiation, for the reasons given earlier, only operates to the extent that the non-repudiating party acts upon the repudiation by not performing. It does not preclude the repudiating party from relying upon any conditions to their obligations—or in this case, from relying upon any conditions to the exercise of a power—if the non-repudiating party chooses to ignore the renunciation and persist with performance. In *The Simona* it could not be said that the non-completion of the contract was the fault of the charterers in the sense that it was caused by their repudiation. As Lord Ackner said: '[t]he non-readiness of the vessel by the cancelling date was in no way induced by the charterers' conduct. It was the result of the owners['] decision to load other cargo first.'[186]

5.90 But in reaching this decision, Lord Ackner appears to have lost sight of the original principle and, in an attempt to explain the absolving effects of an unaccepted repudiation, he rejected waiver of conditions only to reintroduce promissory estoppel to reach the same result. In particular, the question arose as to what would have happened if, despite not having accepted the repudiation, the owners had, due to the continuing renunciation of the charterers, abstained from presenting the vessel in time? While correctly stating that this was not what had occurred in this case, Lord Ackner said:

> Of course, it is always open to A . . . to contend that in relation to a particular right or obligation under the contract, B is estopped . . . If B represents to A that he no longer intends to exercise that right or requires that obligation to be fulfilled by A and A acts upon that representation, then clearly B cannot be heard thereafter to say that he is entitled to exercise that right or that A is in breach of contract by not fulfilling that obligation.[187]

5.91 The result of this passage appears to be that where one party 'refuses to accept'[188] the other's repudiation then even if the repudiating party persists in his repudiation, the repudiating party does not waive the conditions to their obligation.[189] However, according to Lord Ackner, it may be possible to establish a promissory estoppel.

5.92 What is not clear is the precise scope of this estoppel. Lord Ackner appears to have required a representation by the repudiating party that they would

[186] ibid 806.
[187] ibid 805.
[188] An 'ambiguous expression': see JW Carter, 'Discharge as the Basis for Termination for Breach of Contract' (2012) 128 Law Quarterly Review 283, 301.
[189] Bridge (n 19) 511–13 [9-018]–[9-019].

not seek to rely upon their rights if the non-repudiating party chose not to perform—this gives the estoppel a narrow scope. In the decision of the High Court of Australia in *Foran v Wight*,[190] Brennan J expressed the scope of the estoppel differently, requiring only 'an intimation by one party that tender of performance by the other will be nugatory'.[191] The difference in opinion appears to be in relation to the 'ease with which the requirements of representation and reliance may be satisfied in order to give rise to an estoppel'.[192]

Neither approach is wholly satisfactory. Lord Ackner's approach appears to be too narrow in requiring a representation that the non-repudiating party need not perform and not merely that it would be useless for them to do so. Take the case of a contract for the sale of title to land where in the face of a repudiation prior to completion, the non-repudiating party chooses not to tender a useless performance on the date for completion (without necessarily accepting the repudiation). These are, shorn of complications, the facts of *Foran v Wight*.[193] On Lord Ackner's approach it would be necessary to find that '[a] statement in the form "I refuse [to] perform" is impliedly a statement "You are not required to perform"'.[194] But as Professor John Carter has observed, '[t]hat is simply fiction upon fiction. It uses a fiction (the estoppel) which is based on a fictional characterisation of the promisor's conduct.'[195] So either the approach is too narrow, or it is completely fictional. **5.93**

The approach of Brennan J appears to fare better by requiring simply 'an intimation by A that he does not intend to perform which conveys to B that performance by him would be nugatory'.[196] But while it reaches a result that is consonant with the understanding of this principle of waiver as it developed, it would appear to be inconsistent with the requirements of the modern doctrine of promissory estoppel. In particular, there appears to be no necessity for A to represent or promise to B that A will not insist upon their strict legal rights. Indeed, there is not even a need for a representation that B need not perform. Instead, it is enough that A intimates that *A* does not intend to perform irrespective of what B may do. Lord Mustill, writing extra-judicially, described it as 'a quite new kind of estoppel'.[197] **5.94**

[190] (1989) 168 CLR 385.
[191] ibid 421.
[192] Bridge (n 19) 513 [9-019].
[193] (1989) 168 CLR 385.
[194] Carter (n 188) 301.
[195] ibid.
[196] *Foran v Wight* (1989) 168 CLR 385, 422.
[197] Mustill (n 2) 68.

5.95 There is simply no need to invoke promissory estoppel. The principle of waiver of conditions on a repudiation, properly understood, could deal with this situation perfectly well. It was only the misunderstanding of that principle that led to undesirable results and ultimately to a confusion of thought. The approach of Lord Ackner is ahistorical and appears to have lost sight of the fact that the principle of waiver never depended upon a representation of the kind ordinarily necessary to found an estoppel. If the principle of waiver of conditions on a repudiation is to be treated as a case of promissory estoppel, it needs to be accepted that an estoppel can sometimes be made out without any representation that one party will not insist upon their strict legal rights—it is enough to state 'I will not perform'. But this is then a very different kind of estoppel.

5.96 The more serious problem is when all of this history is completely forgotten. In *Diab v Regent Insurance Co Ltd*,[198] the claimant had insured commercial premises against the risk of fire damage. The premises were subsequently destroyed by fire. At an initial meeting with the insurer, the insurer repudiated their liability under the policy because they believed that any claim made would be fraudulent (on the basis of a belief that the fire was deliberately lit). The question for the Privy Council was whether, as the claimant argued, this repudiation of liability by the insurer relieved the claimant from the necessity of complying with a condition precedent to give the insurer written particulars of a claim within fifteen days of the loss or damage occurring. The insured had not done so because of the insurer's repudiation of liability and intimation that they would consider any such claim to be fraudulent.

5.97 The Privy Council appears not to have been referred to any of the cases discussed in this section and instead was taken only to decisions from the United States and Canada that appeared to lay down a rule that a repudiation of liability by an insurer relieves the insured of having to comply with conditions precedent regarding the submission of a formal claim, such as providing written notice.[199] The Board then stated that any such rule formed no part of the law of the United Kingdom.[200] However, their Lordships then went on to note that the possibility of waiver by election. They said:

> It may be, however, that the circumstances in which the repudiation has taken place and the repudiatory words in question justify the inference of a

[198] [2007] 1 WLR 797.
[199] ibid 805 [24].
[200] ibid.

waiver by the insurer of its right to insist on compliance by the insured with the contractual provisions in question.[201]

But this claim was rejected because there was nothing that had been said in the meeting that could be construed as a statement that the insured need not comply with the condition before pursuing a claim under the policy.[202] A claim for estoppel was said to 'founder[] on the same rock': there was no representation that the insurer 'would not hold him to the conditions of the policy'.[203] No reference was made to *The Simona*, but the approach of the Privy Council is consistent with the narrow estoppel set out by Lord Ackner.

Conclusion

This chapter has considered the waiver of conditions by prevention of fulfilment and waiver of conditions on a repudiation. In relation to the former, we have seen that the principle of waiver of conditions must be distinguished from the fictional fulfilment of conditions. Waiver does not deem the condition to have been satisfied—it only precludes the party preventing its fulfilment from relying on the condition. English law should not recognise any fiction of fulfilment but it does and should recognise a principle of waiver. **5.98**

As for waiver of conditions on a repudiation, continuing the theme from the previous chapter, we have seen that the attempted integration of waiver of conditions into promissory estoppel, once again, has not been altogether satisfactory. If waiver of conditions on a repudiation is, in some form, to be treated as an instance of promissory estoppel, it may be that the time has come for us to revisit the suggestion that promissory estoppel is in fact a unified doctrine.[204] **5.99**

Finally, a key point that emerges from the consideration of both forms of waiver in this chapter is that not all conditions can be waived for all purposes. Crucially, a condition cannot be waived for the purpose of an action for the price if the performance of the condition is the consideration for the promise it qualifies. **5.100**

[201] ibid.
[202] ibid 805 [25].
[203] ibid 805 [26].
[204] See Ben McFarlane, 'Understanding Equitable Estoppel: From Metaphors to Better Laws' (2013) 66 Current Legal Problems 267; Ben McFarlane, 'Promissory Estoppel and Debts' in Andrew Burrows and Edwin Peel (eds), *Contract Formation and Parties* (OUP 2010) 115.

6

Frustration

Introduction

This chapter defends the view that the doctrine of frustration is an instance of discharge for failure of condition. The central argument is that in cases of frustration the reason the parties are discharged from further performance of their contractual obligations is that the parties have agreed that their obligations are conditional upon the existence of particular facts or the occurrence of particular events, which no longer exist or have not occurred. This is why it is often said that frustration 'brings the contract to an end forthwith, without more and automatically'.[1] The only qualification to this statement is that 'the contract' is not at an end. The parties are discharged from their contractual obligations, but the contract remains in existence and continues to regulate the parties' relationship.[2] **6.1**

In advancing this claim, this chapter proceeds as follows. First, it considers and explains the development of the various conditions in play in cases of frustration. Understanding the various conditions in play, and their historical development, is essential to understanding the claim that this instance of discharge is also an instance of failure of condition. In particular, it will be seen that in cases of frustration—contrary to modern orthodoxy—although both parties are discharged, they are often discharged for the failure of different conditions. **6.2**

[1] *Hirji Mulji v Cheong Yue Steamship Co Ltd* [1926] AC 497, 505.

[2] JA Weir, 'Nec Tamen Consumebatur . . .—Frustration and Limitation Clauses' (1970) 28 Cambridge Law Journal 189, 191.

Discharge of Contractual Obligations. Jordan English, Oxford University Press. © Jordan English 2025.
DOI: 10.1093/9780198906704.003.0006

Secondly, the chapter criticises the development of a unified doctrine of frustration and explains the problems that have arisen from thinking about this instance of discharge in this way. The third part of this chapter seeks to defend the claim that in cases of frustration the parties' obligations are implicitly conditional. The fourth and final part of this chapter addresses a question often posed by asking whether frustration is invariably 'automatic'.[3] In this chapter, the question takes a slightly different form, which is whether it is possible to waive the relevant condition(s) in cases of frustration.

The Conditions in Cases of Frustration

6.3 '[T]he term "frustration" has an embarrassing width of meaning.'[4] As this section shows, cases said to fall within the ambit of the doctrine of frustration in fact involve the failure of several different conditions commonly found in contracts. The first, which can be called the 'possibility condition', is the condition of a party's obligation, generally but not always found, that it is possible to perform it.[5] Failure of this condition discharges the party who was to render the performance. The second condition is what this book has called the 'substantial-benefit condition'[6] and, as we saw in Chapter 3, this discharges the party who was to receive the performance (which may be unforthcoming due to impossibility or simply because one party fails or refuses to perform). Finally, there are a very limited number of cases where a condition is implied that discharges both parties from their respective obligations to perform because 'the circumstances in which performance is called for would render it a thing radically different from that which was undertaken by the contract. . . . It was not this that I promised to do'.[7] The precise content of this particular condition adapts to the case and contract at hand.

6.4 The key insight of this approach is that in cases of frustration the parties are, in fact, often discharged for the failure of different conditions Unfortunately,

[3] See, eg, GD Goldberg, 'Is Frustration Invariably Automatic?' (1972) 88 Law Quarterly Review 464.

[4] Roy Granville McElroy, *Impossibility of Performance: A Treatise on the Law of Supervening Impossibility of Performance of Contract, Failure of Consideration, and Frustration* (Glanville L Williams ed, CUP 1941) xxxiii.

[5] eg, *Taylor v Caldwell* (1863) 3 B & S 826, 122 ER 309.

[6] eg, *Jackson v Union Marine Insurance Co Ltd* (1874) LR 10 CP 125. It will be argued that this is also the best explanation of *Krell v Henry* [1903] 2 KB 740.

[7] *Davis Contractors Ltd v Fareham Urban District Council* [1956] AC 696, 729.

this proposition has not been fully appreciated in English law with the modern position being that there is a single doctrine of frustration and test for when frustration occurs. The problems with the 'unified doctrine of frustration' are explored at [6.74]–[6.82].

The possibility condition

There is no principle in English law that prevents parties from contracting to do that which is impossible.[8] Where an unconditional (or 'absolute') promise is or becomes impossible to perform, this does not discharge a party from their obligation to perform.[9] As Sir Frederick Pollock observed in 1876: **6.5**

> It is a rule admitted by all the authorities, and supported by positive decisions, that impossibility of this kind is no excuse for the failure to perform an unconditional contract, whether it exists at the date of the contract, or arises from events which happen afterwards.[10]

But to say that 'impossibility' does not discharge a party from his or her unconditional obligation to perform, while true, assumes that the obligation was in fact unconditional.[11] Yet, 'it must, of course, always be a matter of construction what the contractual obligation was'.[12] As Lord Porter observed in *Joseph Constantine Steamship Line Ltd v Imperial Smelting Corp Ltd*,[13] '[t]he very fact, however, that in certain cases impossibility of performance is an excuse shows that in those cases there is no absolute promise. It is conditional on something, ie, the possibility of performance.' In most contracts, the parties' obligations are not absolute and unconditional; neither party has promised to perform 'come what may', guaranteeing performance in all circumstances. More often than not,[14] one party's promise to perform—at least where it is not concerned **6.6**

[8] *Thornborow v Whitacre* (1705) 2 Ld Raym 1164, 1165; 92 ER 270, 271; *Clifford v Watts* (1870) LR 5 CP 577, 588. See also Edwin Peel, *Frustration and Force Majeure* (4th edn, Sweet & Maxwell 2021) 1–3 [1-002].

[9] *Baily v De Crespigny* (1869) LR 4 QB 180, 185; *Grant, Smith & Co & McDonnell Ltd v Seattle Construction and Dry Dock Co* [1920] AC 162, 169.

[10] Frederick Pollock, *Principles of Contract at Law and in Equity* (1st edn, Stevens and Sons 1876) 330.

[11] McElroy (n 4) 6; Michael Bridge, 'Frustration and Excused Non-Performance' (2021) 137 Law Quarterly Review 580, 583.

[12] McElroy (n 4) 6.

[13] [1942] AC 154, 204–05.

[14] But see Robert Stevens, 'Objectivity, Mistake and the Parol Evidence Rule' in Andrew Burrows and Edwin Peel (eds), *Contract Terms* (OUP 2007) 102, 106.

with the payment of a sum of money[15]—is implicitly conditional upon it being possible to perform.[16]

6.7 It is true that this was not always the position. As we have seen in Chapter 2,[17] at one time, courts were reluctant to find conditions unless they were expressly stated in the contract. This was because it was supposed that if a party had wished to protect themselves, that party could have limited their own promise 'by the use of appropriate words of condition'.[18] And where the parties' promises were not expressly conditional, 'the justice of that day required each one to be enforced as it was made';[19] impossibility was no defence.[20] On this approach, each party had promised to perform 'no matter what'.

Paradine v Jane

6.8 The case often referred to in this context, as authority for the 'doctrine of absolute contracts',[21] is *Paradine v Jane*.[22] In that case, the plaintiff landlord brought an action in debt against the defendant tenant for three years of rent due under a lease of land. The defendant pleaded in response to the action that 'a certain German prince, by name Prince Rupert, an alien born, enemy to the King and kingdom, had invaded the realm with an hostile army of men'[23] and forced the defendant out of possession. This had the result that the defendant could not take the profits of the land. On the plaintiff's demurrer, it was held that this plea was not a sufficient answer to the claim.

6.9 Three grounds were given for the decision, the broadest of which was simply that this provided no defence: 'he ought to pay his rent'.[24] The Court

[15] Rarely does a party promise to pay only if they have the money to do so. Perhaps this is why it is often said that the law does not regard obligations to pay money as capable of being impossible to perform: Michele De Gregorio, 'Impossible Performance or Excused Performance? Common Mistake and Frustration after *Great Peace Shipping*' (2005) 16 King's Law Journal 69, 72; William Herbert Page, 'The Development of the Doctrine of Impossibility of Performance' (1920) 18 Michigan Law Review 589, 595; Cliona Kelly, '*Paradine v Jane*: A Doctrine of Absolute Contractual Liability?' (2004) 12 Irish Student Law Review 64, 66.

[16] *Taylor v Caldwell* (1863) 3 B & S 826, 122 ER 309; *Joseph Constantine Steamship Line Ltd v Imperial Smelting Corp Ltd* [1942] AC 154, 204–05.

[17] See [2.8].

[18] Arthur Corbin, *Corbin on Contracts: A Comprehensive Treatise on the Rules of Contract Law* (West Publishing Co 1960) vol 3A, 136 §654.

[19] ibid 170 §661.

[20] Arthur Corbin, *Corbin on Contracts: A Comprehensive Treatise on the Rules of Contract Law* (West Publishing Co 1962) vol 6, 323 §1320.

[21] Peel (n 8) 17 [2-001]. The phrase 'absolute contracts' is just another way of saying that the parties' obligations are 'unconditional'. See Pollock (n 10) 330, who uses the terms interchangeably in this way.

[22] (1647) Aleyn 26, 82 ER 897. Also reported as *Paradine v Jane* (1647) Style 47, 82 ER 519.

[23] *Paradine v Jane* (1647) Aleyn 26, 26; 82 ER 897, 897.

[24] ibid 27; 897. The first two grounds for this decision were that (i) the defendant's plea provided no answer for one quarter of the rent, which was incurred after the time that Prince Rupert had kept the

distinguished the situation 'where the law creates a duty or charge'[25] and said that 'when the party by his own contract creates a duty or charge upon himself, he is bound to make it good, if he may, notwithstanding any accident by inevitable necessity, because he might have provided against it by his contract'.[26]

The following points should be made about *Paradine v Jane*. The first is that, perhaps ironically, *Paradine v Jane* was not an impossibility case.[27] No question arose as to the landlord fulfilling his obligation to convey the interest in the land, and there is no mention of an express or implied covenant of quiet enjoyment.[28] The only question was as to the tenant's obligation to pay rent, and the basis on which the tenant resisted this claim was not that his performance had become impossible (for he could not argue that it had become impossible to pay rent),[29] but that he had been deprived of the use and enjoyment of the land.[30] As one commentator observed, 'the plea would not be regarded as raising any question of impossibility at modern law'.[31] Strictly speaking, then, the statement in *Paradine v Jane* was obiter.[32] **6.10**

The second point to note is that the dictum contains an ambiguity because it is qualified by the language of 'if he may'.[33] This qualification is open to two interpretations. The first is that it was attempting to preserve impossibility as a ground for non-performance of an unconditional promise. In this sense, 'if he may' would mean 'if he can', 'in the sense of being *able* to do something'.[34] The second is that 'if he may' meant 'if he is allowed', 'in the sense of being legally permitted to do something'.[35] **6.11**

defendant from possession, and (ii) the defendant had not pleaded that the army were all aliens, the reasoning being that to the extent that they were not, he had a remedy against them: see Peel (n 8) 18 [2-002].

[25] *Paradine v Jane* (1647) Aleyn 26, 27; 82 ER 897, 897.
[26] ibid.
[27] Page (n 15) 596; Kelly (n 15) 66.
[28] Corbin (n 20) 330 §1322; Page (n 15) 595.
[29] See the text in n 15.
[30] Corbin (n 20) 330 §1322.
[31] Page (n 15) 595. See also Pollock (n 10) 332.
[32] Kelly (n 15) 65. This same point has been recognised judicially by Lord Porter in *Joseph Constantine Steamship Line Ltd v Imperial Smelting Corp Ltd* [1942] AC 154, 203. See also Page (n 15) 595.
[33] De Gregorio (n 15) 72; John Henry Schlegel, 'Of Nuts, and Ships, and Sealing Wax, Suez, and Frustrating Things—The Doctrine of Impossibility of Performance' (1969) 23 Rutgers Law Review 419, 420; Kelly (n 15) 74–77; Peel (n 8) 26 [2-013].
[34] Peel (n 8) 26 [2-013]. See also HWR Wade, 'The Principle of Impossibility in Contract' (1940) 56 Law Quarterly Review 519, 525.
[35] Peel (n 8) 26 [2-013]. See also *Joseph Constantine Steamship Line Ltd v Imperial Smelting Corp Ltd* [1942] AC 154, 184; Schlegel (n 33) 420.

6.12 The problem with the first view is that it would make the statement 'largely self-contradictory'.[36] As Lord Wright observed in *Joseph Constantine Steamship*,[37] 'the reference to inevitable accident seems inconsistent with reading "if he may" as reserving impossibility'. Moreover, the statement was intended to contrast the situation where a 'party by his own contract creates a duty or charge upon himself' with that 'where the law creates a duty or charge', in which case it was said that if 'the party is disabled to perform it without any default in him, and hath no remedy over, there the law will excuse him'.[38] In other words, for this latter category of case, impossibility was an excuse. The interpretation of 'if he may' as a reference to impossibility fails to give weight to that contrast.[39]

6.13 By contrast, the second interpretation—that 'if he may' meant 'if he is allowed'—merely recognises a limited exception to the proposition,[40] namely supervening illegality, which had been recognised before *Paradine v Jane*.[41] It was stated in the following way in *Brewster v Kitchell*: 'if [a person] covenants to do a thing which is lawful and an Act of Parliament comes in and hinders him from doing it, the covenant is repealed'.[42]

6.14 The third point is that even when *Paradine v Jane* was decided, there were a few instances in which it had been held that performance of a promise that was not expressly unconditional would be excused where its performance had become impossible.[43] These included: (i) the death of a party who had promised to perform personal services[44] (although this would later be explained by Bramwell B[45] and Pollock CB[46]—admittedly both dissenting—as resting upon an implied condition); (ii) the destruction of a chattel that was the subject matter of a contract of bailment;[47] and (iii) as already mentioned, illegality due to a subsequent Act of Parliament. But despite these limited exceptions, '[f]or over two centuries this rule was more or less rigorously applied'.[48]

[36] Peel (n 8) 26 [2-013].
[37] *Joseph Constantine Steamship Line Ltd v Imperial Smelting Corp Ltd* [1942] AC 154, 184.
[38] *Paradine v Jane* (1647) Aleyn 26, 27; 82 ER 897, 897.
[39] McElroy (n 4) 4 fn 6.
[40] Peel (n 8) 26 [2-013].
[41] See *Abbott of Westminster v Clerke* (1536) 1 Dyer 26b, 28b; 73 ER 59, 63.
[42] *Brewster v Kitchell* (1697) 1 Salk 198, 198; 91 ER 177, 178.
[43] Schlegel (n 33) 420 fn 9; McElroy (n 4) 5; *Joseph Constantine Steamship Line Ltd v Imperial Smelting Corp Ltd* [1942] AC 154, 203; De Gregorio (n 15) 72–73; Catharine MacMillan, '*Taylor v Caldwell* (1863)' in Charles Mitchell and Paul Mitchell (eds), *Landmark Cases in the Law of Contract* (Hart Publishing 2008) 167, 185–89.
[44] *Hyde v The Dean and Canons of Windsor* (1597) Cro Eliz 552, 553; 78 ER 798, 798.
[45] *Hall v Wright* (1859) El Bl & El 765, 778; 120 ER 695, 700.
[46] ibid 793; 706.
[47] *Williams v Lloyd* (1628) W Jones 179, 82 ER 95. See also *Coggs v Bernard* (1703) 2 Ld Raym 909, 92 ER 107.
[48] McElroy (n 4) 5.

The final point to make is that the dictum in *Paradine v Jane* needs to be viewed in its historical context. When the case was decided, courts were reluctant to find conditions unless they were expressly stated in the contract. But only a short time later the approach to finding conditions had changed. As we saw in Chapter 2 in the context of promissory conditions, in the second half of the seventeenth century the old approach had been abandoned in favour of an approach focusing on the construction that would best serve the objective intentions of the parties.[49] The problem was that outside the context of promissory conditions—ie in cases of impossibility—*Paradine v Jane* had wrongly come to be seen as authority for the proposition that such conditions as would discharge a party in cases of impossibility ought not to be implied.[50] The tension between these differing approaches was bound to come to a head. Indeed, it led Pollock CB, in his dissenting judgment in *Hall v Wright*,[51] to say that 'it must be conceded on all hands that there are contracts to which the law implies exceptions and conditions which are not expressed'.[52] And only a few years later, the tension arose again in *Taylor v Caldwell*.[53] 6.15

Taylor v Caldwell

In *Taylor v Caldwell*,[54] the defendants, Caldwell and Bishop, agreed to let the plaintiffs, Taylor and Lewis, have use and possession of the Surrey Gardens and Music Hall over four days to give a series of grand concerts and fêtes at the Music Hall and Gardens. The plaintiffs agreed to pay £100 for each day. After the contract had been made, but before the first concert, the Music Hall was destroyed by an accidental fire.[55] The plaintiffs subsequently sued the defendants for breach of duty, alleging that 'they did not nor would allow the plaintiffs to have the use of The Surrey Music Hall and Gardens according to the agreement'.[56] They claimed as damages the expenses incurred in advertising and preparing for the concerts. Blackburn J, delivering the judgment of the Court, held that the defendants were not liable as their obligation to perform was implicitly conditional upon the existence of the music hall. The principle governing the case was expressed as being that: 6.16

[49] See [2.10]–[2.11].

[50] See, eg, *Atkinson v Ritchie* (1809) 10 East 530, 533; 103 ER 877, 878; *Hall v Wright* (1859) El Bl & El 765, 789; 120 ER 695, 704.

[51] *Hall v Wright* (1859) El Bl & El 765, 120 ER 695.

[52] ibid 793; 706.

[53] (1863) 3 B & S 826, 122 ER 309.

[54] For a detailed discussion of the factual history of the case, see MacMillan (n 43) 167.

[55] Without seemingly any fault on Caldwell and Bishop's part: ibid 179–80.

[56] *Taylor v Caldwell* (1863) 3 B & S 826, 827; 122 ER 309, 310.

in contracts in which the performance depends on the continued existence of a given person or thing, a condition is implied that the impossibility of performance arising from the perishing of the person or thing shall excuse the performance.[57]

6.17 In reaching this conclusion, Blackburn J did not purport to depart from *Paradine v Jane*. He stated the general rule that where an obligation to do something is absolute (unconditional) then—provided its performance is not unlawful—'the contractor must perform it or pay damages for not doing it', even if 'the performance of his contract has become unexpectedly burdensome or even impossible'.[58] But Blackburn J then said:

> [T]his rule is only applicable when the contract is positive and absolute, and not subject to any condition either express or implied: and there are authorities which, as we think, establish the principle that where, from the nature of the contract, it appears that the parties must from the beginning have known that it could not be fulfilled unless when the time for the fulfilment of the contract arrived some particular specified thing continued to exist, so that, when entering into the contract, they must have contemplated such continuing existence as the foundation of what was to be done; there, in the absence of any express or implied warranty that the thing shall exist, the contract is not to be construed as a positive contract, but as subject to an implied condition that the parties shall be excused in case, before breach, performance becomes impossible from the perishing of the thing without default of the contractor.[59]

6.18 At no point did Blackburn J suggest that the parties had subjectively turned their minds to the possibility that performance might not be possible. Indeed, he said quite the opposite, noting that '[t]he parties when framing their agreement evidently had not present to their minds the possibility of such a disaster, and have made no express stipulation with reference to it'.[60] But the implied condition was not based upon the parties' subjective understandings, but on the objective construction of the agreement. In explaining that a condition was to be implied, Blackburn J said:

> There seems little doubt that this implication tends to further the great object of making the legal construction such as to fulfil the intention of those who

[57] ibid 839; 314.
[58] ibid 833; 312.
[59] ibid 833–34; 312.
[60] ibid 833; 312.

> entered into the contract. For in the course of affairs men in making such contracts in general would, if it were brought to their minds, say that there should be such a condition.[61]

Blackburn J's approach was not new and 'such an implication had been argued in previous cases'.[62] In his judgment, he referred to the 'much discussed case of *Hall v Wright*',[63] in which the court narrowly held that a condition should not be implied discharging the defendant from his promise to marry on account of him becoming inflicted with a serious disease. The disease had caused severe bleeding in his lungs, rendering him 'incapable of marriage'.[64] The dissenting judges (Pollock CB, Bramwell, and Watson BB) had all been willing to imply a condition but the majority thought that *Paradine v Jane* precluded such an implication. 6.19

The incremental change brought about by Blackburn J's judgment in *Taylor v Caldwell* was to 'revisit the decision in *Hall v Wright*'[65] and to signify a greater willingness to find implied conditions where they had not been expressly stated. In other words, courts became more willing to find that contractual obligations were not absolute and unconditional (the premise upon which the so-called rule in *Paradine v Jane* was based). This was the true principle in *Taylor v Caldwell*, and it was confirmed as such in subsequent cases. Thus, in *Robinson v Davison*,[66] Bramwell B said: 6.20

> It is contended, however, that to [imply a condition] is to engraft a new term on an express contract. But this is really a fallacy . . . The fallacy consists, first, in supposing there is in the first instance an absolute contract; and, secondly, that the new term is a condition added to its express terms; whereas the whole question is what the original contract was, and whether it was a contract with or without a condition.

Unfortunately, at the end of his judgment in *Taylor v Caldwell*, Blackburn J went beyond what was necessary to dispose of the issue in the case (whether the defendants were liable for not giving the plaintiffs the use of the Music Hall) and 6.21

[61] ibid 834; 312.
[62] MacMillan (n 43) 192. See also Schlegel (n 33) 423 fn 22.
[63] *Taylor v Caldwell* (1863) 3 B & S 826, 833; 122 ER 309, 312.
[64] *Hall v Wright* (1859) El Bl & El 765, 773; 120 ER 695, 698. There was discussion about the meaning of this plea and whether it meant 'an unfitness for sexual intercourse' and/or 'an incapacity to bear the fatigue and excitement of the marriage ceremony': *Hall v Wright* (1859) El Bl & El 765, 777; 120 ER 695, 700.
[65] MacMillan (n 43) 199.
[66] (1871) LR 6 Ex 269, 277.

said that 'both parties [were] excused'.[67] The problem is that 'Blackburn J [did] not explain why an event which makes it impossible for only one party to perform [their] promise nevertheless discharges both parties'.[68] Put another way, why were the plaintiffs discharged from their obligation to pay the money? It cannot be because their obligation to make payment had become impossible to perform; the fire 'clearly did not make it impossible for the plaintiffs to perform their principal obligation to make the agreed payments'.[69] The principled answer is that they were discharged because the impossibility of providing the Music Hall meant that they were deprived of substantially the whole benefit of the contract. This is sometimes called 'failure of consideration'[70] but in this book the condition has been labelled the 'substantial-benefit condition'.[71] It is discussed at [6.31]–[6.58].

6.22 Subsequent cases applied the principle in *Taylor v Caldwell* to find that the obligations of the parties were not absolute. In *Appleby v Myers*,[72] the principle was applied to 'excuse'[73] the plaintiffs from an obligation to erect, and keep in repair, machinery on the defendant's premises when the premises were destroyed by an accidental fire. In *Robinson v Davison*,[74] it was held to excuse the defendant's wife, a pianist, from performing at a concert when, on the day, she was unable to perform due to illness.[75] And in *Howell v Coupland*,[76] which concerned a contract to sell 200 tons of potatoes that were specifically to be grown on land belonging to the defendant,[77] the defendant was held not liable for failing to deliver the full 200 tons when only 80 tons were delivered due to disease attacking the crop.[78]

6.23 One minor issue with the judgments in these cases is that, like Blackburn J's in *Taylor v Caldwell*, they did not generally express the condition as being that it should be possible to perform. Rather, they expressed the condition as the

[67] *Taylor v Caldwell* (1863) 3 B & S 826, 840; 122 ER 309, 315.
[68] Peel (n 8) 54 [2-050].
[69] ibid 53–54 [2-050]; Ewan McKendrick, 'Frustration: Automatic Discharge of Both Parties?' in Andrew Dyson, James Goudkamp, and Frederick Wilmot-Smith, *Defences in Contract* (Hart Publishing 2017) 141, 144; McElroy (n 4) 99–100.
[70] Peel (n 8) 56 [2-054]; McKendrick (n 69) 145.
[71] See Chapter 3.
[72] (1867) LR 2 CP 651.
[73] This is a loose sense of the word, but one which was common in judgments at the time.
[74] *Robinson v Davison* (1871) LR 6 Ex 269; compare *Hall v Wright* (1859) El Bl & El 765, 120 ER 695.
[75] Although curiously damages were awarded on the basis that she should have given notice.
[76] (1876) 1 QBD 258.
[77] Importantly, 'there was not an absolute contract to deliver 200 tons of potatoes in September and October, but 200 tons of potatoes grown on particular land': ibid 263.
[78] As McElroy and Williams note, '[t]here might have been an interesting question as to the 80 tons': McElroy (n 4) 25. See the discussion of this issue below at [6.121]–[6.122].

'continued existence' of a given person or thing[79] which, if it should perish, would then make performance impossible. Focusing on the perishing of a given person or thing meant that some massaging of the language was necessary to make the principle applicable to certain cases.[80] Examples of this include: (i) *Robinson v Davidson*,[81] where the person necessary for performance had not 'perished' but was merely ill and for that reason unable to perform; (ii) *Howell v Coupland*,[82] where the thing necessary for performance did not exist at the time of the contract and never came into existence (and so could not have 'perished'); and (iii) *Nickoll & Knight v Ashton Edridge & Co*,[83] where a specific vessel that was to deliver cargo had become stranded (but had not perished) making it impossible to deliver the cargo aboard the ship within a fixed time. It would have been better in all these cases simply to state that often parties contract on the implicit basis that it is possible to perform, while recognising that it would be a matter of construction as to what circumstances of factual impossibility might not cause that condition to fail (such as impossibility arising due to factors within a contracting party's control).

Illegality: impossibility by operation of law?

It is well established that supervening illegality—whether arising from a subsequent change in the law (eg an Act of Parliament) or from a change in circumstances that engages a previously existing law (eg the rule against trading with the enemy during wartime)[84]—can sometimes discharge parties from their respective obligations to perform.[85] As we saw above, even at the time of *Paradine v Jane*, illegality was recognised as an excuse for non-performance. **6.24**

Some texts treat this as a circumstance in which the performance of an obligation becomes 'legally impossible'[86] and then treat it alongside cases in which performance is 'factually impossible'. There is some evident sense in treating the two together given that the effect of the supervening event in each case is the same: one or both parties need not perform. But there are three potential issues with doing so. **6.25**

[79] *Taylor v Caldwell* (1863) 3 B & S 826, 839; 122 ER 309, 314.
[80] See De Gregorio (n 15) 74–75.
[81] *Robinson v Davison* (1871) LR 6 Ex 269.
[82] *Howell v Coupland* (1876) 1 QBD 258.
[83] [1901] 2 KB 126.
[84] The distinction is neatly set out in Peel (n 8) 323 [8-001].
[85] ibid; Edwin Peel, *The Law of Contract* (15th edn, Sweet & Maxwell 2020) 1060 [19-045].
[86] Jack Beatson, Andrew Burrows, and John Cartwright, *Anson's Law of Contract* (31st edn, OUP 2020) 477.

6.26 First, to refer to supervening illegality as 'legal impossibility' is to use 'impossibility' in a sense that does not accord with the ordinary usage of that word. Supervening illegality need not make it impossible to perform;[87] it appears to be based 'on the idea that performance ought not to be (though physically it could be) rendered'.[88] As Willes J said in *Clifford v Watts*:

> If the intercourse with the foreign port had been prohibited by the law of this country, the act would have been illegal, and the defendant would have been excused, not because he could not, but because he ought not to do it.[89]

But if that is the case, it seems better just to say this and refer to 'supervening illegality' rather than 'legal impossibility'.

6.27 Secondly, there are cases of actual legal impossibility that need to be distinguished from cases of supervening illegality, such as a contract for the sale of title to land, where prior to the conveyance the title is compulsorily acquired by the State. This is a true case of legal impossibility and is on all fours with factual impossibility: it is not possible to perform the agreement because the vendor no longer has title to the land. It has nothing to do with supervening illegality.

6.28 Thirdly, referring to supervening illegality as 'legal impossibility' gives the impression that whatever justifies discharge in cases of factual impossibility might also justify discharge in cases of supervening illegality. But although the effects are the same, illegality is different—it is an 'excuse' for non-performance that is recognised 'on grounds of public policy'[90] apart from the parties' agreement.

6.29 To illustrate this last point, it might be thought that where the parties to a contract are discharged from their respective obligations to perform on account of supervening illegality this can also be explained by the conditionality of the parties' obligations to perform. But even where the parties did intend that performance should occur despite the illegality, this does not prevent supervening illegality from excusing performance. An illustration is *Ertel Bieber & Co v Rio Tinto Co Ltd*,[91] in which it was held that contracts of sale between an English company and various Germany companies had ceased to be binding following the outbreak of World War I on account of the prohibition against trading with the enemy.[92] This was so even though each of the contracts contained a clause

[87] Peel (n 8) 325 [8-004].
[88] ibid 324 [8-003].
[89] *Clifford v Watts* (1870) LR 5 CP 577, 586.
[90] Peel (n 8) 324 [8-003].
[91] [1918] AC 260.
[92] See, eg, *Esposito v Bowden* (1857) 7 El & Bl 763, 119 ER 1430.

that merely suspended the parties' respective obligations in the event of a war; indeed, this clause was held to be of no effect, with the result that the contract as a whole was 'avoided'.

In sum, supervening illegality is not an instance of failure of condition. Rather, supervening illegality is a distinct reason for discharge and due to the matters of public policy involved, it 'is governed by a number of special rules'.[93] These rules are not addressed further in this chapter. **6.30**

The substantial-benefit condition (failure of consideration)

There is 'another class of case which is quite distinct'[94] in which the defendant does not seek to justify their non-performance by reference to the impossibility of doing so, but on the ground that the defendant simply did not get what they bargained for. This is often called the 'principle of failure of consideration'[95] and we encountered it in Chapter 3. In this book, it has been called the 'substantial-benefit condition'.[96] It is expressed in shorthand by asking whether one party has got what they bargained for. This is assisted by determining '[w]hat did the parties intend to "buy" and "sell"?'[97] And, as we saw in Chapter 3, the substantial-benefit condition can apply both in cases involving breach and in cases not involving breach.[98] Here, we are concerned with those that do not involve breach. **6.31**

In some cases, the reason there is no breach is that one party has by words in the contract expressly limited the scope of their contractual duty. This is illustrated by *Jackson v Union Marine Insurance Co Ltd*.[99] In that case, the charterers were discharged from their obligation to provide a cargo when the vessel ran aground and failed to arrive in time to carry a cargo of iron rails to San Francisco, which were needed for the construction of a railway. This was because the charterers had bought 'a charter for a definite voyage or adventure'[100] and the delay had deprived them of substantially the whole benefit of the bargain. But the shipowner was not in breach for failing to arrive on time because **6.32**

[93] Peel (n 8) 324 [8-003].
[94] McElroy (n 4) 75.
[95] ibid; De Gregorio (n 15) 76.
[96] *Hongkong Fir Shipping Co Ltd v Kawasaki Kisen Kaisha Ltd* [1962] 2 QB 26, 66.
[97] McElroy (n 4) 88; R G McElroy and Glanville Williams, 'The Coronation Cases—I' (1941) 4 Modern Law Review 241, 247, referring to *Knowles v Bovill* (1870) 22 LT 70, 71.
[98] See [3.20]–[3.35].
[99] *Jackson v Union Marine Insurance Co Ltd* (1874) LR 10 CP 125. See [3.25]–[3.32].
[100] *Jackson v Union Marine Insurance Co Ltd* (1874) LR 10 CP 125, 142.

he had expressly excluded 'dangers and accidents of navigation' from his duty. The charterers thus had no cause of action.

6.33 In other cases, the reason that there is no breach is that one party's obligation to perform is implicitly conditional upon it being possible to perform. So in *Poussard v Spiers*,[101] the defendant, who had engaged the plaintiff's wife to sing and play the principal female part in a new opera, was discharged from his obligation to accept her services when due to illness she missed the final week of rehearsals and was unable to perform on the opening night and the first three days of the following week. The defendant had been deprived of substantially the whole benefit of the bargain.[102] But the wife's illness fell within the scope of the possibility condition, which meant that the plaintiff[103] was not in breach.[104]

6.34 In cases involving discharge for failure of the possibility condition on one side, it is often the substantial-benefit condition that explains discharge on the other. But insofar as the party who is to receive the performance is concerned, the reason for non-performance, strictly speaking, is not relevant to the question of the discharge of that party. As Professor Samuel Williston once explained:

> As the basis for the defendant's excuse where the plaintiff has failed to perform, or is obviously going to fail to perform, is failure of consideration, the reason why the plaintiff fails to perform is immaterial. Even though his failure is caused by excusable impossibility, the result is the same. The defendant has not got what he bargained for and need not perform.[105]

6.35 This is why it was argued in Chapter 3 that Diplock LJ was correct to draw the link between discharge following breach and discharge in cases of frustration in *Hongkong Fir*.[106] The substantial-benefit condition can fail in cases involving breach (which orthodoxy now treats as discharge for breach of an 'innominate term') or it can fail in cases not involving breach (which orthodoxy treats as a case of frustration). It is the failure to distinguish between the promise and the condition that has made it difficult to see the relationship between these two seemingly disparate instances of discharge.

[101] (1876) 1 QBD 410. See [3.33]–[3.34].
[102] *Poussard v Spiers* (1876) 1 QBD 410, 415.
[103] The husband was the plaintiff due to the old doctrine of 'coverture' (abolished by the Married Women's Property Act 1882).
[104] *Poussard v Spiers* (1876) 1 QBD 410, 414.
[105] Samuel Williston, *A Treatise on the Law of Contracts* (Walter HE Jaeger ed, 3rd edn, Baker, Voorhis & Co 1962) vol 6, 131–32 §838.
[106] See [3.76]–[3.78].

The application of the doctrine of frustration to leases

A proper understanding of the substantial-benefit condition may also explain the reluctance of the law to apply the doctrine of frustration to leases. The starting point here is once again *Paradine v Jane*. As we saw above, *Paradine v Jane* was not an impossibility case. The argument of the defendant was that he had been forced out of possession, with the result that he could not take the profits of the land, and that this entitled him to refuse to pay the rent. It was not an argument from impossibility, but (if anything) one of failure of the substantial-benefit condition. **6.36**

Should the argument have succeeded? It is submitted that it should not have succeeded and that *Paradine v Jane* was correctly decided. This is because in *Paradine v Jane* if we ask '[w]hat did the parties intend to "buy" and "sell"',[107] the answer is that the plaintiff was to convey to the defendant the leasehold estate and with it the right to possession, and this he had done.[108] That the lessee was prevented from taking possession by Prince Rupert and his army did not mean that the lessee had not got what he bargained for. **6.37**

This does not mean that the substantial-benefit condition can never, in principle, fail in the context of a lease. To the extent that it was ever suggested that this might be the case, that is no longer the law.[109] But it does mean that such arguments are rarely, if ever, likely to succeed for, ordinarily, if the lessee is granted a leasehold estate in the land then they will have gotten all that they bargained for. **6.38**

It has been suggested that such arguments might succeed in cases where a lease specifies that premises are to be used only for a particular purpose, the suitability of the premises for this use is reflected in the price, and for one reason or another it becomes the case that the premises can no longer be used for that particular purpose. In *National Carriers Ltd v Panalpina (Northern) Ltd*,[110] Lord Wilberforce gave such an example, referring to a passage in *Corbin on Contract* about leases of liquor saloons during the era of prohibition in the United States. In that passage, Professor Arthur Corbin had said: **6.39**

> Many short term leases have been made, in which the purpose of the lessee was to conduct a liquor saloon, a purpose known to the lessor and one which

[107] McElroy (n 4) 88; McElroy and Williams, 'The Coronation Cases—I' (n 97) 247, referring to *Knowles v Bovill* (1870) 22 LT 70, 71.
[108] McElroy and Williams, 'The Coronation Cases—I' (n 97) 257; Corbin (n 20) 330 §1322.
[109] See *National Carriers Ltd v Panalpina (Northern) Ltd* [1981] AC 675.
[110] ibid 695, referring to (an earlier edition of) Corbin (n 20) 472–73 §1356.

> gave to the premises a large part of its rental value. Then followed the enactment of a federal, state, or local prohibitory law preventing the use of the premises for the expected purpose. . . . If the terms of the lease are such that the lessee is restricted to this one use, it has been held in a considerable number of cases that his duty to pay rent is discharged.[111]

6.40 In such cases, there is at least an argument to be made—albeit a difficult one—that the lessee did not bargain merely for a conveyance of an interest in land, but for premises that could be used for that purpose. As Lord Wilberforce observed in *National Carriers Ltd v Panalpina (Northern) Ltd*,[112] '[i]n such a case the lease, or the conferring of an estate, is a subsidiary means to an end, not an aim or end of itself'. If the premises cannot be used for the particular purpose, the lessee does not get what they bargained for and the substantial-benefit condition fails. But these cases are likely to be rare and more recent authorities have suggested that the mere fact that a lessee has agreed only to use the premises for specific purposes does not mean that where the premises cannot be used for that purpose it follows that there has been a failure of the substantial-benefit condition.[113]

6.41 Moreover, even if this argument is open as a matter of construction of the lease on the facts, it should also be noted that whether the substantial-benefit condition fails will depend on the length of the contract and the comparative length of any event that prevents one party from receiving the benefit of performance. This is because the substantial-benefit condition only fails where a party has been deprived of 'substantially the whole' benefit. Anything less than this will not suffice. This is illustrated by *National Carriers Ltd v Panalpina (Northern) Ltd*. In that case, the plaintiffs, who sought to recover arrears of rent, had demised to the defendants a warehouse for a term of ten years. The lease contained a covenant that it was not to be used otherwise than for the purpose of a warehouse without the written consent of the landlord. Five years into the lease, the only vehicular access to the warehouse, a street, was blocked off by the local authority due to the dangerous condition of a 'ruinous Victorian warehouse'.[114] It was proposed that the Victorian warehouse be demolished but because it was heritage listed, that process was likely to take around eighteen to

[111] Arthur Corbin, *Corbin on Contracts: A Comprehensive Treatise on the Rules of Contract Law* (West Publishing Co 1951) vol 6, 388 §1356. For another example, see McElroy and Williams, 'The Coronation Cases—I' (n 97) 258.

[112] *National Carriers Ltd v Panalpina (Northern) Ltd* [1981] AC 675, 695.

[113] See *Bank of New York Mellon (International) Ltd v Cine-UK Ltd; London Trocadero (2015) LLP v Picturehouse Cinemas Ltd* [2022] EWCA Civ 1021 [154]–[155], [157].

[114] *National Carriers Ltd v Panalpina (Northern) Ltd* [1981] AC 675, 685.

twenty months. The effect of the street being blocked off was that the plaintiffs' warehouse had been 'rendered totally useless for the one purpose, that of a commercial warehouse, for which alone it [was] fitted, and for which alone, by the terms of the contract between the parties it [could] be lawfully used'.[115]

While at first glance it might appear that this was a case in which the argument that the substantial-benefit condition had failed might have been possible (ie a case of 'possible frustration'),[116] the limited duration of the interruption precluded it from being one. As Lord Wilberforce explained, 'this does not approach the gravity of a frustrating event. Out of 10 years it will have lost under two years of use: there will be nearly three years left after the interruption has ceased.'[117] **6.42**

Krell v Henry and 'frustration of purpose'

The substantial-benefit condition may also shed light on the decision in *Krell v Henry*,[118] a case often cited as having recognised a 'frustration of purpose' or frustration of the 'common purpose' doctrine.[119] As will be seen, the best understanding of that decision is that it was concerned with the substantial-benefit condition. This understanding of the decision also explains why attempts to invoke *Krell v Henry* in support of cases of 'frustration of purpose' have nearly always failed. **6.43**

In *Krell v Henry*, the plaintiff, by an exchange of letters on 20 June 1902, agreed to let the defendant use his suite of chambers on the third floor of Pall Mall 'during the days (but not the nights)'[120] of 26 and 27 June for the sum of £75. The reason for doing so was to enable the defendant to view the procession in connection with the coronation of King Edward VII, although the letters themselves contained no express reference to the procession. On 24 June, the King fell ill and consequently the procession did not take place on the selected days. The defendant, who had already paid £25, declined to pay the balance of £50, upon which the plaintiff sued. The Court of Appeal (Vaughan Williams LJ, with whom Romer and Stirling LJJ agreed) held that the non-occurrence of the procession meant that the defendant was discharged from his obligation to **6.44**

[115] ibid.
[116] ibid 697.
[117] ibid. A similar conclusion was reached at first instance in *Bank of New York Mellon (International) Ltd v Cine-UK Ltd* [2021] EWHC 1013 (QB) [209(d)(iii)]. There was no appeal from this aspect of the decision (and the appeal was, in any event, dismissed): *Bank of New York Mellon (International) Ltd v Cine-UK Ltd; London Trocadero (2015) LLP v Picturehouse Cinemas Ltd* [2022] EWCA Civ 1021.
[118] *Krell v Henry* [1903] 2 KB 740.
[119] See, eg, Peel (n 8) ch 7.
[120] *Krell v Henry* [1903] 2 KB 740, 741.

pay the remaining £50. The defendant's cross-claim for recovery of the £25 was abandoned on appeal.[121]

6.45 The argument that *Krell v Henry* recognised a 'frustration of purpose' doctrine rests upon the fact that the express provisions of the contract were still literally capable of performance. The postponement of the coronation procession simply meant that the purpose in hiring out the room had been undermined.[122] When viewed in this way, *Krell v Henry* poses a grave threat to the sanctity of contract[123] and runs the risk of being invoked in many cases where supervening events have simply rendered the contract a bad bargain for one of the parties.[124] Apparently for this reason, it has 'scarcely ever been followed in England'.[125]

6.46 On closer examination, however, *Krell v Henry* is justifiable as an application of the substantial-benefit condition. This point was first made by Dr Roy McElroy and Professor Glanville Williams, who observed that '[t]he defendant was held to be excused because there was a total failure of consideration for his promise to pay'.[126] They noted that, although the contract made no express reference to the procession, extrinsic evidence was held to be admissible to identify the subject matter of the contract.[127] In particular, there was an announcement in the windows of the plaintiff's flat, which had induced the defendant to enter into the contract, 'to the effect that windows to view the Royal coronation procession were to be let'.[128] This evidence was admitted by Vaughan Williams LJ who said that 'parol evidence is admissible to shew that the subject of the contract was rooms to view the coronation procession, and was so to the knowledge of both parties'.[129]

6.47 When viewed in this light it is clear that *Krell v Henry* was a case concerned with failure of the substantial-benefit condition. If we ask '"what did he buy?" the answer is that the defendant in *Krell v Henry* bought a "view of the coronation procession."'[130] And clearly he did not get what he bargained for. In other

[121] ibid 754. The decision of Darling J at first instance to allow the defendant to recover the £25 was disapproved of in *Blakeley v Muller & Co* (1903) 19 TLR 186, 187. This would become known as the *Chandler v Webster* 'fallacy' (*Chandler v Webster* [1904] 1 KB 493) and it was not laid to rest until *Fibrosa Spolka Akcyjna v Fairbairn Lawson Combe Barbour Ltd* [1943] AC 32, 45–49.
[122] Peel (n 8) 295 [7-014].
[123] ibid 289 [7-004].
[124] ibid 295 [7-014]; Peel (n 85) 1057 [19-043].
[125] Peel (n 85) 1058 [19-044].
[126] McElroy and Williams, 'The Coronation Cases—I' (n 97) 247.
[127] *Krell v Henry* [1903] 2 KB 740, 753–54.
[128] ibid 750.
[129] ibid 754, quoted in McElroy and Williams, 'The Coronation Cases—I' (n 97) 249.
[130] McElroy and Williams, 'The Coronation Cases—I' (n 97) 249.

words, the defendant, due to no fault on the part of the plaintiff, was deprived of substantially the whole benefit that it was intended he should obtain in consideration of his promise to pay the hire. The failure of this condition meant that his obligation to pay the remainder never fell due.

Subsequent cases have recognised this feature of *Krell v Henry* and explained the case on the basis that '[w]hat the parties were buying and selling was, quite literally, . . . room[s] with a view'.[131] But the position is even stronger than that. What was being bought and sold in *Krell v Henry* was not *rooms* with a view of the coronation procession, but rather a *view* of the coronation procession.[132] That is, in part, shown by the fact that the defendant was to have access to the rooms during the days only. The licence to use the flat in *Krell v Henry* was 'a subsidiary means to an end, not an aim or end of itself'.[133] **6.48**

This feature also explains why it is unlikely that the plaintiff would have been obligated to provide access to the room if the defendant had wished to pay. The plaintiff's obligation to provide access to the rooms was part of an indivisible obligation to provide a view of the procession or, if one prefers, also conditional upon being able to provide a view of the procession. On either view, the impossibility of providing a view of the procession discharged the plaintiff from the obligation to provide access. In the absence of a guarantee that the procession would take place, or a promise to perform even if the procession did not take place, the plaintiff's obligation was conditional upon it being possible to provide a view of the procession. **6.49**

Of course, some might argue that on the facts of *Krell v Henry* this is an implausible construction of the agreement. It could be said that the defendant bargained for access to the rooms and that the view was no more than the reason the defendant wanted access to the rooms. This conclusion would be almost irresistible if, for example, the defendant was to have access to the rooms during the nights as well as the days. **6.50**

But in many ways, this can only show one of two things, neither of which is fatal to the argument being put here. It could show that *Krell v Henry* was wrongly decided on its facts. That would only suggest that the court misapplied the principles, not that the principles are wrong, and that there are **6.51**

[131] *Canary Wharf (BP4) T1 Ltd v European Medicines Agency* [2019] EWHC 335 (Ch) [37(4)]; *Great Peace Shipping Ltd v Tsavliris Salvage (International) Ltd (The Great Peace)* [2003] QB 679, 701 [66]; *Bell v Lever Brothers Ltd* [1932] AC 161, 226. See further, Peel (n 85) 1057–58 [19-043].

[132] See, eg, *Clark v Lindsay* (1903) 88 LT 198, 202.

[133] To borrow the phrase from *National Carriers Ltd v Panalpina (Northern) Ltd* [1981] AC 675, 695.

difficult questions of construction involved about which reasonable minds can disagree. Alternatively, it could show how exceedingly unusual the contract in *Krell v Henry* was. First, as mentioned above, the defendant was only to have access to the rooms during the days but not the nights. Secondly, the plaintiff did not warrant that the procession would take place. This is why the plaintiff was not in breach for failing to provide a view of the procession (though this fact would not change the analysis of whether the defendant had to pay).

6.52 These unique features of *Krell v Henry* can also explain an example given by Vaughan Williams LJ where the hirer would not be discharged from their obligation to pay the price—a cabdriver engaged to take a person to Epsom on Derby Day at a 'suitable enhanced price for such a journey'.[134] Vaughan Williams LJ said that the hirer would not be discharged should the race not go ahead.[135] It is submitted that this would be because the contract could not, in this case, plausibly be construed as one 'to get him to the Derby' (which could not occur if there were no Derby); it would simply be a contract 'to get the passenger to Epsom'.[136] As Marcus Smith J explained in *Canary Wharf (BP4) T1 Ltd v European Medicines Agency*,[137] the ability of the cab driver to charge a premium was due to market forces: it 'was simply a reflection of an excess of demand for cabs over their supply, with the cab driver's price being correspondingly high as a result.' Of course, if the proper construction of the agreement was that the cabdriver had agreed to get the passenger to the 'Derby', then a similar result to *Krell v Henry* should follow. And there may be cases where the high price is indicative of the purpose having been made a part of the contract.

6.53 Similar reasoning explains the decision in *Herne Bay Steam Boat Co v Hutton*,[138] which was delivered only a few days earlier by the same members of the Court of Appeal who sat in *Krell v Henry*. The plaintiff company agreed to make its steamboat available to the defendant on 28 and 29 June so that the defendant could take out paying passengers 'for the purpose of viewing the naval review and for a day's cruise round the fleet'.[139] The naval review, which was part of the same coronation celebrations as *Krell v Henry*, was cancelled. The defendant subsequently chose to have nothing further to do with the agreement, eventually informing the plaintiff on 29 June that he did not require the use of the

[134] *Krell v Henry* [1903] 2 KB 740, 750.
[135] ibid. See also *Herne Bay Steam Boat Co v Hutton* [1903] 2 KB 683, 689.
[136] Peel (n 85) 1058 [19-043].
[137] [2019] EWHC 335 (Ch) [37(1)].
[138] [1903] 2 KB 683.
[139] ibid 684. The quoted words are from the agreement itself.

ship and that he would not pay the balance of the hire. The Court of Appeal held that the defendant was liable to pay damages for his renunciation of his contractual obligations. One explanation of the case, given by McElroy and Williams,[140] was that even if it could be said that the subject matter of the contract was the use of a ship in order to provide a view of the naval review and the fleet, the effect of the naval review not taking place was not to deprive the defendant of substantially the whole benefit of the contract. The fleet was still there and it was not a trivial aspect. As Sir Frederick Pollock observed shortly thereafter, 'the fleet was still there . . . and, as the writer of these lines can bear witness, it was very well worth seeing without the review.'[141]

Another explanation is that the subject matter of the contract was simply the use of the ship, which but for the defendant's renunciation would have been made available to him. That the defendant had wished to use it for the purpose of taking out passengers to view the naval review and the fleet was irrelevant. The defendant was buying the use of a ship with the hope of employing it profitably for paying customers. The only person who could have been selling a 'view' of the naval review and fleet, making it akin to *Krell v Henry*, was the defendant when he contracted with his customers, not the plaintiff company when it contracted with the defendant. **6.54**

Finally, it is submitted that this understanding of *Krell v Henry*, which focuses on the subject matter of the contract, is much more satisfactory than the current orthodoxy that English law has a doctrine of frustration of purpose, though one that will rarely, if ever, succeed. A case in point is the decision in *Canary Wharf (BP4) T1 Ltd v European Medicines Agency*.[142] In that case, the European Medicines Agency (EMA) entered into a twenty-five-year lease of property located at Canary Wharf, London, for the purpose of having its headquarters there. Following the news about the possibility of Brexit occurring, the EMA wrote to Canary Wharf and advised that if Brexit occurred, it would be 'treating that event as a frustration of the [l]ease.'[143] While Brexit was, at that stage, an uncertainty, proceedings were brought to clarify the position if Brexit should occur. One of the arguments the EMA sought to rely upon in support of its case for discharge was the 'frustration of a common purpose'[144] that 'the [p]remises would constitute the EMA's headquarters.'[145] In particular, there was **6.55**

140 McElroy and Williams, 'The Coronation Cases—I' (n 97) 254–55.
141 Pollock, 'Notes' (1904) 20 Law Quarterly Review 1, 4.
142 [2019] EWHC 335 (Ch).
143 ibid [2].
144 ibid [34].
145 ibid [219].

evidence that the premises that were leased had been built in 'such a way as to suit the EMA (and conceivably only the EMA)'.[146]

6.56 If one believed in a frustration of purpose doctrine, it is hard to imagine a better case for it. The whole purpose of the lease was to provide a headquarters for the EMA—an agency of the European Union (EU)—in a member state of the EU. The purpose of the agreement would be frustrated when the United Kingdom ceased to be a part of the EU. Yet, Marcus Smith J held that the lease was not frustrated and said that the case did not even 'come close to a case of frustration of common purpose'.[147] In a telling conclusion, he said that the EMA could not say that 'this is not what it bargained for'.[148]

6.57 On the assumption that there is a frustration of purpose doctrine, it is difficult to see how it could be said—as Marcus Smith J did—that '[t]his is not a case like *Krell v Henry* where the parties had a common purpose going beyond their agreement, which was thwarted'.[149] One answer given was that in this case the parties' purposes were 'divergent', with the EMA being focused on 'bespoke premises' and Canary Wharf focused on 'long-term cash flow, at the highest rate'.[150] But this only exposes a problem with the notion of a common purpose, namely, that there is no 'common purpose' of a contract; 'instead, there are [only] the purposes of the parties to the contract'.[151] And in commercial agreements, these objects will almost always diverge.[152]

6.58 The real reason that the EMA was not discharged from its obligation to pay rent was precisely that identified by Marcus Smith J: the EMA got exactly what it bargained for, namely, a valid legal lease. The subject matter of the contract was simply a lease of commercial or office space. There was no term that the lease could be used only as a headquarters.[153] It would be better if English law recognised that there is no frustration of purpose doctrine, rather than the current approach which merely pays lip service to a doctrine that is never successfully invoked.

[146] ibid [217].
[147] ibid [247].
[148] ibid [248].
[149] ibid [244].
[150] ibid [245].
[151] Corbin (n 20) 326 §1322.
[152] Leon E Trakman, 'Frustrated Contracts and Legal Fictions' (1983) 46 Modern Law Review 39, 47–48. See also McElroy (n 4) 142–43.
[153] A point made by Mr Justice Marcus Smith: *Canary Wharf (BP4) T1 Ltd v European Medicines Agency* [2019] EWHC 335 (Ch) [246].

The 'not-radically-different' condition

6.59 The final category of case is concerned not with a single condition as such, but an amalgamation of conditions that have been implied into contracts. The precise conditions are various and distinct, but common to all is that they involve the implication of a condition to the effect that the circumstances in which performance is called for are 'not radically different' to those that were supposed to obtain at the time of contracting. They are thus referred to in this chapter, in the singular and at the more abstract level which unites them, as the 'not-radically-different condition'.

6.60 The not-radically-different condition arises because often it is not a reasonable construction of the parties' agreement to say that each promises to perform their respective obligations 'no matter what'.[154] Usually, the continued existence to some degree of the conditions prevailing, or supposed to be prevailing, at the time of contracting is a condition on which the contractual obligations of both parties are dependent.[155] As Earl Loreburn explained in *FA Tamplin Steamship Co Ltd v Anglo-Mexican Petroleum Products Co Ltd*:

> [A] Court can and ought to examine the contract and the circumstances in which it was made . . . in order to see whether or not from the nature of it the parties must have made their bargain on the footing that a . . . state of things would continue to exist.[156]

6.61 The precise content of the not-radically-different condition will depend upon the contract under consideration, and the language with which the condition is expressed will necessarily be adapted to the case at hand.[157] At bottom, it reflects the fact that often 'from the nature of the contract it cannot be supposed the parties, as reasonable men, intended it to be binding on them under such altered conditions'.[158] The language of 'not radically different' also reflects a basic fact, to be borne in mind when ascertaining the scope of contractual obligations, that '[s]ome delay or change is very common in all human affairs, and it cannot be supposed that any bargain has been made on the tacit condition that such a thing will not happen in any degree'.[159]

[154] In the context of intentions, see Luca Ferrero, 'Conditional Intentions' (2009) 43 Noûs 700, 700; Gregory Klass, 'A Conditional Intent to Perform' (2009) 15 Legal Theory 107, 107.

[155] Hans Smit, 'Frustration of Contract: A Comparative Attempt at Consolidation' (1958) 58 Columbia Law Review 287, 304.

[156] [1916] 2 AC 397, 403.

[157] ibid 404.

[158] ibid. See also *Metropolitan Water Board v Dick, Kerr & Co Ltd* [1918] AC 119, 131.

[159] *FA Tamplin Steamship Co Ltd v Anglo-Mexican Petroleum Products Co Ltd* [1916] 2 AC 397, 403.

6.62 The not-radically-different condition can be engaged in circumstances where neither the possibility condition, the substantial-benefit condition, nor supervening illegality, would effect a discharge of either party from their contractual obligations. An example is *Metropolitan Water Board v Dick, Kerr & Co Ltd*.[160] In that case, the appellant Water Board had, in July 1914, contracted with the respondent firm of contractors for the construction of a reservoir to be completed within six years, although subject to a provision for extension. In February 1916, however, the Minister of Munitions, through the exercise of powers conferred by the Defence of the Realm Acts and Regulations, directed the contractors to cease work on the contract, which they did. The Water Board subsequently commenced an action seeking a declaration that 'the contract [was] still in existence as a binding contract and had not been determined'.[161] The contractors alleged that the interruption caused by the notice meant that the contract had ceased to be binding. The House of Lords agreed and held that the contractors were discharged because of the failure of an implied condition.

6.63 The case was not—to borrow Lord Dunedin's words—a 'clean case of illegality' where the illegality was permanent.[162] While the notice had been in effect for almost two years at the time of judgment, the illegality was 'only temporary, and [would] some day be withdrawn'.[163] Thus, it could not be said that it would be illegal to perform the contract for its entire duration. Nonetheless, all members of the House agreed that the parties were discharged. Lord Dunedin said that 'the contract when resumed would be a contract under different conditions from those which existed when the contract was begun'.[164] Lord Finlay LC also said that the contract:

> does not cover the case in which the interruption is of such a character and duration that it vitally and fundamentally changes the conditions of the contract, and could not possibly have been in the contemplation of the parties to the contract when it was made.[165]

6.64 In sum, while a reasonable person in the position of parties may have contemplated some disruption to the performance of the contract, the degree of disruption was such that 'from the nature of the contract it could not be supposed the parties, as reasonable men, intended it to be binding on them in such

160 [1918] AC 119.
161 ibid 123.
162 ibid 128.
163 ibid.
164 ibid.
165 ibid 126.

unreasonable conditions'.[166] This is because our obligations to perform are often conditional upon the state of affairs that existed at the time of contracting remaining the same, at least to some degree, at the time of performance.

Of course, the precise point at which the 'not-radically-different' condition will fail is necessarily imprecise and conclusions on this issue may well expose reasonable differences of opinion. An example is the decision in *FA Tamplin Steamship Co Ltd v Anglo-Mexican Petroleum Products Co Ltd*.[167] In that case, the appellant owners agreed to charter their steamship to the respondents for five years from December 1912 for the carriage of oil. The charterparty contained an exception for restraint of princes and rulers. In February 1915,[168] the steamer was requisitioned by the British Government for use as a troopship in the war. The owners claimed that the parties had been discharged from their obligations (or at least that their obligations had been suspended) by the requisitioning of the vessel. The charterers, who were willing to pay the agreed freight, claimed that the parties had not been discharged. The reason the parties took these (at first glance, surprising) positions was that the hire fee paid by the British Government (which both sides sought to claim) was higher than the sums due under the charter. **6.65**

The House of Lords held, by a majority, that neither party had been discharged by the requisition. Earl Loreburn said that he could not infer that the interruption was, or would be, 'such as makes it unreasonable to require the parties to go on' and observed that '[t]here [might] be many months during which the ship [would] be available for commercial purposes before the five years [had] expired'.[169] By contrast, Lord Atkinson (in dissent) thought that the 'imposition of the restraint for a lengthened period create[d] a condition of things to which the charterparty [was] inapplicable'.[170] **6.66**

The majority may have been influenced by the fact that owners were seeking to benefit from the higher rate of compensation payable by the government.[171] The only point that needs to be made here is that the question about when this condition is engaged is one on which reasonable minds can differ. Indeed, it **6.67**

[166] ibid 131.
[167] [1916] 2 AC 397.
[168] The ship had previously been requisitioned in December 1914 but there was no dispute in relation to that requisition, which was accepted by both parties 'as a merely temporary burden upon their rights under the charterparty': ibid 409.
[169] ibid 405.
[170] ibid 421.
[171] Peel (n 8) 227–29 [5-060]. See also *Metropolitan Water Board v Dick, Kerr & Co Ltd* [1918] AC 119, 129.

has been observed that, although the majority and minority disagreed on the facts, the principles applied by each were 'identical'.[172]

6.68 Another case that illustrates this condition—and the difficult line-drawing exercise that its application can involve—is *Bank Line Ltd v Arthur Capel & Co*.[173] In February 1915, the appellant owners agreed to charter a steamship to the respondents for twelve months from the time at which the vessel was delivered and put at the disposal of the charterers. The ship was to be delivered by April 1915, but if it was not delivered by the end of the month the charterers were given an option to cancel the charter. The charterparty also provided that if the ship, through unforeseen circumstances, could not be delivered by the end of April, the charterers, if required by the owners, were to state whether they intended to cancel or take delivery of the vessel. Finally, the charterers were also given the option of cancelling if the vessel were 'commandeered' by the government during the charter.

6.69 The vessel was not delivered by the end of April 1915 (although the contract was not cancelled) and in early May 1915 it was requisitioned by the British government. Efforts were made by both parties to get the vessel released but these ceased in June 1915. The owners later received an offer to purchase the vessel and, after they arranged to provide the government with another vessel, they procured the vessel's release in September 1915. At this point, the charterers claimed that the owners were obliged to deliver the vessel and they sought damages for its non-delivery. In response, the owners argued that the requisition discharged the parties from their obligations to perform.

6.70 Importantly, the owners could not rely upon the possibility condition as permanently discharging them, rather than temporarily suspending their obligations, because the obligations of the parties were not permanently impossible to perform. Nonetheless, the House of Lords, by a majority, held that the owners were discharged and that the requisitioning of the vessel made the 'charter, as a matter of business a totally different thing'.[174] No member of the majority thought that the provision for such events in the contract precluded the implication.[175]

[172] *Bank Line Ltd v Arthur Capel & Co* [1919] AC 435, 443; *Metropolitan Water Board v Dick, Kerr & Co Ltd* [1918] AC 119, 127.

[173] [1919] AC 435.

[174] ibid 460 (Lord Sumner). See also 444 (Lord Finlay LC).

[175] ibid 443 (Lord Finlay LC), 456 (Lord Sumner), 462 (Lord Wrenbury). Lord Shaw did not address the issue.

By contrast, Viscount Haldane, who dissented, would have held that the parties remained bound. In particular, he pointed to the facts that the vessel was to be used for twelve months 'not from a definite date, but from the date when the steamer was delivered to the charterers' and 'that they intended to use her for the carriage of coal across the Channel, a use which they could put her to at any period that was likely to call for it'.[176] He also noted that the contract expressly provided for the parties' rights if the ship were requisitioned, which demonstrated 'that such commandeering was contemplated by the parties as an event which would not necessarily put an end to the basis of their contract'.[177] **6.71**

Viscount Haldane's view is the better one, but again this only shows a difference in the construction and application of this condition, rather than a difference in principle. Whether one agrees with the result in each of these cases, the question is not, as it was in the previous sections, whether an obligation has become impossible to perform or whether one party has been deprived of substantially the whole benefit of the bargain. The question is whether the circumstances in which performance is now called for are so far beyond the contemplated state of affairs at the time of contracting that the parties are discharged from their unperformed contractual obligations. This is because our contractual obligations are often conditional upon the state of affairs that existed at the time of contracting remaining the same, at least to some degree, at the time performance is called for. **6.72**

Unconditional agreements

Of course, in rare cases, where it has been expressed sufficiently clearly, the parties really do promise to perform 'no matter what'. Thus in *Salam Air SAOC v Latam Airlines Group SA*,[178] Foxton J, on an application for an injunction, was faced with the question of whether there was a sufficiently arguable case that the obligations of a lessee to pay rent under three six-year aircraft leases had been discharged when authorities, in response to the Covid-19 pandemic, placed significant restrictions on flights into and out of Oman (where the lessee and aircraft were based). The difficulty for the lessee was that this **6.73**

[176] ibid 447.
[177] ibid 445.
[178] [2020] EWHC 2414 (Comm).

was a 'dry' lease—a lease in which the lessee undertakes all risks and responsibility for the aircraft and in which the lessor's obligation, aside from delivery, is limited to not interfering with the use, possession, and quiet enjoyment of the aircraft.[179] Moreover, the obligation to pay rent was expressed to 'be absolute and unconditional irrespective of any contingency whatever'[180]—a clause which is known as a 'hell or highwater' clause.[181] Unsurprisingly, Foxton J held that this clause—which had expressly made the obligation to pay rent unconditional—was 'fundamentally inconsistent' with any suggestion that the regulations had the effect of 'freeing [the lessor] of its obligation to pay rent'.[182]

A Unified Doctrine of Frustration?

6.74 A key feature of cases involving frustration that becomes apparent from analysing the relevant conditions at work is that the parties are often, although not always, discharged for failure of different conditions.[183] So, in *Taylor v Caldwell*, the defendants were discharged from the obligation to give the plaintiffs the use of the musical hall due to impossibility (ie failure of the possibility condition). But had the owners been suing for the rent, it would seem absurd to say that the parties obliged to pay the money were discharged because of impossibility—it was perfectly possible for them to perform their obligation to pay the money.[184] They would be discharged because the impossibility of providing the Music Hall meant that they were deprived of substantially the whole benefit of the contract; the substantial-benefit condition had failed.

6.75 Yet the modern trend has been to regard these cases as revealing 'one single, fused doctrine of "frustration"'[185] with a single test for when frustration occurs.

[179] ibid [48]; *Wilmington Trust SP Services (Dublin) Ltd v Spicejet Ltd* [2021] EWHC 1117 (Comm) [4].

[180] *Salam Air SAOC v Latam Airlines Group SA* [2020] EWHC 2414 (Comm) [12], [51].

[181] *Bitumen Invest AS v Richmond Mercantile Ltd FZC* [2017] 1 Lloyd's Rep 219, 221 [8].

[182] *Salam Air SAOC v Latam Airlines Group SA* [2020] EWHC 2414 (Comm) [51]. cf *Wilmington Trust SP Services (Dublin) Ltd v Spicejet Ltd* [2021] EWHC 1117 (Comm) [61], [65], in which Miss Julia Dias QC assumed without deciding that such a clause did not 'exclude the possibility of frustration'. However, the Deputy High Court Judge was very clear that she 'express[ed] no view one way or the other'.

[183] See generally, McElroy (n 4) xxvii, 140; Corbin (n 20) 326 §1322; Weir (n 2) 191; John Stannard, 'Frustrating Delay' (1983) 46 Modern Law Review 738, 741–43. Compare Peel (n 8) 53–56 [2-050]–[2-054]; McKendrick (n 69) 144–46, 152–54.

[184] McElroy (n 4) xxvii; Corbin (n 20) 326 §1322; Peel (n 8) 53–54 [2-050]; McKendrick (n 69) 144.

[185] De Gregorio (n 15) 78. See Arnold D McNair, *Legal Effects of War* (CUP 1920) 82; Arnold D McNair, 'Frustration of Contract by War' (1940) 56 Law Quarterly Review 173, 182 fn 40.

The start of this trend is usually identified as the 'war cases'—in particular, the decision in *Tamplin*,[186] discussed in the previous section.[187] In these cases, a number of the old decisions were 'rationalised' and 'transmuted . . . into the modern idea that a frustrating event displaced the contract itself'.[188] A consequence is that today there is said to be a 'general test for frustration',[189] namely, that given by Lord Radcliffe in *Davis Contractors Ltd v Fareham Urban District Council*:

> frustration occurs whenever the law recognizes that without default of either party a contractual obligation has become incapable of being performed because the circumstances in which performance is called for would render it a thing radically different from that which was undertaken by the contract. *Non haec in foedera veni*. It was not this that I promised to do.[190]

Of course, in a sense, the argument that there is a single reason which unites cases of frustration is consistent with the argument being put forward in this chapter. Except for supervening illegality, which for the reasons given above is based upon different principles, each is an example of failure of condition. The issue with the unified doctrine of frustration, however, is that it fails to appreciate that there are multiple conditions (and in this sense multiple reasons) in play that can operate together to discharge the parties from their respective obligations to perform. The modern approach instead looks for a single reason, in all cases, that discharges both parties from their obligations to perform. This is incorrect as a matter of principle and, as the next two sub-sections explain, this 'unification' has had some unfortunate side effects.[191] 6.76

First side effect: 'contracts' discharged instead of 'obligations'

First, the notion of a doctrine of frustration has led courts and commentators to speak of 'contracts' rather than 'obligations' being 'frustrated' or discharged.[192] 6.77

[186] *FA Tamplin Steamship Co Ltd v Anglo-Mexican Petroleum Products Co Ltd* [1916] 2 AC 397. Now see *Davis Contractors Ltd v Fareham Urban District Council* [1956] AC 696, 729 (Lord Radcliffe).

[187] See McNair, *Legal Effects of War* (n 185) 82; HC Gutteridge, 'Contract and Commercial Law' (1935) 51 Law Quarterly Review 91, 110; McNair, 'Frustration of Contract by War' (n 185) 182 fn 40; McElroy (n 4) 162; Stannard (n 183) 749; Andrew Tettenborn, 'From Chaos to Cosmos—Or Is it Confusion' [2002] 2 Web Journal of Current Legal Issues; De Gregorio (n 15) 77–78.

[188] Tettenborn (n 187).

[189] *Canary Wharf (BP4) T1 Ltd v European Medicines Agency* [2019] EWHC 335 (Ch) [22].

[190] *Davis Contractors Ltd v Fareham Urban District Council* [1956] AC 696, 729 (emphasis added).

[191] McElroy (n 4) 162.

[192] See also the Law Reform (Frustrated Contracts) Act 1943, s 1. The problems with this Act are beyond the scope of this chapter but for a conditions-based critique of this Act, see Robert Stevens,

This tendency was described by Tony Weir as 'a characteristically sloppy English ellips[is]'.[193] In explaining that in *Taylor v Caldwell* it was the '*promise* [of each party] that was conditional, not the whole *contract*',[194] he said:

> So when the hall accidentally burnt down, this had an effect on the *promises* of both parties. But the *contract* need not somehow get consumed in the flames. It can survive, quite uncharred, in its own metaphysical world, and continue thence to regulate the rights and liabilities of the parties of which it is the source. . . . Instead of that, we have in English law the doctrine that *force majeure* makes the whole contract evanish like a Fifoot and Cheshire cat . . .[195]

6.78 It might be thought that this complaint is merely semantic, but it has contributed to courts making errors. Thus, in *Hirji Mulji v Cheong Yue Steamship Co Ltd*,[196] it contributed to the Privy Council's conclusion that the 'frustration of the contract' meant that an arbitrator did not have jurisdiction to hear a dispute arising under it. Lord Sumner said that 'frustration brings the contract to an end forthwith, without more and automatically'[197] and that 'a contract that has been determined is in the same position as one that has never been concluded at all. It founds no jurisdiction.'[198] The House of Lords was rightly critical of this conclusion in *Heyman v Darwins Ltd*,[199] and *Hirji Mulji* was not followed in *Kruse v Questier & Co Ltd*.[200] Other common law courts have also noted that Lord Sumner was 'mistaken'[201] on this point. In fairness, and to not overstate the point, when orthodoxy refers to frustration automatically terminating 'the contract', what is meant is that the parties are prospectively discharged from the further performance of their obligations. The mistake here was in treating this situation as identical to one where no contract had been concluded at all. That is no doubt correct, but the notion of frustration bringing an end to 'the contract' is at least partly to blame for the confusion.

'Repeal the Law Reform (Frustrated Contracts) Act 1943' in Edwin Peel and Rebecca Probert, *Shaping the Law of Obligations: Essays in Honour of Professor Ewan McKendrick KC*' (OUP 2023) 125.

193 Weir (n 2) 191.
194 ibid.
195 ibid (emphasis in original).
196 [1926] AC 497.
197 ibid 505.
198 ibid 502.
199 [1942] AC 356, 366, 373, 383, 401.
200 [1953] 1 QB 669, 679. See generally McKendrick (n 69) 149. It is now dealt with by the Arbitration Act 1996, s 7.
201 *Codelfa Construction Pty Ltd v State Rail Authority of New South Wales* (1982) 149 CLR 337, 365.

Second side effect: separate treatment of 'frustration' and 'excuses'

A second side effect of the unified doctrine of frustration is that it has led to the separate treatment of 'frustration' and 'excuses' falling short of frustration,[202] with the latter being neglected, save in specialist texts.[203] It is said that in English law '[t]here is no such concept as partial or temporary frustration on account of partial or temporary impossibility'[204] yet, at the same time, 'partial or temporary impossibility which occurs without the fault of one party may . . . give . . . an excuse for non-performance'.[205] 6.79

To illustrate partial impossibility, suppose a seller promises to sell to the buyer a particular tonnage of a crop to be grown specifically on the seller's land but, due to no fault of the seller, a portion of the crop fails. As we will see at [6.121], the authorities appear to demonstrate that subject to the obligation being 'severable' (in that it can be broken down into individual obligations), the seller will not be liable for failing to deliver the failed proportion of the crop,[206] but may be liable for failing to deliver the successful proportion of the crop.[207] 6.80

An example of temporary impossibility is illness. It has been said that although the temporary illness of an employee might not be 'of such a duration as to frustrate his contract of employment, the employee would not be in breach of the contract through failing to work while he was ill'.[208] Thus, in *Poussard v Spiers*,[209] Madame Poussard's temporary illness 'was not any breach of contract by the plaintiff'[210] but it seems that had the defendant requested that Madame Poussard perform when she had recovered, she would have been bound to do so.[211] 6.81

The modern approach, 'with its focus on the discharge of contracts rather than obligations . . . consigns these cases to a sort of no-man's land'.[212] By contrast, 6.82

[202] See generally Bridge (n 11).
[203] See, eg, Peel (n 8).
[204] ibid 199 [5-007]. See also *Bank of New York Mellon (International) Ltd v Cine-UK Ltd* [2021] EWHC 1013 (QB) [211]–[212]; *London Trocadero (2015) LLP v Picturehouse Cinemas Ltd* [2021] EWHC 2591 (Ch) [168]. There was no appeal from this aspect of the decision (and the appeal was, in any event, dismissed): *Bank of New York Mellon (International) Ltd v Cine-UK Ltd; London Trocadero (2015) LLP v Picturehouse Cinemas Ltd* [2022] EWCA Civ 1021.
[205] Peel (n 8) 199 [5-007].
[206] *Howell v Coupland* (1876) 1 QBD 258.
[207] *HR and S Sainsbury Ltd v Street* [1972] 1 WLR 834.
[208] Peel (n 8) 232 [5-067].
[209] *Poussard v Spiers* (1876) 1 QBD 410, discussed in Bridge (n 11) 597–98 and Peel (n 8) 233–34 [5-071].
[210] *Poussard v Spiers* (1876) 1 QBD 410, 414.
[211] Bridge (n 11) 598. For another example, see *Minnevitch v Café de Paris (Londres) Ltd* [1936] 1 All ER 884, referred to in Peel (n 8) 233 [5-069].
[212] Bridge (n 11) 589.

on the approach put forward in this book, the relationship between cases of 'excuses' and cases of 'frustration' is clear and explained by the conditionality of the parties' respective obligations. In cases of partial impossibility, the often-conditional nature of the obligation that is impossible to perform means that the party is under no immediate duty to perform that obligation, but this does not necessarily mean that they need not perform other contractual obligations. As for cases of temporary impossibility, so long as the impossibility persists that party will not be required to perform provided the possibility condition is in play. If the impossibility is permanent, then the condition has failed and that party will be discharged for failure of the condition.[213] Cases involving 'frustration' and cases involving 'excuses' are not expressing a fundamentally different idea; the different result is simply a feature of the different impact an event can have on the relevant condition.

Does the not-radically-different condition cover the field?

6.83 As mentioned above, the unified doctrine of frustration appears to derive from a number of the war cases, which were concerned with the not-radically-different condition. Expressed at this level of generality, this condition covers a range of conditions that have been implied into contracts. In fairness then, might it be argued that this condition covers the field—in particular, the possibility condition and the substantial-benefit condition—and in that sense there is a unified doctrine? Indeed, expressing all the conditions in this way, in essence as a test for frustration, 'has the advantage of being flexible and capable of application to a wide range of circumstances'.[214]

6.84 While initially attractive, the problem with treating all cases as subsumed under the not-radically-different condition is that it does not reveal in cases of impossibility or failure of the substantial-benefit condition why the circumstances in which performance is called for are 'radically different'. In many cases, expressing the condition at the level of generality of 'not radically different' will only obscure the true reason for discharge.[215] It is true that in some cases, ie those falling outside of these two categories, often the most that can be said of the relevant condition is that the circumstances in which performance is called for shall not become radically different (and that will be the best way

[213] On this distinction between 'suspension' and 'discharge', see [1.50]–[1.51].
[214] *Codelfa Construction Pty Ltd v State Rail Authority of New South Wales* (1982) 149 CLR 337, 380.
[215] Stannard (n 183) 743.

to express the condition), but these cases are exceptional and at the margin. Whenever possible to do so, the condition should be stated with precision.

Defending the Implied Condition View

The implied condition view defended in this chapter is just one view which ascribes the effects of 'frustration' to an implicature in the parties' agreement. Another view, which is not the same as that adopted here, is that the effects of frustration are best explained by an implied 'term' by which the parties are taken to have positively agreed to discharge or terminate their unperformed contractual obligations in the events that have happened. This 'implied term' view differs from the implied condition view because rather than stating (negatively) that the parties simply did not agree to perform in all circumstances, it states (positively) that the parties agreed that in the events that have happened, there should be an additional term that each party is discharged from further performance. **6.85**

While it is the implied condition view that this chapter defends, it is fair to say that neither the implied condition view nor the implied term view represents current orthodox thinking. Indeed, both views are often dismissed on the basis that they are fictitious.[216] In *Ocean Tramp Tankers Corp v V/O Sovfracht (The Eugenia)*,[217] Lord Denning said that 'the theory of an implied term has now been discarded by everyone, or nearly everyone, for the simple reason that it does not represent the truth'. And in *James Scott & Sons Ltd v R&N Del Sel*,[218] Lord Sands famously said that the theory of an implied condition involves 'a pious fiction—a fiction because it does not correspond with anything that was in the minds of parties at the time; pious because it seeks to do homage to a very sacred legal principle, the sanctity of contract'. **6.86**

Unfortunately, the criticisms of these views—particularly insofar as they apply to the implied condition view—have tended to attack a straw man. This section shows (i) how the criticisms have distorted the implied condition view, (ii) how they have rejected it based upon a false premise, and (iii) how the view that has been adopted in its stead, the 'construction theory', is just the implied condition view by another name. It is only once this ground is cleared that we **6.87**

[216] See, eg, Trakman (n 152) 41; PS Atiyah, 'Judicial Techniques and the English Law of Contract' (1968) 2 Ottawa Law Review 337, 361; Beatson, Burrows, and Cartwright (n 86) 480.
[217] [1964] 2 QB 226, 238.
[218] [1922] SC 592, 596.

can fairly assess whether the implied condition view is convincing (and it is submitted that it is). Before doing this, however, it is worth clarifying an important feature of the implied condition view being put forward here.

Clarification

6.88 It is sometimes assumed that any condition must be a condition subsequent operating to defeat 'the contract', rather than a condition precedent to the unperformed obligations of the parties. This has led judges—even those minded to adopt the implied condition view—to suggest that it is 'easier to imply a condition precedent defeating a contract before its execution has commenced than a condition subsequent defeating the contract when it is part performed'.[219]

6.89 The suggestion that it is the 'contract' that is subject to the condition flows from the tendency to speak of 'contracts' rather than 'obligations' being discharged. Meanwhile, the suggestion that the condition must be a 'condition subsequent' seems to flow from the failure to draw the distinction—explored in Chapter 1—between an obligation that has fallen due and therefore calls for immediate performance and an obligation that requires performance only at some future date.[220] MacKenna J illustrated this distinction in *HR and S Sainsbury Ltd v Street* when he said:

> 'He *shall* be under an obligation to deliver in the future if he produces . . .' would be in form a condition precedent. 'He *is* under an obligation to deliver in the future but that obligation shall be discharged if he does not produce . . .' would be in form a condition subsequent. The difference is a matter of words, not of substance.[221]

6.90 When cast in the form of a condition precedent, the italicised language of 'shall' refers to the obligation that will fall due in the future (ie the immediate duty of performance). But when cast in the form of a condition subsequent, the italicised language of 'is' refers to the more general obligation to perform in the future that can be described as a present duty. As explained in Chapter 1, the only difference between the two is in the level of abstraction at which the obligation is described.[222]

219 *FA Tamplin Steamship Co Ltd v Anglo-Mexican Petroleum Products Co Ltd* [1916] 2 AC 397, 423.
220 See [1.20]–[1.21].
221 *HR and S Sainsbury Ltd v Street* [1972] 1 WLR 834, 839 (emphasis added).
222 See [1.21].

6.91 The reason, aside from clarity, that it is important to note that there is an implied condition precedent to the unperformed obligations of the parties is that thinking in terms of a condition subsequent to 'the contract' renders the implied condition view less plausible. It seems less plausible to say that the parties positively agreed (as would be the case with a condition subsequent) that if some unforeseen event should occur, 'the contract' should cease—which implies foresight of the precise event in question—than it is to say, negatively (as is the case with a condition precedent), that the parties simply did not agree to perform in all circumstances: '*non haec in foedera veni*. It was not this I promised to do'.[223] On the implied condition view, the parties do not agree to 'terminate the contract'; they just do not promise to perform in all circumstances. Having made this clarification, we can now move on to consider the problems with objections to the implied condition view.

Condition stated with needless precision

6.92 The first problem is that objections to the implied condition view have often stated the condition 'with needless precision'.[224] A good example is Lord Sands' 'tiger days excepted' example. He said:

> A tiger has escaped from a travelling menagerie. The milkgirl fails to deliver the milk. Possibly the milkman may be exonerated from any breach of contract; but, even so, it would seem hardly reasonable to base that exoneration on the ground that 'tiger days excepted' must be held as if written into the milk contract.[225]

6.93 In *Davis Contractors Ltd v Fareham Urban District Council*,[226] Lord Reid relied upon this example to illustrate the 'artificiality of the theory of an implied term'. The problem with it is that 'the exception is specified with needless precision'.[227] As Dr Frederick Wilmot-Smith has noted, '[i]f the exception were phrased in more abstract terms—if, for example, the exception were: "unless performance is impossible"—the objection is denuded of much of its power'.[228]

[223] *Davis Contractors Ltd v Fareham Urban District Council* [1956] AC 696, 729 (emphasis added). This distinction between a positive and negative agreement is taken (with modification) from Frederick Wilmot-Smith, *Failure of Condition* (DPhil thesis, University of Oxford 2013) 251–57; Frederick Wilmot-Smith, 'Termination after Breach' (2018) 134 Law Quarterly Review 307, 314.
[224] Wilmot-Smith, 'Termination after Breach' (n 223) 319.
[225] *James Scott & Sons Ltd v R&N Del Sel* [1922] SC 592, 596.
[226] *Davis Contractors Ltd v Fareham Urban District Council* [1956] AC 696, 720.
[227] Wilmot-Smith, 'Termination after Breach' (n 223) 318.
[228] ibid 318–19.

Rejected as not corresponding to 'subjective' intentions of parties

6.94 Another problem—and a striking feature of the rejections of the implied condition view—is that often the implied condition view is rejected because it does not correspond with the subjective intentions of the parties. So it is said that 'the actual intention of the parties was nowhere to be found',[229] that 'we have little ground for supposing that the parties thought of the possibility of fire [in *Taylor v Caldwell*]',[230] or that 'there is something of a logical difficulty in seeing how the parties could even impliedly have provided for something which ex hypothesi they neither expected nor foresaw'.[231] But implication and construction do not depend upon the subjective or 'actual' intentions of the parties.[232] As Oliver Wendell Holmes Jr memorably wrote, 'nothing is more certain than that parties may be bound by a contract to things which neither of them intended'.[233] Dr Jonathan Morgan has put it his way:

> Once we accept that the meaning of contracts does not depend on what either party actually (subjectively) believed, thought or intended, there is no necessary illogicality in implying a term about an unusual occurrence that *ex hypothesi* the actual parties had not considered—contrary to the superficially attractive reasoning in the *Davis Contractors* case.[234]

6.95 Admittedly, there are some judicial statements that suggest that the implied condition theory was based upon the subjective intentions of the parties. In *Hirji Mulji v Cheong Yue Steamship Co Ltd*,[235] for example, Lord Sumner said that 'the law is only doing what the parties really (though subconsciously) meant to do themselves'. But these statements run into the problem, mentioned above, that the 'general test for implication of terms on the facts is not subjective but objective'.[236] Moreover, proponents of this view 'did not put forward a purely subjective version'.[237] In *FA Tamplin Steamship*,[238] Earl Loreburn,

[229] Trakman (n 152) 42.
[230] Corbin (n 20) 356 §1331.
[231] *Davis Contractors Ltd v Fareham Urban District Council* [1956] AC 696, 728.
[232] For implication, see *Marks and Spencer plc v BNP Paribas Securities Services Trust Co (Jersey) Ltd* [2016] AC 742, 754 [21]; *Equitable Life Assurance Society v Hyman* [2002] 1 AC 408, 459. For interpretation, see *Investors Compensation Scheme Ltd v West Bromwich Building Society* [1998] 1 WLR 896, 912–13.
[233] Mr Justice Holmes, 'The Path of the Law' (1897) 10 Harvard Law Review 457, 463.
[234] Jonathan Morgan, 'Common Mistake in Contract: Rare Success and Common Misapprehensions' (2018) 77 Cambridge Law Journal 559, 561.
[235] *Hirji Mulji v Cheong Yue Steamship Co Ltd* [1926] AC 497, 504.
[236] Beatson, Burrows, and Cartwright (n 86) 480.
[237] Peel (n 85) 1101 [19-124].
[238] *FA Tamplin Steamship Co Ltd v Anglo-Mexican Petroleum Products Co Ltd* [1916] 2 AC 397, 404; quoted in Peel (n 85) 1101 [19-124], 1103 [19-127].

focused on the question '[w]hat, in fact, was the true meaning of the contract?', and said that 'from the nature of the contract it cannot be supposed the parties, as reasonable men, intended it to be binding on them under such altered conditions'. On this approach, criticisms premised on the notion that the test is subjective have misunderstood the implied condition view.

A false distinction between implication and construction

Perhaps more surprising is that the view which has taken the implied condition view's place as orthodoxy is that whether the parties are discharged for frustration is a matter of construction. The leading statement is that of Lord Reid in *Davis Contractors Ltd v Fareham Urban District Council*: **6.96**

> [F]rustration depends, at least in most cases ... on the true construction of the terms which are in the contract read in light of the nature of the contract and of the relevant surrounding circumstances when the contract was made.... The question is whether the contract which they did make is, on its true construction, wide enough to apply to the new situation: if it is not, then it is at an end.[239]

Lord Radcliffe expressed a similar idea; he spoke of the circumstances in which performance is called for being 'radically different from that which was undertaken by the contract. Non haec in foedera veni. It was not this that I promised to do'.[240]

The reason that this is surprising is that to say that on the occurrence of some uncertain event the contractual obligations of the parties cease to bind—because, as a matter of construction, the contract was not intended to be binding in these circumstances—is just another way of saying that the obligations of the parties are conditional. This appears to have been noticed judicially. In *Canary Wharf*,[241] Marcus Smith J said that the construction theory is simply a 'more sophisticated variant' of the 'implied term or implied condition theory'. Academically, it has been said that this theory 'seems to involve nothing other than a process of necessary implication'.[242] And Lord Hoffmann, speaking of the construction theory, has also said: **6.97**

[239] *Davis Contractors Ltd v Fareham Urban District Council* [1956] AC 696, 720–21.
[240] ibid 729 (emphasis added).
[241] *Canary Wharf (BP4) T1 Ltd v European Medicines Agency* [2019] EWHC 335 (Ch) [26(4)].
[242] Goldberg (n 3) 467.

But that does not mean that the judges who adopted the implied term theory of frustration were wrong. They were also right because the implication of any implied term in fact is also a question of construction. The ultimate question remains: is this what the contract means?[243]

6.98 The invocation of Lord Hoffmann will no doubt bring to mind the familiar debate about whether there is a meaningful distinction between implication and construction.[244] While space does not permit a full analysis of the issue, it seems clear that Lord Hoffmann's view was the better one despite having been rejected by Lord Neuberger in *Marks and Spencer plc v BNP Paribas Securities Services Trust Co (Jersey) Ltd*.[245] Lord Neuberger's statement that '[w]hen one is implying a term or a phrase, one is not construing words, as the words to be implied are ex hypothesi not there to be construed'[246] fails to appreciate that '[t]he meaning which a document (or any other utterance) would convey to a reasonable man is not the same thing as the meaning of its words'.[247] In life and in law, 'people often mean more than they say'.[248] A further problem with the rejection of this view in *Marks and Spencer* is that nowhere is it suggested what the justification is for the implication of terms, if not to ascertain the meaning of the contract as a whole.

6.99 But the argument here does not depend on accepting this. Even if one agrees with Lord Neuberger generally, the distinction between implication and construction (if any) in this specific context is vanishingly small. This is because the question whether the parties' express promises are implicitly conditional could be seen, not as involving the implication of a new 'term', but simply as establishing an implicit meaning of an express term,[249] similar to Ludwig Wittgenstein's 'game'[250] example (discussed below). Thus, construing the contract or implying a condition 'are in these cases only alternative ways of describing the same process'.[251] And if the construction theory today provides the 'most satisfactory explanation of the doctrine of frustration',[252] then it seems

[243] Lord Hoffmann, 'Anthropomorphic Justice: The Reasonable Man and His Friends' (1995) 29 The Law Teacher 127, 140.
[244] See, eg, *Attorney General of Belize v Belize Telecom Ltd* [2009] 1 WLR 1988 and *Marks and Spencer plc v BNP Paribas Securities Services Trust Co (Jersey) Ltd* [2016] AC 742.
[245] [2016] AC 742.
[246] ibid 756 [27].
[247] *Investors Compensation Scheme Ltd v West Bromwich Building Society* [1998] 1 WLR 896, 913.
[248] Lord Hoffmann, 'Language and Lawyers' (2018) 134 Law Quarterly Review 553, 564.
[249] See Frederick Wilmot-Smith, 'Express and Implied Terms' (2023) 43 Oxford Journal of Legal Studies 54.
[250] Ludwig Wittgenstein, *Philosophical Investigations* (rev 4th edn by PMS Hacker and Joachim Schulte, Wiley-Blackwell 2009) 38.
[251] Peel (n 85) 1103 [19-127]. See also Hoffmann (n 243) 140.
[252] Peel (n 8) 1103 [19-127].

the implied condition view has simply been accepted under a different name. We have come full circle—as Sir Frederick Pollock said in 1881, 'the modern tendency . . . is to reduce all the rules on this subject to rules of construction'.[253]

Is the implied condition view nonetheless fictitious?

If it is accepted that the construction theory is the currently preferred explanation in the cases[254] then, as a matter of positive law, it seems clear that frustration is a product of the parties' agreement. And, as explained above, the construction theory is, in substance, no different to the implied condition view. But is the idea that the conditions are found in the parties' agreement convincing? **6.100**

One problem said to arise with the implied condition view 'is that it turns on a test of what the parties would have said in response to the interjection of the "officious bystander" at the moment of the parties' agreement'.[255] In *Denny, Mott & Dickson Ltd v James B Fraser & Co Ltd*,[256] Lord Wright said: **6.101**

> It is not possible, to my mind, to say that, if they had thought of it, they would have said: 'Well, if that happens, all is over between us.' On the contrary, they would almost certainly on the one side or the other have sought to introduce reservations or qualifications or compensations.

This criticism has been repeated in a number of cases.[257] But it suffers from two key defects. First, like we noted above, it often expresses the relevant event with too great a degree of specificity. So, in *National Carriers Ltd v Panalpina (Northern) Ltd*,[258] Lord Hailsham LC spoke of the officious bystander pointing out 'a temporary closure of Kingston Street pending a public local inquiry into a proposal for demolition after the lease had been running for over five years' and then said, unsurprisingly, 'I have not the least idea what they would have said'. Not only does this express the event with too great a degree **6.102**

[253] Frederick Pollock, *Principles of Contract: Being a Treatise on the General Principles Concerning the Validity of Agreements in the Law of England* (3rd edn, Stevens and Sons 1881) 381.

[254] cf *Canary Wharf (BP4) T1 Ltd v European Medicines Agency* [2019] EWHC 335 (Ch) [26(5)], but see Peel (n 85) 1103–04 [19-128].

[255] *Canary Wharf (BP4) T1 Ltd v European Medicines Agency* [2019] EWHC 335 (Ch) [26(1)]. The reliance on the 'officious bystander' appears, in this context, to have originated from Earl Loreburn in *FA Tamplin Steamship Co Ltd v Anglo-Mexican Petroleum Products Co Ltd* [1916] 2 AC 397, 404.

[256] [1944] AC 265, 275.

[257] See also *The Eugenia* [1964] 2 QB 226, 238; *Davis Contractors Ltd v Fareham Urban District Council* [1956] AC 696, 720; *National Carriers Ltd v Panalpina (Northern) Ltd* [1981] AC 675, 687.

[258] [1981] AC 675, 687.

of precision, it should also be noted that in *National Carriers Ltd v Panalpina (Northern) Ltd* the 'contract' was not 'frustrated', so Lord Hailsham LC's answer is unsurprising.

6.103 The second defect with this criticism flows from the use of the 'officious bystander' test in the first place. As evidenced by the statements made when raising the criticism, the 'officious bystander' test runs the risk of focusing on the actual parties, even though the inquiry is 'irrespective of the individuals concerned, their temperaments and failings, their interest and circumstances'.[259] As Lord Hoffmann explained:

> The vividness of the scene which [the invocation of the officious bystander] creates mean that we cannot avoid having our minds predispositions influenced by what we know of the actual characters of the contracting parties. And yet we know that it is a fundamental principle of the English law of contract that on a question of construction, the characters, minds and subjective intentions of the actual parties are irrelevant and inadmissible.[260]

In other words, '[b]y conjuring up the image of the *actual* parties in such vivid reality, the officious bystander distracts the court from the objectivity with which it should interpret the text'.[261]

6.104 The combination of these two defects has given unmerited strength to the objections against the implied condition view based on the use of the officious bystander. But when the metaphor of the officious bystander is removed, the position becomes clearer. The fact that had the individual parties known the precise means by which (i) an obligation would become impossible to perform, (ii) one party would be deprived of substantially the whole benefit of the bargain, or (iii) the circumstances would become radically different, they may have bargained for something different, or indeed not bargained at all, is beside the point. The question is what a reasonable person would have understood the parties to mean, and that question is to be assessed objectively at the time of contracting.

6.105 The strongest objection is that the implied condition view depends on too capacious a notion of agreement, even when assessed objectively, to be plausible. Wilmot-Smith has noted that whether frustration can be explained in this way 'depends, in particular, upon the plausibility of building a generic exception,

[259] *Hirji Mulji v Cheong Yue Steamship Co Ltd* [1926] AC 497, 510.
[260] Hoffmann (n 243) 139.
[261] ibid 140 (emphasis in original).

such as [the possibility condition] into parties' agreements'.[262] While expressly not engaging in that project, he notes that 'the widespread rejection of the implied terms thesis of frustration illustrates that few believe the contracting parties' agreement is capable of bearing the semantic load Blackburn J [in *Taylor v Caldwell*] must have supposed'.[263]

It will not be possible in this chapter to address the 'deep questions in the philosophy of action'[264] raised by Wilmot-Smith's doubts.[265] But a few brief points can be made. To begin, and to put the debate into its context, it is well accepted that our utterances can have meanings that are not explicitly or consciously stated. Take Wittgenstein's famous example: **6.106**

> Someone says to me, 'Show the children a game.' I teach them gambling with dice, and the other says, 'I didn't mean that sort of game'. In that case, must he have had the exclusion of the game with dice before his mind when he gave the order?[266]

The point of the example is that the background context limits the meaning of the words used, even if the speaker did not 'consciously formulate dice as an exclusion'.[267] The answer to the question therefore is 'no'. And as Wilmot-Smith notes, this 'insight is, in substance, widely accepted in the law of contract'.[268] That is why 'the meaning of [a] document is what the parties using those words against the relevant background would reasonably have been understood to mean'.[269] The precise debate in this context is 'about quite *how much* work the more robust concept of meaning can do'.[270] **6.107**

The debate boils down to whether 'background assumptions' can constitute a condition of our promises to perform. The premise of this debate appears to be that expressions of intentions, or agreements, are construed objectively in a manner consistent with how we understand our subjective intentions to be formed. If our subjective intentions are not conditioned by background assumptions, it seems unlikely that a reasonable person would understand our **6.108**

[262] Wilmot-Smith, 'Termination after Breach' (n 223) 319.
[263] ibid.
[264] ibid.
[265] Although see Alexander Georgiou, 'Mistaken Payments, Quasi-Contracts, and the "Justice" of Unjust Enrichment' (2022) 42 Oxford Journal of Legal Studies 606; Ferrero (n 154).
[266] Wittgenstein (n 250) 38.
[267] Wilmot-Smith, *Failure of Condition* (n 223) 56.
[268] ibid 56.
[269] *Investors Compensation Scheme Ltd v West Bromwich Building Society* [1998] 1 WLR 896, 913; quoted ibid 56.
[270] Wilmot-Smith, *Failure of Condition* (n 223) 56 (emphasis in original).

statements of intentions or promises to be implicitly conditional upon background assumptions remaining true. So, an understanding of how conditional intentions are formed helps us understand how a reasonable person would construe a promise to perform and whether it is implicitly conditional.

6.109 An example of a background assumption was given by Professor Lon Fuller:

> The absentminded professor stepping from his office into the hall as he reads a book 'assumes' that the floor of the hall will be there to receive him. His conduct is conditioned and directed by this assumption, even though the possibility that the floor has been removed does not 'occur' to him; that is, it is not present in his conscious mental processes.[271]

6.110 Wilmot-Smith argues that these ideas—of a 'condition' and a 'background assumption'—'must be kept apart'.[272] But he accepts that '[t]he distinction between a conditional intention and an intention formed on the basis of a background assumption is an extremely difficult one to draw in individual cases' and that '[t]he precise line between the two is determined by how robust a concept of implicit intention we employ'.[273] Nonetheless, he argues that in cases of frustration 'the underlying normative principle seems to be closer to a background assumption'.[274] By contrast, Alexander Georgiou argues that all background assumptions form part of our conditions of intention—a much wider claim than we need to accept here—but that only those that are expressly communicated or would be obvious to a reasonable person in the position of the other party form part of any agreement.[275]

6.111 In the context of 'frustration', it seems true to say that there is, at least in principle, a distinction between 'conditions' and 'background assumptions'. Not every assumption constitutes a condition of a party's obligation to perform. In *Canary Wharf*, the assumption that the United Kingdom would remain a member of the European Union and therefore that the premises could be used as headquarters, while known to both parties, was not a condition of the EMA's obligation to pay rent. Indeed, the rejection of a broader 'frustration of purpose' doctrine in this chapter, if correct, means that it cannot be the case that every background assumption, known to both parties, is a condition of the

[271] Lon L Fuller and Melvin Aron Eisenberg, *Basic Contract Law* (8th edn, West Academic Press 2006) 732–33; quoted in Melvin A Eisenberg, *Foundational Principles of Contract Law* (OUP 2018) 628.
[272] Wilmot-Smith, *Failure of Condition* (n 223) 61.
[273] ibid 63.
[274] ibid 250.
[275] Georgiou (n 265).

obligation to perform. But that does not mean that no background assumption can form part of the conditions to be found in the agreement.

Ultimately, it is submitted that this more robust concept of meaning can still explain the conditions identified in this chapter. To start with the easiest case first—the substantial-benefit condition—it has long been recognised that 'in a bilateral contract parties enter into contracts in order to secure the performance of the return promise rather than bargain for a lawsuit'.[276] Would a reasonable person in the position of the parties in *Taylor v Caldwell* have supposed that the plaintiffs were promising to pay even if not provided the use of the Music Hall? Absent any express or implied promise to do so, the answer to this would seem to be no. 6.112

As for impossibility, the question of construction appears simply to be whether the parties have promised to perform in the event of an impossibility of the kind that has arisen or not.[277] Did the parties promise to perform 'come Hell or High Water',[278] in which case their respective promises will be construed as absolute and unconditional?[279] In some cases, such as where one party has taken on the risk that performance will not be possible, this will be the case. But often this will not be the proper construction. Parties enter into agreements with the background knowledge that a party will be unable to perform an impossibility, and unless one party has promised for one reason or another that they will perform no matter what, or that they will perform in these particular circumstances of impossibility, then the most natural conclusion is that they did not promise to perform an impossibility. And if there is no promise, then there must be a condition.[280] This might be why in *Taylor v Caldwell*, Blackburn J conditioned his proposition on 'the absence of any express or implied warranty that the thing shall exist'.[281] 6.113

The hardest cases are those falling under the umbrella of the not-radically-different condition. This is where the distinction between a background assumption and a condition seems most relevant. Indeed, that is why care must be taken to ensure that the not-radically-different condition is only found to have failed in the most 'radical' of cases. As noted earlier, 'it cannot be supposed 6.114

[276] Francis Dawson, 'Readiness and Willingness under the Contractual Remedies Act' (2017) 23 New Zealand Business Law Quarterly 61, 65.
[277] See JC Smith, 'Contracts—Mistake, Frustration and Implied Terms' (1994) 110 Law Quarterly Review 400, 403.
[278] Borrowed from Weir (n 2) 191.
[279] See [6.73] above.
[280] Smith (n 277) 403.
[281] *Taylor v Caldwell* (1863) 3 B & S 826, 833; 122 ER 309, 312.

that any bargain has been made on the tacit condition that [change] will not happen *in any degree*'.[282] But it does seem that some cases can be conceived of in which it would seem fair to say that one party did not promise to perform in the circumstances in which the parties find themselves. Thus, in the example of the escaped tiger from the travelling menagerie given above—which is arguably an instance of this condition—it seems unlikely that a reasonable person would have understood the milk delivery person to be promising to perform at risk to life and limb.

6.115 Of course, in all these cases if the parties had wished to make their respective promises conditional, they could have done so expressly. That was the thinking behind the old approach in *Paradine v Jane*. But the 'seductive idea that a contract can . . . [expressly] articulate every contingency that might arise before, during, or after performance is sheer fantasy'.[283] Put another way: '[I]n contracting, as in other areas of life, some things go without saying. And a central characteristic of things that go without saying is—they are not said.'[284]

Summary

6.116 In summary, the implied condition view can explain the discharge of the parties' respective obligations to perform in cases of frustration. The objections to this view have tended to attack a strawman. They have stated the condition with needless precision and have rejected the implied condition view on an incorrect basis—that we are concerned with what the parties subjectively intended. Moreover, the view which now appears to be favoured judicially and academically—the 'construction theory'—properly understood, is the implied condition view in all but name. In particular, the distinction (if any) between implication and construction in this context is meaningless once it is appreciated that this view can be seen not as involving the implication of a new term, but as establishing an implicit meaning of an express term. While this does involve a capacious notion of agreement, it is well accepted in life and in law that our utterances can have meanings that are not explicitly or consciously stated. As for how much work this notion of agreement can do, if one accepts that some background assumptions can form part of the conditions of our

[282] *FA Tamplin Steamship Co Ltd v Anglo-Mexican Petroleum Products Co Ltd* [1916] 2 AC 397, 403 (emphasis added).
[283] Randy E Barnett and Nathan B Oman, *Contracts: Cases and Doctrine* (6th edn, Wolters Kluwer 2017) 1065; quoted in Eisenberg, *Foundational Principles of Contract Law* (n 271) 629.
[284] Eisenberg, *Foundational Principles of Contract Law* (n 271) 629.

intentions, then there is no reason why they cannot form part of the conditions found in our agreements. And if this is right, then the conditions in cases of frustration can be found in the parties' agreement.

None of this is to say that understanding frustration in this way makes it any easier to determine the scope of the relevant conditions and when they will fail. The implied condition view is not a panacea for these difficult questions of construction, which will often involve line-drawing and differences of opinion. The importance of understanding this view, however, is that it helps us understand why the parties are discharged, and how this form of discharge relates to other instances of discharge in contract law. **6.117**

Is Frustration Invariably Automatic?[285]

The final part of this chapter deals briefly with a question often raised in connection with the relationship between discharge following breach and discharge in cases of frustration: 'is frustration invariably automatic'?[286] On the orthodox approach, discharge following breach depends upon an election to exercise the power to terminate, whereas frustration 'brings the contract to an end forthwith, without more and automatically'.[287] On the view put forward in this book, however, the distinction between these two instances of discharge is much less significant than it at first sight appears. This is because in both cases the party whose obligation was conditional is discharged immediately upon the failure of the condition. In this limited sense, both discharge following breach and discharge following frustration are 'automatic'. **6.118**

But even on this view, the question arises in another form. In the context of breach, it was said that ordinarily (subject to the limits discussed in Chapter 5)[288] the innocent party may waive the condition and continue to perform and insist upon performance. Is it then possible for the parties in a case of frustration to waive the relevant conditions and continue performing?[289] In *BP Exploration Co (Libya) Ltd v Hunt (No 2)*,[290] Robert Goff J answered this question in the negative. He said: **6.119**

[285] See Goldberg (n 3).
[286] ibid. See Wilmot-Smith, 'Termination after Breach' (n 223) 314–16; McKendrick (n 69).
[287] *Hirji Mulji v Cheong Yue Steamship Co Ltd* [1926] AC 497, 505.
[288] See [5.52]–[5.63].
[289] This difficulty was identified in Wilmot-Smith, *Failure of Condition* (n 223) 258.
[290] [1979] 1 WLR 783, 809–10.

> [I]t is well established that, if a contract is frustrated, it is forthwith determined as a matter of law.... That being the case, it is somewhat difficult to talk in terms of one party in such circumstances 'waiving frustration of the agreement or any right to rely thereon' or being 'estopped from relying thereon' against the other party.[291]

In a similar vein, in *Joseph Constantine Steamship*,[292] Lord Wright said: 'in the case of frustration the contract is ended and dead, simply by the frustrating event. If the parties choose to go on with it, that is in truth entering into a new contract.'

6.120 It is apparent from these statements that the reason it is not seen as possible for the parties to continue performance in cases of frustration is that 'the contract' has been determined. But as Professor John Stannard has argued in this context, '[t]his sort of reasoning leads to muddle and confused thinking'.[293] It acts '[a]s if there were some entity called "the contract" which could be "in existence" one moment and "gone" the next moment!'[294] The conclusion follows from the premise, but the premise is wrong.

6.121 In principle, parties ought to be able to waive the conditions of their obligations to perform—frustration need not be 'invariably automatic'.[295] Take a case in which a seller promises to sell to the buyer 100 tons of a crop specifically to be grown on the seller's land but, due to no fault of the seller, most of the crop fails and only 10 tons is harvested. There are three possibilities:

(1) It may be that, on a proper construction of the contract, the price is 'severable', meaning that delivery of 100 tons is not a condition precedent to payment and that each delivery of a ton satisfies the condition precedent to payment of the severed proportion of the price.[296] In such a case, it would make sense to say that the obligation to deliver is also severable (in that it can be broken down into individual obligations), such that the possibility condition only discharges the seller pro tanto.[297] The result would be that the seller is bound to deliver the 10 tons harvested,

[291] ibid.
[292] *Joseph Constantine Steamship Line Ltd v Imperial Smelting Corp Ltd* [1942] AC 154, 188.
[293] Stannard (n 183) 746.
[294] ibid.
[295] Goldberg (n 3). See also McElroy (n 4) 96–98, 106, 221–31.
[296] See, eg, *Ritchie v Atkinson* (1808) 10 East 295, 103 ER 787.
[297] See, eg, *Howell v Coupland* (1876) 1 QBD 258 (although note the ambiguity as to whether the seller was required to deliver the successful proportion, which he had done; the only issue was in respect of the unsuccessful proportion).

and the buyer is bound to accept (and pay for) the 10 tons. Waiver is not relevant in this scenario.

(2) Alternatively, although the price and the obligation to deliver are severable, it may be that delivery of 100 tons is a condition of the buyer's obligation to accept (and pay for) the crop. In such a case, the buyer would be under no duty to accept anything less than 100 tons. The seller, on the other hand, would again be discharged only pro tanto by the possibility condition, but prima facie bound to deliver the 10 tons harvested. This would present the buyer with a choice: either the buyer could refuse to accept the delivery (in which case the seller would be discharged due to the failure of the concurrent condition that the buyer be ready, willing, and able to accept delivery), or the buyer could waive the condition of delivery of 100 tons and accept the 10 tons harvested (in which case the seller would be bound to deliver and liable in damages for failing to deliver the 10 tons). This appears to have been the result reached in *HR and S Sainsbury Ltd v Street*.[298] Buyers agreed to purchase 275 tons of barley that was to be grown on the seller's farm. The crop, due to no fault of the seller, only produced 140 tons, which was then sold to a third party. The buyers brought an action for damages for the failure to deliver the 140 tons. MacKenna J held that the seller was liable and that the buyers had the option of requiring delivery of the crops produced.

(3) Finally, it may be that neither the price nor the obligation to deliver are severable in the sense described above, and that on a proper construction of the agreement the seller only promised to deliver 100 tons (no more, no less) and the buyer only promised to accept (and pay for) 100 tons (no more, no less). In such a case, if the seller waives the condition of possibility, the buyer is still under no duty to accept and pay for the goods. If the buyer waives the condition that 100 tons are delivered, the seller is still under no duty to provide the goods. This was the result reached in *Lovatt v Hamilton*.[299] A contract for the sale of 50 tons of palm oil to arrive onboard a particular vessel was entered into but only seven tons arrived. The Court held that the arrival of the oil was a condition precedent and that the buyers were not entitled to the seven tons which had arrived on the basis that it was an 'entire contract'.[300] In such a case, both parties must agree to waive the relevant conditions for

[298] [1972] 1 WLR 834.
[299] (1839) 5 M & W 639, 151 ER 271.
[300] ibid 644–54; 273.

it to have any operative effect. But in many cases, the result of this will be to create a new agreement. And here, the difference between a view that says in principle both parties can waive and a view that says they must enter into a new agreement—while a difference nonetheless—is marginal.

6.122 There is thus no reason why, in appropriate cases, it should not be possible to waive the relevant conditions, though there may be some limits beyond those considered in Chapter 5. For example, it would make little sense for a seller to waive a condition so as to render themselves liable in damages when it is not possible to perform at all—and it might be said that in cases of total impossibility no person would be held to such a representation.

6.123 By way of a postscript, sometimes on the orthodox approach the opposite question is asked: '[w]hy is termination not automatic',[301] particularly in cases where the breach deprives one party of substantially the whole benefit of the contract? The answer that has been offered is that this is a manifestation of the 'fundamental legal and moral rule that a man should not be allowed to take advantage of his own wrong'.[302] But, as we have seen in Chapter 2, the modern view that it is necessary to terminate the contract is simply the result of a series of missteps flowing from loose language, the practical steps which often need to be taken in order to negate any suggestion of waiver of the condition, and the tendency to apply statements about needing to accept a repudiation (in the sense of renunciation) to cases of actual breach. Orthodoxy starts from the position that the effects of the two events (discharge following breach and discharge in cases of frustration) are very different and then seeks to offer an explanation for that difference. But on the approach taken here, the effects should not be different and they ought to be treated the same.

Conclusion

6.124 This chapter has been concerned with defending the view that the best explanation of the discharge of each party in cases of frustration is the failure of an implied condition. This is the explanation that has been given traditionally and is consistent with the repeated statements over the years that 'no Court has an

[301] Wilmot-Smith, 'Termination after Breach' (n 223) 314.

[302] *Hongkong Fir Shipping Co Ltd v Kawasaki Kisen Kaisha Ltd* [1962] 2 QB 26, 66. See also Wilmot-Smith, 'Termination after Breach' (n 223) 314–16.

absolving power'.[303] The first part of this chapter sought to demonstrate the operation of the various conditions in play. The second explained the unfortunate side effects of the modern unified doctrine of frustration which came about as a result of the war cases. The third, and arguably the most important part, defended the view that these are conditions to be found in the parties' agreement. It was seen that objections to this view have tended to attack a straw man and that the preferred 'construction theory' is simply a variant of the implied condition view. Finally, the chapter concluded by explaining why, at least in principle, the parties ought to be able to waive the conditions of their obligations to perform.

The purpose of this analysis is not to cling to the past. Some legal developments are desirable. But unfortunately the law of frustration has developed in a way that obscures its proper basis and its relationship with other instances of discharge. Once frustration is understood as an instance of failure of condition, the relationship between it and other forms of discharge becomes much clearer. Often, the only difference between instances of discharge for failure of condition considered elsewhere in this book[304] and in this chapter is that the former involves a breach of duty (ie a breach of contract). And in the next chapter, it will be seen that in cases of common mistake the only feature that sets those cases apart from cases of frustration is timing. In cases of frustration, the condition fails after the contract is formed; in cases of common mistake, the condition fails from the beginning. **6.125**

[303] *FA Tamplin Steamship Co Ltd v Anglo-Mexican Petroleum Products Co Ltd* [1916] 2 AC 397, 404; *Joseph Constantine Steamship Line Ltd v Imperial Smelting Corp Ltd* [1942] AC 154, 185; *Denny, Mott & Dickson Ltd v James B Fraser & Co Ltd* [1944] AC 265, 281; *Metropolitan Water Board v Dick, Kerr & Co Ltd* [1918] AC 119, 127; *British Movietonews Ltd v London and District Cinemas Ltd* [1952] AC 166, 183.

[304] Such as those considered in Chapter 3.

7
Common Mistake

Introduction

A widespread view is that English law recognises a 'doctrine of common mistake' which provides that '[w]here both parties share the same mistake of fact or law . . . the contract may be void'.[1] By contrast, the central argument of this chapter is that the best explanation of the doctrine of common mistake is it is not a doctrine based on 'mistake' but rather that it simply depends on implied conditions to be found in the parties' agreement.[2] Whether the parties were 'mistaken' ultimately has no impact at all on what is a question of construction: did the **7.1**

[1] Jack Beatson, Andrew Burrows, and John Cartwright, *Anson's Law of Contract* (31st edn, OUP 2020) 296. See too John Cartwright, *Misrepresentation, Mistake and Non-Disclosure* (6th edn, Sweet & Maxwell 2022) 580–81 [15-19]. Compare Hugh Beale, 'Common Mistake' in Hugh Beale (ed), *Chitty on Contracts* (35th edn, Sweet & Maxwell 2023) vol 1 751, 756–57 [9-011]; Edwin Peel, *The Law of Contract* (15th edn, Sweet & Maxwell 2020) 356 [8-006].

[2] S Martin Leake, *A Digest of Principles of the Law of Contracts* (3rd edn, Stevens and Sons Ltd 1892) 282–90; CJ Slade, 'The Myth of Mistake in the English Law of Contract' (1954) 70 Law Quarterly Review 385, 396–403; KO Shatwell, 'The Supposed Doctrine of Mistake in Contract: A Comedy of Errors' (1955) 33 Canadian Bar Review 164, 178–82; Arthur L Goodhart, 'Mistake and Frustration in English Contract Law' in *Aequitas und Bona Fides—Festgabe Zum 70 Geburtstag Von August Simonius* (Helbing & Lichtenhahn 1955) 99; JC Smith, 'Contracts—Mistake, Frustration and Implied Terms' (1994) 110 Law Quarterly Review 400; Stephen A Smith, *Contract Theory* (OUP 2004) 297–304; Jonathan Morgan, 'Common Mistake in Contract: Rare Success and Common Misapprehensions' (2018) 77 Cambridge Law Journal 559. For the similar, if not identical, view that it is a matter of the construction of the agreement see: PS Atiyah, '*Couturier v Hastie* and the Sale of Non-existent Goods' (1957) 73 Law Quarterly Review 340; PS Atiyah and FAR Bennion, 'Mistake in the Construction of Contracts' (1961) 24 Modern Law Review 421; Robert Stevens, 'Objectivity, Mistake and the Parol Evidence Rule' in Andrew Burrows and Edwin Peel (eds), *Contract Terms* (OUP 2007) 101, 105–06; Robert Stevens, 'The Meaning of Words and the Intentions of Persons' in Simone Degeling, James Edelman, and James Goudkamp (eds), *Contract in Commercial Law* (Lawbook Co 2016) 167, 178–79.

Discharge of Contractual Obligations. Jordan English, Oxford University Press. © Jordan English 2025.
DOI: 10.1093/9780198906704.003.0007

parties agree to perform in all events? And, as we saw in the previous chapter, rarely do the parties promise to perform 'no matter what'. Instead, often the obligations of each party are conditional on the existence of particular facts or the occurrence of particular events. Where those facts do not exist or the events cannot occur at the time the agreement is made, the obligations of the parties are 'inoperative'.[3] In this sense, there is, or at least ought not to be, any doctrine of common mistake that depends on the parties being 'mistaken'.

7.2 The chapter proceeds in four sections. The first section clarifies why, on the view put forward here, the contract is not 'void' other than in a loose sense of the term. The second section illustrates the different conditions that operate in cases said to be within the doctrine of common mistake and how those cases can instead be explained on the implied condition view. It will be seen that the conditions here mirror the conditions identified in Chapter 6. The third section—in light of the rejection of this view by the Court of Appeal in *Great Peace Shipping Ltd v Tsavliris Salvage (International) Ltd*[4] (*The Great Peace*)—responds to common objections to the implied condition view and explains the problems with the supposed doctrine of common mistake. Finally, the fourth section considers briefly whether there should be a doctrine of common mistake in equity[5] and concludes that there should not.

Inoperative Not Void

7.3 An initial difficulty with the view put forward in this chapter is that orthodoxy suggests that common mistake renders a contract 'void'.[6] The word 'void' is ambiguous. A contract can be void in one of two ways: either because there is no agreement or because there is an agreement but, for some reason, it takes no effect as a contract. In the context of unilateral mistake, which is not the focus of this chapter, it is said that the contract is void because mistake operates to 'negative'[7] consent (to show that there never was an agreement at all). By contrast, in cases of common mistake, the contract is said to be void because the shared mistake of the parties operates to 'nullify'[8] consent. There is

[3] Atiyah and Bennion (n 2) 427.
[4] [2003] QB 679.
[5] eg *Solle v Butcher* [1950] 1 KB 671, but see now ibid 725 [157].
[6] See, eg, *Bell v Lever Brothers Ltd* [1932] AC 161, 217–18; *Associated Japanese Bank (International) Ltd v Crédit du Nord SA* [1989] 1 WLR 255, 268.
[7] *Bell v Lever Brothers Ltd* [1932] AC 161, 217.
[8] ibid.

an agreement, but its terms are completely ineffective and it takes no effect as a valid contract.[9]

How then can the implied condition view put forward in this chapter be reconciled with the idea that in cases of common mistake the contract is void, ie of no effect? As Professor Patrick Atiyah and Francis Bennion noted, '[t]he circularity of saying that a contract is void, that is to say totally ineffective, because of the effect of one of its terms, is obvious'.[10] If the effect of common mistake is to render the contract void, in the sense of it having no effect, then this view looks doomed from the start. 7.4

One response is to suggest that the condition is to be implied not into the contract but into the offer and acceptance.[11] This was the argument of Sir Christopher Slade: 'there is consensus but at no time is there a contract'.[12] On this view, and contrary to the sense in which condition has been used in the rest of this book, the condition would be an 'external condition' (a condition to the formation of a contract) rather than an 'internal condition' (a condition that qualifies an obligation to perform).[13] It is akin to saying that the parties have not reached a binding agreement because, objectively construed, each only intended to contract if the relevant condition was satisfied. The contract would then be void in a similar sense to that used in unilateral mistake cases. 7.5

The problem with this response is that it seems misleading to suggest that there is no binding agreement in common mistake cases. As we shall see, in cases said to fall within the doctrine of common mistake, the parties have agreed on all the essential terms of the contract, even if the contractual obligations of the parties are not to be performed unless certain conditions are satisfied.[14] The better view is that there is an agreement which has taken effect as a perfectly valid contract, the contract contains the relevant conditions, and where those conditions have already failed at the time of contracting the parties are discharged from their obligations ab initio.[15] To put it another way, the obligations of the parties are 'inoperative'[16] because, properly construed, their 7.6

[9] See generally, Cartwright (n 1) 567–68 [15-03].
[10] Atiyah and Bennion (n 2) 427. See also Slade (n 2) 399 fn 67.
[11] Slade (n 2) 399.
[12] ibid 399 fn 67.
[13] See the discussion at [1.32]–[1.37].
[14] Smith, 'Contracts—Mistake, Frustration and Implied Terms' (n 2) 410; Atiyah and Bennion (n 2) 427.
[15] Shatwell (n 2) 182.
[16] Atiyah and Bennion (n 2) 427; Smith, 'Contracts—Mistake, Frustration and Implied Terms' (n 2) 410.

promises do not apply to the circumstances that have obtained. On this view, to say that the contract is 'void' is simply a loose way of saying that the contractual obligations of the parties are inoperative. It does not mean that there is no contract at all.

7.7 This approach also avoids difficulties that arise on the view that the contract is 'void' in the more usual sense of that term (ie that there is no valid contract). One such difficulty is the effect of clauses that are not premised upon performance, such as arbitration and jurisdiction clauses.[17] In *Harrison & Jones Ltd v Bunten & Lancaster Ltd*,[18] it was accepted by Pilcher J that if the contracts there in issue were 'void on the ground of mutual fundamental mistake' then 'there never were any contracts and consequently, . . . there never was an arbitration clause under which the parties could arbitrate their disputes'. This problem has now been remedied by legislation,[19] but it could have been avoided altogether. That is because on the view taken in this chapter, the reason the parties are not required to perform in cases of common mistake is that most (but not all) of their obligations are conditional. An arbitration clause, which itself is premised upon non-performance for whatever reason, is not usually conditional and thus can take effect. The contract is not void in the usual sense of that term. There is a perfectly valid contract and unconditional obligations or other terms that are not premised upon performance can take effect.

The Conditions in Cases of Common Mistake

7.8 The central argument of this chapter is that the doctrine of common mistake is best explained as a matter of construing the parties' agreement and determining the implicit conditions contained in it. But as with the cases said to fall within the doctrine of frustration, there are certain conditions that are commonly found in contracts that can explain the discharge of one or both parties in cases of common mistake. These include the 'possibility condition', the 'substantial-benefit condition', and the 'not-radically-different condition'. That the same conditions are commonly in play in cases of frustration and cases of

[17] See Stevens, 'The Meaning of Words and the Intentions of Persons' (n 2) 179.
[18] [1953] 1 QB 646, 653.
[19] Arbitration Act 1996, s 7.

common mistake is not surprising, given that the distinction between the two is simply a matter of timing, as is discussed further below.[20]

The possibility condition

It will be recalled that the 'possibility' condition is the condition of a party's obligation, generally but not always found, that it is possible to perform the obligation.[21] In Chapter 6, we dealt with cases where the condition failed after the making of the agreement (subsequent impossibility). In this section, we deal with cases where the condition, unbeknownst to the parties,[22] has already failed at the time the agreement is made (antecedent impossibility). The principles are, however, no different. Whether this condition is found is ultimately a question of construction. Two early cases that demonstrate this are *Bute v Thompson*[23] and *Clifford v Watts*.[24] **7.9**

In *Bute v Thompson*, the plaintiff demised his interest in a coal mine to the defendants for fifty years. The defendants in return covenanted that they would mine 13,000 tons of coal each year and pay a royalty equating to 8d per ton as a fixed rent 'whether the coals shall be worked or not'.[25] In an action by the plaintiff, it was alleged that the defendants had breached the covenant to mine 13,000 tons of coal in each year and had failed to pay the rent. The defendants responded by pleading that at the beginning of the period for which rent was due the mine was 'greatly exhausted' and that only a small amount of coal, less than a quarter of the 13,000 tons, remained to be worked out of the ground.[26] On a demurrer, Pollock CB held that this was no defence. Focusing on the fact that there was a 'fixed rent', he said that the covenant: **7.10**

> does not carry with it, by any implication, a condition that there shall be coals to that amount capable of being wrought. . . . [W]e cannot import into that covenant a condition that there should be coals to that extent. If that was the intention of the parties, they should so have expressed it.[27]

[20] See [7.96]–[7.99].

[21] See, eg, *Taylor v Caldwell* (1863) 3 B & S 826, 122 ER 309.

[22] cf where the impossibility was objectively apparent: Frederick Pollock, *Principles of Contract at Law and in Equity* (1st edn, Stevens and Sons 1876) 324. See also *Clifford v Watts* (1870) LR 5 CP 577, 588.

[23] (1844) 13 M & W 487, 153 ER 202.

[24] (1870) LR 5 CP 577.

[25] *Bute v Thompson* (1844) 13 M & W 487, 488; 153 ER 202, 203. Plus 9d per ton for any quantity above 13,000 tons.

[26] ibid 489; 204.

[27] ibid 494; 206.

7.11 This was not, strictly speaking, an impossibility case. Although a breach of the covenant to mine 13,000 tons of coal each year was alleged, the true nature of the action was one for the recovery of the rent, and it was not impossible to perform the obligation to pay the money. But the case is analogous to one in which the possibility condition is relied upon because the question was whether the obligation to pay the rent was conditional upon it being possible to raise 13,000 tons of coal out of the ground. The answer to this question was 'no' because the fixed rent was expressed to be payable whether the coal was mined or not.

7.12 By contrast, *Clifford v Watts* was an impossibility case. The plaintiff demised to the defendant a clay pit. The defendant in return undertook to dig no less than 1,000 tons per year and to pay a royalty of 2s 6d per ton. The plaintiff sued the defendant for breach of the covenant to dig 1,000 tons per year. The defendant denied the breach on the basis that there was not enough clay in the land to dig 1,000 tons per year and thus the performance of the defendant's covenant was, at the time of making it, impossible.

7.13 The Court of Common Pleas (Willes, Montague Smith, and Brett JJ), on a demurrer, found for the defendant and held that the plea was a good defence to the action. Willes J said that the question was 'whether the defendant ha[d] by this covenant contracted to perform an impossibility'.[28] He thought that the most 'natural and ordinary construction of the covenant' was that it was inapplicable if '[i]t turned out that there was no clay of the descriptions mentioned on the land'.[29] The covenant therefore had not been breached. Montague Smith J agreed and said that 'the covenantor did not undertake to perform an impossibility, but merely to dig and remove such clay as should be found in the land, to the extent stipulated for.'[30]

7.14 The Court distinguished *Bute v Thompson* on the basis that in that case there was a covenant for a minimum rent, irrespective of whether the coal was worked or not.[31] But although there was a covenant for minimum rent 'whether the coals shall be worked or not' in *Bute v Thompson*, it is likely that this was 'intended merely to reinforce the covenant to extract the coal'[32] and that the clause itself presupposed that there was in fact coal to be extracted. As Atiyah and Bennion explained, a better explanation for the difference between

[28] *Clifford v Watts* (1870) LR 5 CP 577, 583.
[29] ibid 585.
[30] ibid 588. See also 588 (Brett J).
[31] ibid 587 (Willes J), 588 (Montague-Smith J).
[32] Atiyah and Bennion (n 2) 436.

these two cases is that 'by the time *Clifford v Watts* was decided a change had taken place in the attitude of courts towards reading implied [conditions] into the literal contract'.[33] In particular, by this time *Taylor v Caldwell*, which was relied upon by counsel in argument,[34] had been decided. As we saw in Chapter 6, the incremental change brought about by *Taylor v Caldwell* was to indicate a greater willingness on the part of courts to find implied conditions where they had not been expressly stated.[35]

Whatever view one takes of the results in *Bute v Thompson* and *Clifford v Watts*, these cases demonstrate that whether impossibility operates to discharge a party from their obligation to perform ultimately depends upon whether that party has promised to perform an impossibility of the kind raised or not.[36] In *Clifford v Watts*, it was expressly stated by Willes J[37] and Brett J[38] that there is no principle which prevents a person from contracting to do that which is impossible. **7.15**

Decisions in other common law jurisdictions also demonstrate that whether an agreement contains the possibility condition is a question of construction. The most important is the decision of the High Court of Australia in *McRae v Commonwealth Disposals Commission*.[39] The Commonwealth Disposals Commission agreed to sell to the plaintiffs a wrecked oil tanker and its contents, which were believed to be lying on Jourmaund Reef, 100 miles north of Samarai Island, Papua New Guinea. As it turned out, there was no oil tanker near that location. The plaintiffs, sharing the defendants' belief that there was a tanker, entered into the contract, paid the purchase price, and then expended a large sum of money fitting a ship with diving and salvage equipment and engaging workers to proceed to New Guinea, which the workers did.[40] Upon discovering that there was no tanker, the plaintiffs claimed damages for 'breach of a contract to sell a tanker lying at a particular place'.[41] The High Court upheld the plaintiffs' claim and rejected the defendants' argument that the contract was 'void' for common mistake.[42] **7.16**

[33] ibid 435–36.
[34] *Clifford v Watts* (1870) LR 5 CP 577, 580. A point noted in ibid 436 fn 41.
[35] See [6.19]–[6.20].
[36] See Atiyah and Bennion (n 2) 435. Contrast *Sheikh Bros Ltd v Ochsner* [1957] AC 136 and see Atiyah and Bennion (n 2) 436.
[37] *Clifford v Watts* (1870) LR 5 CP 577, 585–86.
[38] ibid 588.
[39] (1951) 84 CLR 377.
[40] ibid 400.
[41] ibid.
[42] ibid 402–10.

7.17 Dixon and Fullagar JJ (with whom McTiernan J agreed) said that 'the problem is fundamentally one of construction'[43] and that when asking 'whether a promisor was excused from performance by existing or supervening impossibility', the common law:

> has always regarded the fundamental question as being: 'What did the promisor really promise?' Did he promise to perform his part at all events, or only subject to the mutually contemplated original or continued existence of a particular subject-matter?[44]

7.18 It was held that it was not possible to imply a condition precedent into the parties' agreement. This was because the 'terms of the contract and the surrounding circumstances clearly exclude[d] any such implication'.[45] Instead, '[t]he only proper construction of the contract [was] that it included a promise by the Commission that there was a tanker in the position specified'.[46] And the existence of the promise, meant that there was no room for a condition.[47]

The substantial-benefit condition (failure of consideration)

7.19 In Chapter 6, we saw how a number of cases within the scope of the doctrine of frustration were concerned with the substantial-benefit condition—the condition that renders one party's obligation to perform conditional upon that party receiving 'substantially the whole benefit which it was the intention of the parties as expressed in the contract that [they] should obtain as the consideration for performing those undertakings'.[48] The same is true of cases involving the doctrine of common mistake. This section outlines the cases that are best seen as instances of the application of the substantial-benefit condition. But this section also serves a subsidiary purpose. As we shall see, it so happens that almost all of the leading cases on common mistake fall into this category. This section therefore also tells a story, namely, how it is that English law came to recognise a doctrine of common mistake. Through this section it will be seen how a number of cases involving the substantial-benefit condition illustrate a conflict between the implied condition approach and a doctrine of common mistake.

[43] ibid 408, referring to *Clifford v Watts* (1870) LR 5 CP 577.
[44] *McRae v Commonwealth Disposals Commission* (1951) 84 CLR 377, 408.
[45] ibid 409.
[46] ibid 410.
[47] Smith, 'Contracts—Mistake, Frustration and Implied Terms' (n 2) 402–03.
[48] *Hongkong Fir Shipping Co Ltd v Kawasaki Kisen Kaisha Ltd* [1962] 2 QB 26, 66. See [6.31]–[6.58].

A question of construction

The application of the substantial-benefit condition is ultimately a question of whether one party got what they bargained for. This question in turn depends upon the construction of the contract. An early case that illustrates this proposition is *Couturier v Hastie*.[49] The plaintiffs sold a cargo of corn being shipped from Salonica (Thessaloniki) through the defendants, who were agents, on a *del credere* commission—a relationship in which the agent 'undertakes to indemnify the seller against the non-payment by the buyer of the price or other sums for which the buyer may be liable under the contract'.[50] Unknown to any of the parties involved in the sale, before the agreement was entered into, the cargo had become overheated and was sold off at Tunis to prevent further deterioration. The purchaser, upon discovering this, repudiated his liability under the contract and the plaintiffs brought an action for the price against the defendants on the basis of the commission. The defendants denied that the purchaser was bound on the grounds that the contract was for the sale of a specific cargo of corn and the corn did not exist in a form capable of being sold at the time the agreement was made.[51] The plaintiffs, in contrast, argued that the contract was for the purchase of the shipping documents and the chance of the cargo being in existence.[52] The Court of Exchequer Chamber and the House of Lords, disagreeing with the Court of Exchequer, held that the purchaser was not bound and the plaintiffs' claim failed. 7.20

At all levels, the judges agreed that the 'the whole question turn[ed] upon the construction of the contract which was entered into between the parties'.[53] In the House of Lords, Lord Cranworth LC said: 7.21

> The contract plainly imports that there was something which was to be sold at the time of the contract, and something to be purchased. No such thing existing, I think the Court of Exchequer Chamber has come to the only reasonable conclusion upon it . . .[54]

If we ask 'what did the parties intend to buy and sell', the answer given by the Court of Exchequer Chamber and the House of Lords is that the parties 7.22

[49] (1852) 8 Ex 40, 155 ER 1250 (Exch); (1853) 9 Ex 102, 156 ER 43 (Exch Chamb); (1856) 5 HLC 673, 10 ER 1065 (HL).

[50] Michael Bridge (ed), *Benjamin's Sale of Goods* (12th edn, Sweet & Maxwell 2023) 154–55 [3-004].

[51] See, eg, *Couturier v Hastie* (1852) 8 Ex 40, 48; 155 ER 1250, 1254.

[52] ibid 52–53; 1256.

[53] *Couturier v Hastie* (1856) 5 HLC 673, 681; 10 ER 1065, 1068. See also *Couturier v Hastie* (1852) 8 Ex 40, 53; 155 ER 1250, 1256; *Couturier v Hastie* (1853) 9 Ex 102, 107; 156 ER 43, 45.

[54] *Couturier v Hastie* (1856) 5 HLC 673, 681–82; 10 ER 1065, 1069.

intended to buy and sell a specific cargo of corn. The fact that the specific cargo of corn could not be provided was enough to discharge the purchaser (and therefore the defendants as *del credere* agents) from his obligation to pay the price. He did not get what he bargained for and therefore was not liable. Analysed in this way, *Couturier v Hastie* is a simple application of the substantial-benefit condition. As Pollock put it, '[h]ere the question was reducible to this: what were the parties dealing with, a real deliverable cargo or the chance of the cargo being delivered?'[55]

7.23 For some time, however, *Couturier v Hastie* was 'commonly treated in the textbooks as a case of a contract avoided by mutual mistake'.[56] Indeed, the belief that 'the sale was held to be void'[57] caused Sir Mackenzie Chalmers to draft s 6 of the Sale of Goods Act 1893, which provided (and still provides in its current form) that '[w]here there is a contract for the sale of specific goods, and the goods without the knowledge of the seller have perished at the time when the contract is made, the contract is void.'[58]

7.24 That this was the interpretation given to *Couturier v Hastie* is surprising because (i) 'mistake' is not mentioned in any of the arguments of counsel, or by any of the judges that heard the case,[59] and (ii) it was not necessary to decide, and no judge did decide, whether the contract was void, the sole issue being whether the purchaser was liable to pay the price.[60] In fact, had the liability of the vendors been in issue, it is possible that the court would have held that the vendors were liable to pay damages for breach on the basis that they had implicitly 'promised that the goods were in existence'.[61]

7.25 It is now generally accepted that *Couturier v Hastie* was not decided on the ground of a mistake rendering the contract void.[62] Properly understood, the

[55] Frederick Pollock, *Revised Reports: Being a Republication of Such Cases in the English Courts of Common Law and Equity, from the Year 1785, as are Still of Practical Utility* (Sweet & Maxwell 1908) vol 101, vi.

[56] *McRae v Commonwealth Disposals Commission* (1951) 84 CLR 377, 402. See, eg, Sir William R Anson, *Principles of the English Law of Contract* (1st edn, Clarendon Press 1879) 121. See further David Ibbetson, *A Historical Introduction to the Law of Obligations* (OUP 2001) 228.

[57] MD Chalmers, *The Sale of Goods Act, 1893, including The Factors Acts, 1889 & 1890* (William Clowes and Sons Ltd 1894) 17.

[58] See now Sale of Goods Act 1979, s 6.

[59] Atiyah (n 2) 342–43; Peel (n 1) 358 [8-009]; Beatson, Burrows, and Cartwright (n 1) 302.

[60] Atiyah (n 2) 346; Beale (n 1) 761–62 [9-019]; *McRae v Commonwealth Disposals Commission* (1951) 84 CLR 377, 406–07.

[61] *McRae v Commonwealth Disposals Commission* (1951) 84 CLR 377, 407 (emphasis removed). See also Beale (n 1) 762 [9-019]. cf *Barrow, Lane and Ballard Ltd v Phillip Phillips and Co Ltd* [1929] 1 KB 574, 582; Peel (n 1) 358 [8-009].

[62] Beale (n 1) 761–62 [9-019]; Atiyah (n 2); *McRae v Commonwealth Disposals Commission* (1951) 84 CLR 377, 402–08. Although cf the suggestion in Beatson, Burrows, and Cartwright (n 1) 302.

case makes clear that whether one party is discharged on the ground that they did not get what they bargained for depends on what precisely was the consideration for (and therefore the condition of) their promise. It is a question of construction, not one of a supposed doctrine of common mistake.

Two conflicting approaches

The cases considered thus far, involving the impossibility condition and the substantial-benefit condition, have illustrated the common law approach of treating issues that might today be analysed under the label of mistake as involving a question of construction. In the next case, however, Blackburn J, drawing on the civil law, took a very different approach. It is here that we find the origins of the supposed doctrine of common mistake.[63] But it will be argued below that this case too could have been explained as an instance of the substantial-benefit condition. Moreover, as will be seen, it is the introduction of this different approach that has led to the conflict that can be found in the authorities as to how best to rationalise cases of mistake. **7.26**

The plaintiff in *Kennedy v Panama, New Zealand, and Australian Royal Mail Co Ltd*[64] had been induced to buy shares by a statement in the defendant company's prospectus that the company had entered into a valuable contract with the government of New Zealand. When the plaintiff found out that the contract was disputed—and it was ultimately held to be ultra vires—he claimed that he was no longer a shareholder. He brought an action seeking to recover instalments on the shares he had paid, while the company brought an action to recover the remaining instalment due. **7.27**

The plaintiff's argument was put on two bases.[65] First he argued that the statement was a misrepresentation made fraudulently 'on the part of the directors'.[66] This latter part of the plea was necessary as the case was heard by a common law court in 1867 prior to the procedural fusion of law and equity effected by the Judicature Acts and the decision in *Redgrave v Hurd*,[67] which clearly recognised the power to rescind for any misrepresentation, whether fraudulent or innocent.[68] Secondly, the plaintiff argued that the statement in the prospectus **7.28**

63 Catharine MacMillan, *Mistakes in Contract Law* (Hart Publishing 2010) 190.
64 (1867) LR 2 QB 580.
65 See further MacMillan (n 63) 199–200.
66 *Kennedy v Panama, New Zealand, and Australian Royal Mail Co Ltd* (1867) LR 2 QB 580, 581.
67 (1881) 20 Ch D 1, 12–13.
68 See John Cartwright, 'The rise and fall of mistake in the English law of contract' in Ruth Sefton-Green (ed), *Mistake, Fraud and Duties to Inform in European Contract Law* (CUP 2005) 65, 70 fn 20; FH Lawson, 'Error in Substantia' (1936) 52 Law Quarterly Review 79, 88; Daniel Friedmann, 'The Objective Principle and Mistake and Involuntariness in Contract and Restitution' (2003) 119 Law Quarterly Review 68, 76.

'amounted to a condition, and was not a mere representation'.[69] On this basis, the plaintiff would simply never have come under any immediate duty to pay the instalments of the price for the shares. The company's response to both arguments was that 'the statement in the prospectus was a mere representation honestly made, and not a condition the non-performance of which avoided the contract of [the plaintiff] to take the new shares'.[70]

7.29 The Court (Cockburn CJ, Blackburn, Mellor, and Shee JJ) gave judgment for the company. Blackburn J, who delivered the Court's judgment, held on the first issue of misrepresentation that the directors had made 'an honest mistake, and not a fraudulent misrepresentation'.[71] As for the second issue, Blackburn J 'did not consider [the plaintiff's] condition precedent argument in the way in which it had been argued'.[72] Indeed, he appeared to reject an approach based upon implied conditions or, at the very least, only treat it as 'analogous'.[73] Instead, Blackburn J characterised the plaintiff's argument as being that he 'was entitled to return the shares . . . on the ground that he had applied for one thing and got another'.[74] Treating cases of innocent 'misrepresentation' as equivalent to cases of 'misapprehension', he said:

> where there has been an innocent misrepresentation or misapprehension, it does not authorize a rescission, unless it is such as to shew that there is a complete difference in substance between what was supposed to be and what was taken, so as to constitute a failure of consideration.[75]

7.30 This statement, particularly the reference to 'failure of consideration' could be seen as a simple application of the substantial benefit condition. The plaintiff had got what he bargained for and therefore had to pay the price—the substantial-benefit condition had not failed. But instead of relying upon a common law rule of construction, as had occurred in *Couturier v Hastie*, Blackburn J instead relied upon the 'civil law' to support this proposition. He noted that the Digest of Justinian laid down the general rule that 'where the parties are not at one as to the subject of the contract there is no agreement',[76] and he observed that this rule applies where there is a 'misapprehension as to

69 *Kennedy v Panama, New Zealand, and Australian Royal Mail Co Ltd* (1867) LR 2 QB 580, 581.
70 ibid 581–82.
71 ibid 586.
72 MacMillan (n 63) 202.
73 *Kennedy v Panama, New Zealand, and Australian Royal Mail Co Ltd* (1867) LR 2 QB 580, 588.
74 ibid 586.
75 ibid 587.
76 ibid.

the substance of the thing'[77] (*error in substantia*). After referring to the Digest, he said: 'the principle of our law is the same as that of the civil law'.[78] Ultimately, he held that the plaintiff could not succeed on this argument because he 'got [the] shares in the very company for shares in which he had applied'.[79] The 'misapprehension' concerned 'a material part of the motive'[80] of the plaintiff in buying the shares, but it did not prevent the plaintiff from getting in substance what he had bargained for.

On the assumption that Blackburn J intended to import a doctrine of *error in substantia* into English law, it has been argued that the doctrine was misapplied by him[81] and that which he purported to recognise was not the same as the 'civil law' doctrine.[82] More charitably, it has been suggested that Blackburn J 'intended only to support the common law approach to a failure of consideration with an analogy to the elegance of Roman jurisprudence'.[83] After all, Blackburn J had referred to the 'civil law' in the past in support of common law jurisprudence,[84] including in *Taylor v Caldwell*.[85] So understood, *Kennedy v Panama* could be explained as an instance of failure of the substantial-benefit condition which, as we have noted, often travels under the label of 'failure of consideration'.[86] **7.31**

Whichever the correct interpretation may be, one thing is clear: *Kennedy v Panama* ultimately contributed to the suggestion that there is a doctrine of mistake.[87] But Blackburn J's reliance on a 'civil law' doctrine also **7.32**

[77] ibid 588.
[78] ibid.
[79] ibid 589.
[80] ibid.
[81] Lawson (n 68) 88–89; *The Great Peace* [2003] QB 679, 699 [59].
[82] Cartwright (n 68) 71; Michele De Gregorio, 'Impossible Performance or Excused Performance? Common Mistake and Frustration after *Great Peace Shipping*' (2005) 16 King's Law Journal 69, 79.
[83] MacMillan (n 63) 203.
[84] See Cartwright (n 68) 68–71.
[85] (1863) 3 B & S 826, 834–35; 122 ER 309, 312–13.
[86] Although Blackburn J appears not to have treated failure of consideration as resting upon an implied condition.
[87] MacMillan (n 63) 205–07. It was in this same year (1867) that discussions of 'mistake' began to appear in textbooks: see Cartwright (n 68) 71; AWB Simpson, 'Innovation in Nineteenth Century Contract Law' (1975) 91 Law Quarterly Review 247, 267. This appears, however, to have been coincidental, given that (i) the first text to discuss 'mistake' did not refer to *Kennedy v Panama, New Zealand, and Australian Royal Mail Co Ltd* (1867) LR 2 QB 580 and (ii) the same text maintained that the question was 'whether the agreement is made absolutely, or only conditionally upon and with reference to the state of circumstances supposed by mistake, so that upon the real state of circumstances the agreement is inoperative and void': Stephen Martin Leake, *The Elements of the Law of Contracts* (1st edn, Stevens and Sons 1867) 176. The second edition, which refers to *Kennedy v Panama*, is in materially similar terms: Stephen Martin Leake, *An Elementary Digest of the Law of Contracts* (2nd edn, Stevens and Sons 1878) 339.

created a conflict between the approach taken by the civil law and the approach that had hitherto been taken by the common law. While '[c]ontinental doctrines . . . treated mistake as a way of showing that there was no consensus, and therefore no contract' the common law said that there was a consensus:

> [b]ut the agreement, the consensus, included an implied condition to the effect that the state of affairs existed; if it did not, the contract was not off because the parties had failed to agree, but because that was what the parties had agreed.[88]

The conflict between these two approaches continued throughout the nineteenth and twentieth century and still lingers today.

7.33 This conflict is well illustrated by two cases arising out the cancelled coronation procession for King Edward VII: *Clark v Lindsay*[89] and *Griffith v Brymer*.[90] These cases are also explicable in terms of the substantial-benefit condition.

7.34 In *Clark v Lindsay*, the plaintiff agreed to pay £50 to obtain the use of the defendant's rooms in Ludgate Hill for the purpose of viewing the coronation procession scheduled for 27 June 1902. It was a term of the agreement that the rooms were to be 'used only for the purpose of viewing the Coronation Procession'.[91] The agreement was entered into on 24 June and the plaintiff paid around 12 noon that day. Twenty minutes later, it was announced that the procession would be postponed due to the King's ill health. It was found that, at the time of contracting, the King's health was such that the procession could not go ahead (albeit that this fact was not known to the parties).[92] After seeing the announcement, the plaintiff immediately went back to the defendant. He initially demanded his money back but after negotiations, and on the assumption that the postponement would only be for a day or two, agreed to the insertion of a term that in the event the coronation procession was postponed, the plaintiff would have the use of the rooms on similar terms. When the postponed procession did not take place as planned,[93] the plaintiff sought recovery of the £50 paid. The case was concerned with the recovery of money paid, but the assumption appears to have been that if 'the contract was altogether inoperative'

[88] Simpson (n 87) 268 (emphasis removed).
[89] (1903) 88 LT 198.
[90] (1903) 19 TLR 434.
[91] *Clark v Lindsay* (1903) 88 LT 198, 199.
[92] ibid 199–200.
[93] The plaintiff argued that the postponement agreement contemplated '[t]he Coronation Procession with the foreign princes, and so forth', which never took place: ibid 200.

then 'the party who had paid his money was entitled to get it back'.[94] The focus was therefore on the two agreements made between the parties.

7.35 The High Court held that if matters had stood as they were after the original agreement was concluded, the plaintiff would have been able to recover the money paid. Unfortunately for the plaintiff, Lord Alverstone CJ (with whom Wills J agreed, Channell J concurring) held that the effect of the second agreement for a postponed procession, a procession which on the plaintiff's argument was subsequently abandoned,[95] was to bring it within the then-current rule in *Blakeley v Muller & Co*.[96] That rule precluded recovery of money paid pursuant to a contract in cases of subsequent impossibility (ie cases of frustration) 'unless there be a condition providing for the return of the money paid or payable before that event has been ascertained'.[97] This would later become known as the rule in *Chandler v Webster*,[98] and it was not overturned until the decision of the House of Lords in *Fibrosa Spolka Akcyjna v Fairbairn Lawson Combe Barbour Ltd*.[99] But there is perhaps a better explanation for the result. Channell J said that at the time of the second agreement '[t]he doubt was known and each party took his chance', with the result that no condition could be implied.[100]

7.36 In any event, our focus here is on the first agreement. Lord Alverstone CJ, after stating that '[t]he first thing in all these cases is to ascertain what the contract really is',[101] said:

> [I]t seems to me quite impossible to say that the procession was only the object or motive that induced the persons to enter into this contract.... [I]t really is the happening of the event—namely, the procession taking place—which is the substance of that which is contracted about and is contracted for.[102]

7.37 The references in Lord Alverstone CJ's judgment to the 'substance' of the contract appear to be references to *Kennedy v Panama* in which the same language was used by Blackburn J.[103] This potentially appears to support the existence of a doctrine of common mistake. But Channell J, who wished to be clear that he

[94] ibid 202.
[95] See n 93.
[96] (1903) 19 TLR 186.
[97] *Clark v Lindsay* (1903) 88 LT 198, 201.
[98] [1904] 1 KB 493.
[99] [1943] AC 32.
[100] *Clark v Lindsay* (1903) 88 LT 198, 202. See too Edwin Peel, *Frustration and Force Majeure* (4th edn, Sweet & Maxwell 2021) 294 [7-011].
[101] *Clark v Lindsay* (1903) 88 LT 198, 201.
[102] ibid.
[103] See the argument of counsel: ibid 200.

'[did] not in any way differ from what ha[d] been said by' the Chief Justice, said that the case fell within the principle in *Taylor v Caldwell* as depending upon an 'implied condition' and that '[t]he principle of the matter is exactly the same whether the thing contracted for is or is not in existence at the time the contract is entered into'.[104] Channell J said that the contract was a 'good contract' but:

> as originally made . . . was subject to an implied condition that, if the intention to hold the procession which existed, as the parties believed, at the time of the contract being made, was subsequently abandoned, then neither party was to be further bound by the contract.[105]

Channell J added that just as where the procession was abandoned after the making of the contract, 'if the procession had been abandoned before the contract was made, the contract was altogether inoperative, and . . . the party who had paid his money was entitled to get it back.[106]

7.38 Channell J's implied condition approach was followed in *Griffith v Brymer*.[107] In that case, the plaintiff sought to recover £100 paid by him pursuant to an oral agreement reached at 11am on June 24. The decision to operate on the King was reached at 10am, making it the case that at the time the agreement was made the procession could not take place. Neither party was aware of the postponement, which was not announced until later that day. Wright J held that the plaintiff was entitled to recover. He is reported as having 'expressed his agreement with the law as laid down by Mr Justice Channell in "*Clark v Lindsay*" '[108] although, perhaps adding to the confusion between the civil and common law approaches, he said that the contract was 'void'.

7.39 *Clark v Lindsay* and *Griffith v Brymer* are both illustrations of the substantial-benefit condition. The question is whether the party seeking to recover money or to resist payment (as the case may be) got what they bargained for. And, in these cases, the parties had not bargained for 'the letting of rooms for a few hours on a particular day'[109] but for a 'view of the procession'. These cases also strengthen the argument made in Chapter 6 that *Krell v Henry*—another coronation case—is simply an application of the substantial benefit condition and is not support for a broader 'frustration of purpose doctrine'.[110] In *Clark v*

[104] ibid 202.
[105] ibid.
[106] ibid.
[107] (1903) 19 TLR 434.
[108] ibid 434.
[109] *Clark v Lindsay* (1903) 88 LT 198, 202.
[110] See [6.43]–[6.58].

Lindsay, it was expressly stated that if the relevant event affects only the 'purpose which leads to the contract and which induces the parties to enter into it', it 'does not or cannot affect the rights of the parties in the same way as when it forms part of the subject of the contract'.[111] This is because whether one approaches the matter as Blackburn J did in *Kennedy v Panama* or from the perspective of the substantial benefit condition, the purpose of one party or both parties is irrelevant unless it is part of the contract.

Bell v Lever Brothers Ltd

The distinction between the common law and civilian approaches came to the fore in the decision in *Bell v Lever Brothers Ltd*.[112] The decision is valuable for its discussion of these approaches. It is also discussed here because, as will be seen, the best explanation of this leading case is that it had nothing to do with 'mistake' and everything to do with the substantial-benefit condition. **7.40**

The case concerned two defendants, Bell and Snelling, who had acted as directors and as the Chairman and Vice-Chairman (respectively) of the Niger Company, which traded in West African products, including cocoa. Lever Brothers held 99.5 per cent of the shares in the Niger Company. Both directors were appointed and maintained by Lever Brothers (in its capacity as the majority shareholder) pursuant to separate contracts of service. In 1929, the Niger Company merged with its primary competitor, and a new company was formed. There was no need for the two defendants in this new company. As such, an agreement was reached pursuant to which both defendants would 'retire from the Boards of the Niger Company and its subsidiaries'[113] in exchange for which Lever Brothers would pay Bell £30,000 and Snelling £20,000 in full satisfaction of any claims they might have against Lever Brothers, the Niger Company, or any associated company. **7.41**

After the agreements had been performed, it came to light that a couple of years earlier, Bell and Snelling had engaged in coca dealings on their own account, and kept these dealings and the resultant profits secret from the Niger Company. These breaches of duty by Bell and Snelling meant that Lever Brothers would have been 'justified in stopping any further payments to them, and would [have been] relieved from the obligation of further maintaining them in their offices'.[114] Lever Brothers brought an action seeking to recover **7.42**

[111] *Clark v Lindsay* (1903) 88 LT 198, 201.
[112] [1932] AC 161.
[113] ibid 178, 179.
[114] ibid 173.

the amounts that had been paid to each of the defendants on the ground that the agreements were entered 'into under such mutual mistake of fact as to render them not binding'.[115]

7.43 There was an issue as to whether an argument about 'mutual mistake' was open to Lever Brothers in light of the pleadings and how the case was run at trial. In the House of Lords, Lord Blanesburgh dismissed the case on that basis and Lord Atkin said that 'much may be said for [the] contention' that the argument was not open to Lever Brothers.[116] In any event, a majority of the House of Lords (Lord Atkin and Lord Thankerton, Lord Blanesburgh agreeing; Lord Warrington and Lord Hailsham dissenting) held that the claim could not succeed on the ground of 'mutual mistake'.

7.44 Lord Atkin expressed his conclusion on two alternative bases, reflecting the two approaches discussed above. The first basis was that there are some cases of mistake that 'nullify' (as opposed to 'negative')[117] consent. Such cases would include mistakes as to the existence of the subject-matter of the contract[118] and mistakes as to title.[119] He then added:

> Mistake as to quality of the thing contracted for raises more difficult questions. In such a case a mistake will not affect assent unless it is the mistake of both parties, and is as to the existence of some quality which makes the thing without the quality essentially different from the thing as it was believed to be.[120]

7.45 Applying the 'law as to mistake' to the present case, Lord Atkin said:

> [I]t would be wrong to decide that an agreement to terminate a definite specified contract is void if it turns out that the agreement had already been broken and could have been terminated otherwise. The contract released is the identical contract in both cases, and the party paying for release gets exactly what he bargains for. It seems immaterial that he could have got the same result in another way, or that if he had known the true facts he would not have entered into the bargain.[121]

[115] *Lever Brothers Ltd v Bell* [1931] 1 KB 557, 561. Importantly, the jury negatived any finding of fraud and found that 'the conduct complained of was not present to [the defendants'] mind[s] when the cancellation agreement was being negotiated': at 569.
[116] *Bell v Lever Brothers Ltd* [1932] AC 161, 217.
[117] ibid 217 (emphasis added).
[118] See, eg, *Couturier v Hastie* (1856) 5 HLC 673, 10 ER 1065; Sale of Goods Act 1979, s 6.
[119] See, eg, *Cooper v Phibbs* (1867) LR 2 HL 149.
[120] *Bell v Lever Brothers Ltd* [1932] AC 161, 218.
[121] ibid 223–24.

The second basis of Lord Atkin's speech was stated as 'the alternative mode of expressing the result of a mutual mistake',[122] namely, that there is an implied condition in the contract.[123] However, Lord Atkin warned: **7.46**

> The implications to be made are to be no more than are 'necessary' for giving business efficacy to the transaction, and it appears to me that, both as to existing facts and future facts, a condition would not be implied unless the new state of facts makes the contract something different in kind from the contract in the original state of facts.[124]

After suggesting that this gave 'a common standard for mutual mistake, and implied conditions whether as to existing or as to future facts', Lord Atkin concluded that 'in the present case the identity of the subject-matter was not destroyed'.[125] **7.47**

It thus appears that Lord Atkin saw the two approaches as different ways of getting to the same result. Lord Thankerton, by contrast, rejected the implied condition approach,[126] but it is fair to say that Lord Atkin's speech has certainly been the most influential. It should also be noted that the other member of the majority, Lord Blanesburgh, agreed with both Law Lords. At its highest, *Bell v Lever Brothers Ltd* appears to be supportive of both approaches. **7.48**

The result in *Bell v Lever Brothers Ltd* has been described as 'controversial',[127] 'quite exceptional',[128] and 'puzzling'.[129] Starting from the premise that the subject-matter of each contract was the 'contract of service',[130] it has been argued that there is 'an apparent contradiction'[131] between Lord Atkin's statement in relation to 'mistakes as to quality' and the decision in the case. For example, Sir John Cyril Smith argued: **7.49**

> The subject-matter, as the parties believed it to be, was worth £30,000; as it in fact was, it was worth nothing. As it is impossible to envisage a mistake as to quality which is more fundamental that that in *Bell v Lever Bros*, it is argued

[122] ibid 224.
[123] ibid 224–27.
[124] ibid 226.
[125] ibid 226–27.
[126] *Bell v Lever Brothers Ltd* [1932] AC 161, 237.
[127] Atiyah and Bennion (n 2) 438.
[128] *Associated Japanese Bank (International) Ltd v Crédit du Nord SA* [1989] 1 WLR 255, 267.
[129] Smith, 'Contracts—Mistake, Frustration and Implied Terms' (n 2) 411.
[130] See, eg, ibid 412; Peel (n 1) 363 [8-018].
[131] Smith, 'Contracts—Mistake, Frustration and Implied Terms' (n 2) 411. See also De Gregorio (n 82) 85.

that no common assumption as to the quality of the subject-matter will be regarded as sufficiently basic to avoid the contract.[132]

7.50 But the result is readily justifiable when one looks at what precisely the parties were buying and selling (to continue the sale analogy). According to the terms of the contract, Lever Brothers paid £50,000 total to Bell and Snelling in return for them 'retir[ing] from the Boards of the Niger Company and its subsidiaries'.[133] This is exactly what Bell and Snelling did. The fact that, due to the breaches of duty by Bell and Snelling, Lever Brothers could have used its voting powers as shareholders of Niger to remove them without being in breach of their agreement does not change the fact that the consideration for Lever Brothers' undertaking to pay was in fact the directors stepping down. This is precisely what occurred. On this view, Lever Brothers got exactly what it bargained for. In other words, the substantial-benefit condition had not failed.

7.51 Part of the key to understanding the case in this way is that Lever Brothers had the power to remove the directors at any time by virtue of it being a majority shareholder of the Niger Company. The service agreements were simply agreements to maintain Bell and Snelling in those positions 'so long only as they fulfilled their prescribed duties as officers of Niger'.[134] As Lord Blanesburgh was at pains to point out:

> So soon as they defaulted in these respects Levers would be justified in stopping any further payments to them, and would be relieved from the obligation of further maintaining them in their offices. But that would be all. For results more drastic Levers had to rely only on their voting power as shareholders of Niger.[135]

7.52 Suppose that the service agreements had never existed at all. Could it be said that if Lever Brothers agreed to pay £50,000 to the directors in exchange for them stepping down, and they did, that Lever Brothers had not got what it bargained for? Of course not. It might be said to be a bad deal given that Lever Brothers could remove them by the exercise of its shareholder voting powers for free, but this does not change the construction of the agreement. The position should not change simply because there is a service agreement and Lever Brothers mistakenly believed that it would be in breach of that agreement if it

[132] Smith, 'Contracts—Mistake, Frustration and Implied Terms' (n 2) 412.
[133] *Bell v Lever Brothers Ltd* [1932] AC 161, 178–79.
[134] ibid 172.
[135] ibid 172–73.

removed the directors. Lever Brothers bargained for the two directors to step down, and the two directors did. The fact that they could have got it for free is neither here nor there.

The above demonstrates that the result in *Bell v Lever Brothers Ltd* is readily explicable as an instance of the non-failure of the substantial-benefit condition. Although the result is also explicable in terms of Lord Atkin's narrow doctrine of mistake, it is submitted that references to 'mistake', based upon theories of subjective consent, only serve to obscure what is a simple question involving the substantial-benefit condition: did the party get what it bargained for? For example, Professor Catharine MacMillan has said: **7.53**

> If we base our doctrine of mistake upon a consensual theory of contract, which Lord Atkin clearly does, it is hard to imagine a more destructive force to consent. This is not a case where change makes the bargain less desirable; it is a case where the bargain would never be made.[136]

Quite so. But it is only when one looks at the case through the prism of 'mistake' that the result looks so odd. If one focuses on the proper construction of the agreement, and on when the substantial-benefit condition fails, the result is entirely orthodox.

Nonetheless, despite being explicable in terms of the substantial-benefit condition, the reference in *Bell v Lever Brothers Ltd* to a doctrine of mistake has led to the continued tension between the traditional common law approach of implying conditions and the civilian-inspired approach of recognising a doctrine of mistake. **7.54**

The Great Peace

The most recent leading case that can be analysed as turning upon the application of the substantial-benefit condition, and as illustrating the continuing conflict between the two approaches to the issue of mistake, is the decision of the Court of Appeal in *The Great Peace*.[137] In that case a vessel, the *Cape Providence*, was damaged in the South Indian Ocean. The defendants were a salvage company that had offered their services. They engaged a firm of brokers and asked them to find a vessel in the vicinity of the *Cape Providence* that could assist. The brokers were informed by a third party company that there **7.55**

[136] Catharine MacMillan, 'How temptation led to mistake: an explanation of *Bell v Lever Brothers Ltd*' (2003) 119 Law Quarterly Review 625, 658.

[137] [2003] QB 679.

were four vessels in the area and were given the estimated position of the *Great Peace*. The brokers thereupon contacted the *Great Peace's* managers and said that they believed the *Great Peace* was the closest vessel to *Cape Providence*.

7.56 The defendants agreed through their brokers to charter the *Great Peace* for a minimum period of five days at a rate of US $16,500 per day. Shortly after the contract was concluded, it came to light that the vessels were in fact 410 miles away from each other. Had the information from the third party company been correct the vessels would only have been 35 miles away from each other. Upon discovering this, the defendants told their brokers that they were 'looking to cancel the "Great Peace", but not yet'[138] because they wanted to 'know if there was a nearer available vessel which could provide assistance'.[139] By chance, shortly thereafter a vessel that was being chartered by the charterers of the *Cape Providence* passed by. The defendants thus instructed their brokers to cancel the charter of the *Great Peace*, which they did. The plaintiffs claimed $82,500, representing five days' loss of hire. The defendants, among other things, pleaded that the agreement was 'void in law for fundamental mistake', the relevant mistake being that 'both parties proceeded on the fundamental assumption of fact that the "Great Peace" was "in close proximity" to the "Cape Providence" when she was not'.[140] At first instance and on appeal, it was held that the defendants were liable to pay the $82,500.

7.57 At first instance, Toulson J explained that the 'effect of a mutual mistake . . . depends on the proper analysis of the contract and the rights and obligations thereby created'.[141] He said:

> [T]he contractual specification of the services to be provided by the Great Peace involved the necessary implication that the Great Peace was capable of providing the services specified. If, to take an extreme case, the Great Peace had been 5 days' sailing away from the 'Cape Providence', there would have been a failure of that implied condition precedent.[142]

7.58 Toulson J went on to say, however, that the condition had not failed. He noted that the *Great Peace* could have changed course[143] and he thought that the

[138] *The Great Peace* [2001] EWHC 529 (QB) [21].
[139] ibid.
[140] ibid [27(i)].
[141] ibid [50].
[142] ibid [55].
[143] ibid [56], although note the criticism of this suggestion in the Court of Appeal: *The Great Peace* [2003] QB 679, 727 [164].

reaction of the defendants upon learning of the vessels' true position was telling: 'Evidently the defendants did not regard the contract as devoid of purpose, or they would have cancelled at once'.[144]

Toulson J's decision was upheld by the Court of Appeal (Lord Phillips MR, May, and Laws LJJ). After a lengthy examination of the authorities and after rejecting the proposition that 'the doctrine of common mistake can be satisfactorily explained by an implied term'[145]—a point which will be discussed in the next section—Lord Phillips MR asked: '[w]as the distance between the two vessels so great as to . . . render the contractual adventure impossible of performance?'[146] The answer to that question was 'no'. Lord Phillips MR agreed with Toulson J that the defendants' reaction to learning of the true position of the vessels was a 'telling indication' that the services to be provided by the *Great Peace* were not 'essentially different from those which the parties had envisaged when the contract was concluded'.[147] The distance between the vessels 'did not mean that it was impossible to perform the contractual adventure'.[148] **7.59**

The language here of the 'impossibility' of performing the 'contractual adventure' should not be taken to suggest that this case was concerned with the possibility condition. The party seeking to be discharged here was the party who was to receive the performance and they sought to be discharged from their obligation to pay. This is a question involving the substantial-benefit condition: would the distance between the vessels, now discovered, mean that the defendants would not get what they bargained for? The answer both courts gave to that question was 'no'. **7.60**

A number of the leading cases therefore can be explained as turning upon the application of the substantial-benefit condition. But it is also in these cases that we find the origins of the doctrine of common mistake. The difficulties with the doctrine of common mistake are discussed below. Before considering those difficulties, however, it is necessary to consider one final condition—the not-radically-different condition. **7.61**

[144] *The Great Peace* [2001] EWHC 529 (QB) [56].
[145] *The Great Peace* [2003] QB 679, 704 [82].
[146] ibid 726 [162].
[147] ibid 727 [165].
[148] ibid.

The 'not-radically-different' condition

7.62 As explained in the previous chapter,[149] this final category is not a single condition but a more abstract label referring to an amalgamation of different conditions that have been held in various cases to be implicit in contracts. These are cases that cannot be explained by the possibility condition or the substantial-benefit condition, but where nonetheless the continued existence to some degree of the circumstances supposed to be prevailing at the time of contracting was a condition on which the contractual obligations of both parties are dependent.

7.63 One such case is *Associated Japanese Bank (International) Ltd v Crédit du Nord SA*.[150] Mr Bennett had entered into two contracts to sell and leaseback four machines with the plaintiff, Associated Japanese Bank. This was a means of raising finance. The defendant, Crédit du Nord, had guaranteed the obligations of Mr Bennett under the leaseback agreement. It later turned out that Mr Bennett was a fraudster and, despite the assumptions made by the plaintiff and the defendant, the machines did not exist. Mr Bennett was subsequently adjudged bankrupt and the plaintiff sought to recover from the defendant under the terms of the guarantee. The Court held that the plaintiff could not recover.

7.64 Steyn J based his decision on two grounds.[151] The first was based on clause 6 of the guarantee, which provided that the plaintiff's rights were not to be affected 'by the substitution of any other goods comprised in [the lease]'[152] provided the defendant consented to the substitution. Steyn J thought that clause 6 'contemplated the existence of the machines' and that therefore 'the guarantee was subject to an express condition precedent that there was a lease in respect of four existing machines'.[153] The second ground was that if this conclusion were wrong, 'the guarantee contained an implied condition precedent that the lease related to existing machines'.[154]

[149] See [6.59].
[150] [1989] 1 WLR 255.
[151] There is an argument that the contract was in fact a unilateral one and that there was no contract because the act of acceptance—the leasing of the machines—was never done: Smith, 'Contracts—Mistake, Frustration and Implied Terms' (n 2) 404–05. But this argument was not made.
[152] *Associated Japanese Bank (International) Ltd v Crédit du Nord SA* [1989] 1 WLR 255, 263.
[153] ibid.
[154] ibid.

7.65 Although it was not necessary to do so to resolve the case, given the role that the arguments had played in the hearing,[155] Steyn J then went on to discuss the law regarding common mistake. He said:

> For both parties the guarantee of obligations under a lease with non-existent machines was essentially different from a guarantee of a lease with four machines which both parties at the time of the contract believed to exist. . . . In my judgment the stringent test of common law mistake is satisfied: the guarantee is void ab initio.[156]

7.66 As Smith has noted, the implied condition view 'is in one respect supported, but in another, contradicted'[157] by Steyn J's judgment. On the one hand, as will be explored fully below,[158] the implied condition view left no room for an independent doctrine of common mistake. On the other hand, Steyn J did clearly separate the two ideas.[159] In any event, the case is readily explicable as turning upon a specific instance of the not-radically-different condition. This is because to say that the guarantee 'contemplated the existence of the machines'[160] is simply a more specific way of saying that 'the guarantee of obligations under a lease with non-existent machines was essentially different from a guarantee of a lease with four machines'.[161] The specific condition found by Steyn J is merely a specific instance of the group of conditions that have been referred to in this book, in the singular, as the 'not-radically-different' condition.

7.67 It should also be noted, for completeness, that the language of 'essentially different' was used in this case in a different sense to the way in which it was used in *Bell v Lever Brothers Ltd*. In the latter case, the language of 'essentially different' was a proxy for whether the plaintiff got what they bargained for—Lord Atkin referred to 'the thing contracted for'[162] as being that which must be essentially different. By contrast, in *Associated Japanese Bank*, the language of 'essentially different' was being used by one party to say that the performance of its guarantee obligations in these circumstances would be essentially different; in other words, that the circumstances in which performance would be called for were 'essentially' or 'radically' different from those which were supposed to

155 ibid 264.
156 ibid 269.
157 Smith, 'Contracts—Mistake, Frustration and Implied Terms' (n 2) 400.
158 See [7.91]–[7.94].
159 GH Treitel, 'Mistake in Contract' (1988) 104 Law Quarterly Review 501, 503.
160 *Associated Japanese Bank (International) Ltd v Crédit du Nord SA* [1989] 1 WLR 255, 263.
161 ibid 269.
162 *Bell v Lever Brothers Ltd* [1932] AC 161, 218.

be prevailing at the time of contracting. That is why the case can be analysed as involving the not-radically-different condition.

7.68 Another case which can be seen as involving the not-radically-different condition is the decision in *The Great Peace*, which was examined above. As we saw, the case is explicable primarily as an application of the substantial-benefit condition. But the defendants had also pleaded their case as being that it was a fundamental assumption of fact that the *Cape Providence* was in close proximity to the *Great Peace* when in truth it was not. Could it be argued that this circumstance, supposed by both parties to have obtained at the time of contracting, was a condition upon which the obligation of both parties was dependent?

7.69 The answer that Toulson J gave was 'no'. He thought that it would be 'wrong in the circumstances to elevate the facts reported . . . into terms of the subsequent contract between the parties'[163] and that '[i]f the defendants had wished for a contractual stipulation from the claimants as to the position of the Great Peace, they could have asked for it.'[164] This conclusion seems correct and reflects the fact, noted in the previous chapter,[165] that it is not a tacit condition of every agreement that some change will not happen 'in any degree'.[166] Although the vessels were further apart than supposed, it did not radically change the circumstances in which performance of either party was called for. Similar conclusions have been reached in circumstances involving the closure of the Suez Canal which, in order for the contracts to be performed, would have required the vessels to go around the Cape of Good Hope.[167] In *The Eugenia*, a case in which the charterers under a time charter sought to escape liability, Lord Denning MR said that '[t]he voyage round the Cape made no great difference except that it took a good deal longer and was more expensive for the charterers than a voyage through the canal'.[168] A similar argument could be made here.

7.70 A final case that illustrates a specific instantiation of the not-radically-different condition is *British Red Cross v Werry*.[169] The case concerned an agreement to settle an action under the Inheritance (Provision for Family and Dependants) Act 1975. The action had been brought by the unmarried partner (Miss Deeley) of the deceased (Mr Harding) against individuals that

[163] *The Great Peace* [2001] EWHC 529 (QB) [60].
[164] ibid [61].
[165] See [6.61].
[166] *FA Tamplin Steamship Co Ltd v Anglo-Mexican Petroleum Products Co Ltd* [1916] 2 AC 397, 403.
[167] See *Tsakiroglou & Co Ltd v Noblee Thorl GmbH* [1962] AC 93; *Ocean Tramp Tankers Corp v V/O Sovfracht (The Eugenia)* [1964] 2 QB 226.
[168] *The Eugenia* [1964] 2 QB 226, 240.
[169] [2017] EWHC 875 (Ch).

received property under the intestacy rules (the 'intestacy beneficiaries') 'on the basis that the rules of intestacy left [Miss Deeley] without reasonable provision for her maintenance.'[170] After Miss Deeley's death a few years later, and in the course of cleaning out the family home which both had occupied, Mr Harding's will was discovered. The will gave Miss Deeley considerably more than she had obtained under the settlement agreement.

The beneficiaries of Miss Deeley's will—five charities—sought leave to appeal from the order approving the settlement agreement on the basis that the agreement was 'void' for common mistake. Deputy Judge Elizabeth Cooke allowed the appeal on the basis that it was 'beyond dispute that the settlement agreement was entered into on the basis of a common mistake'.[171] She said that 'the mistake [was] as fundamental as . . . where a party contracted to purchase land that he or she already owned'.[172] **7.71**

This is a case in which the circumstances in which the agreement took effect were radically different from those which were supposed to be prevailing at the time of contract. But it is clear that the condition can be expressed with a greater degree of specificity than this: the obligations of the parties under the agreement were simply conditional upon there being an intestacy, the existence of which 'was necessarily the basis for the compromise agreement'.[173] **7.72**

Unconditional agreements

It was stated at the beginning of this chapter that rarely do the parties promise to perform 'no matter what'. But, as we saw in Chapter 6,[174] where the parties really do promise to perform 'no matter what', effect will be given to that expression of intention. The position is no different in cases said to be concerned with the doctrine of common mistake. Thus, in *Triple Seven Msn 27251 Ltd v Azman Air Services Ltd*,[175] the claimants leased to the defendant two aircrafts, each for a period of five years. The purpose, known to both parties, of the defendant in entering into the agreements was to 'transport passengers from West Africa to the Kingdom of Saudi Arabia for the Hajj and Umrah pilgrimages'.[176] **7.73**

170 ibid [6].
171 ibid [23]. The order was unopposed: [17].
172 ibid [22].
173 Morgan (n 2) 568.
174 See [6.73].
175 [2018] 4 WLR 97.
176 ibid [2].

A few days before the lease agreements were entered into—but unbeknownst to either party—the General Authority of Civil Aviation of Saudi Arabia sent a letter refusing permission for the defendant to participate in the transport of pilgrims to Saudi Arabia for the 2016 Hajj pilgrimage. The letter was received by the defendant a few hours after the agreements had been entered into. When the defendant failed to take delivery of the aircraft or pay the first instalments of rent, the claimant terminated the contractual obligations of the parties pursuant to a clause in the contract and commenced proceedings, among other things, seeking damages for breach of contract. The defendant's primary defence was that the leases were 'void' for common mistake.

7.74 Peter MacDonald Eggers QC, sitting as a Deputy High Court Judge, ultimately held that the 'mistaken assumption shared by the parties was not sufficiently fundamental' to render the lease agreements 'void'.[177] But even if this had not been the case, he would not have found that the lease agreements were void in part due to a clause in the agreements which provided that the lessee's obligations were 'absolute and unconditional, irrespective of any contingency or circumstance whatsoever'.[178] This clause meant that the lessor really did promise to perform 'no matter what'. And where that is the case, the parties ought to be held to their contracts.

Defending the Implied Condition View

7.75 As the previous section showed, not only can cases involving common mistake be explained on the basis of an implied condition, there was significant judicial support for this view prior to the decision in *The Great Peace*. Indeed, it is well recognised that the early cases, such as *Clifford v Watts* and *Couturier v Hastie*, 'tended to reason not from a doctrine of mistake, but from the construction of the terms of the agreement'.[179] In later cases too, this was at least one dominant way of explaining the result. We saw this in the coronation cases—*Clark v Lindsay* and *Griffith v Brymer*—which turned upon an implied condition, and in *Bell v Lever Brothers Ltd*, where Lord Atkin saw the implied condition approach as being at least an 'alternative mode of expressing the result of a mutual mistake'.[180] Similarly, at first instance in *The Great Peace*, Toulson J said

[177] ibid [89].
[178] ibid [91(2)].
[179] Cartwright (n 68) 67.
[180] *Bell v Lever Brothers Ltd* [1932] AC 161, 224.

that 'to speak of a mistake vitiating a contract is an alternative mode of analysing the effects of a mistake according to the true interpretation of the contract'.[181] There is also, as we have seen, significant academic support for the implied condition view.[182]

Despite this significant judicial and academic support, the implied condition view was rejected by the Court of Appeal in *The Great Peace* for reasons similar to those given for the rejection of this view of frustration in *Davis Contractors Ltd v Fareham Urban District Council*.[183] Lord Phillips MR said: **7.76**

> [T]he theory of the implied term is as unrealistic when considering common mistake as when considering frustration. Where a fundamental assumption upon which an agreement is founded proves to be mistaken, it is not realistic to ask whether the parties impliedly agreed that in those circumstances the contract would not be binding.[184]

It would be plausible to think that the Court of Appeal was rejecting the implied condition view here in favour of a doctrine of common mistake concerned with what the parties subjectively intended. But curiously, it seems that this is not the case. In *Dana Gas PJSC v Dana Gas Sukuk Ltd*,[185] Leggatt J observed that *The Great Peace* had rejected 'the conception of the doctrine of mistake which treats the subjective beliefs of the parties as relevant'. Instead, as Leggatt J noted,[186] Lord Phillips MR in *The Great Peace* stated that the doctrine was based on 'a rule of law under which, if it transpires that one or both of the parties have agreed to do something which it is impossible to perform, no obligation arises out of that agreement'.[187] This rejection of the subjective doctrine of common mistake leads to the odd result that there apparently is a doctrine of common mistake but it has nothing to do with actual mistakes. Mistakes are necessarily subjective—they depend upon a state of mind. If the rule is not based on the subjective beliefs of the parties then it is, quite simply, not a rule about mistakes. The apparent justification for the doctrine, based on impossibility, is discussed below.[188] **7.77**

181 *The Great Peace* [2001] EWHC 529 (QB) [98].
182 See n 2.
183 [1956] AC 696, 728. See Morgan (n 2) 561.
184 *The Great Peace* [2003] QB 679, 703 [73].
185 [2018] 1 Lloyd's Rep 177, 186 [60].
186 ibid.
187 *The Great Peace* [2003] QB 679, 703 [73].
188 See [7.87]–[7.90].

Common objections

7.78 The argument of this chapter, of course, is that both the rejection of the implied condition view and the theory adopted in its stead are wrong. The problems with the supposed doctrine of common mistake—however it is conceived—are examined below. As for the objections to the implied condition view, the common objections to this view in the context of frustration have already been addressed in Chapter 6[189] and the responses given there apply with equal force here. In particular, in relation to the possible objection that in cases of common mistake the implication of a condition is unrealistic because the parties did not turn their mind to the possibility that the relevant assumption was not true, the objection only bites if implication or construction depends upon the subjective or actual intentions of the parties. They plainly do not.[190] As Professor Jonathan Morgan has noted:

> If the alleged contract's binding operation is implicitly dependent on a particular fact's existence, on its proper construction, it matters not that the parties never turned their minds to this point. For that is most assuredly not the test for implying a term.[191]

7.79 Moreover, at least one recent case has rejected the view that common mistake rests 'on the notion that the parties have impliedly agreed what is to happen in the event that an assumption underlying the contract proves to be false', only to go on immediately to say that:

> [Common mistake] does, however, involve a question of construction of the contract. It is only where it is to be inferred from the terms of the contract or the surrounding circumstances that the contract was never intended to apply in the situation which in reality existed when the contract was made that the doctrine will apply.[192]

7.80 To repeat what was said in Chapter 6 in relation to the 'construction theory' of frustration,[193] to say that 'the contract was never intended to apply in the situation which in reality existed'[194] is just another way of saying that the obligations of the parties were conditional. It is true that it seems less plausible to say that the parties positively agreed that if the facts were not as they were

[189] See [6.85]–[6.117].
[190] See [6.94]–[6.95].
[191] Morgan (n 2) 561.
[192] *Dana Gas PJSC v Dana Gas Sukuk Ltd* [2018] 1 Lloyd's Rep 177, 186 [61].
[193] See [6.96]–[6.99].
[194] *Dana Gas PJSC v Dana Gas Sukuk Ltd* [2018] 1 Lloyd's Rep 177, 186 [61].

supposed to be then 'the contract' should cease. But the implied condition view does not say this. It states, negatively, that the parties do not promise to perform in all circumstances—'that is, after all, what non-satisfaction of a condition precedent means'.[195]

Problems with the doctrine of common mistake

Not only is the implied condition view capable of explaining the positive law, there are in fact several problems with the supposed doctrine of common mistake, all of which demonstrate that the implied condition view is to be preferred. **7.81**

Subjective mistake inconsistent with common law's objective approach

The first problem is that 'the doctrine of mistake, whatever it is, is . . . one intimately associated with the now repudiated doctrine of reality of consent'.[196] The very idea that a common mistake should invalidate a contract is one which was influenced by the 'will theory' of contract and the writings of the French jurist Robert Joseph Pothier.[197] Pothier's theory was that 'contractual liability stemmed from the mutual [subjective] assent of the parties'[198] and that where this assent was not present there was no contract. This principle covered not just cases where the parties were at cross-purposes, but 'situations in which the contract had been entered into under some material misapprehension'.[199] **7.82**

This theory, however, has always been in tension with the common law's objective approach to contract formation and interpretation.[200] The leading authority is the decision in *Smith v Hughes*,[201] which stands for the proposition that, absent fraud or misrepresentation, there is no principle of English law that prevents a person from relying upon a mistake made by the other as to the subject-matter of the contract.[202] In a statement that is often quoted as embodying the objective approach, Blackburn J said: **7.83**

[195] Frederick Wilmot-Smith, *Failure of Condition* (DPhil thesis, University of Oxford 2013) 257.
[196] Simpson (n 87) 269.
[197] See generally, ibid 264–69; Ibbetson (n 56) 225–29.
[198] Ibbetson (n 56) 220. See also Goodhart (n 2) 99, 100.
[199] Ibbetson (n 56) 226. See Robert Joseph Pothier, *A Treatise on Obligations, Considered in a Moral and Legal View* (Francois-Xavier Martin tr, Martin & Ogden 1802) 14.
[200] Cartwright (n 68) 72. See *Dana Gas PJSC v Dana Gas Sukuk Ltd* [2018] 1 Lloyd's Rep 177, 186 [60].
[201] (1871) LR 6 QB 597.
[202] The position in relation to a belief as to the 'terms' of the contract is slightly more complicated. The position appears to be that if A knows that B is contracting in the subjective belief that A is *promising* (ie

> If, whatever a man's real intention may be, he so conducts himself that a reasonable man would believe that he was assenting to the terms proposed by the other party, and that other party upon that belief enters into the contract with him, the man thus conducting himself would be equally bound as if he had intended to agree to the other party's terms.[203]

7.84 Whatever may be said of other legal systems, it is clear that the will theory does not represent English contract law.[204] And if the doctrine of mistake is—as it is commonly supposed to be—a doctrine based upon the subjective beliefs of the parties, then there is no role for it in 'a system which interprets its contracts by a purely objective standard'.[205] As Dixon and Fullagar JJ put the point in *McRae v Commonwealth Disposals Commission*: 'once the common law had made up its mind that a promise supported by consideration ought to be performed, it was inevitable that the theorisings of the civilians about "mistake" should mean little or nothing to it'.[206]

7.85 Moreover, a doctrine that is based upon the parties subjectively having made a common mistake cannot easily explain those cases in which both parties are mistaken but there is no relief.[207] A case in point is *Barr v Gibson*.[208] The defendant had sold to the plaintiff title to a ship and covenanted that he had the power to sell. Unbeknownst to both parties, the ship had run ashore. Despite

warranting) some matter, then A cannot rely upon the objective agreement. A can only rely upon the objective agreement where A does not know, or ought not to know, that B is contracting on the faith of this belief: ibid 608; *Hartog v Colin & Shields* [1939] 3 All ER 566; Peel (n 1) 382–83 [8-047]. This is sometimes referred to as a 'mistake as to terms', but it is perhaps better understood simply as a circumstance where A can no longer rely upon the objective meaning of the agreement, if 'he knows that the objective impression of agreement created is false': Stevens, 'Objectivity, Mistake and the Parol Evidence Rule' (n 2) 104. Further, it is usually suggested that the contract is 'void' or that there was 'never a contract at all' (see, eg, *Statoil ASA v Louis Dreyfus Energy Services LP (The Harriette N)* [2008] 2 Lloyd's Rep 685, 694 [87]), but there is a powerful argument that that contract should be 'treated as binding on the terms as understood by the party who believed that the promise was given to him': Friedmann (n 68) 73. See also Paul S Davies, *JC Smith's Law of Contract* (3rd edn, OUP 2021) 16–17 and compare *A Roberts & Co Ltd v Leicestershire County Council* [1961] Ch 555 with *Statoil ASA v Louis Dreyfus Energy Services LP (The Harriette N)* [2008] 2 Lloyd's Rep 685.

[203] *Smith v Hughes* (1871) LR 6 QB 597, 607. Blackburn J here actually appears to have been subscribing to a subjective theory of assent and he relied upon estoppel as a rule of evidence for this statement of principle. See Ibbetson (n 56) 222 fn 9. Despite this, the objective approach is not a principle of estoppel: see Davies (n 202) 19. For a more recent endorsement of the objective approach without relying on estoppel, see *RTS Flexible Systems Ltd v Molkerei Alois Müller GmbH & Co KG (UK Production)* [2010] 1 WLR 753, 771 [45].

[204] Goodhart (n 2) 101.

[205] ibid 102.

[206] (1951) 84 CLR 377, 407.

[207] Atiyah and Bennion (n 2) 422.

[208] (1838) 3 M & W 390, 150 ER 1196. *McRae v Commonwealth Disposals Commission* (1951) 84 CLR 377 is another example.

the fact that both parties were clearly mistaken, Parke B held that the transfer purported to be absolute and therefore that if the ship had been physically destroyed or had ceased to answer the description of a ship then the defendant would have been in breach of the covenant.[209]

Of course, the answer given by proponents of the doctrine of common mistake is that the doctrine does not apply if the contract expressly allocates the risk or if one party warrants the existence of the state of affairs.[210] But that response only reveals that the doctrine has nothing to do with subjective mistakes, for a party may give an express warranty about purported facts as to which both parties are mistaken.[211] **7.86**

No justification for the doctrine

For the reasons given above, the doctrine cannot be one based upon the subjective common mistake of the parties. But, as was noted in the previous section, according to Leggatt J in *Dana Gas PJSC*,[212] 'the conception of the doctrine of mistake which treats the subjective beliefs of the parties as relevant has not been accepted' in English law. This then leads to the next problem: what is the justification for a doctrine of common mistake? After all, 'no Court has an absolving power'[213] and 'the court has no power to improve upon the instrument which it is called upon to construe'.[214] **7.87**

One justification which has been offered is that common mistake is a doctrine concerned with 'impossibility'. As noted above, in *The Great Peace*, Lord Phillips MR suggested that the doctrine of common mistake: **7.88**

> results from a rule of law under which, if it transpires that one or both of the parties have agreed to do something which it is impossible to perform, no obligation arises out of that agreement.[215]

There are two reasons to doubt this justification. The first is that there has been confusion about what Lord Phillips MR meant by this and, in particular, about the apparent requirement that 'the non-existence of the state of affairs **7.89**

[209] On the facts, it was held that the ship had not ceased to exist for this purpose.
[210] *The Great Peace* [2003] QB 679, 703 [75].
[211] Atiyah and Bennion (n 2) 425–26.
[212] *Dana Gas PJSC v Dana Gas Sukuk Ltd* [2018] 1 Lloyd's Rep 177, 186 [60].
[213] *FA Tamplin Steamship Co Ltd v Anglo-Mexican Petroleum Products Co Ltd* [1916] 2 AC 397, 404; *Joseph Constantine Steamship Line Ltd v Imperial Smelting Corp Ltd* [1942] AC 154, 185; *Denny, Mott & Dickson Ltd v James B Fraser & Co Ltd* [1944] AC 265, 281; *Metropolitan Water Board v Dick, Kerr & Co Ltd* [1918] AC 119, 127; *British Movietonews Ltd v London and District Cinemas Ltd* [1952] AC 166, 183.
[214] *Attorney General of Belize v Belize Telecom Ltd* [2009] 1 WLR 1988, 1993 [16].
[215] *The Great Peace* [2003] QB 679, 703 [73].

must render performance of the contract impossible'.[216] Later in his judgment he spoke of 'a fundamental assumption which renders performance of the *essence* of the obligation impossible'.[217] Most recent cases have treated this statement as merely one formulation of when a 'mistake is sufficiently fundamental'.[218]

7.90 The second, more fundamental, reason to doubt Lord Phillips MR's justification is that, as we saw in Chapter 6, there is no principle in English law that prevents parties from contracting to do that which is impossible.[219] In *Clifford v Watts*,[220] Brett J said that 'it is not competent to a defendant to say that there is no binding contract, merely because he has engaged to do something which is physically impossible.' There is no 'rule of law' that no obligation arises out of an agreement that is impossible to perform.

No room for a doctrine of common mistake

7.91 The third problem with a doctrine of common mistake is that it is unnecessary. Smith famously argued that 'there is no room for the application of a distinct doctrine of mistake'.[221] He had in mind the decision of *Associated Japanese Bank*, where Steyn J had said:

> Logically, before one can turn to the rules as to mistake, whether at common law or in equity, one must first determine whether the contract itself, by express or implied condition precedent or otherwise, provides who bears the risk of the relevant mistake. It is at this hurdle that many pleas of mistake will either fail or prove to have been unnecessary. Only if the contract is silent on the point, is there scope for invoking mistake.[222]

7.92 In *Associated Japanese Bank*, Steyn J had in fact gone on to consider whether the contract might be void for common mistake. But, as he noted in the quote

[216] ibid 703 [76]. See *Brennan v Bolt Burdon* [2005] QB 303, 316 [22], 323 [58]–[60]; *Kyle Bay Ltd t/a Astons Nightclub v Underwriters Subscribing under Policy No. 019057/08/01* [2007] 1 CLC 164, 169–70 [21]–[25]; *Apvodedo NV v Collins* [2008] EWHC 775 (Ch) [43]–[46]; *Dana Gas PJSC v Dana Gas Sukuk Ltd* [2018] 1 Lloyd's Rep 177, 187 [65]; *Triple Seven Msn 27251 Ltd v Azman Air Services Ltd* [2018] 4 WLR 97 [60]–[65], [75]–[76].

[217] *The Great Peace* [2003] QB 679, 704 [82] (emphasis added).

[218] *Dana Gas PJSC v Dana Gas Sukuk Ltd* [2018] 1 Lloyd's Rep 177, 187 [65]. The other formulation is when the mistake renders 'the subject-matter of the contract essentially and radically different from the subject-matter which the parties believed to exist': *Associated Japanese Bank (International) Ltd v Crédit du Nord SA* [1989] 1 WLR 255, 268. See *Kyle Bay Ltd t/a Astons Nightclub v Underwriters* [2007] 1 CLC 164, 170 [24]–[25]; *Dana Gas PJSC v Dana Gas Sukuk Ltd* [2018] 1 Lloyd's Rep 177, 187 [65]; *Triple Seven Msn 27251 Ltd v Azman Air Services Ltd* [2018] 4 WLR 97 [75]–[76].

[219] See [6.5].

[220] *Clifford v Watts* (1870) LR 5 CP 577, 588.

[221] Smith, 'Contracts—Mistake, Frustration and Implied Terms' (n 2) 400. See also Morgan (n 2).

[222] *Associated Japanese Bank (International) Ltd v Crédit du Nord SA* [1989] 1 WLR 255, 268.

above, this was unnecessary. In *Graves v Graves*,[223] an argument was advanced that a lease between a landlord and his former wife was void for common mistake. In particular, the tenancy had been granted on the basis that the rent would be paid by the wife from the receipt of a housing benefit. The housing benefit was not payable. The Court of Appeal (Thomas LJ with whom Hughes LJ and Coleridge J agreed) held that it was unnecessary to consider whether the contract was void for common mistake[224] because there was 'an implied condition that if housing benefit was not payable, the tenancy would come to an end'.[225]

To be fair, in *Associated Japanese Bank* Steyn J clearly contemplated that a plea of mistake could pass this hurdle,[226] but herein lies the problem: once it has been ascertained whether the obligations of the parties are or are not conditional, the risk has been allocated and the contract should 'bind according to its terms'.[227] To hold otherwise would 'contradict the intention of the parties' as expressed in the contract.[228] In Smith's words: **7.93**

> Suppose that the court in the *Japanese Bank* case had found that there was no express or implied condition precedent that the machines existed. It would then have established that the parties did *not* intend that the contract should be invalidated if it turned out that the machines did not exist. That, it is submitted, should have been the end of the matter.[229]

Similarly, at first instance in *The Great Peace*, Toulson J noted that if the guarantee in *Associated Japanese Bank* had not been intended to be conditional on the existence of the machines then it is 'hard to see how the defendant bank would have been entitled to refuse performance of the guarantee on an independent doctrine of mistake'.[230] In this sense, there is no room for a doctrine of common mistake. **7.94**

Obscures the relationship with other areas of contract law

The last problem with the supposed existence of a separate doctrine of common mistake is that it leads to an arbitrary line being drawn between cases of common mistake and cases of frustration. It also leads to false analogies **7.95**

[223] [2007] EWCA Civ 660.
[224] ibid [43].
[225] ibid [41].
[226] Treitel (n 159) 503.
[227] Morgan (n 2) 568 (emphasis removed).
[228] Smith, 'Contracts—Mistake, Frustration and Implied Terms' (n 2) 407.
[229] ibid 407–08. See also *The Great Peace* [2001] EWHC 529 (QB) [98].
[230] *The Great Peace* [2001] EWHC 529 (QB) [98].

being drawn with other areas in an attempt to unify the different cases of 'mistake' in the law of contract.

7.96 To take the first proposition, on the current orthodoxy there is no doubt that there is a close relationship between the doctrine of frustration and the doctrine of common mistake. In *The Great Peace*, the Court of Appeal recognised that 'the law of frustration and common mistake had advanced hand in hand on the foundation of a common principle'.[231] Yet orthodoxy refuses to go further[232] and recognise that these are simply two instances of failure of condition, differentiated only by the point in time at which the condition fails.[233]

7.97 That the difference between frustration and common mistake is only a matter of timing is illustrated by contrasting coronation cases such as *Griffith v Brymer*[234] and *Krell v Henry*.[235] In *Griffith v Brymer*, the contract was entered into at 11am on 24 June, one hour after the decision had been made to operate on the King (thus, postponing the procession). According to orthodoxy, this is a case of common mistake. By contrast, in *Krell v Henry*, the agreement was entered into four days before the decision was made. On the orthodox approach, this is a case of frustration. Yet, the only difference between these two cases is the timing of the agreements; in other words, when the condition fails.

7.98 This difference is also helpfully illustrated by *Amalgamated Investment & Property Co Ltd v John Walker & Sons Ltd*.[236] On 25 September 1973, the plaintiffs entered into a contract to purchase title to land on which a warehouse was situated. On 26 September, the day after the contract, the vendor was notified that the property had been selected for inclusion on a list of buildings of special architectural or historical significance, which was about to be given legal effect. The list was signed on behalf of the Secretary of State on 27 September. The listing of the building significantly impacted the redevelopment potential of the site such that, so long as it was listed and building consent could not be obtained, the value of the land would be reduced from £1.7 million to £200,000. The purchasers subsequently argued that the contract was void for common mistake and argued that the relevant event was the inclusion of the property on the list for signing, which had occurred before the contract was

[231] *The Great Peace* [2003] QB 679, 700 [61].
[232] See, eg, Andrew Burrows, *A Casebook on Contract* (7th edn, Hart Publishing 2020) 791.
[233] Smith, 'Contracts—Mistake, Frustration and Implied Terms' (n 2) 402; Stevens, 'Objectivity, Mistake and the Parol Evidence Rule' (n 2) 105; Wilmot-Smith (n 195) 220.
[234] (1903) 19 TLR 434.
[235] [1903] 2 KB 740.
[236] [1977] 1 WLR 164.

concluded. The Court of Appeal, agreeing with the primary judge, held that there was no mistake at the time of the contract because the relevant event was not the inclusion of the property on the list, but the signing of that list on behalf of the Secretary of State and that occurred on 27 September (two days after the contract was concluded). The Court therefore went on to apply the law relating to frustration, though ultimately it held that the purchasers were not entitled to succeed.[237]

It makes no sense for the question whether one doctrine or the other applies to turn upon such fine and arbitrary distinctions.[238] By contrast, on the approach taken in this book, both frustration and common mistake are instances of failure of condition in which the court's role is to ascertain what were the conditions to each party's obligation to perform and whether those conditions have failed. As Professor Robert Stevens has noted, '[t]he court's essential task does not differ according to whether the unforeseen event occurred ten minutes before or ten minutes after the contract is entered into'.[239] **7.99**

A related, and in some ways inverse, problem with a doctrine of common mistake is that it leads to attempts to analogise with other apparent instances of mistake in contract law—in particular, 'unilateral mistake' and its sub-category 'mutual mistake'.[240] When these cases are treated together, the relationship between them is uneasy. As Professor Hugh Beale notes, 'it is certainly hard to discern a single "doctrine" of mistake when the two categories of case . . . are subject to quite different rules'.[241] **7.100**

Moreover, it seems that neither category—common mistake on the one hand and unilateral or mutual mistake on the other—has anything to do with mistake. In particular, an argument which cannot be developed here, is that most cases that fall under the umbrella of unilateral or mutual mistake fall to be treated alongside the cases on offer and acceptance.[242] In *The Law of Contract*, Professor Edwin Peel states that '[i]n some respects, therefore, unilateral mistake and common mistake are not that closely related to each other and might have been assessed separately in other parts of this book'.[243] Attempts to unify these separate instances and create a unified doctrine of mistake in the law of **7.101**

[237] ibid 173.
[238] cf Peel (n 1) 1106–07 [19-131]–[19-133].
[239] Stevens, 'Objectivity, Mistake and the Parol Evidence Rule' (n 2) 106.
[240] See, eg, Beatson, Burrows, and Cartwright (n 1) ch 8.
[241] Beale (n 1) 757 [9-011].
[242] Slade (n 2) 386–90; Shatwell (n 2) 188–93; PS Atiyah, 'Judicial Techniques and the English Law of Contract' (1968) 2 Ottawa Law Review 337, 344–50.
[243] Peel (n 1) 352 [8-001].

contract will only serve to hinder rather than assist our understanding of the subject.

Summary

7.102 The implied condition view is 'superior in principle'[244] to an alternative approach based upon a doctrine of mistake. As this section explained, it commands significant judicial and academic support and the alternative approach faces a number of objections. First, if based upon the parties' subjective beliefs and a theory of subjective assent, it is inconsistent with the common law's objective approach to contract formation and interpretation. Secondly, if not based upon the parties' subjective beliefs, there appears to be no plausible justification for the doctrine. Contrary to Lord Phillips MR's suggestion, there is no principle of English law that no obligation can arise out of an agreement to do the impossible. Thirdly, if one begins by construing the agreement and asking whether the parties' obligations are conditional, there is no need for a doctrine of common mistake: 'the additional stage is unnecessary, indeed unhelpful.'[245] Finally, as we have just seen, the suggestion of a doctrine of common mistake causes us both to fail to draw connections between related cases and to draw false connections between unrelated ones.

A Doctrine of Common Mistake in Equity?

7.103 The last part of this chapter briefly considers whether there ought to be a doctrine of common mistake in equity. The point of departure in any discussion of this topic is the decision of the Court of Appeal in *Solle v Butcher*,[246] in which Denning LJ recognised a doctrine of common mistake in equity that renders a contract voidable and liable to be set aside (on terms if necessary).

7.104 Denning LJ's starting point was that at common law, where the parties had objectively reached an agreement, neither party could rely upon a mistake to say that a contract was 'a nullity from the beginning'[247] whether one party knew about the mistake and '[a] fortiori, if the other party did not know of the

[244] Morgan (n 2) 561.
[245] ibid 560.
[246] [1950] 1 KB 671.
[247] ibid 691.

mistake, but shared it'.[248] The cases, he said, really involved 'contracts which [were] not void for mistake but [were] void by reason of an implied condition precedent'.[249] This starting point is consistent with the thesis of this chapter that instances of common mistake are just particular instances of failure of condition.

However, Denning LJ then went on to consider 'mistakes which render a contract voidable, that is, liable to be set aside on some equitable ground'.[250] Relying principally upon the House of Lords decision in *Cooper v Phibbs*,[251] Denning LJ thought that the authorities supported a jurisdiction in equity to set aside a contract for a 'fundamental' common mistake and, where necessary, on terms.[252] **7.105**

The decision in *Solle v Butcher* was then followed in '[a] number of cases, albeit small in number'[253] in the fifty years following the decision.[254] But it was also met with criticism.[255] First, an important practical problem with the doctrine was 'how serious a mistake must be to justify equitable intervention (when it does not make the contract void at law)'.[256] The best guidance given was that the mistake had to be 'fundamental',[257] that '[e]quity [would] give relief against common mistake in cases where the common law [would] not',[258] and that 'equity [could] have regard to a wider and perhaps unlimited category of "fundamental" mistake'.[259] **7.106**

A second criticism—but one which it seems was ultimately unfounded—was that it was doubtful whether the cases upon which Denning LJ relied really did establish an equitable jurisdiction to set aside a contract for a common **7.107**

[248] ibid.
[249] ibid.
[250] ibid 692.
[251] (1867) LR 2 HL 149.
[252] *Solle v Butcher* [1950] 1 KB 671, 693–94.
[253] *The Great Peace* [2003] QB 679, 724 [153].
[254] *Grist v Bailey* [1967] Ch 532 (Ch); *Magee v Pennine Insurance Co Ltd* [1969] 2 QB 507; *Laurence v Lexcourt Holdings Ltd* [1978] 1 WLR 1128. See also *Associated Japanese Bank (International) Ltd v Crédit du Nord SA* [1989] 1 WLR 255 and the discussion in *The Great Peace* [2003] QB 679, 719–24 [133]–[153].
[255] Atiyah and Bennion (n 2) 440–42; Slade (n 2) 403–07; AL Goodhart, 'Rescission of Lease on the Ground of Mistake' (1950) 66 Law Quarterly Review 169; Smith, 'Contracts—Mistake, Frustration and Implied Terms' (n 2) 417–19.
[256] Treitel (n 159) 504. See also Smith, 'Contracts—Mistake, Frustration and Implied Terms' (n 2) 418; *The Great Peace* [2003] QB 679, 719 [131]; *The Great Peace* [2001] EWHC 529 (QB) [117]–[118]; Beale (n 1) 782–83 [9-057].
[257] *Solle v Butcher* [1950] 1 KB 671, 693.
[258] *Associated Japanese Bank (International) Ltd v Crédit du Nord SA* [1989] 1 WLR 255, 270.
[259] *William Sindall Plc v Cambridgeshire County Council* [1994] 1 WLR 1016, 1042.

mistake—or at least one as broad as he suggested.[260] An example can be found in the discussion of *Cooper v Phibbs*,[261] the leading decision upon which Denning LJ relied. In that case, a nephew entered into an agreement to lease a fishery with the trustee of a settlement for his uncle's five daughters. Prior to his death, the uncle had represented to the nephew that the uncle held the fee simple to the fishery outright. As it turned out, the uncle only held the fee simple as trustee for the nephew, who was an equitable life tenant under a strict settlement. The House of Lords held that the nephew was entitled to have the agreement for lease set aside. Lord Westbury, who gave one of two reasoned speeches, said:

> [I]f parties contract under a mutual mistake and misapprehension as to their relative and respective rights, the result is, that that agreement is liable to be set aside as having proceeded upon a common mistake.[262]

7.108 Slade, who doubted whether this case really established an equitable jurisdiction to rescind a contract for mistake, argued that Lord Westbury's comments here were merely obiter, on the ground that there had been an 'active, albeit innocent, misrepresentation on the part of [the uncle]'[263] and that 'the court had undoubted jurisdiction to grant rescission on that ground'.[264] In particular, Lord Cranworth, who gave the only other reasoned speech, said 'in this case the [nephew] was led into the mistake by the misinformation given to him by his uncle, who is now represented by [the trustee and the uncle's five daughters]'.[265]

7.109 But to be fair to Denning LJ, Lord Cranworth only offered misrepresentation as an alternative ground for his decision, primarily basing his decision on the fact that the nephew had 'entered into the agreement under a common mistake, and [was] entitled to be relieved from the consequences of it'.[266] Moreover, Lord Cranworth relied upon the earlier decision in *Bingham v Bingham*[267] in support of that proposition. That was a case in which the plaintiff sought to have moneys refunded following the purported sale of an estate by the defendant, which it turned out the plaintiff already held. The report to the case states that 'there was a plain mistake, such as the court was warranted to relieve against,

[260] Goodhart (n 255); Slade (n 2) 403–07; FMB Reynolds, 'Reconsider the Contract Textbooks' (2003) 119 Law Quarterly Review 177, 179.
[261] (1867) LR 2 HL 149.
[262] ibid 170.
[263] Slade (n 2) 405.
[264] ibid.
[265] *Cooper v Phibbs* (1867) LR 2 HL 149, 164.
[266] ibid.
[267] (1748) 1 Ves Sen 126, 27 ER 934.

and not to suffer the defendant to run away with the money in consideration of the sale of an estate, to which he had no right'.[268] In *Cooper v Phibbs*, Lord Cranworth said of *Bingham v Bingham*, that 'the doctrine there acted upon was perfectly correct'.[269] It seems therefore, contrary to Slade's view, that the ground of the decision in *Cooper v Phibbs* was common mistake.[270]

The third criticism of the decision in *Solle v Butcher*, however, was that it was not clear how the decision was to be reconciled with *Bell v Lever Brothers*, in which *Cooper v Phibbs* was discussed, and no mention was made of the equitable doctrine.[271] It was principally for this last reason that the Court of Appeal in *The Great Peace* 'effectively overruled'[272] *Solle v Butcher*, which was described as an attempt by Denning LJ to 'outflank'[273] *Bell v Lever Brothers*. Lord Phillips MR said that it was 'impossible to reconcile' the two decisions and that coherence could only 'be restored to this area of law . . . by declaring that there is no jurisdiction to grant rescission of a contract on the ground of common mistake where that contract is valid and enforceable on ordinary principles of contract law'.[274] **7.110**

On balance, the overruling of *Solle v Butcher* should be supported but subject to two qualifications. First, as a matter of precedent, it is questionable whether it was open to the Court of Appeal to depart from *Solle v Butcher*, which was also a decision of the Court of Appeal, even if it was inconsistent with the earlier decision of the House of Lords in *Bell v Lever Bros Ltd*.[275] **7.111**

Secondly, contrary to some of the criticisms outlined above,[276] it has been demonstrated persuasively by Professor Catharine MacMillan that, historically, equity did have a jurisdiction to rescind agreements entered into as a result of a mistake.[277] Although as she explains: **7.112**

> Equitable relief for mistake was not based upon a failure of consent in the formation of the contract. . . . Equity recognised mistake as a factor, like fraud, accident or surprise, which could affect the conscience of the individual.[278]

[268] ibid 127; 934.
[269] *Cooper v Phibbs* (1867) LR 2 HL 149, 164.
[270] As the Court of Appeal accepted in *The Great Peace* [2003] QB 679, 713 [109]. See also MacMillan (n 63) 62–65.
[271] Smith, 'Contracts—Mistake, Frustration and Implied Terms' (n 2) 418.
[272] *Pitt v Holt* [2013] 2 AC 108, 153 [115].
[273] *The Great Peace* [2003] QB 679, 718 [126]. See also *The Great Peace* [2001] EWHC 529 (QB) [69].
[274] *The Great Peace* [2003] QB 679, 725 [157]. See also 726 [160].
[275] SB Midwinter, '*The Great Peace* and precedent' (2003) 119 Law Quarterly Review 180; Davies (n 202) 350.
[276] See n 260.
[277] MacMillan (n 63) 61–67.
[278] ibid 38. See also 314.

Given that equity did have such a jurisdiction, it seems that if the overruling of *Solle v Butcher* is to be defended it must be 'on the grounds of legal policy and not on precedent'.[279]

7.113 The overruling of *Solle v Butcher*, however, should be supported as a matter of legal policy. It is difficult to see what the justification is for a jurisdiction to relieve against the consequences of a common mistake in circumstances where there is an agreement supported by consideration.[280] As we have seen, once the court has determined, on a proper construction of the contract, that performance was to occur in the circumstances that have arisen, the court's role is to give effect to the parties' agreement,[281] at least by way of making available an action for damages. If the obligations of the parties are unconditional, then the parties ought to be held to that agreement, no more and no less than if their obligations were conditional. There is no injustice in this result and therefore no need for equity to supplement the common law.[282]

7.114 This is not to say that 'mistake' cannot have any role in equity. The fact that one or both parties were mistaken may be a reason for a court to refuse to award specific performance and confine one party to damages.[283] Similarly, if a mistake of one party is induced by a representation by the other party, even if that other party is mistaken, it may be a ground for setting the contract aside for misrepresentation.[284] It may even be palatable for rescission to be available in equity, as it is in Australia, where one party is:

> aware that circumstances exist which indicate that the [other] party is entering the contract under some serious mistake or misapprehension about either the content or subject matter of that term and deliberately sets out to ensure that the [other] party does not become aware of the existence of his mistake or misapprehension.[285]

7.115 But this would be a limited principle, and not merely based upon the fact that one party was 'mistaken'. Moreover, it would have no application in the cases that have been the focus of this chapter, namely, cases where both parties entered into the contact labouring under a 'common' mistake. There is no need

279 ibid 316.
280 Compare *Pitt v Holt* [2013] 2 AC 108.
281 Smith, 'Contracts—Mistake, Frustration and Implied Terms' (n 2) 407–08.
282 See further Stevens, 'Objectivity, Mistake and the Parol Evidence Rule' (n 2) 106.
283 *Malins v Freeman* (1837) 2 Keen 25, 48 ER 537.
284 *Redgrave v Hurd* (1881) 20 Ch D 1.
285 *Taylor v Johnson* (1983) 151 CLR 422, 432. See also *Solle v Butcher* [1950] 1 KB 671, 692.

or room for a doctrine of common mistake in equity. As a matter of legal policy therefore it should not exist.

Conclusion

The aim of this chapter has been to reject the now-orthodox position that English law recognises a doctrine of common mistake that renders a contract void. Instead, it has been argued that the doctrine of common mistake is simply an instance of failure of condition. As we have seen, the early cases strongly supported this view. Unfortunately, despite the significant judicial and academic support for the implied condition view, it was rejected by the Court of Appeal in *The Great Peace*. But the reasons it gave for rejecting the implied condition view in this context were the same 'superficial'[286] reasons that had been given for rejecting this view in the context of frustration, and they do not withstand scrutiny. Similarly, the supposed doctrine of common mistake faces several problems. The end result is that cases of common mistake are best explained without reference to mistake at all. They are simply cases in which the parties' respective obligations to perform were conditional upon facts that did not exist or events that could not occur. There is certainly no need for a doctrine of common mistake at law, and the position is no different in equity. **7.116**

[286] Morgan (n 2) 561.

8
Anticipatory Breach

Introduction

8.1 The preceding chapters have dealt with the discharge of contractual obligations following a breach of contract, and in cases of frustration and common mistake. This chapter deals with an equally important topic: the doctrine of anticipatory breach. According to that doctrine, where one party, in advance of the time for performance, renounces their obligations under the contract or disables themselves from performing—both commonly referred to as a 'repudiation'[1]—the other party can, on 'acceptance', treat the repudiation as an event discharging the parties from their contractual obligations to perform and immediately bring an action for damages for breach of contract.

8.2 The doctrine of anticipatory breach is one that has proved eminently sensible in practice but exceedingly difficult to justify as a matter of theory. The well-known theoretical difficulties with the doctrine ultimately boil down to a single question: how can one party breach an obligation to perform when the performance of that obligation has not yet fallen due?[2] As Kelly CB put it in *Frost v Knight*:[3] 'One contracts in 1870 to pay to another 1000l on the 1st

[1] See [2.47].

[2] Sir Michael Mustill, 'Anticipatory Breach of Contract: The Common Law at Work' in *Butterworth Lectures 1989–90* (Butterworths 1990) 40; Francis Dawson, 'Metaphors and Anticipatory Breach of Contract' (1981) 40 Cambridge Law Journal 83, 83; Paul Mitchell, '*Hochster v De La Tour* (1853)' in Charles Mitchell and Paul Mitchell (eds), *Landmark Cases in the Law of Contract* (Hart Publishing 2008) 135, 135.

[3] *Frost v Knight* (1870) LR 5 Ex 322, 327. cf *Frost v Knight* (1872) LR 7 Ex 111 (Court of Exchequer Chamber).

Discharge of Contractual Obligations. Jordan English, Oxford University Press. © Jordan English 2025.
DOI: 10.1093/9780198906704.003.0008

of January, 1871. To say that the contract is broken before the year 1870 is at end is undeniably and self-evidently untrue.' These difficulties have led some to conclude that the concept of anticipatory breach cannot be explained at all and must be seen as an entrenched oddity in our law, justified on the grounds of practical convenience alone.[4]

8.3 Against this background, this chapter proceeds in three parts. The first considers the development of the doctrine of anticipatory breach and in particular the decision of the Court of Queen's Bench in *Hochster v De La Tour*.[5] The second part examines the different explanations that have been offered for the doctrine of anticipatory breach on the orthodox power to terminate model. Ultimately, it will be seen that no explanation can perfectly account for the features of the doctrine as applied in English law today. The third part of this chapter therefore considers whether a failure of condition model might provide a better analysis of the doctrine of anticipatory breach. In this area once again the problems faced today have arisen from the failure to appreciate that the events that can operate to discharge one party from their obligation to perform need not also give that party an action for damages.[6] In other words, there is a vital distinction between promises and conditions.

The Development of the Doctrine of Anticipatory Breach

The older cases: waiver of conditions on a repudiation

8.4 As we saw in Chapter 5,[7] the forerunners to the modern doctrine of anticipatory breach were a number of older cases in which it was held that a disablement or renunciation by one party to a contract operated as a waiver of the conditions to the obligation that they were unable or had refused to perform.[8] Repudiation therefore operated as an 'excuse' for non-compliance with a condition.[9]

[4] Michael Mustill, 'The Golden Victory—Some Reflections' (2008) 124 Law Quarterly Review 569, 584.

[5] (1853) 2 El & Bl 678, 118 ER 922.

[6] Mustill (n 2) 43; Qiao Liu, 'Claiming Damages upon an Anticipatory Breach: Why Should an Acceptance Be Necessary' (2005) 25 Legal Studies 559, 563.

[7] See [5.37]–[5.97].

[8] See generally, Mustill (n 2) 14–26; Mitchell (n 2) 136–46; Qiao Liu, *Anticipatory Breach* (Hart Publishing 2011) 14–20.

[9] JW Carter, Wayne Courtney, and Gregory Tolhurst, 'Two Models for Discharge of a Contract by Repudiation' (2018) 77 Cambridge Law Journal 97, 103.

This principle was applied in a number of cases involving disablement.[10] In *Bowdell v Parsons*,[11] for example, the defendant, who was to deliver 12 stacks of hay as and when the plaintiff requested, had allegedly delivered only one load before he sold the residue to other buyers. In an action for damages for non-delivery, it was argued that the plaintiff had not pleaded a request—this being a condition precedent to the obligation to deliver. Lord Ellenborough CJ rejected this argument, stating that 'by the defendant's selling and disposing of the rest of the hay to other persons, he disqualified himself from delivering it to the plaintiff: and therefore no request was necessary.'[12] Similarly in *Amory v Brodrick*,[13] the defendant who had covenanted with the plaintiff, the assignee of a bond, that he would 'at the request of the plaintiff, avow, ratify, and confirm all such actions' that the plaintiff lawfully brought against the debtor of the bond, was held to have dispensed with the need for a request when he executed a general release in favour of the debtor and disabled himself from bringing any action on the bond. **8.5**

The same idea was relied upon in cases concerned with breach of promises to marry, where the defendant had promised to marry the claimant upon request but in the meantime had married another person.[14] In *Short v Stone*,[15] it was held that in such a case 'if a party puts himself out of the condition in which a request could properly be made, he dispenses with the request.'[16] In *Caines v Smith*,[17] it was similarly held that it was not necessary for the plaintiff to plead a request to marry.[18] **8.6**

The principle was also applied in cases involving a renunciation. In *Hochster* itself it was recognised that a 'renunciation . . . by one party dispenses with a condition to be performed in the meantime.'[19] Examples of the application of this principle include *Ripley v M'Clure*[20] and *Cort v Ambergate Railway Co.*[21] In *Ripley v M'Clure*, the defendant had agreed to buy one third of a cargo of **8.7**

[10] See generally, *Sir Anthony Main's Case* (1596) 5 Co Rep 20b, 77 ER 80; *Bowdell v Parsons* (1808) 10 East 359, 103 ER 811; *Amory v Brodrick* (1822) 5 B & Ald 712, 106 ER 1351; *Ford v Tiley* (1827) 6 B & C 325, 108 ER 472; *Short v Stone* (1846) 8 QB 358, 115 ER 911; *Lovelock v Franklyn* (1846) 8 QB 371, 115 ER 916; *Caines v Smith* (1847) 15 M & W 189, 153 ER 816; *Sands v Clarke* (1849) 8 C B 751, 137 ER 703.
[11] (1808) 10 East 359, 103 ER 811.
[12] ibid 361; 812 (in argument).
[13] (1822) 5 B & Ald 712, 106 ER 1351.
[14] For a general discussion of these cases see Mitchell (n 2) 136–39.
[15] (1846) 8 QB 358, 115 ER 911.
[16] ibid 369; 915.
[17] (1847) 15 M & W 189, 153 ER 816.
[18] ibid 190; 817.
[19] *Hochster v De La Tour* (1853) 2 El & Bl 678, 693–94; 118 ER 922, 927–28.
[20] (1849) 4 Ex 345, 154 ER 1245; affirmed on appeal (1850) 5 Ex 140, 155 ER 60.
[21] (1851) 17 QB 127, 117 ER 1229. Both cases are discussed in more detail at [5.48]–[5.51].

tea from the plaintiff on the arrival of a vessel with the cargo in Belfast but, before the arrival of the vessel, the defendant refused to perform. The Court of Exchequer (affirmed on appeal) held that the refusal to perform, unretracted at the time of performance, operated to waive the condition that the plaintiff be ready, willing, and able to deliver the cargo. In *Cort v Ambergate Railway Co*, the defendants renounced their obligation to accept further delivery of chairs that they had contracted to be manufactured and supplied by the plaintiffs. The Court of Queen's Bench held that this renunciation operated to waive the condition that the plaintiffs actually make and offer to deliver the chairs before the defendant's obligation to accept the residue could fall due.

8.8 As Professor Paul Mitchell has observed, the principle of waiver of conditions on a repudiation provided 'a powerful tool for releasing innocent parties from pointless performance and allowing them to sue immediately'.[22] But in all of these cases, the action was brought after the time for performance had fallen due.[23] Although the principle's practical effect was to enlarge the scope of the repudiating party's obligation to perform,[24] because the defendant could no longer rely upon the condition, their obligation to perform had in theory actually fallen due.[25] There was therefore an actual breach. The older cases on waiver of conditions on a repudiation were not cases involving a doctrine of anticipatory breach.

Hochster v De La Tour

8.9 The facts of *Hochster v De La Tour*[26] are quite simple. Hochster had been hired by De La Tour to accompany him as a courier on a tour across continental Europe for three months from 1 June 1852. On 11 May, De La Tour wrote to tell Hochster that he had changed his mind and would not need his services. This was a renunciation of De La Tour's obligations under the contract. On 22 May—ie before the services were due to commence on 1 June—Hochster commenced an action seeking damages for breach of contract. Hochster subsequently found employment with Lord Ashburton on similar terms but this did not commence until 4 July.

[22] Mitchell (n 2) 139.
[23] ibid 147; Mustill (n 2) 19.
[24] Arthur Corbin, *Corbin on Contracts: A Comprehensive Treatise on the Rules of Contract Law* (West Publishing Co 1960) vol 3A, 480 §752. See also Mitchell (n 2) 138.
[25] Liu (n 8) 14–15.
[26] (1853) 2 El & Bl 678, 118 ER 922.

8.10 As counsel for Hochster put it, the question that arose for consideration was 'whether in law it is possible to break a contract before the day for its performance comes'.[27] This was the first occasion on which the question had properly arisen for consideration.[28] Two 'formidable obstacle[s]'[29] to the plaintiff's case were the dicta of Parke B in *Phillpotts v Evans*[30] and *Ripley v M'Clure*.[31] In *Phillpotts v Evans*, a case concerned with an action for non-acceptance of a delivery of wheat, the defendant had given notice of his intention not to accept the wheat while the goods were still in transit. The case was concerned with the proper measure of damages and ultimately held that the proper measure of damages was the difference between the market price and the contract price at the time when the goods were actually tendered and refused, not the time when notice of the intended refusal was given. But speaking of the refusal while the goods were still in transit, Parke B said:

> I think no action would then have lain for the breach of the contract, but that the plaintiffs were bound to wait until the time arrived for delivery of the wheat, to see whether the defendant would then receive it. . . . His contract was not broken by his previous declaration that he would not accept them; it was a mere nullity, and it was perfectly in his power to accept them nevertheless; and, vice versa, the plaintiffs could not sue him before.[32]

In *Ripley v M'Clure*, discussed above,[33] Parke B again said that 'if the jury had been told that a refusal before the arrival of the cargo was a breach, that would have been incorrect. We think that point rightly decided in *Philpotts* [sic] *v Evans*'.[34]

8.11 With this powerful dicta behind them, counsel for De La Tour must have been confident in their prospects of success. Counsel argued that 'an announcement of an intention to break the contract when the time comes is no more than an offer to rescind'.[35] But when pressed by the Court as to why Hochster could not then go out and seek alternative employment, counsel argued that if Hochster 'adopt[ed] [De La Tour's] notice, which is in legal effect an offer, to rescind, he must adopt it altogether',[36] meaning that he must forsake any claim for

27 ibid 682; 923.
28 Mustill (n 2) 38.
29 Liu (n 8) 10.
30 (1839) 5 M & W 475, 151 ER 200.
31 (1849) 4 Ex 345, 154 ER 1245.
32 *Phillpotts v Evans* (1839) 5 M & W 475, 477; 151 ER 200, 202.
33 See [8.7].
34 *Ripley v M'Clure* (1849) 4 Ex 345, 359; 154 ER 1245, 1251.
35 *Hochster v De La Tour* (1853) 2 El & Bl 678, 686; 118 ER 922, 925.
36 ibid.

damages. In all likelihood, it was in this moment that De La Tour lost his case.[37] Lord Campbell CJ interjected: 'you say the plaintiff, to preserve any remedy at all, was bound to remain idle.'[38] And Erle J said:

> Suppose the defendant, after the plaintiff's engagement with Lord Ashburton, had retracted his refusal and required the plaintiff to travel with him on 1st June, and the plaintiff had refused to do so, and gone with Lord Ashburton instead? Do you say that the now defendant could in that case have sued the now plaintiff for a breach of contract?[39]

8.12 Counsel for the defendant remained steadfast in his response: the plaintiff must either accept the offer and lose the right to damages or remain ready, willing, and able to perform. According to Professor Arthur Corbin, counsel instead should have offered a third possibility, namely, that following a repudiation the innocent party is discharged from further performance of their contractual obligations without forfeiting their right to damages, but that such a right does not exist until performance has or would have actually fallen due under the contract.[40] But such a possibility was never raised and was not before the Court.

8.13 Faced with the options of finding for De La Tour and requiring Hochster to have remained on standby until the time for performance had actually arrived, and finding for Hochster and holding that the renunciation operated to discharge Hochster immediately and give him an immediate right of action for breach, the Court unsurprisingly opted for the latter conclusion.[41] While noting that the arguments of counsel for De La Tour were powerfully made, Lord Campbell CJ said: 'But it cannot be laid down as a universal rule that, where by agreement an act is to be done on a future day, no action can be brought for a breach of the agreement till the day for doing the act has arrived.'[42] He added:

> [I]t is surely much more rational, and more for the benefit of both parties, that, after the renunciation of the agreement by the defendant, the plaintiff should be at liberty to consider himself absolved from any future performance of it,

[37] Arthur Corbin, *Corbin on Contracts: A Comprehensive Treatise on the Rules of Contract Law* (West Publishing Co 1951) vol 4, 857–59 §960; Mustill (n 2) 40–41.

[38] *Hochster v De La Tour* (1853) 2 El & Bl 678, 686; 118 ER 922, 925.

[39] ibid.

[40] Corbin (n 37) 857–58 §960; Mustill (n 2) 41; JW Carter, *Carters' Breach of Contract* (2nd edn, Hart Publishing 2018) 286 [7-02].

[41] See also Mustill (n 2) 40.

[42] *Hochster v De La Tour* (1853) 2 El & Bl 678, 688; 118 ER 922, 926.

> retaining his right to sue for any damage he has suffered from the breach of it.... [A]nd it seems reasonable to allow an option to the injured party, either to sue immediately, or to wait till the time when the act was to be done ...[43]

Judgment was therefore given for Hochster, who was able to succeed on the basis that De La Tour's renunciation had discharged him immediately from his obligation to be ready, willing, and able to perform and given him an immediate right to damages.

8.14 The decision in *Hochster v De La Tour* was controversial and it was not universally embraced at first. In *Frost v Knight*,[44] the Court of Exchequer (Kelly CB, Channell B; Martin B dissenting) refused to apply the doctrine in *Hochster* to a contract of marriage. In that case, the defendant had promised to marry the plaintiff upon his father's death, it being anticipated that his father would oppose the marriage. The defendant subsequently renounced his promise during his father's lifetime, causing the plaintiff to bring an action for breach. Importantly, the father was still alive at the time the action was brought.

8.15 Kelly CB was critical of *Hochster* despite being bound to apply it.[45] He began his judgment by stating that '[n]othing can be more certain, as a matter of fact, than that a promise to marry upon an event which has not yet happened is not broken by the defendant declaring that he will not perform his promise.'[46] The Chief Baron identified four problems with *Hochster*. First, the judgment appeared to assume that a renunciation was itself a breach of contract, which would simply rely on a fiction.[47] Secondly, the result was 'unsupported by any previous authority' and 'directly opposed to the principle of several cases.'[48] Thirdly, the effect of the rule in *Hochster*, if applied to contracts of marriage would be to substitute for the parties' original contract 'another contract which they have never entered into and never contemplated.'[49] As applied to a contract of marriage, damages would be given for breach of a contract that may not have fallen due for performance until the plaintiff and defendant were in their sixties and seventies, at which point the defendant may have lost all his health, fortune, and rank in life while the plaintiff may have lost her health or character.[50]

43 ibid 690–91; 926–27.
44 (1870) LR 5 Ex 322.
45 *Hoschter v De La Tour* had previously been applied by the Exchequer Chamber in *Danube and Black Sea Railway and Kustendjie Harbour Co Ltd v Xenos* (1863) 13 CB (NS) 825, 143 ER 325.
46 *Frost v Knight* (1870) LR 5 Ex 322, 326.
47 ibid 328, 331.
48 ibid 331.
49 ibid 334.
50 ibid 334–35.

This also gave rise to a fourth problem: it would be 'absolutely impossible to do more than merely conjecture the damages which would have been sustained if no renunciation of the contract had ever been made, and the breach had taken place upon the death of the father.'[51]

8.16 Nonetheless when the case got to the Exchequer Chamber the judgment was reversed and *Hochster* was applied.[52] Cockburn CJ considered that the case fell within the principle of *Hochster* and it was just and convenient for the rule be applied.[53] Apart from authority, allowing the promisee to act on the repudiation immediately meant that measures could be taken by the promisee to reduce any eventual loss.[54] Moreover, the difficulties with measuring damages prospectively were not unique to the *Hochster* doctrine and were outweighed by the advantages of the rule (namely, expediency).[55] The decision of the Exchequer Chamber in *Frost v Knight* represented the crystallisation of the doctrine of anticipatory breach in English law. The existence of the doctrine has never been questioned seriously since.[56]

On acceptance

8.17 One feature of the doctrine of anticipatory breach that has not yet been mentioned is the requirement of 'acceptance'. It is 'trite law'[57] that a statement by one party in advance of performance that they will not perform, on its own, does not discharge the other party from their obligation to perform and give rise to an immediate action for breach. For a repudiation to have these effects it must be 'accepted'.[58] As Asquith LJ said in *Howard v Pickford Tool Co Ltd*,[59] '[a]n unaccepted repudiation is a thing writ in water and of no value to anybody: it confers no legal rights of any sort or kind.'[60]

[51] ibid 335.
[52] *Frost v Knight* (1872) LR 7 Ex 111.
[53] ibid 113, 114.
[54] ibid 115.
[55] ibid 117.
[56] Mustill (n 2) 48.
[57] *Jafari-Fini v Skillglass Ltd (in admin)* [2006] EWHC 77 (Ch) [164]; *Harcap Limited v FK Generators & Equipment Ltd* [2017] EWHC 2765 (Comm) [59].
[58] For criticism of this language see, JC Smith, 'Anticipatory Breach of Contract' in E Lomnicka and C Morse (eds), *Contemporary Issues in Commercial Law: Essays in Honour of A G Guest* (Sweet & Maxwell 1997) 175, 184–88.
[59] [1951] 1 KB 417, 421.
[60] See also ibid 420–21 (Evershed MR); *Golding v London & Edinburgh Insurance Co Ltd* (1932) 43 Ll L Rep 487, 488. It should, however, be noted that this statement, unqualified, is misleading: Mustill (n 2) 61–62. See further [5.37]–[5.97].

Yet the requirement of acceptance did not originate in *Hochster*—the plaintiff had acted upon the repudiation immediately so no such issue arose. The requirement of acceptance is derived from the decision of the Court of Exchequer (affirmed in the Exchequer Chamber) in *Avery v Bowden*.[61] In that case, the plaintiff shipowner had agreed to sail to Odessa to load a cargo from the defendant's agents. The ship arrived in Odessa on 11 March 1854. Shortly thereafter, the defendant's agents told the captain of the ship that they had no cargo for him and that he should leave. The captain continued to insist on a cargo. On 28 March, war was declared between Great Britain and Russia as part of the Crimean War, which made performance of the contract illegal. The ship eventually sailed away without a cargo on 17 April before the lay days had expired. **8.18**

In an action for breach for not providing a cargo, the defendant relied upon the outbreak of the war before the expiry of the lay days as discharging them from their obligation to provide a cargo. The plaintiff argued that the agent's statement prior to the outbreak of the war amounted to a renunciation giving rise to an immediate right of action. The Court found that the language used by the agent did not amount to a renunciation of the contract and this was the ultimate ground of the decision. However, in obiter, Lord Campbell CJ said that if the language had been stronger then 'the captain might have treated this as a breach and renunciation of the contract . . . whereupon the plaintiff would have had a right to maintain an action on the charter party', but 'it could not be considered as constituting a cause of action after the captain still continued to insist upon having a cargo in fulfilment of the charter party.'[62] **8.19**

Although these comments were only obiter, they were quickly accepted as binding statements of principle.[63] This may have in part been due to a mistake in the headnote of the report to the case,[64] which provided as the holding of the case: 'the refusal of the agent before the time for loading had expired, not being acted on as a renunciation of the contract, was not a cause of action.'[65] As Sir Michael Mustill observed, 'the view of *Avery v Bowden* adopted by judges and **8.20**

[61] *Avery v Bowden* (1855) 5 El & Bl 714, 119 ER 647 (affirmed in *Avery v Bowden* (1856) 6 El & Bl 953, 119 ER 1119).

[62] *Avery v Bowden* (1855) 5 El & Bl 714, 728; 119 ER 647, 652–53.

[63] Liu (n 8) 22–23.

[64] ibid 23, citing L Vold, 'Anticipatory Breach of Contracts and Necessity of Election' (1927–28) 26 Michigan Law Review 502, 519.

[65] *Avery v Bowden* (1855) 5 El & Bl 714, 714; 119 ER 647, 647.

commentators ever since is that a renunciation is ineffectual unless treated as such by the innocent party. Thus it is, as Asquith LJ was to say a century later, "a thing writ in water".[66]

8.21 In this sense, the doctrine of anticipatory breach may represent the first historically true example of an election to terminate. In *Frost v Knight*,[67] Cockburn CJ summarised the now-accepted position in the following way:

> The promisee, if he pleases, may treat the notice of intention as inoperative, and await the time when the contract is to be executed, and then hold the other party responsible for all the consequences of non-performance: but in that case he keeps the contract alive for the benefit of the other party as well as his own . . . On the other hand, the promisee may, if he thinks proper, treat the repudiation of the other party as a wrongful putting an end to the contract, and may at once bring his action as on a breach of it . . .

In other words, in order to bring about a discharge of their contractual obligations and to have an immediate right of action for damages, the innocent party had to 'accept' the repudiation, that is, choose to bring the contractual performances of the parties to an end.

8.22 But, importantly, the requirement of acceptance came about precisely because anticipatory breach was not dealing with an actual breach of contract. A statement made in advance of the time for performance was not itself a breach of contract. It would only have that effect if accepted by the other party. The principle of acceptance therefore had no application to discharge following actual breach. Despite this, we have already seen in Chapter 2 how the requirement of acceptance for anticipatory breach, discussed in *Heyman v Darwins Ltd*,[68] appears to have influenced the modern lawyer's understanding of discharge following an actual breach.[69] In brief, lawyers and textbook writers appear to have mistakenly assumed that because acceptance is required for discharge following an anticipatory breach, acceptance is also required for discharge following an actual breach, ie that the innocent party must elect to terminate.

[66] Mustill (n 2) 45.
[67] *Frost v Knight* (1872) LR 7 Ex 111, 112–13.
[68] [1942] AC 356.
[69] See [2.46]–[2.52].

Justifications for Anticipatory Breach

The doctrine of anticipatory breach faces the obvious objection that was highlighted at the beginning of this chapter: how can one party be said to have breached an obligation to perform when the performance of that obligation has not yet fallen due?[70] The simple answer is that they cannot: 'the breach of a promise is impossible except by non-performance in accordance with its terms'.[71] Nonetheless, it is clear that the doctrine of anticipatory breach has a lot to commend it from a practical perspective.[72] As Professor Qiao Liu had observed, the doctrine 'avoid[s] waste', 'free[s] resources from fruitless or inefficient use', and 'encourage[s] early mitigation of loss'.[73] In *Hochster* itself, Lord Campbell CJ said: **8.23**

> Thus, instead of remaining idle and laying out money in preparations which must be useless, [the plaintiff] is at liberty to seek service under another employer, which would go in mitigation of the damages to which he would otherwise be entitled for a breach of the contract.[74]

The question then is whether in light of these clearly beneficial practical outcomes, a satisfactory theoretical explanation can be given of the doctrine. Is it possible to construct an explanation of the doctrine of anticipatory breach that coheres with the rest of contract law, the discharge of contractual obligations in particular? Or must we contend, as Mustill did, that 'logic has collapsed under the weight of a desire to reach a humanly acceptable solution, in the face of principles of orthodox contract law'?[75] **8.24**

Actual breach (an implied promise theory)

The first possibility is that the cases applying the doctrine of anticipatory breach are in fact concerned with an actual, present breach caused by the renunciation or disablement.[76] The most prominent version of this theory **8.25**

[70] Mustill (n 2) 40; Dawson (n 2) 83; Mitchell (n 2) 135.
[71] Corbin (n 37) 859 §961.
[72] *Moschi v Lep Air Services* [1973] AC 331, 356 ('Whatever theoretical criticism can be advanced, the rule is really the only one which is practicable'). See also Liu (n 8) 13; Mitchell (n 2) 163.
[73] Liu (n 8) 37.
[74] *Hochster v De La Tour* (1853) 2 El & Bl 678, 690; 118 ER 922, 926.
[75] Mustill (n 2) 48.
[76] See generally, Corbin (n 37) 897–900 §971; Dawson (n 2) 96–100; Smith (n 58) 178–82; Liu (n 8) 31–33; John Stannard and David Capper, *Termination for Breach of Contract* (2nd edn, OUP 2020) 205–06 [7.30]–[7.31]; Carter (n 40) 295–96 [7-21]; Peter Benson, *Justice in Transactions: A Theory of Contract Law* (Harvard University Press 2019) 254.

postulates that each party impliedly promises not to do anything to prejudice the contractual relationship between the parties and it is this obligation that is breached when one party renounces their obligations or disables themselves from performing.[77] In *Hochster*, Lord Campbell appealed to this theory when he suggested:

> [I]t may be, that, where there is a contract to do an act on a future day, there is a relation constituted between the parties in the meantime by the contract, and that they impliedly promise that in the meantime neither will do any thing to the prejudice of the other inconsistent with that relation.[78]

Similarly, in *Frost v Knight*,[79] Cockburn CJ said that there is 'a breach of the contract when the promisor repudiates it and declares he will no longer be bound by it', adding:

> The promisee has an inchoate right to the performance of the bargain, which becomes complete when the time for performance has arrived. In the mean time he has a right to have the contract kept open as a subsisting and effective contract.[80]

8.26 The actual breach theory is the dominant view of the doctrine in the United States[81] and it has on occasion garnered support in England. In *Maredelanto Compania Naviera SA v Bergbau-Handel GmbH (The Mihalis Angelos)*,[82] Lord Denning MR stated that '[t]he words "anticipatory breach" are misleading. The cause of action is not the future breach. It is the renunciation itself.' And building on this explanation, Sir John Cyril Smith argued that '[t]he injured party is not anticipating a breach' but rather is anticipating the loss that will be incurred consequent upon an actual, present breach.[83]

8.27 The fundamental difficulty with the actual breach or implied promise theory, however, is that it is an anathema to the learning of generations of English lawyers who have been taught that an unaccepted repudiation is not a breach of contract: it is a 'thing writ in water'.[84] Of course, the answer to this could simply

77 Smith (n 58) 178–82.
78 *Hochster v De La Tour* (1853) 2 El & Bl 678, 689; 118 ER 922, 926.
79 (1872) LR 7 Ex 111, 114.
80 ibid.
81 Carter (n 40) 295–96 [7-21]. See American Law Institute, *Restatement of the Law Second: Contracts 2d* (American Law Institute Publishers 1981) 286 §253.
82 [1971] 1 QB 164, 196.
83 Smith (n 58) 179.
84 *Howard v Pickford Tool Co Ltd* [1951] 1 KB 417, 421. See also *Frost v Knight* (1872) LR 7 Ex 111, 118; *Johnstone v Milling* (1886) 16 QBD 460, 467, 472–73. '[T]he notion that an anticipatory

be that 'these statements are wrong; anticipatory breach is as immediately actionable as any other breach'.[85] This book is no stranger to the argument that certain contract paradigms need to be rethought. But it has never historically been the law, nor presently is it the law, that an unaccepted repudiation gives rise to an action for damages. Moreover, it has generally been accepted that a claimant is not required to mitigate their loss unless and until they accept the repudiation because mitigation is only relevant to conduct post-breach.[86] None of this would be true if an unaccepted repudiation were in fact an actual breach of contract.

Similarly, the doctrine cannot be founded on the idea of a continuing obligation to remain ready, willing, and able to perform.[87] A promisor is not under a duty to remain ready, willing, and able to perform prior to the time at which performance is due. As Mustill observed, 'this cannot be the general law, for it is trite that a vendor has only to be able to deliver on the day, and that it is no breach if he is not ready until then'.[88] The actual breach theory therefore seems to struggle to explain the features of English contract law as they exist today. **8.28**

Offer to terminate

The second possible justification for the doctrine of anticipatory breach is that a repudiation is, in essence, an offer to terminate the contract which can then be 'accepted' by the innocent party.[89] In *Denmark Productions Ltd v Boscobel Productions Ltd*,[90] Winn LJ relied upon this theory when he said: **8.29**

> Where A and B are parties to an executory contract, if A intimates by word or conduct that he no longer intends, or is unable, to perform it, or to perform it in a particular manner, he is, in effect, making an offer to B to treat the contract as dissolved or varied so far as it relates to the future. If B elects to treat the contract as thereby repudiated, he is deemed, according to the language of many decided cases, to 'accept the repudiation' ...

repudiation is not a breach until accepted as such by the innocent party' is 'cardinal to the English doctrine': E Tabachnik, 'Anticipatory Breach of Contract' (1972) 25 Current Legal Problems 149, 155.

[85] Smith (n 58) 180.
[86] cf *White and Carter (Councils) Ltd v McGregor* [1962] AC 413.
[87] cf Stannard and Capper (n 76) 206 [7.31].
[88] Mustill (n 2) 74. See also *Phillpotts v Evans* (1839) 5 M & W 475, 477; 151 ER 200, 202.
[89] See generally, Mustill (n 2) 33–36; Smith (n 58) 184–88; Liu (n 8) 11–14; Carter (n 40) 293–94 [7-18].
[90] [1969] 1 QB 699, 731.

8.30 It has been said that the offer and acceptance theory is the 'least satisfactory basis' for the doctrine.[91] The principal reason for this theory's rejection is that it is fanciful to suppose that the conduct of the repudiating party amounts to an 'offer' to terminate the contract, at least in the same sense that the term is used in the context of the contractual rules on offer and acceptance. As applied to renunciation, a statement by one party that they will not perform cannot sensibly be construed as a mere offer to discharge both parties' contractual obligations if only the other party agrees:

> [I]n the anticipatory breach cases the promisor was not inviting agreement; he was telling the promisee, "it's off." To hold otherwise would be a fiction which should have no place in modern law, especially commercial law in which anticipatory breach has come to feature so prominently.[92]

Indeed, Corbin, commenting on *Hochster*, observed that there was no doubt that De La Tour would have happily had Hochster agree to a 'mutual rescission of the contract'.[93] But De La Tour's conduct was not an offer of this kind. Instead, his 'repudiation was a manifestation of [De La Tour's] intention to commit a breach of the contract, even though [Hochster] would not assent to a rescission.'[94]

8.31 There is an even more fundamental problem when the offer and acceptance theory is applied to the other form of anticipatory breach, disablement. For here, the theory does not work unless the disablement consists of overt conduct from which an offer to terminate can plausibly be construed.[95] An example of where there was no such overt conduct is *Universal Cargo Carriers Corp v Citati*.[96] In that case, a ship had been chartered to load a quantity of scrap iron at Basrah and arrived in time to do so but the charterer failed to nominate an effective shipper or loading birth, and failed to provide a cargo. Three days before the lay days had expired, the shipowners rechartered the vessel to another party. On a special case from the arbitrator, the shipowners sought to justify their conduct by reference to the charterer's actual or anticipatory breach. On the issue of anticipatory breach,[97] the Court held that the shipowners were entitled to succeed on the basis of disablement if it could

[91] Carter (n 40) 293 [7-18].
[92] Smith (n 58) 184–85. See also Carter (n 40) 293 [7-18].
[93] Corbin (n 37) 857 §960.
[94] ibid.
[95] Mustill (n 2) 74, 78.
[96] [1957] 2 QB 401.
[97] The discussion of this case in Chapter 3 focused on the issue of actual breach: see [3.51]–[3.55].

be shown that 'the charterer was unable to load a cargo within such a time as would not have frustrated the object of the venture . . . notwithstanding that that was not a conclusion which they would have been justified in drawing from the facts known to them at the time'.[98] In particular, the prior findings of the arbitrator were that a reasonable ship owner would have concluded that 'the charterer was always willing to perform if he could'.[99] The problem for the offer and acceptance theory is that there was no conduct from which an offer to terminate could be inferred. As Mustill put it: 'the charterers had said and done nothing which could be construed as an intimation that they did not want to go ahead with the contract: quite the reverse.'[100]

A further problem is that the offer and acceptance theory cannot explain why damages are payable for an anticipatory breach. If the offer and acceptance theory were true it would be a case of discharge by agreement—a 'consensual termination'[101]—for which no damages would be payable. A person who makes an offer to the other party to terminate the contract commits no wrong whether the offer is accepted or not.[102] Indeed, an earlier version of the offer to terminate theory—which treated the offer as being an offer to rescind *ab initio* rather than terminate[103]—was in fact deployed unsuccessfully by counsel for the defendant in *Hochster* to argue that no damages ought to be payable. It will be recalled that in *Hochster* counsel argued that 'an announcement of an intention to break the contract when the time comes is no more than an offer to rescind' and that if Hochster 'adopt[ed] [De La Tour's] notice, which is in legal effect an offer, to rescind, he must adopt it altogether',[104] meaning that he must forsake any claim for damages. The Court rejected this argument. **8.32**

Finally, as a matter of authority, the offer and acceptance theory has been rejected at the highest level. In *Sinhalese Film Industrial Corp Ltd v Madanayake*,[105] Lord Diplock, delivering the advice of the Privy Council, said that although the decision to accept a repudiation 'is often described as an election to rescind the contract . . . the non-repudiating party's obligation to perform the contract any further is terminated by operation of law and not as the result of any agreement between the parties to rescind it'. In *Vitol SA v Norelf Ltd*,[106] Lord Steyn **8.33**

[98] *Universal Cargo Carriers Corp v Citati* [1957] 2 QB 401, 450.
[99] ibid 410, 439.
[100] Mustill (n 2) 74.
[101] Carter (n 40) 293 [7-18].
[102] Corbin (n 37) 934–35 §980.
[103] Mustill (n 2) 33–36.
[104] *Hochster v De La Tour* (1853) 2 El & Bl 678, 686; 118 ER 922, 925.
[105] (1971) 74 NLR 289, 291.
[106] [1996] AC 800, 812.

(with whom the other Law Lords agreed) conceded that 'the analogy of offer and acceptance is imperfect'. Finally, in *Hurst v Bryk*,[107] Lord Millett (again with whom the other Law Lords agreed) said: 'The theory that a repudiatory breach of contract is an offer to terminate the contract which can be accepted by the offeree, thereby bringing the contract to an end by mutual consent, is discredited.' The offer and acceptance theory is therefore a poor justification for the doctrine of anticipatory breach and can be rejected.

Inevitable breach

8.34 A third possible theory—and one that is at first sight more attractive—is that the doctrine of anticipatory breach allows the innocent party to anticipate what is an inevitable breach.[108] The law does not insist that parties wait for a factually or legally inevitable[109] breach, but rather accelerates the legal remedies that would be available if a breach of that kind were to occur. On this view, the phrase 'anticipatory breach' is a misnomer—it is a doctrine of liability in anticipation of breach.[110]

8.35 The idea has early antecedents. In *Frost v Knight*,[111] Cockburn CJ explaining the doctrine—albeit that he had earlier subscribed to an actual breach analysis—said that 'the eventual non-performance may therefore, by anticipation, be treated as a cause of action'. The best explanation of this view, however, was given almost 200 years later in *Universal Cargo Carriers Corp v Citati*.[112] In that case, the Court said:

> The two forms of anticipatory breach have a common characteristic that is essential to the concept, namely, that the injured party is allowed to anticipate an inevitable breach. If a man renounces his right to perform and is held to his renunciation, the breach will be legally inevitable; if a man puts it out of his power to perform, the breach will be inevitable in fact—or practically inevitable, for the law never requires absolute certainty and does not take account of bare possibilities.[113]

[107] [2002] 1 AC 185, 195.
[108] See generally, Mitchell (n 2) 165–66; Carter (n 40) 296–97 [7-22].
[109] *Universal Cargo Carriers Corp v Citati* [1957] 2 QB 401, 438.
[110] This phrase can be attributed to Professor Robert Stevens who has often framed the issue in this way in BCL/MJur Commercial Remedies seminars at the University of Oxford.
[111] *Frost v Knight* (1872) LR 7 Ex 111, 114.
[112] [1957] 2 QB 401.
[113] ibid 438.

8.36 The distinction between a factually and a legally inevitable breach is designed to reflect the distinction between disablement and renunciation. Where a person has disabled themselves from performing, their eventual non-performance and therefore the breach is said to be factually inevitable. Where a person has renounced their obligation to perform their eventual non-performance and breach is legally inevitable. By 'legal inevitability', what is meant is that it is not certain that the breach would have in fact occurred. For example, in *Hochster* 'the defendant might have changed his mind before 1 June and taken on Hochster after all'.[114] But by accepting the renunciation, the law permits the claimant to hold the defendant to their word that they will not perform and treat the breach as inevitable.[115] As Lord Campbell CJ said in *Hochster*:

> It seems strange that the defendant, after renouncing the contract, and absolutely declaring that he will never act under it, should be permitted to object that faith is given to his assertion, and that an opportunity is not left to him of changing his mind.[116]

8.37 On this view, the role of acceptance is to enable the claimant to take the defendant at their word. Until acceptance, the defendant is free to retract their renunciation and there is no liability because a breach is not inevitable. But upon acceptance of a renunciation, the defendant is held to their word that they will not perform.

8.38 As attractive as this theory is as an explanation for the vast majority of cases, the difficulty is that even with the qualification for legal inevitability (eg that following acceptance, the law does not permit the defendant to change their mind) and the fact that the law does not require absolute certainty for factual inevitability, the breach in a number of the leading cases was not inevitable.[117] In *Avery v Bowden*, for example, the Crimean War broke out before the lay days had expired discharging the defendant from their obligation to provide a cargo. But had the plaintiff renounced their obligations prior to this event and had the defendant accepted this repudiation, Lord Campbell CJ appears to have thought that an action would have been available.[118] This was the case

[114] Mustill (n 2) 42.
[115] *Universal Cargo Carriers Corp v Citati* [1957] 2 QB 401, 437. See also *Geden Operations Ltd v Dry Bulk Handy Holdings Inc (The Bulk Uruguay)* [2014] 2 All ER (Comm) 196, 201–04 [15]–[18].
[116] *Hochster v De La Tour* (1853) 2 El & Bl 678, 690; 118 ER 922, 926.
[117] Mustill (n 2) 73; Mitchell (n 2) 166; Carter (n 40) 296–97 [7-22]; Ewan McKendrick, 'Termination for Breach' in Hugh Beale (ed), *Chitty on Contracts* (35th edn, Sweet & Maxwell 2023) 2133, 2185 [28-071] (although cf 2187–88 [28-075]).
[118] *Avery v Bowden* (1855) 5 El & Bl 714, 728; 119 ER 647, 652–53.

notwithstanding that it was clear that the effect of the war breaking out before the time for loading had expired was that there would have been no breach; the breach was not bound to occur.

8.39 The inevitable breach theory was rejected for this reason in *The Mihalis Angelos*.[119] The owners of the *Mihalis Angelos* had agreed under a charterparty to arrive at a port in Haiphong, Vietnam to load a quantity of apatite (a phosphate mineral). The ship was to arrive in Haiphong and be ready to load by 1 July 1965. Clause 11 of the charterparty provided that if the vessel was not ready to load on or before 20 July, the charterers had the option to cancel the contract. The ship did not in fact arrive on 1 July and on 17 July, while the ship was still in Hong Kong, the charterers (incorrectly believing that the contract had been frustrated) repudiated the contract. The owners accepted this repudiation. Although this was an anticipatory breach, the ship did not in fact finish loading at Hong Kong until July 23 and it was found in a special case stated by the arbitrators that 'if the ship, after discharge at Hong Kong, had proceeded to Haiphong, the charterers would beyond doubt . . . have cancelled the charter, on the ground that the ship had missed her cancelling date.'[120] The charterers argued that the anticipatory breach, as it turned out, had deprived the owners of nothing—a worthless charter—and for that reason the damages payable should be nominal only.

8.40 In the High Court, Mocatta J applied the inevitable breach theory to reach the conclusion that the damages payable by the charterers should be £4,000. With 'some regret',[121] he held that because the law assumes that there will be an inevitable breach he could not take into account the circumstance that the charterers would have cancelled the contract pursuant to the express clause and not been in breach. He said: 'It is in relation to that assumed future breach of contract, which by law is anticipated, that damages have to be assessed.'[122]

8.41 The Court of Appeal, however, disagreed. Lord Denning MR, who, subscribing to the actual breach theory, saw 'the renunciation itself' as 'the breach', said 'the damages must be measured by compensating the injured party for the loss he has suffered by reason of the renunciation. You must take into account all contingencies which might have reduced or extinguished the loss.'[123] Edmund

119 [1971] 1 QB 164.
120 ibid 174.
121 ibid 183.
122 ibid 182.
123 ibid 196.

Davies LJ agreed and stated that the approach adopted by Mocatta J led 'to a result so manifestly unrealistic that there must surely be something wrong with it.'[124] Megaw LJ similarly said that '[w]hen a logical argument leads to such a conclusion, one is bound to consider whether the premise is sound.'[125] In his view, following acceptance of a repudiation, the innocent party was entitled to recover 'the true value of the contractual rights which he has thereby lost; subject to the duty to mitigate.'[126] In an important passage, he said:

> If the contractual rights which he has lost were capable by the terms of the contract of being rendered either less valuable or valueless in certain events, and if it can be shown that those events were, at the date of acceptance of the repudiation, predestined to happen, then in my view the damages which he can recover are not more than the true value, if any, of the rights which he has lost, having regard to those predestined events.[127]

The inevitable breach theory thus appears to have been comprehensively rejected in *The Mihalis Angelos*. Yet despite its seeming rejection, cases continue to discuss and rely on it.[128] This seems to reflect the theory's intuitive attractiveness as an explanation of the doctrine. But, as intuitive as it may seem, the inevitable breach theory still faces the insuperable problem that a breach is not, in all cases, inevitable. It therefore cannot, without some modification, be an explanation for the doctrine. **8.42**

It remains to note the related view that has been put forward by Professor Qiao Liu, which he terms the 'inferential breach analysis'.[129] This appears to be the inevitable breach view but with some slight differences. In particular, it does not depend upon the inevitability of the breach but rather a reasonable 'inference that a prospective fundamental breach is likely, on the balance of probabilities, to materialise at the time for performance.'[130] Liu suggests that two steps are required: **8.43**

[124] ibid 202.
[125] ibid 209.
[126] ibid 210.
[127] ibid.
[128] *Thunderbird Industries LLC v Simoco Digital UK Ltd* [2004] EWHC 209 (Ch) [22]–[23]; *Geden Operations Ltd v Dry Bulk Handy Holdings Inc (The Bulk Uruguay)* [2014] 2 All ER (Comm) 196, 201–04 [15]–[18]; *Spar Shipping AS v Grand China Logistics Holding (Group) Co Ltd* [2015] 1 All ER (Comm) 879, 926 [144]; *Teekay Tankers Ltd v STX Offshore and Shipbuilding Co Ltd (No 2)* [2017] 1 Lloyd's Rep 387, 430 [217].
[129] See Qiao Liu, 'Inferring Future Breach: Towards a Unifying Test of Anticipatory Breach of Contract' (2007) 66 Cambridge Law Journal 574; Liu (n 8) 33–39.
[130] Liu, 'Inferring Future Breach' (n 129) 598.

> First, the party alleging an anticipatory breach must satisfy the court that a legal inference may be drawn that a future breach is likely to occur. Secondly, the party must also satisfy the court that the inferred breach is sufficiently serious to compel an acceleration of the legal remedies for it.[131]

8.44 The key difference between Liu's theory and the inevitable breach theory is that Liu appears to accept that it is theoretically possible to have a present breach of a future obligation.[132] Thus he says that 'there is nothing in either principle or reason that compels the conclusion that a breach of contract must be an actual breach'; 'an anticipatory breach is a present breach, a breach committed presently, because it is embodied in a party's "present" words or conduct'; '[i]t is a present breach of a future obligation'; and he distinguishes between the actual breach that will occur when the time for performance comes and the present 'anticipatory breach' that 'exists only while the anticipated breach is still anticipated'.[133] With the greatest of respect, this is all very difficult to understand and there appear to be very good reasons in principle and reason why a breach of contract must be an actual breach. To say that one has breached a contractual obligation is to say that the obligation has fallen due and it has not been performed. If the obligation has not yet fallen due, then it cannot be breached. Liu's view is not a satisfactory explanation of the doctrine of anticipatory breach.[134]

No explanation

8.45 The final possibility—at least on the power to terminate account of the discharge of contractual obligations—is that no rational explanation can be given for the doctrine of anticipatory breach other than practical convenience.[135] This was the view of Mustill who concluded: 'The concept of anticipatory breach cannot be rationalised, but must be seen as a piece of positive law, firmly established but not anchored in or deducible from the ordinary course of the law of contract.'[136]

[131] Liu (n 8) 37.
[132] ibid 35–37.
[133] ibid 35–36.
[134] See also the criticisms in Neil Andrews, Andrew Tettenborn, Graham Virgo, 'Contractual Duties: Performance, Breach, Termination and Remedies (4th edn, Sweet & Maxwell 2023) 136–37 [7-023]–[7-024], 169–170 [7-112]–[7-116].
[135] See generally, Mitchell (n 2) 163–64; Mustill (n 4) 571, 584.
[136] Mustill (n 4) 584.

This would not necessarily entail the rejection of the doctrine. The way in which the common law develops means that it may not always be possible to construct a theory that explains every feature of a doctrine. Anticipatory breach is perhaps the best example of this.[137] No one seriously contends that Hochster should have lost his case and been required to remain idle. As Lord Simon once said, '[w]hatever theoretical criticism can be advanced, the rule is really the only one which is practicable'.[138] **8.46**

A Failure of Condition Model

The discussion thus far has been premised on the orthodox power to terminate model of the discharge of contractual obligations. But as has been seen throughout this book, in the discharge of contractual obligations there is a vital, but often obscured, distinction between promises (duties) and conditions. The distinction is important because, while a breach of duty always gives rise to an action for damages, it does not necessarily discharge a party from their obligation to perform.[139] On the failure of condition model, discharge depends upon the failure of a condition not a breach of duty. And it is not necessary for there to be a breach of duty for a condition to fail.[140] **8.47**

It is not surprising then to find that in relation to anticipatory breach, part of the difficulty in coming up with a satisfactory rationale has arisen due to the failure to distinguish between promises and conditions.[141] As Mustill put it in a tour de force on anticipatory breach: '[w]ith respect to the judges of distinction who have tackled this problem over the centuries, it seems to me that at crucial moments some of them have failed to recognise that the non-occurrence of the condition is not necessarily a breach'.[142] He then added: **8.48**

> [T]he problems have arisen from the assumption, often correct but not invariably so, that if the non-performance by B of his obligation . . . has the effect of discharging A from his duty to perform . . . it must necessarily follow that B is also liable in damages to A.[143]

[137] Mustill (n 2) 76; Carter (n 40) 292 [7-17].
[138] *Moschi v Lep Air Services Ltd* [1973] AC 331, 356.
[139] Sir William R Anson, *Principles of the English Law of Contract* (1st edn, Clarendon Press 1879) 266.
[140] See [1.40]–[1.49].
[141] Samuel Williston, 'Repudiation of Contracts—II' (1901) 14 Harvard Law Review 421, 434; Mustill (n 2) 12–14, 76; Liu (n 6) 563.
[142] Mustill (n 2) 12.
[143] ibid 13.

Put another way, a number of the problems that have arisen could have been avoided 'by separating discharge from cause of action'[144]—promises from conditions.

8.49 The problem has also been noted by Professor Samuel Williston, who once wrote that '[t]he difference between conditions and promises is so radical in its consequence that there is no excuse for a nomenclature which fails to recognize the distinction'.[145] Writing on *Hochster*, he said that there is a 'distinction between a defence and a right of action':

> This seems obvious, but it is frequently lost sight of, as it was in that case. Every consideration of justice requires that repudiation or inability to perform should immediately excuse the innocent party from performing, nor is any technical rule violated if the excuse is allowed. But it does not follow from this that he has an immediate right of action.[146]

8.50 But as we have already seen,[147] there is another way in which the law could have developed had counsel provided a different answer to the Court's question in *Hochster*. As Corbin argued, counsel should have said that following a repudiation the innocent party is discharged from further performance of their contractual obligations, but that their right to damages does not exist until performance has or would have actually fallen due under the contract.[148] Alternatively, it could have been said that the innocent party can bring an immediate action for damages (as well as being discharged from further performance) but if by the time of trial it becomes clear that a breach would not have occurred, their right to damages should be extinguished.

8.51 Drawing this distinction between discharge and damages, between promises and conditions, gives us a new way of explaining the doctrine of anticipatory breach and in particular allows us to rehabilitate the inevitable breach theory in a way that explains why it is intuitively attractive and perhaps why it continues to be relied on by judges. In particular, although it cannot be said that in all cases a *breach* is inevitable, what can be said to be inevitable is the *non-performance*. As Popplewell J said in *Geden Operations Ltd v Dry Bulk Handy Holdings Inc (The Bulk Uruguay)*:[149]

[144] ibid 76.
[145] Samuel Williston, *The Law of Contracts* (Baker, Voorhis & Co 1921) vol 2, 1282 §665.
[146] Williston (n 141) 434.
[147] See [8.12].
[148] Corbin (n 37) 857–58 §960; Mustill (n 2) 41; Carter (n 40) 286 [7-02].
[149] [2014] 2 All ER (Comm) 196, 203 [17].

> [T]he rationale for treating both renunciation and self induced impossibility as entitling the innocent party to treat the contract as at an end prior to the time for performance is the inevitability of non performance . . . [T]he reason for the rule is that a party is allowed to anticipate an inevitable event and is not obliged to wait until it happens . . .

According to this view, which we can call the 'inevitable non-performance' view, where a contracting party disables themselves from performing their non-performance is factually inevitable, discounting bare possibilities (such as the possibility that a vendor of land who disables themselves from performing by selling the title to the land might repurchase it). Equally, if one party renounces their obligation to perform and the other party accepts that renunciation, the law permits the other party to hold the renouncing party to their word that they will not perform and their non-performance is legally inevitable. On a failure of condition model of the discharge of contractual obligations, if the parties' obligations to perform are conditional then irrespective of whether the innocent party's obligation is subject to a condition precedent or subsequent, they can, in anticipation of the eventual non-performance by the other party, treat themselves as discharged from their obligation to perform. **8.52**

Of course what is not inevitable on this view is that there will be a breach. As *Avery v Bowden* and *The Mihalis Angelos* demonstrate, subsequent events may have provided the repudiating party with an excuse for non-performance when the time for performance came, in which case there would have been no breach. But on the failure of condition model and the inevitable non-performance view, this goes to whether there is a breach of duty and not to the separate question of discharge. In other words, it goes solely to the question of whether there should be a claim for damages which is distinct from the question of whether the innocent party should be discharged from their obligation to perform. The non-performance is inevitable and can be treated as discharging the party immediately, even if the breach is not inevitable. **8.53**

Now, the obvious point at which the positive law diverges from this analysis is that, because of the conflation of promises and conditions, it treats an acceptance of a repudiation as not just giving rise to the discharge of the innocent party but as also giving rise to an immediate action for damages. This is difficult to explain on this view because the breach is clearly not inevitable in all cases. Yet even here there have been positive developments. More recent cases, building on *The Mihalis Angelos*, have held that damages are to be assessed on the basis of events that did in fact occur and not on the assumption **8.54** that a breach was inevitable. In *Golden Straight Corp v Nippon Yusen Kubishika Kaisha (The Golden Victory)*,[150] owners of a tanker chartered the vessel for a period of seven years. The charterparty contained a war clause that permitted the owners and the charterers to cancel the contract if war should break out between, relevantly, the United States of America, the United Kingdom, and Iraq. In December 2001, when the charterparty still had nearly four years left to run, the charterers repudiated the charterparty, a repudiation which the owners accepted. The owners claimed damages but by the time the case reached arbitration, the Second Gulf War had broken out in March 2003 and it was accepted that the charterers would have cancelled the charterparty relying on the war clause if the contract had been in force at that point. The issue for the House of Lords was whether damages should be reduced on the basis that the charterers would have lawfully terminated the charterparty in March 2003 or whether damages should be payable for the full four years remaining on the charterparty, ignoring events subsequent to the repudiation. A majority of the House of Lords (Lords Scott, Carswell, and Brown; Lords Bingham and Walker dissenting) held that damages should be reduced to take into account events that were now known to have occurred.

8.55 *The Golden Victory* suggests that in cases of anticipatory breach, if it in fact becomes clear that no breach would have occurred, damages should be nominal only.[151] Although the case was concerned with an actual breach, which may suggest the principles discussed do not apply to anticipatory breach, the basis for termination in the case was not the breach of some condition or innominate term (to use the orthodox language) but rather the fact that the form the actual breach took amounted to a renunciation of the charterers' future obligations. The complexity here arises because, as we saw in Chapter 2,[152] sometimes the conduct to infer a renunciation of future obligations is in fact the way in which a present obligation is breached. Thus an anticipatory breach can also involve an actual breach. Seen in this way, the principles in *The Golden Victory* are clearly applicable to anticipatory breach. This conclusion is fortified by the fact that the House of Lords in *The Golden Victory* referred extensively to *The Mihalis Angelos*, which was concerned with anticipatory breach.

8.56 If it is correct that *The Golden Victory* applies to anticipatory breach cases, then the only difference between the inevitable non-performance view and the

[150] [2007] 2 AC 353.

[151] Brian Coote, 'Breach, anticipatory breach, or the breach anticipated?' (2007) 123 Law Quarterly Review 503.

[152] See [2.50].

positive law as it stands is that on the inevitable non-performance view if it becomes clear that there would have been no breach, there should be no right to damages at all, not even nominal damages. On the positive law at present, if a repudiation is accepted but it subsequently becomes clear that there would have been no breach, damages are still awarded but they are nominal. In other words, on the inevitable non-performance view, the excusing event goes to liability whereas on the positive law at present it goes to the quantum of damages payable.[153]

This is a difference but it is a marginal one. Due to more recent developments such as *The Golden Victory*, the positive law at present is almost identical to the position that ought to have obtained if a distinction had been drawn between promises and conditions, ie between discharge and damages. To use the old expression, the common law works itself pure.[154] **8.57**

Conclusion

As this chapter has shown, on the power to terminate model the doctrine of anticipatory breach is all but impossible to justify. Yet the difficulties in explaining the doctrine stem from the perennial failure of English lawyers to distinguish promises from conditions. When this is done, it is possible to come up with a much more satisfactory explanation of the doctrine (although admittedly one that renders the label 'anticipatory breach' misleading). That is, that a party is able to anticipate an inevitable non-performance by one party to discharge themselves from their own obligation to perform. Any right to damages, however, even if immediately actionable in anticipation, must be conditional on whether the future breach was in fact inevitable. If it is known at the time of trial that a breach would not have occurred then damages ought not to be payable—the breach was not inevitable. That is, in all material respects other than the payment of nominal damages, the position that obtains on the positive law today. **8.58**

[153] See Coote (n 151) 511, making a similar point in the context of the effect of excusing events when a repudiation is accepted versus when it is not accepted.

[154] Ronald Dworkin, *Law's Empire* (reprint, Hart Publishing 1998) 400.

9

Restitution for Failure of Condition

Introduction

The core focus of this book has been on the discharge of contractual obligations for failure of condition. But the arguments presented in the previous chapters about the discharge of contractual obligations also have important consequences beyond the law of contract. In particular, the emphasis that has been placed on the nature and operation of conditions has significant implications for how we understand the doctrine of failure of consideration in the law of restitution or—as it is commonly referred to today—restitution for failure of condition.[1] **9.1**

There are three important implications for the law of restitution that result from the arguments made in this book. First, as was already noted in Chapter 1,[2] '[i]t is a source of confusion of thought that the word condition is frequently used without exact recognition of what the supposed condition qualifies'.[3] By asking 'what does the condition qualify?', this chapter resolves an important question in the law of restitution, namely, what exactly is conditional in failure **9.2**

[1] See, eg, *Barton v Morris* [2023] AC 684, 758 [231] (Lord Burrows) ('[W]hat has traditionally been called failure of consideration but is now often referred to as failure of condition or failure of basis'); *Anderson v McPherson (No 2)* [2012] WASC 19 [235] (Edelman J) ('[T]he doctrine of failure of consideration has been described as failure of "condition".'). See also Frederick Wilmot-Smith, 'Replacing Risk-taking Reasoning' (2011) 127 Law Quarterly Review 610, 618–19; Frederick Wilmot-Smith, 'Reconsidering "Total" Failure' (2013) 72 Cambridge Law Journal 414, 416.

[2] [1.19].

[3] Samuel Williston, *The Law of Contracts* (Baker, Voorhis & Co 1921) vol 2, 1283 §666.

Discharge of Contractual Obligations. Jordan English, Oxford University Press. © Jordan English 2025.
DOI: 10.1093/9780198906704.003.0009

of condition cases. The answer given is that in the common context of contractual performances it is the obligation that is conditional. The effect of a condition failing on this view is that the obligation—which provided the juristic reason for the performance—either never imposed any immediate duty of performance on the claimant seeking restitution (condition precedent) or no longer imposes such a duty (condition subsequent). The result is an absence of basis (or a lack of any justifying ground) for the performance that has been rendered.

9.3 Secondly, this chapter explains why restitution for failure of condition does not contradict the law of contract in cases where there is an underlying valid contract and that contract appears, at first glance, to entitle the defendant to receive the performance in question. It is generally supposed that a claim in restitution cannot 'override a valid and subsisting legal obligation of the claimant to confer the benefit on the defendant'.[4] The answer given in this chapter is that the conflict between restitution and contract in these cases is more apparent than real. This is because where one party performs pursuant to an apparent obligation to do so and subsequently discovers that a condition precedent to that obligation had not been fulfilled there was, as it turns out, simply no immediate duty to perform. And obligations to perform in advance are often subject to a condition subsequent extinguishing the duty of performance if the agreed exchange is not received. If, on the other hand, the obligation is unconditional, then restitution is, and should be, denied. Restitution for failure of condition therefore does not contradict the law of contract.

9.4 Finally, this book has argued that the power to terminate is, at most, an unnecessary add-on in the law of contract; that the discharge of contractual obligations can be explained as instances of failure of condition. The final part of this chapter therefore engages with the question of whether it is necessary to terminate the contract in order to bring a claim for restitution for failure of condition. Unsurprisingly, the answer given is that termination is not a necessary prerequisite to a claim in restitution.

[4] *Dargamo Holdings Ltd v Avonwick Holdings Ltd* [2022] 1 All ER (Comm) 1244, 1261–62 [70]. See also *Kleinwort Benson Ltd v Lincoln City Council* [1999] 2 AC 349, 408; *Fairfield Sentry Ltd (in liq) v Migani* [2014] UKPC 9 [18]; *DD Growth Premium 2X Fund (in official liquidation) v RMF Market Neutral Strategies (Master) Ltd* [2017] UKPC 36 [62]; *Bank of New York Mellon (International) Ltd v Cine-UK Ltd; London Trocadero (2015) LLP v Picturehouse Cinemas Ltd* [2022] EWCA Civ 1021 [144]–[146].

What is Conditional in Failure of Condition Claims?

It is well established that, irrespective of what label is used, claims for restitution for 'failure of consideration', 'failure of basis', or 'failure of condition' are based on the conditional nature of the transfer, payment, or service.[5] In the leading case of *Fibrosa Spolka Akcyjna v Fairbairn Lawson Combe Barbour Ltd*,[6] Lord Wright said: **9.5**

> The payment was originally conditional. The condition of retaining it is eventual performance. Accordingly, when that condition fails, the right to retain the money must simultaneously fail.[7]

Although judges and academics have often used different terminology, the core idea of conditionality is clear. As Carr LJ observed in this context in *Dargamo Holdings Ltd v Avonwick Holdings Ltd*,[8] 'whichever terminology is used, the legal content is the same'.

What is less clear is what the condition supposedly qualifies. This is a fundamental question: what exactly is conditional in failure of condition cases? Take the simple example of money paid pursuant to a contract. There are at least five possibilities as to what the condition could qualify for the purpose of a claim in restitution. The condition could qualify: (i) the subjective intention of the claimant making the payment; (ii) the defendant's title to the money; (iii) the defendant's 'right to retain' the money; (iv) the 'payment'; or (v) the claimant's obligation to pay. Each of these will be considered in turn. **9.6**

[5] Peter Birks, 'Restitution and the Freedom of Contract' (1983) 36 Current Legal Problems 141, 151; Wilmot-Smith, 'Reconsidering "Total" Failure' (n 1) 415–16; Andrew Burrows, 'Conditional Intention as an Unjust Factor' in Elise Bant, Kit Barker, and Simone Degeling (eds), *Research Handbook on Unjust Enrichment and Restitution* (Edward Elgar Publishing 2020) 345, 346–47; Charles Mitchell, Paul Mitchell, and Stephen Watterson (eds), *Goff & Jones on Unjust Enrichment* (10th edn, Sweet & Maxwell 2022) 461 [12-01]; Robert Stevens, *The Laws of Restitution* (OUP 2023) 109–10.

[6] [1943] AC 32, 65.

[7] This is not an isolated statement. Numerous other judges have taken this view. In England, see *School Facility Management Ltd v Governing Body of Christ the King College* [2020] EWHC 1118 (Comm) [419]; *Dargamo Holdings Ltd v Avonwick Holdings Ltd* [2022] 1 All ER (Comm) 1244, 1263 [79]; *Thurcroft Power Ltd v Volta Energy Group Ltd* [2022] EWHC 338 (Comm) [226]; *Barton v Morris* [2023] AC 684, 716–17 [78]. In Australia, see *McDonald v Dennys Lascelles Ltd* (1933) 48 CLR 457, 477; *Baltic Shipping Co v Dillon* (1993) 176 CLR 344, 351–52, 385, 389; *Roxborough v Rothmans of Pall Mall Australia Ltd* (2001) 208 CLR 516, 538 [58], 538–39 [60]; *Anderson v McPherson (No 2)* [2012] WASC 19 [234]–[235]; *Redland City Council v Kozik* (2024) 98 ALJR 544, 579–80 [183]–[184].

[8] [2022] 1 All ER (Comm) 1244, 1263 [78]. See also *Barnes v Eastenders Cash & Carry plc* [2015] AC 1, 42 [105]; *Guinness Mahon & Co Ltd v Kensington and Chelsea Royal London Borough Council* [1999] QB 215, 239–40; *Haugesund Kommune v Depfa ACS Bank* [2012] QB 549, 574 [62] (the latter two cases making a similar point in relation to 'absence of consideration' versus 'failure of consideration').

Intention?

9.7 The first possibility is that what is conditional in failure of condition claims is the subjective intention of the claimant making the payment. Thus, Professor Andrew Burrows, writing shortly before his appointment to the Supreme Court, said:

> [T]he law of unjust enrichment requires there to be restitution because the claimant's intention to benefit the defendant was conditional and that condition has not occurred. In the circumstances, the claimant did not intend the defendant to retain the benefit conferred, after the condition has failed, and the defendant should therefore make restitution of the value of the benefit.[9]

9.8 The view that it is the claimant's intention that is conditional is part of a broader project that seeks to align 'failure of condition' with the unjust factors of mistake, undue influence, and duress.[10] The latter are said to be cases in which the claimant's intention to confer a benefit was 'vitiated', whereas failure of condition is said to be a case in which the claimant's consent was 'qualified'.[11]

9.9 The immediate difficulty with this view, however, is that '[a] condition in the claimant's head (i.e., a subjective condition) is insufficient'.[12] The 'condition' for the purpose of a claim in restitution is assessed objectively.[13] And in cases where there is a contract between the parties, the question of contractual construction and the question of identifying the 'basis' or 'condition' for the purpose of the restitutionary claim are the same.[14]

9.10 The usual answer to this difficulty is to suggest that a claimant who does not make the condition of their intention known to the defendant is a 'risk-taker' and therefore underserving of restitution.[15] But as Dr Frederick Wilmot-Smith

[9] Burrows (n 5) 346–47. See also Mitchell, Mitchell, and Watterson (n 5) 461 [12-01] ('[T]he claimant's intention to confer the benefit is genuine, but it is conditional').

[10] See, eg, Peter Birks, *An Introduction to the Law of Restitution* (rev'd edn, Clarendon Press 1990) 101, 219; James Edelman and Elise Bant, *Unjust Enrichment* (2nd edn, Hart Publishing 2016) 251; Burrows (n 5) 347; Stevens (n 5) 110–11 (albeit critical of this view).

[11] Birks (n 10) 218. See also *Dargamo Holdings Ltd v Avonwick Holdings Ltd* [2022] 1 All ER (Comm) 1244, 1263 [79].

[12] Burrows (n 5) 347.

[13] *Giedo Van der Garde BV v Force India Formula One Team Ltd (formerly Spyker F1 Team Ltd (England))* [2010] EWHC 2373 (QB) [285]–[286]; *BP Oil International Ltd v Vega Petroleum Ltd* [2022] 1 Lloyd's Rep 89, 110 [208]. See also Edelman and Bant (n 10) 253–54; Mitchell, Mitchell, and Watterson (n 5) 477–79 [13-02]–[13-04].

[14] *BP Oil International Ltd v Vega Petroleum Ltd* [2022] 1 Lloyd's Rep 89, 110 [206]–[208]. See also *Dargamo Holdings Ltd v Avonwick Holdings Ltd* [2022] 1 All ER (Comm) 1244, 1274 [133].

[15] Birks (n 10) 101, 219; Felicity Maher, 'A New Conception of Failure of Basis' (2004) 12 Restitution Law Review 96, 100–01; Edelman and Bant (n 10) 253–54; Burrows (n 5) 347.

has observed, the conclusion that a claimant is a risk-taker is circular—it begs the question as to why they should not be able to recover.[16] As he notes:

> To say the result depends on whether the claimant took the risk she would not recover is circular: she will only take this risk if she has no action in unjust enrichment. Therefore, the conclusion (that there is no action) drives the argument (that the claimant is a risk-taker) to reach that conclusion. This merely begs the question.[17]

The view, therefore, that the condition qualifies the claimant's subjective consent is untenable as a matter of description and as a matter of theory. **9.11**

Title?

A second possibility is that the condition qualifies the defendant's title to the money. Thus in the decision of the High Court of Australia in *McDonald v Dennys Lascelles Ltd*,[18] Dixon J spoke of the defendant's 'title to retain the money' being not absolute but 'conditional upon the subsequent completion of the contract', a statement which was repeated by Lord Goff in *Stocznia Gdanska SA v Latvian Shipping Co*.[19] **9.12**

It should be noted that it is not entirely clear that 'title' here is being used in the sense of a right to a thing (ie a property right). It is plausible that in the statement above 'title' is being used in the sense of an 'entitlement' to retain the money—the third possibility considered below—not in the proprietary sense. But even putting this doubt to one side, the view that the condition qualifies the defendant's title to the money is obviously false for two reasons. **9.13**

First, when we speak of legal title, ordinarily we mean a right to a physical thing. But in the classic case of payment of money on a condition that fails, the payment will usually not have been made in cash (a physical thing to which a person can have title) but rather by way of bank transfer. And although it is commonly said that a person has 'cash in the bank', the reality is that a bank account is 'merely a single debt of an amount equal to the final balance standing **9.14**

[16] Wilmot-Smith, 'Replacing Risk-taking Reasoning' (n 1) 613. See also James Edelman, 'Liability in Unjust Enrichment where a Contract Fails to Materialize' in Andrew Burrows and Edwin Peel (eds), *Contract Formation and Parties* (OUP 2010) 159, 160–62.

[17] Wilmot-Smith, 'Replacing Risk-taking Reasoning' (n 1) 613.

[18] (1933) 48 CLR 457, 477. See also *Baltic Shipping Co v Dillon* (1993) 176 CLR 344, 352, 385.

[19] [1998] 1 WLR 574, 589.

to the credit of the account holder'.[20] This is not a physical thing, but a right; a chose in action. There is no 'thing' to which the defendant could have a conditional title.

9.15 Secondly, even in cases where there is a physical thing to which a claimant could have title, if it were true that what is conditional is the claimant's title then following a failure of condition there should be a revesting of rights or, at the very least, a trust. But this view has been emphatically rejected.[21] Professor Peter Birks once advocated for a trust to arise in cases of failure of condition,[22] to which Lord Goff in *Westdeutsche Landesbank Girozentrale v Islington London Borough Council*[23] replied: 'His thesis is avowedly experimental, written to test the temperature of the water. I feel bound to respond that the temperature of the water must be regarded as decidedly cold'. Lord Browne-Wilkinson similarly said that he was 'not persuaded'.[24]

9.16 Both of these objections appear to be fatal to the view that it is the defendant's title that is conditional.

Entitlement to retain?

9.17 There are a number of statements in the cases and the academic literature that might suggest a third possibility: namely, that it is the defendant's 'entitlement to retain' the money that is conditional. As we saw earlier, in the classic statement of the doctrine in *Fibrosa*, Lord Wright said that when the condition fails 'the right to retain the money must simultaneously fail'.[25] Similarly, in the Australian case of *Baltic Shipping Co v Dillon*,[26] Mason CJ, Gaudron J, and McHugh J all suggested that it is the 'right to retain' a payment that is conditional.[27] And in a passage that has been approved of by the Court of Appeal in *Dargamo*,[28] the editors of *Goff & Jones on Unjust Enrichment*

[20] *Foskett v McKeown* [2001] 1 AC 102, 128. See also *Croton v The Queen* (1967) 117 CLR 326, 330, quoted in *Parsons v The Queen* (1999) 195 CLR 619, 626–27 [17].

[21] *Westdeutsche Landesbank Girozentrale v Islington London Borough Council* [1996] AC 669, 689–90, 708–09.

[22] Peter Birks, 'Restitution and Resulting Trusts' in Stephen Goldstein (ed), *Equity: Contemporary Legal Developments* (Hebrew University of Jerusalem 1992) 335.

[23] [1996] AC 669, 689.

[24] ibid 709.

[25] *Fibrosa Spolka Akcyjna v Fairbairn Lawson Combe Barbour Ltd* [1943] AC 32, 65.

[26] (1993) 176 CLR 344.

[27] *Baltic Shipping Co v Dillon* (1993) 176 CLR 344, 351 (Mason CJ), 385 (Gaudron J), 389 (McHugh J).

[28] *Dargamo Holdings Ltd v Avonwick Holdings Ltd* [2022] 1 All ER (Comm) 1244, 1263 [79]. See also *Barton v Morris* [2023] AC 684, 716–17 [78].

write: 'The core underlying idea of failure of basis is simple: a benefit has been conferred on the joint understanding that the recipient's right to retain it is conditional.'[29]

The most detailed exposition of this view has been provided by Justice James Edelman and Professor Elise Bant. They argue that where there is a juristic reason to receive an enrichment—a contractual obligation, an obligation contained in a deed, a gift, the terms of a statute, and so on—restitution should generally be denied.[30] To permit restitution would be to contradict another area of law.[31] But '[e]xceptionally', despite there being 'a valid juristic reason to *receive* an enrichment', this may not necessarily entitle 'a defendant to *retain* the enrichment'.[32] As an example of this phenomenon they say: **9.18**

> a plaintiff may be entitled to restitution of a benefit conferred pursuant to an otherwise valid contractual obligation, where the basis for that contractual obligation has itself wholly failed. The contractual obligation provided a *right to receive* the enrichment but when the basis for that obligation failed, there was no *right to retain* the enrichment.[33]

The difficulty with this view is that it is just not clear what an 'entitlement to retain' is. Provided that a person has a valid title or a valid right, English law does not require a person to justify that they are entitled to retain things or rights that they hold. English law simply recognises no concept. As Dr Timothy Pilkington notes, the term 'entitlement' is most commonly used to describe a Hohfeldian '(claim-)right': **9.19**

> But it is incorrect to regard, for example, a payee as having a conditional right to a payment after the payment has been made. This is because there is no corresponding duty the payor owes in respect of the payment after it has been made.[34]

Moreover, to the extent that a person can be said not to have an entitlement to retain a payment because they must make restitution, ie, because they have

[29] Mitchell, Mitchell, and Watterson (n 5) 461 [12-01]. See also Rory Gregson, 'All or Nothing' (2024) 83 Cambridge Law Journal 27, 28.
[30] See generally Edelman and Bant (n 10) ch 7.
[31] Edelman and Bant (n 10) 140.
[32] ibid 166 (emphasis added). See also Burrows (n 5) 348–49 (seemingly endorsing this view).
[33] Edelman and Bant (n 10) 166 (emphasis added).
[34] Timothy Pilkington, *Restitution for Failure of Condition* (DPhil thesis, University of Oxford 2023) 64.

a 'liability', then to say that the defendant's entitlement to retain a payment is conditional is circular: it begs the question why restitution is required.

9.20 Another difficulty is that for failure of condition claims in respect of services, services are not 'things or rights and are therefore incapable of being retained or kept'.[35] In *Cobbe v Yeoman's Row Management Ltd*,[36] the House of Lords allowed a claim in restitution where the claimant had performed services for the defendant in obtaining planning permission on a condition (that the land would be sold to him) that failed. In no meaningful way can it be said that the defendant's entitlement to retain these services was conditional as these services were not a 'thing' that could be retained. It might be said that the defendant's entitlement to retain the *benefit* of the service was conditional, but then this is just to rephrase the view that restitution is required—it is question begging.

9.21 This difficulty leads Pilkington to argue that 'what is conditional upon D's performance of the services is what can alternatively be referred to as D's *deservingness* against C of the payment made'.[37] But with respect, this faces the same problem identified in [9.19] above. English law does not have a concept of a defendant's 'deservingness' to a payment and to the extent that the concept is simply suggesting that restitution ought to be made it is circular. This is because to say that a defendant is not deserving of a payment, or is only deserving conditionally, asserts what it seeks to prove. Inevitably, in explaining why the defendant is not deserving, such a view would need to collapse into one of the other four views set out in this section.

9.22 The suggestion therefore that in cases of restitution of payments for failure of condition the defendant has a conditional entitlement to retain the payment seems only to be restating the conclusion: that restitution is required. It still does not answer the question: what is conditional in a failure of condition claim?

The payment?

9.23 A fourth possibility is that the 'payment' is conditional in the sense that the parties have (implicitly) agreed that if the performance does not occur, the

[35] ibid 64.
[36] [2008] 1 WLR 1752.
[37] Pilkington (n 34) 64 (emphasis added).

money is to be repaid. This is what appears to be suggested by some scholars[38] and is the view definitively taken by others.[39]

9.24 The most 'startling' feature of this view is that, if correct, it means that 'English lawyers have been too quick to dismiss the language of quasi-contract'.[40] Indeed, as Alexander Georgiou argues, this liability 'ought to be regarded as a form of agreement-based liability—and the language of "quasi-contract" was perhaps not so far wide of the mark after all.'[41] To put the point more forcefully, if such an agreement can be found 'then the category would not be failure of condition. It would be an instance where restitution is expressly or impliedly agreed.'[42] On this view, quasi-contract was off the mark not because claims in restitution for failure of condition cannot be analogised to contract claims (as if there were a contract), but because they are contractual claims.

9.25 None of this is necessarily a reason to reject the claim if the view is otherwise plausible. However, to adopt it requires one to accept an extremely capacious notion of agreement, even broader than the notion that was adopted in Chapter 6 when defending the implied condition view of frustration. This is because beyond stating, negatively, that the parties simply did not agree to perform in all circumstances (as was said in Chapter 6), it requires the parties to have agreed, positively, that if some condition should fail (such as counter-performance) then the payee agrees to pay the money back. It is the positive aspect of this agreement that appears to be implausible. It does not follow from the fact that the parties did not agree to perform in all circumstances that they positively agree that restitution should follow if one party fails to perform.[43]

9.26 But as a matter of descriptive analysis, this claim also suffers from the weakness that it does not describe the law as we find it. If restitution in failure of condition

[38] For example, Professor Robert Stevens has argued that restitution for failure of condition is required because 'not to do so would be contrary to the agreement between them. Without restitution, a payment agreed to be conditional would become an unconditional one': Stevens (n 5) 109. In his review of this book, Justice Edelman writes that '[t]he double negative in this proposition might suggest a contrived implied term; an agreement that restitution must follow a failure of the condition': James Edelman, 'The Laws of Restitution' (2024) 140 Law Quarterly Review 321, 325.

[39] Alexander Georgiou, 'Mistaken Payments, Quasi-Contracts, and the "Justice" of Unjust Enrichment' (2022) 42 Oxford Journal of Legal Studies 606.

[40] ibid 630.

[41] ibid. The quoted statement is about recovery of mistaken payments but Georgiou argues that the same is true of failure of condition claims: at 631.

[42] Edelman (n 38) 325.

[43] See also the criticisms in Peter Chau and Lusina Ho, 'Agreement and Restitutionary Liability for Mistaken Payments' in Warren Swain and Sagi Peari (eds), *Rethinking Unjust Enrichment: History, Sociology, Doctrine, and Theory* (OUP 2023) 181, 182–89.

claims were based on a positive, tacit agreement to make restitution, then restitution would not be available in cases where the contract is unenforceable or void. This is because on this view such claims are, in essence, contractual claims. But it is well accepted that restitutionary claims for failure of condition are available where the contract is unenforceable. The decision of the High Court of Australia in *Pavey & Matthews Pty Ltd v Paul*[44] is an illustrative example. In that case, building work had been done pursuant to an oral building contract. The relevant statutory provision rendered building contracts not in writing unenforceable. A majority of the Court allowed a claim in restitution by the builder for the value of the work done precisely because liability in restitution did not depend on an implied contract. Mason and Wilson JJ said that 'the true foundation of the right to recover on a quantum meruit does not depend on the existence of an implied contract',[45] while Deane J said that 'the action was not based upon a genuine agreement at all'.[46]

9.27 It is also accepted that restitutionary claims for failure of condition are available where the contract is void. To hold otherwise, would be to return the law to the days of *Sinclair v Brougham*,[47] in which the House of Lords held that depositors could not recover deposits made with a building society that ran a banking business ultra vires the society's purposes because the depositors' contracts with the building society were void. The Court reasoned that it could not imply even a fictional promise to repay because any such promise would have been ultra vires and therefore void.[48] *Sinclair v Brougham* was overruled in *Westdeutsche Landesbank Girozentrale v Islington London Borough Council*,[49] a case which was also concerned with recovery for failure of condition in the context of ultra vires (and therefore void) contracts. Importantly for present purposes, Lord Browne-Wilkinson said:

> The common law restitutionary claim is based not on implied contract but on unjust enrichment: in the circumstances the law imposes an obligation to repay rather than implying an entirely fictitious agreement to repay . . . It follows that in *Sinclair v Brougham* the depositors should have had a personal claim to recover the moneys at law based on a total failure of consideration.[50]

[44] (1987) 162 CLR 221.
[45] ibid 227.
[46] ibid 256.
[47] [1914] AC 398.
[48] ibid 417, 433–34, 440, 452.
[49] [1996] AC 669, 710–11. See also *Haugesund Kommune v Depfa ACS Bank* [2012] QB 549, 582 [87].
[50] *Westdeutsche Landesbank Girozentrale v Islington London Borough Council* [1996] AC 669, 710.

Therefore in addition to being implausible, the idea that it is the payment that is conditional, in the sense that there is an implicit promise to repay if the condition fails, suffers from the problem that it has been rejected in the cases. 9.28

The obligation?

The final possibility, which this chapter adopts, is that in the context of a payment made pursuant to a contract it is 'the obligation to pay . . . [that] is conditional'.[51] The effect of a condition failing on this view is that the obligation—which provided the juristic reason for the payment of the money—either never imposed any immediate duty of performance on the claimant seeking restitution (condition precedent) or no longer imposes such a duty (condition subsequent). A 'juristic reason',[52] a 'good reason',[53] or a 'justifying ground'[54] is that which justifies a person being entitled to receive a performance or some other benefit. If such a reason exists, then restitution will, and should, be denied. The 'obligation rule', discussed in the next section, is an example of this phenomenon. By contrast, where no such ground exists, the reason why a performance or conferral of a benefit is reversed 'is the lack of any good reason justifying it'.[55] 9.29

In other words, where an obligation, which constitutes the juristic reason for a payment, is conditional and that condition fails, the obligation cannot justify the payment that has been made. The payment has been made for no good reason or, if one prefers, in the absence of a valid ground. The effect of the condition failing therefore is to create an absence of basis. 9.30

This view has some academic support.[56] It also has the benefit of explaining a number of features of claims in restitution for failure of condition. First, it is consistent with the propositions seen above that the condition is to be assessed objectively rather than subjectively and that the question of contractual construction and the question of identifying the basis or condition for the 9.31

[51] *Baltic Shipping Co v Dillon* (1993) 176 CLR 344, 385.
[52] See, eg, Edelman and Bant (n 10) 130–37, although speaking principally in terms of juristic reasons to *retain* an enrichment.
[53] See, eg, Stevens (n 5) 78–79.
[54] Mitchell, Mitchell, and Watterson (n 5) ch 3.
[55] Stevens (n 5) 9.
[56] Robert Stevens, 'Is there a Law of Unjust Enrichment?' in Simone Degeling and James Edelman (eds), *Unjust Enrichment in Commercial Law* (Thomson Reuters 2008) 11, 24–30 (although cf Stevens (n 5) ch 7); Tariq Baloch, *Unjust Enrichment and Contract* (Hart Publishing 2009) 175–78.

restitutionary claim are the same.[57] As Professor Robert Stevens has observed, 'the law is, and ought to be, that the condition is found in the agreement between the parties.'[58] And secondly, as the next section details, this view also explains why restitution for failure of condition does not contradict the law of contract where there is an underlying valid contract and that contract appears, at first glance, to entitle the defendant to receive the performance in question.

9.32 An immediate objection to this view is that not all instances of restitutionary claims for failure of condition are claims in the context of a valid underlying contract.[59] Therefore it cannot be the obligation that is conditional because in some cases there is no obligation. However, a small clarification avoids this objection. The clarification is that an obligation is just one instance of what may constitute a juristic reason. The matters that can constitute juristic reasons are non-exhaustive and include contractual obligations, an obligation contained in a deed, a gift, a will, the terms of a statute, and court judgments.[60] And importantly for present purposes, a juristic reason can also include a non-contractual agreement.

9.33 This last point is more difficult to see in English law, because unlike in some civilian systems, where a broader range of agreements are recognised as having particular legal effects,[61] it is usually assumed that outside of enforceable and valid contracts, a non-contractual agreement has no effect at all. But 'it is a mistake to believe that the law of contracts (ie of *enforceable* agreements) exhausts the law of agreement.'[62] There are many situations in which a non-contractual agreement provides the legal justification for the conferral of a benefit and provided no condition has failed, it will preclude restitution.[63]

9.34 An example of a non-contractual agreement constituting a justifying ground was given in *Lipkin Gorman v Karpnale Ltd*.[64] There Lord Goff referred to gambling contracts which, at the time the case was decided, were void under s 18 of the Gaming Act 1845.[65] He said:

[57] See [9.9] above.
[58] Stevens (n 5) 110.
[59] See, eg, *Cobbe v Yeoman's Row Management Ltd* [2008] 1 WLR 1752; *Benedetti v Sawiris* [2014] AC 938.
[60] For similar lists, see Stevens (n 5) 78–79; Edelman and Bant (n 10) 132.
[61] See the discussion in this context in Gerhard Dannemann, 'Unjust Enrichment as Absence of Basis: Can English Law Cope?' in Andrew Burrows and Lord Rodger of Earlsferry (eds), *Mapping the Law: Essays in Memory of Peter Birks* (OUP 2006) 363, 364–367.
[62] Stevens (n 5) 111.
[63] See Dannemann (n 61) 364–67.
[64] [1991] 2 AC 548. See also Stevens (n 5) 97.
[65] This is no longer the position. See Gambling Act 2005, s 335(1).

> [C]ontracts by way of gaming or wagering are void in English law. What is the effect of this? It is obvious that each time a bet is placed by the gambler, the agreement under which the bet is placed is an agreement by way of gaming or wagering, and so is rendered null and void.... Of course, the gambler cannot recover the money from the casino on the ground of failure of consideration; for he has relied upon the casino to honour the wager—he has in law given the money to the casino, trusting that the casino will fulfil the obligation binding in honour upon it and pay him if he wins his bet—though if the casino does so its payment to the gambler will likewise be in law a gift.[66]

The reference to the payment being 'in law a gift' (as the justifying ground), rather than simply a payment made pursuant to a non-contractual agreement, demonstrates the difficulties English law has in recognising the force of non-contractual agreements. But the example usefully illustrates that in the absence of a relevant failure of condition, a non-contractual agreement can operate as a juristic reason for the payment in question.

It is therefore no objection that failure of condition claims exist outside of the context of valid contracts. This is because an obligation is just one instance of a juristic reason for a performance or a conferral of a benefit. However, in the common context of contractual performances, the juristic reason for the performance is usually the obligation and it will therefore be the obligation that is conditional. Our focus is on this context. **9.35**

Why Does Restitution Not Contradict the Law of Contract?

As mentioned in the previous section, the benefit of seeing the obligation as being that which is conditional in many failure of condition claims is that it helps explain why claims in restitution for failure of condition do not contradict the law of contract, even where there is a valid underlying contract that would appear to entitle the defendant to receive the performance in question. **9.36**

Conditions precedent

An example of a case where restitution was permitted despite there being a valid contract that, at first glance, appeared to entitle the defendant to **9.37**

[66] *Lipkin Gorman v Karpnale Ltd* [1991] 2 AC 548, 577.

the payment in question is the decision of the High Court of Australia in *Roxborough v Rothmans of Pall Mall Australia Ltd*.[67] In that case, tobacco retailers purchased tobacco products from a wholesaler. The purchase price for each sale included a cost component and another amount, separately identified on each invoice as a 'tobacco licence fee'.[68] This amount was to cover a periodic licence fee that had been imposed by the State of New South Wales. This licence fee was subsequently held to be unconstitutional and invalid on the basis that it was, in truth, an excise duty within the meaning of s 90 of the Australian Constitution and therefore beyond the legislative powers of the state governments.[69] In an action for restitution for failure of consideration, a majority of the Court (Gleeson CJ, Gaudron, Gummow, Hayne, and Callinan JJ; Kirby J dissenting) held that the retailers were able to recover the amounts as having being paid on a basis—that the licence fee was due and owing—that had failed.

9.38 The difficulty posed by *Roxborough* is that the contract was perfectly valid and had not been rescinded, terminated, or otherwise rendered unenforceable or void. Indeed, it was on this basis that Kirby J dissented. Accordingly, it is sometimes said that *Roxborough* is an example of where 'restitution has been allowed despite the fact that the claimant's payment was made pursuant to a valid obligation'.[70] On this view, while the existence of a legal obligation to make a payment will usually preclude restitution, sometimes an 'unjust factor overrides the claimant's legal obligation to the defendant so as to allow restitution'.[71] But as Dr Tariq Baloch has pointed out, this view 'dangerously expands the province of unjust enrichment and has the capacity to disturb other areas of law. This is because it is not clear why in some situations a claim founded on unjust enrichment can trump a valid obligation.'[72]

9.39 The contradiction in *Roxborough*, however, was only apparent and not real. The apparent conflict arises from the assumption that the obligation to pay the licence fee component of the purchase price in *Roxborough* was not conditional on the tax being valid. The better view is that the obligation to pay the licence fee component of the purchase price was conditional on the tax being

[67] (2001) 208 CLR 516.
[68] ibid 522 [4].
[69] In *Ha v New South Wales* (1997) 189 CLR 465.
[70] James Edelman and Charles Mitchell, 'Restitution' (2006) All England Annual Review 337, 343 [20.17], quoted in Baloch (n 56) 160. See also Andrew Burrows, *A Restatement of the English Law of Unjust Enrichment* (OUP 2012) 34.
[71] Burrows (n 70) 33.
[72] Baloch (n 56) 160–61.

valid.[73] Although the point was not discussed in detail,[74] Gummow J appeared to recognise this when he referred to 'the conditional nature of the licence fee payments'.[75]

This interpretation removes the apparent contradiction between the existence of a valid contract and restitution being permitted for failure of condition. There is simply no contradiction in cases where one party performs pursuant to an apparent obligation to do so and subsequently discovers that a condition precedent to that obligation had not been fulfilled. There was, as it turns out, no immediate duty to perform. As Professor Charles Fried explained: 9.40

> If your promise is conditional, then unless the condition is met you are under no obligation. . . . There just is no obligation. It is gone. And if the person with a conditional obligation happened to make prepayment, then the [law] would allow him to obtain restitution of that prepayment, since that prepayment was given pursuant to an obligation that no longer exists.[76]

That there was no immediate duty of performance can be shown by considering what the position would have been if the case were reversed and the wholesaler was suing for the payment of the price. As Stevens has explained, '[i]f the wholesalers had not been paid and had been suing the retailers for payment of the price, exactly the same end result ought to be reached'.[77] This is because the obligation to pay the licence fee component of the purchase price never fell due as a result of the failure of the condition precedent. 9.41

Conditions subsequent

More difficult are cases involving obligations to pay in advance where restitution is nonetheless allowed, as is often the case with advance payments. In *Fibrosa*,[78] for example, the claimant, a Polish company, agreed to purchase flax-hackling machines for £4,800 from the defendant, an English company. Delivery of the machines to Poland was not to occur until some three or four months later, but the contract required payment of one third of the purchase 9.42

[73] ibid; Stevens (n 5) 126.

[74] Baloch (n 56) 161.

[75] *Roxborough v Rothmans of Pall Mall Australia Ltd* (2001) 208 CLR 516, 538 [58]. See also 538–539 [60].

[76] Charles Fried, *Contract as Promise* (2nd edn, OUP 2015) 121. See also Stevens, 'Is there a Law of Unjust Enrichment?' (n 56) 24–25.

[77] Stevens (n 5) 126.

[78] *Fibrosa Spolka Akcyjna v Fairbairn Lawson Combe Barbour Ltd* [1943] AC 32.

price in advance. The claimant paid £1,000 pursuant to this clause in advance. Shortly thereafter, and before the machines were delivered, Germany invaded Poland and war was declared between Great Britain and Germany.

9.43 The House of Lords held that the parties were discharged from the performance of their further contractual obligations on account of the 'legal impossibility'[79] caused by the war but that the claimant could recover the advance payment in restitution for a 'total failure of consideration'. The claimant was therefore able to recover in restitution despite the fact that the obligation to make the payment had fallen due before the frustrating event and despite the fact that frustration, on the orthodox account, only operates to discharge future contractual obligations.

9.44 The results in the advance payment cases appear to contradict the proposition that a claim in restitution cannot 'override a valid and subsisting legal obligation of the claimant to confer the benefit on the defendant'.[80] This has been referred to by Carr LJ in *Dargamo* as the 'Obligation Rule'.[81] In that case, the parties had entered into a deed under which the seller agreed to transfer shares to the purchasers in consideration for US$950 million.[82] The only obligation of the seller under the deed was to transfer the shares, but it was common ground between the parties that the purchase price was intended to include payment for the future transfer of a number of other assets not covered by the agreement.[83] However, for reasons unknown, the parties deliberately omitted any obligation to transfer the further assets from the deed and the further assets were not part of the consideration identified in the deed.[84] The shares were duly transferred and the $950 million paid but the further assets were never transferred to one of the purchasers, who claimed repayment of the proportion of their contribution to the purchase price that they alleged represented the value of those further assets ($82.5 million). On appeal, their claim was solely framed as a claim in restitution for a total failure of consideration.

[79] See [6.24]–[6.30].

[80] *Dargamo Holdings Ltd v Avonwick Holdings Ltd* [2022] 1 All ER (Comm) 1244, 1261–62 [70]. See also *Kleinwort Benson Ltd v Lincoln City Council* [1999] 2 AC 349, 408; *Fairfield Sentry Ltd (in liq) v Migani* [2014] UKPC 9 [18]; *DD Growth Premium 2X Fund (in official liquidation) v RMF Market Neutral Strategies (Master) Ltd* [2017] UKPC 36 [62]; *Bank of New York Mellon (International) Ltd v Cine-UK Ltd; London Trocadero (2015) LLP v Picturehouse Cinemas Ltd* [2022] EWCA Civ 1021 [144]–[146].

[81] *Dargamo Holdings Ltd v Avonwick Holdings Ltd* [2022] 1 All ER (Comm) 1244, 1261–62 [70].

[82] The transfer was triggered by the exercise of an option but that is immaterial.

[83] *Dargamo Holdings Ltd v Avonwick Holdings Ltd* [2022] 1 All ER (Comm) 1244, 1250 [17], 1269–70 [107].

[84] ibid 1271 [112].

The Court of Appeal (Carr LJ, Asplin LJ, and Sir Timothy Lloyd) rejected the restitutionary claim. Whatever their extracontractual understanding was, the obligation to pay the purchase price was only conditional on the transfer of the shares and this had been done. This was a case to which the Obligation Rule applied. As Carr LJ said, 'there is no scope for the law of unjust enrichment to intervene by reference to a basis which is not only alternative and extraneous, but which also directly contradicts the express contractual terms'.[85] **9.45**

The Obligation Rule is eminently justified. The law of restitution should not contradict other areas of law.[86] As Lord Hope observed in *Kleinwort Benson Ltd v Lincoln City Council*,[87] 'the payee cannot be said to have been unjustly enriched if he was entitled to receive the sum paid to him'. In other words, the obligation to confer the benefit 'provide[s] a legal ground for performance received'.[88] In *Portman Building Society v Hamlyn Taylor Neck*,[89] Millett LJ said that 'the continuing validity of the transaction under which the money was paid' is 'fatal' to a claim in restitution. **9.46**

But, as noted above, the advance payment cases appear to contradict the Obligation Rule. One response to the contradiction, put forward by Professor Burrows[90] and accepted by the Court of Appeal on two occasions[91] and the Supreme Court on one,[92] is to suggest that the Obligation Rule is subject to exceptions and that sometimes 'the unjust factor overrides the claimant's legal obligation to the defendant so as to allow restitution'.[93] But as we saw when considering this argument at [9.38] above, this view gives unjust enrichment a dangerously expansive role.[94] It is not clear why a claim in restitution should 'override' a contractual obligation and, as Burrows himself has admitted, '[t]his "clash" between contract and unjust enrichment is not easy to explain'.[95] **9.47**

Another response to avoid the conflict is based on the idea of circuity of action. The argument is that: **9.48**

[85] ibid 1271 [116].
[86] Edelman and Bant (n 10) 141.
[87] [1999] 2 AC 349, 408.
[88] Stevens, 'Is there a Law of Unjust Enrichment?' (n 56) 24.
[89] [1998] 4 All ER 202, 208.
[90] Burrows (n 70) 33–34.
[91] *Dargamo Holdings Ltd v Avonwick Holdings Ltd* [2022] 1 All ER (Comm) 1244, 1262 [72]–[73]; *Bank of New York Mellon (International) Ltd v Cine-UK Ltd; London Trocadero (2015) LLP v Picturehouse Cinemas Ltd* [2022] EWCA Civ 1021 [144]–[146].
[92] *International Energy Group Ltd v Zurich Insurance plc UK Branch* [2016] AC 509, 550–52 [68]–[72].
[93] Burrows (n 70) 33.
[94] Baloch (n 56) 160–61.
[95] Burrows (n 5) 348.

> if a party would be entitled to recover back money if it had been paid under a contract, [they] should not remain liable to pay such sums which had become due, as it would make no sense to hold [them] liable in one action for payment which [they] could then claim back in another.[96]

This was the view taken by Lord Atkin in *Fibrosa*,[97] repeated by Lord Goff in *Stocznia Gdanska SA v Latvian Shipping Co*,[98] and seemingly applied by the Court of Appeal in *Rover International Ltd v Cannon Film Sales Ltd*.[99]

9.49 But there are two problems with this response. First, an argument based on circuity of action does not explain why it is that the circle should be broken so that the restitutionary claim prevails over the contract one. Why not break the circle so that the contract claim prevails over the restitutionary one? As Stevens put it:

> It would indeed be 'absurd that the prospective payee could sue for the money because it was due before breach, while the payor could then sue for its return because part payments can be recovered back by the payor'. However, if there is a circle there are again two ways in which it can be broken. Why should the payor's right to repayment trump the payee's right to be paid? The argument can be turned on its head. If the payee were entitled to sue for what is due it would be absurd to allow the payor to be able to recover it back once it is paid.[100]

9.50 Secondly, on one view that has been expressed in the cases, the argument based on circuity of action does not actually resolve the conflict. In *London Trocadero (2015) LLP v Picturehouse Cinemas Ltd*,[101] a landlord sought to recover unpaid rent in respect of leases of cinema premises. The tenants (and their guarantor) argued that they were not liable to pay the rent as, owing to restrictions imposed in response to the Covid-19 pandemic, the premises could not be used as a cinema and there had therefore been a failure of basis. Although the claim ultimately failed because there was no failure of basis, at first instance Deputy Judge Vos accepted the argument that 'it would make no commercial sense to require the payer to make the payment and then commence a claim for a return

[96] Stevens, 'Is there a Law of Unjust Enrichment?' (n 56) 26; Stevens (n 5) 125. To be clear, Stevens does not support the argument.
[97] *Fibrosa Spolka Akcyjna v Fairbairn Lawson Combe Barbour Ltd* [1943] AC 32, 53.
[98] [1998] 1 WLR 574, 587.
[99] [1989] 1 WLR 912, 932, 936. See also *McDonald v Dennys Lascelles Ltd* (1933) 48 CLR 457, 479.
[100] Stevens, 'Is there a Law of Unjust Enrichment?' (n 56) 26–27. See also Stevens (n 5) 125.
[101] [2021] EWHC 2591 (Ch).

of the payment in unjust enrichment'.[102] But ultimately, he thought that failure of basis would not provide a 'direct defence' to a contractual claim but rather 'should be pleaded by way of counterclaim in unjust enrichment and set-off'[103] (the Court of Appeal did not consider the issue).[104] The issue is that if, on the circuity of action argument, failure of condition only provides a counter-claim and not a direct defence to (denial of) the debt then the argument does not resolve the conflict between contract and restitution at all. It just asserts the priority of the restitutionary claim without more.

9.51 A further response still is the argument noted earlier in this chapter by Edelman and Bant. They avoid the apparent conflict between allowing restitution and the existence of the contractual obligation by stating that '[t]he contractual obligation provided a *right to receive* the enrichment but when the basis for that obligation failed, there was no *right to retain* the enrichment'.[105] But this explanation founders on the same rock we identified when asking what is conditional in failure of condition claims. English law has no concept of an 'entitlement to retain' that can be conditional in this way. If the defendant has a right to receive the enrichment that should be the end of the story.

9.52 The better view is to recognise that, like the cases involving the failure of a condition precedent examined in the previous sub-section, the conflict between restitution and contract in these cases is more apparent than real. That is because even obligations to perform in advance are often subject to a condition subsequent extinguishing the duty of performance if the agreed exchange is not received.[106] As Professor Samuel Williston argued:

> In fact, however, no promise in a bilateral contract the performance of which on one side is agreed upon as the equivalent exchange for performance on the other side, is wholly independent. Though performance of one promise may be due first, it is still true that the later performance is the agreed exchange, and if the court is satisfied that the agreed exchange will not be forthcoming, the first performance is excused.[107]

[102] ibid [162].
[103] ibid [160]–[173].
[104] *Bank of New York Mellon (International) Ltd v Cine-UK Ltd; London Trocadero (2015) LLP v Picturehouse Cinemas Ltd* [2022] EWCA Civ 1021 [39]–[41].
[105] Edelman and Bant (n 10) 166 (emphasis added). See also at 252, quoted with approval in Burrows (n 5) 348–49.
[106] See, eg, *Jozovich v Central California Berry Growers* 183 Cal App 2d 216 (1960) (California CA), discussed in Arthur Corbin, *Corbin on Contracts: A Comprehensive Treatise on the Rules of Contract Law* (West Publishing Co 1962) vol 6, 24 §1256 fn 23.
[107] Williston (n 3) 1581 §828. See also Corbin (n 106) 23–25 §1256.

9.53 The mere fact therefore that an obligation has fallen due is not determinative. A distinction needs to be drawn between obligations that have fallen due but are still subject to a condition subsequent and obligations that have fallen due but are not subject to any further conditions. This is sometimes expressed as a distinction between 'a sum of money which has fallen conditionally due and one which is unconditionally earned'.[108] In *McDonald v Dennys Lascelles Ltd*,[109] Dixon J described the latter, from the perspective of the obligee, as rights which have been 'unconditionally acquired'.

9.54 That an obligation may sometimes only fall due conditionally can explain why restitution in *Fibrosa* did not contradict the contractual obligation to pay one-third of the purchase price in advance. This amount had fallen due, but the obligation to pay was subject to a condition subsequent that the machines were delivered. As Dixon J explained in *McDonald v Dennys Lascelles Ltd*:

> It appears to me inevitably to follow from the principles upon which instalments paid are recoverable that an unpaid overdue instalment ceases to be payable by the purchasers when the contract is discharged.[110]

When the outbreak of the war prevented delivery from happening in *Fibrosa*, the condition failed and the obligation was discharged—the duty of performance that had fallen due was extinguished. Restitution was rightly permitted because there was no longer a contractual obligation that supported the payment that had been made. In other words, there was no juristic reason for the payment.

9.55 Of course, in some cases an obligation will have fallen due unconditionally and the unconditional nature of that obligation will provide a good reason for the payment and preclude restitution. An example is *Stocznia Gdanska SA v Latvian Shipping Co*.[111] The plaintiff shipbuilders entered into six shipbuilding contracts, the price being payable in four instalments by the defendant buyers. Work began on two of the ships but the defendants failed to pay the second instalments, which were due after notice had been given that the keel of each ship had been laid. In the face of this refusal, the plaintiffs exercised express powers to terminate and commenced an action in debt seeking to recover the second instalments. The defendants argued that even if there were a contractual right to the money, it would have been recoverable

[108] Stevens, 'Is there a Law of Unjust Enrichment?' (n 56) 28. See too Baloch (n 56) 177–78.
[109] (1933) 48 CLR 457, 477.
[110] ibid 479.
[111] [1998] 1 WLR 574.

immediately for a total failure of consideration.[112] Ultimately, the argument failed because according to the House of Lords there had been no 'total' failure of consideration; this was not a simple contract of sale but a contract to design and build a ship.[113]

But another explanation for the case, which finds support in the speech of Lord Goff,[114] is that the buyers remained liable to pay the second instalments because the obligations to pay had fallen unconditionally due: '[u]nlike a standard contract of sale, the part payment was earned not by the passing of property but by the laying of the keel.'[115] In other words, the obligation to pay the second instalment in each contract was not subject to a condition subsequent that the ship be delivered. The obligation provided a juristic reason for the payment and precluded restitution from being available. **9.56**

Sometimes an obligation that has fallen due is conditional in some respects but unconditional in others. A good example is provided by the law in relation to deposits. A deposit, being made in earnest of performance by the buyer, is an unconditional payment except insofar as the seller does not perform for reasons not attributable to the buyer's breach. If, therefore, the purchaser refuses to complete they 'can have no right to recover the deposit'.[116] The obligation to pay was unconditional and provides a juristic reason for the payment. Equally, if the deposit has not yet been paid, 'the deposit is recoverable [by the buyer] as an agreed sum, earned without more'.[117] By contrast, if the seller fails to complete due to their own default, then the deposit is recoverable by the buyer in an action for restitution.[118] The obligation to pay the deposit was subject to a condition subsequent that the seller complete unless non-completion was due to the fault of the buyer. **9.57**

An objection to this view has been put forward by Pilkington, who argues that 'it is conceptually problematic to maintain that an obligation can remain conditional after it has been performed.'[119] He writes that in cases of discharge by performance: **9.58**

[112] ibid 587.
[113] ibid 588.
[114] See ibid 589 and the discussion of *Hyundai Heavy Industries Co Ltd v Papadopoulos* [1980] 1 WLR 1129.
[115] Stevens, 'Is there a Law of Unjust Enrichment?' (n 56) 26; Stevens (n 5) 125. See also Baloch (n 56) 162–63.
[116] *Howe v Smith* (1884) 27 Ch D 89, 95.
[117] Stevens (n 5) 136, citing *Hinton v Sparkes* (1868) LR 3 CP 161.
[118] Mitchell, Mitchell, and Watterson (n 5) 501 [14-01].
[119] Pilkington (n 34) 40.

what it means for an obligation to be discharged is that the obligation, while having previously existed, no longer does. Given that an obligation no longer exists after it has been discharged, it cannot be that the obligation can remain conditional after the obligation has been discharged through performance. Something that no longer exists cannot remain conditional.[120]

9.59 But as was observed in Chapter 1,[121] performance of a contractual obligation does not make that obligation, or the duty of performance it creates, disappear. The performing party is discharged from their contractual obligation because the obligation no longer requires anything from that party. The obligation and the duty of performance still exist, but the obliged party has complied with their obligation by performing. So long as the conditions to that obligation remain fulfilled, the duty it creates will act as a juristic reason for any performances rendered pursuant to it. But, as this section has shown, if a condition subsequent to that obligation fails, then it will extinguish the duty of performance created by that obligation and with it the juristic reason for any performance.

Nothing new under the sun

9.60 The view that a valid contractual obligation will, and should, provide a justifying ground for a performance received, but if that obligation is subject to a condition (precedent or subsequent) that has failed, then it will not, is not new. It has previously been argued that 'a valid and enforceable contract will not provide a legal ground for the receipt of a benefit if that benefit was subject to a condition precedent which has not been satisfied or a condition subsequent which has failed'.[122] But this view has arguably been obscured in the literature and case law by a lack of emphasis on the conditionality of contractual obligations to perform and, in particular, the assumption that where an obligation has fallen due it has unconditionally fallen due. As this section has sought to demonstrate, there is no reason to make that assumption. And by focusing on the conditionality of contractual obligations to perform it can be seen that there is no conflict in cases where restitution for failure of condition is permitted and there is a valid underlying contract, provided that the obligation to

[120] ibid.
[121] See [1.53].
[122] Stevens, 'Is there a Law of Unjust Enrichment?' (n 56) 25. See too Andrew Burrows, *The Law of Restitution* (3rd edn, OUP 2011) 329.

perform was conditional. If the obligation to perform was unconditional then restitution, rightly, is denied.

Is It Necessary to Terminate?

It has sometimes been suggested that it is necessary to terminate in order to bring a claim in restitution for failure of condition.[123] That suggestion, if true, presents a problem for the thesis presented in this book, namely, that 'termination' is an unnecessary add-on in the law of contract; that the discharge of contractual obligations can be explained as instances of failure of condition. Fortunately, as others have recognised, 'termination is neither a sufficient nor a necessary condition of restitution. The important question is always whether the agreed condition of performance has failed.'[124] **9.61**

That termination is insufficient is shown by the decision in *Stocznia Gdanska SA v Latvian Shipping Co* examined at [9.55]–[9.56] above. Following the exercise of express powers to terminate by the plaintiff shipbuilders, the buyers remained liable to pay the second instalments because the obligations to pay had fallen unconditionally due. There was no relevant failure of condition. And even on the orthodox account of termination, '[b]oth parties are discharged from the further performance of the contract, but rights are not divested or discharged which have already been *unconditionally* acquired.'[125] **9.62**

Birks in his final work suggested that the termination of the contract was sufficient to show that there was an absence of basis justifying restitution.[126] But in doing so he appears to have ignored accrued, ie unconditional, contractual rights in respect of which the termination of the contract is not sufficient.[127] The mistake Birks made was to treat the 'continued validity of the contract' as 'the basis of the payment'.[128] The obligation, rather than the contract, provides **9.63**

[123] Jack Beatson and Graham Virgo, 'Contract, Unjust Enrichment and Unconscionability' (2002) 118 LQR 352, 355–56; Peter Birks, *Unjust Enrichment* (2nd edn, OUP 2003) 125–26; Burrows (n 122) 327–28; Graham Virgo, 'Restitution' in Hugh Beale (ed), *Chitty on Contracts* (35th edn, Sweet & Maxwell 2023) 2563, 2576–77 [33-016] fn 109, 2613–15 [33-067]. See too *BP Oil International Ltd v Vega Petroleum Ltd* [2022] 1 Lloyd's Rep 89, 110 [205], although cf *Anron Bunkering DMCC v Glencore Energy UK Ltd* [2023] 1 WLR 1912, 1924–25 [45].

[124] Stevens (n 5) 124.

[125] *McDonald v Dennys Lascelles Ltd* (1933) 48 CLR 457, 476–77 (emphasis added).

[126] Birks (n 123) 125–27.

[127] Stevens, 'Is there a Law of Unjust Enrichment?' (n 56) 24. See also the criticisms in Baloch (n 56) 175–78.

[128] Birks (n 123) 126. See Stevens, 'Is there a Law of Unjust Enrichment?' (n 56) 24. There is of course a further problem here in that termination does not render a contract 'invalid'.

the basis for the payment, and the termination of the contract does not necessarily affect that obligation unless it was conditional.

9.64 By contrast, that termination is not necessary is illustrated by the decision in *Roxborough*, which was approved of by the Court of Appeal in *Dargamo*.[129] As we saw there, a majority of the High Court of Australia held that a claim in restitution for failure of condition could succeed notwithstanding that the contract had not been terminated. This was because the obligation to pay the licence fee component of the purchase price was subject to a condition that the tax was valid. The tax was not valid and so there was no obligation to pay. In *Anron Bunkering DMCC v Glencore Energy UK Ltd*,[130] Mr Simon Colton KC (sitting as a Deputy High Court Judge) said that 'it is not a requirement that the contract in question be terminated in a sale of goods case before a claim in unjust enrichment can be brought'.[131]

9.65 At its highest, it might be said on the orthodox approach that termination may, in some cases, be necessary to indicate that the condition has failed. This was suggested in *Anron* by Deputy Judge Simon Colton KC, who said:

> To be clear, there will be circumstances where the test [for restitution] is not met without termination: for example, where defective goods are delivered, the buyer cannot recover an advance payment, or an instalment, unless and until it has decided to reject the goods . . . Similarly, in the case of late delivery, if delivery remains a possibility under the contract, then it may not be possible to conclude that there is a failure of basis unless and until delivery ceases to be a possibility – which may, in reality, be only if and when the contract is brought to an end.[132]

9.66 But the first example given about deciding whether to reject the goods, if anything, indicates that termination is not necessary. This is because, on the orthodox account, rejection of goods is not the same thing as the termination of the contract. For example, in instalment contracts, a defect in the goods delivered as part of one instalment will entitle the buyer to 'reject' that instalment, but it may not entitle the buyer to 'terminate' the contractual obligations of the parties.[133] Nonetheless, if the money had been paid, a claim in restitution

[129] *Dargamo Holdings Ltd v Avonwick Holdings Ltd* [2022] 1 All ER (Comm) 1244, 1261 [67], 1272 [121]. See also Stevens (n 5) 126.

[130] [2023] 1 WLR 1912, 1924 [45].

[131] cf *BP Oil International Ltd v Vega Petroleum Ltd* [2022] 1 Lloyd's Rep 89, 110 [205], which was disapproved of in this case.

[132] *Anron Bunkering DMCC v Glencore Energy UK Ltd* [2023] 1 WLR 1912, 1924–25 [45].

[133] Michael Bridge (ed), *Benjamin's Sale of Goods* (12th edn, Sweet & Maxwell 2023) 633–34 [12-029].

for failure of condition could succeed in respect of that instalment despite the fact that the contract as a whole has not been terminated.[134]

As for the second example, it is true to say that termination on the orthodox account provides a way of evidencing that delivery will not take place and therefore that the condition has failed. But the existence of a power to terminate is not necessary to reach that conclusion. The buyer's obligation to accept delivery is conditional upon delivery within such time so as to give them substantially the whole benefit of the contract.[135] If that delivery does not occur by that time, and the buyer negates any inference of waiver, the buyer will never be obligated to accept delivery and the court can treat the condition as having failed. The power to terminate is an otiose way of demonstrating something which can be shown through the traditional failure of condition model. Termination is unnecessary. 9.67

In sum, termination is neither sufficient nor necessary for a claim in restitution to succeed. It may be that in some cases, on the orthodox account of discharge of contractual obligations, termination can serve an evidentiary role in indicating that the relevant condition has failed. But on a discharge of contractual obligations for failure of condition model, the additional step of termination is simply unnecessary. 9.68

Conclusion

This chapter has been concerned with the implications of the arguments made in this book about the discharge of contractual obligations for the law of restitution. Three key claims were made. The first was that what is conditional in failure of condition claims, at least in the context of contractual performances, is the obligation to perform. The effect of a condition failing is that the obligation, which on its face provided a juristic reason or basis for the performance rendered, either never did (where it was subject to a condition precedent) or no longer does (where it was subject to a condition subsequent). 9.69

[134] The purpose being served by rejection here then is not to terminate the contract but to negate any inference of waiver of the condition that the goods be free from defects. As we saw in [2.42]–[2.45], practically speaking, the buyer will need to take steps to reject the goods in order to negate any suggestion of waiver of the condition. But this is not for the purpose of terminating the contract but rather negating any inference of waiver. It is the rule found in s 11(4) of the Sale of Goods Act 1979.

[135] See the discussion in [2.96]–[2.98].

9.70 The second claim was that restitution for failure of condition does not contradict the law of contract in cases where restitution is permitted and there is a valid underlying contract, provided that the obligation to perform was conditional. The conflict between contract and restitution is more apparent than real. This is because where a condition precedent fails, the claimant seeking restitution, as it turns out, had no duty to confer the benefit in question on the defendant, who correspondingly had no right to receive it. And where a condition subsequent fails, the duty that previously provided the justifying ground for the conferral of the benefit by the claimant on the defendant no longer does so. Where the obligation was unconditional, however, restitution should be, and is, denied.

9.71 Finally, this chapter argued that (i) termination is not sufficient to enable a claim in restitution to succeed, (ii) termination is not necessary for a claim to succeed, and (iii) although termination may sometimes serve an evidentiary function of indicating that a condition has failed on the orthodox model, on the failure of condition model this additional step is unnecessary.

9.72 These are just three implications for the law of restitution. A focus on conditions more generally can, and has, provided ways of dealing with other problems in the law of restitution that are not touched upon in this chapter.[136] But more importantly, these implications illustrate that becoming attuned to the nature of conditions, how they operate, and what they qualify has importance not just for contract law but for other areas of law as well. It might be an overstatement to say that conditions are everywhere, but a renewed focus on conditions, and increasing our collective sensitivity to them, might help resolve a number of problems beyond those examined in this chapter.[137]

[136] Such as the problems with the traditional requirement of a 'total' failure of consideration. Conditions are binary: they either fail or they do not. A condition cannot 'partially' fail: Burrows (n 5) 347–48; Stevens (n 5) 115–16.

[137] To give two areas that merit further exploration with a view to analysing them in terms of conditions: (i) the control of discretionary powers in private law and the equitable doctrine of 'fraud on a power'; and (ii) the consequences of non-compliance with statutory procedures for the exercise of a power or acquisition of a right. On the former, see Philip Sales, 'Use of Powers for Proper Purposes in Private Law' (2020) 136 Law Quarterly Review 384. On the latter, see *Elim Court RTM Co Ltd v Avon Freeholds Ltd* [2018] QB 571, 585–89 [49]–[59], which was considered and qualified in *A1 Properties (Sunderland) Ltd v Tudor Studios RTM Co Ltd* [2024] 3 WLR 601.

10
Conclusion

Introduction

The book finishes where it started: orthodoxy. Current orthodoxy holds that English law has a doctrine of termination for breach, a doctrine of frustration, and a doctrine of common mistake. These doctrines, it is said, have distinct justifications and consequently distinct doctrinal rules. None depend on the conditional nature of obligations to perform. **10.1**

The central claim of this book has been that this needs to be reconsidered. Discharge following breach, frustration, and common mistake traditionally have been, still can be, and should be explained as instances of the discharge of contractual obligations for failure of condition. Parties, generally speaking, do not promise to perform 'come what may' but instead make their promises subject to all kinds of express and implied conditions. The agreed conditionality of contracting parties' obligations to perform can explain each of these seemingly disparate areas of contract law. **10.2**

Admittedly, academics are often tempted to reject orthodoxy in order to make their work exciting or novel. A colleague of mine once did some teaching where a student, who had clearly picked up this habit, objected to a statement he made by saying: 'but Professor, that view is too orthodox'. But there is a danger here. 'Lawyers are not in the business of making new discoveries.'[1] That is why this work has sought to make clear that the criticism is only of the *currently* accepted view. In particular, the primary claims advanced in this book are not **10.3**

[1] Robert Stevens, *The Laws of Restitution* (OUP 2023) 297.

Discharge of Contractual Obligations. Jordan English, Oxford University Press. © Jordan English 2025.
DOI: 10.1093/9780198906704.003.0010

new and have been made before.[2] This book should be seen not as a rejection of tradition in favour of novelty but as a return to an earlier and better understanding—a return to the contract law that modern contract lawyers seem to have forgotten.

10.4 Even here, concessions have had to be made. The aim of this book has been to help judges, practitioners, and academics understand the law, not to propose a model that, while interesting, they cannot apply. Thus, in Chapter 2, it was recognised that a wholesale return to the failure of condition model and the rejection of the power to terminate model is unlikely. Too much water has passed under that particular bridge. But the insight developed in that chapter was that in cases involving discharge following breach and non-compliance with a promissory condition there are *two* questions that courts should be asking and not one: first, was the performance of the duty that has been breached a condition precedent to, or a concurrent condition of, the other party's obligation to perform; and secondly, is this particular term a 'condition' such that its breach gives rise to a power to terminate? Not enough, if any, emphasis is placed on the first question in the modern law, yet as this book has shown, the first question is arguably the more important.

10.5 By contrast, cases on frustration and common mistake can still be rationalised wholly as instances of discharge for failure of condition in a way that is broadly consistent with the tenor of modern law. And the benefit of doing so is that it shows how these different forms of discharge of contractual obligations fit together: they are unified by the fact that they are all forms of discharge for failure of condition.

10.6 In the remainder of this brief chapter, this book does three things. First, it reiterates the essential distinction between promises and conditions. Secondly, it indicates the parallels that can be drawn between the claims made in this book and the law of contract as it exists in the United States. Finally, it sets out the academic and practical implications of the arguments that have been made.

Promises and Conditions

10.7 The distinction between promises (ie duties) and conditions has permeated every aspect of this book. The distinction is fundamental. A breach of a duty

[2] See [1.2] and the authors cited there.

always gives rise to an action for damages, but it does not follow that the other party is discharged from their obligation to perform. On the model put forward in this book, this will only occur if there is a failure of a condition. A breach of duty may cause a condition to fail but equally it may not. And inversely, there may be a failure of condition without there being a breach of duty, as in the areas of frustration and common mistake.

The conflation of promises and conditions has led to a number of problems that have been explored in this book. In Chapter 2, we saw that it has caused lawyers to speak of 'breaches of conditions',[3] which, strictly speaking, is nonsensical. One cannot breach a condition if 'condition' is understood to refer to an uncertain fact or event upon which the existence of one party's immediate duty of performance depends. One breaches *duties*, not conditions.[4] To speak of a 'breach of condition' originally was a contraction: it referred to the breach of a promise, the performance of which was a condition.[5] But this loose language ultimately set English law down a path of confusion. And it is a path from which it may not easily return. **10.8**

The failure to notice the distinction has also caused English lawyers to lose sight of the relationship between discharge following breach and discharge in cases of frustration and common mistake. As Chapter 3 explained, authors who have noticed the link between frustration and discharge following breach have sought to reject it or 'play it down'.[6] Yet Diplock LJ in *Hongkong Fir Shipping Co Ltd v Kawasaki Kisen Kaisha Ltd*[7] 'could not have asserted more clearly the consistency of the rules governing discharge by frustration and discharge for breach'.[8] Further, if a clear distinction were drawn between promises and conditions, and conditions were studied more closely in their own right, then the relationship between frustration and common mistake, which was explored in Chapters 6 and 7, would be easier to see as well. **10.9**

[3] See [2.38].

[4] Arthur Corbin, 'Supervening Impossibility of Performing Conditions Precedent' (1922) 22 Columbia Law Review 421, 423.

[5] Robert Bradgate, 'Termination for Breach' in John Birds, Robert Bradgate, and Charlotte Villiers (eds), *Termination of Contracts* (Wiley Chancery 1995) 17, 42.

[6] Ewan McKendrick, 'Innominate Terms Revisited' in Louise Gullifer and Stefan Vogenauer (eds), *English and European Perspectives on Contract and Commercial Law: Essays in Honour of Hugh Beale* (Hart Publishing 2014) 183, 191.

[7] [1962] 2 QB 26.

[8] Donal Nolan, '*Hongkong Fir Shipping Co Ltd v Kawasaki Kisen Kaisha Ltd, The Hongkong Fir* (1961)' in Charles Mitchell and Paul Mitchell (eds), *Landmark Cases in the Law of Contract* (Hart Publishing 2018) 269, 286. See also 295–96.

10.10 We have even seen, in Chapter 8, that the problems in the area of anticipatory breach have arisen from the failure to appreciate that the events that can operate to discharge one party from their obligation to perform need not also give that party an action for damages. In other words, the doctrine of anticipatory breach might have developed more coherently if the distinction between promises and conditions were more clearly drawn.

10.11 The distinction between promises and conditions is therefore vital to understanding the discharge of contractual obligations. It is one of the foundational building blocks of contract law. There has been a natural tendency in the exposition of contract law to condense complex ideas and to simplify explanations of existing doctrines. But simplicity should not be sought at the risk of obscuring the distinct concepts in play. The law should be as simple as possible, but no simpler.[9]

The United States

10.12 This book has not been a book of comparative law. It has focused on the English law of contract. However, the astute reader would have noticed that a number of the claims made in this book, particularly in relation to discharge following breach and waiver of conditions, have parallels in the rules of contract law as developed in the United States. In that jurisdiction,[10] discharge following breach is generally understood to rest upon the failure of a condition precedent or concurrent condition. The *Restatement (Second) of Contract*, for example, states that 'a material failure of performance, including defective performance as well as an absence of performance, operates as the non-occurrence of a condition.'[11]

10.13 Similarly, in *Farnsworth on Contracts*, although referring to the 'suspension' and 'termination' of the contract, the current editor writes that, '[i]n developing these rules, courts have relied on the concept of a *condition*, an event that must occur before performance of a contractual duty becomes due.'[12] The

[9] A paraphrase attributable to Einstein. See Albert Einstein, 'On the Method of Theoretical Physics' (1934) 1 Philosophy of Science 163, 165.

[10] Or rather in those jurisdictions, given that there are fifty states and the District of Columbia, each with their own contract law.

[11] American Law Institute, *Restatement of the Law Second: Contracts 2d* (American Law Institute Publishers 1981) 215 §237, comment (a).

[12] E Allan Farnsworth, *Farnsworth on Contracts* (Zachary Wolfe ed, 4th edn, Wolters Kluwer 2023–24 supplement) vol 2, §8.01.

editor later adds that '[i]n order for a breach to justify the injured party's suspension of performance, the breach must be significant enough to amount to the nonoccurrence of a constructive condition of exchange'[13] and, when referring to the rules on 'termination' and 'total breach', he says 'the breach is treated as the nonoccurrence of a condition'.[14]

A detailed account of why the law has developed in the way that it did in the United States is beyond the scope of this work, but at a glance, it seems to have been strongly influenced by the likes of Professor Samuel Williston and Professor Arthur Corbin, who did not conflate promises with conditions. In fact, both were critical of English lawyers for doing precisely that. Professor Williston wrote that '[t]he difference between conditions and promises is so radical in its consequence that there is no excuse for a nomenclature which fails to recognize the distinction', and immediately added: **10.14**

> In the English books there has sprung up an astonishing usage of the word 'condition' in the law of sales as meaning a certain kind of promise and this usage has to some extent been followed in the United States. It cannot be too strongly deprecated.[15]

The learning of this jurisdiction therefore provides a valuable source of ideas as to how to deal with modern problems on a failure of condition model. The story told in this book may also serve as a valuable lesson for American lawyers today—that is, the importance of not overlooking the distinction between promises and conditions. **10.15**

Implications

The claims made in this book are important for both the theory and the practice of contract law. To begin with the theory, Chapters 2, 3, 6, and 7 showed that discharge following breach, frustration, and common mistake share a unity and can each be explained as instances of failure of condition justified by the parties' agreement. That is the central and most important theoretical claim in this book. But it is not the only claim. Chapter 4, for example, showed that the instances of waiver of condition are not all uniform, and cannot all be explained, despite modern attempts, as instances of estoppel. Chapter 5 **10.16**

[13] ibid §8.17.
[14] ibid §8.17. See Chapter 8 of this text generally.
[15] Samuel Williston, *The Law of Contracts* (Baker, Voorhis & Co 1921) vol 2, 1282–83 §665.

showed that an unaccepted repudiation, historically at least, was *not* a thing 'writ in water'[16] and also that English law should recognise a principle of waiver of conditions by prevention of fulfilment, but should not recognise the civilian 'fiction of fulfilment'.[17] Chapters 6 and 7 specifically argued that the implied condition view of frustration and common mistake has been unfairly maligned.[18] Chapter 8 showed that the existing justifications for the doctrine of anticipatory breach cannot account for the features of the doctrine as applied in English law today.[19] And Chapter 9 explained why restitution for failure of condition does not contradict the law of contract in cases where there is an underlying valid contract and that contract appears, at first glance, to entitle the defendant to receive the performance in question.[20]

10.17 It would be a mistake, however, to think that the implications of the arguments presented in this book are only academic. The approach to discharge following breach in Chapters 2 and 3 helped solve a number of practical problems, including: (i) whether a party themselves in breach can terminate for the other party's breach;[21] (ii) how promissory warranties work in the insurance context;[22] (iii) when and why a party should be entitled to damages for the loss of a bargain;[23] (iv) whether, in light of the 'intermediate' or 'innominate' term, English law should continue to recognise a third category of term, namely, 'warranties';[24] (v) whether multiple innominate terms can be breached in a way that, collectively but not individually, discharges the other party from their obligation to perform;[25] and (vi) whether one party is discharged from performance where an event that deprives them of substantially the whole benefit of the contract is partly due to a breach and partly due to something that is not a breach of any duty.[26] On the failure of condition model, some of these problems were easily resolved; others were not problems at all.

10.18 Similarly for waiver of conditions, in Chapter 4 we saw that courts, at a practical level, need to grapple with the distinction between waiver of conditions by election and waiver of conditions by estoppel to determine when a waiver is

[16] See [5.37]–[5.97].
[17] See [5.4]–[5.36].
[18] See, in particular, [6.85]–[6.116] and [7.78]–[7.80].
[19] See [8.23]–[8.46].
[20] See [9.36]–[9.60].
[21] See [2.116].
[22] See [2.117].
[23] See [2.118]–[2.133].
[24] See [3.66]–[3.75].
[25] See [3.72].
[26] See [3.73].

irrevocable on account of the principle of finality and when a waiver is revocable (provided that there has not been detrimental reliance).[27] Chapter 5 also demonstrated the important proposition that conditions cannot be waived for all purposes. In particular, a condition cannot be waived for the purpose of an action for the price if the performance of the condition is the consideration for the promise it qualifies.[28]

The practical implications also extended to the approach taken to the discharge of contractual obligations in cases of frustration and common mistake. Chapters 6 and 7 argued that the failure of condition approach means that a contract cannot be frustrated and should not be 'void' for common mistake where one party has unconditionally promised to perform (as seen in the cases dealing with 'hell or high water' clauses).[29] Chapter 6 also argued that frustration should not invariably be automatic—the assumption that the contract is killed off, as if it were a metaphysical entity, and therefore that it is not possible to waive conditions in cases of frustration, is mistaken.[30] Chapters 6 and 7 also solved the problem of why some clauses, such as arbitration and jurisdiction clauses, 'survive' the termination of the contract.[31] The mistake again is in the metaphor. Contracts do not live or die; clauses do not survive. The question is simply whether the clause's intended operation was or was not conditional and therefore whether it operates in the circumstances that have obtained. **10.19**

Finally, travelling beyond the law of contract, Chapter 9 gave an account of why the termination of the contract is neither necessary nor sufficient before bringing a claim in restitution for failure of condition. Termination therefore is not a prerequisite to a claim in restitution for failure of condition: 'The important question is whether the agreed condition of performance has failed.'[32] **10.20**

Conclusion

When and why parties are discharged from their contractual obligations for reasons other than performance of those obligations is a crucial question at the heart of contract law. Moreover, it is a question that contract lawyers have been grappling with for centuries. Yet much of the law discussed in this book, such **10.21**

[27] See [4.43]–[4.48].
[28] See [5.52]–[5.63].
[29] See [6.73] and [7.73]–[7.74].
[30] See [6.118]–[6.123].
[31] See [6.77]–[6.78] and [7.7].
[32] Stevens (n 1) 124.

as the 'old law' on independent and dependent promises and the law on waiver of conditions, has been forgotten, confined to the dustbin of history. This is unfortunate. When dealing with seemingly modern problems, we should always check whether there is an old solution. If we do, we might find that our modern problems are simply old problems under a different guise or indeed that they should not be problems at all.

Index

References in the index are to paragraph numbers. Footnotes are indicated by n. after the paragraph number. Only a selection of the most significant cases are cited in the index: for a complete list of cases and their citations, see the Table of Cases on p.xvii.